SAGE was founded in 1965 by Sara Miller McCune to support the dissemination of usable knowledge by publishing innovative and high-quality research and teaching content. Today, we publish over 900 journals, including those of more than 400 learned societies, more than 800 new books per year, and a growing range of library products including archives, data, case studies, reports, and video. SAGE remains majority-owned by our founder, and after Sara's lifetime will become owned by a charitable trust that secures our continued independence.

Los Angeles | London | New Delhi | Singapore | Washington DC | Melbourne

TRANSLATIONAL RESEARCH AND APPLIED PSYCHOLOGY IN INDIA

Thank you for choosing a SAGE product!
If you have any comment, observation or feedback,
I would like to personally hear from you.

Please write to me at **contactceo@sagepub.in**

Vivek Mehra, Managing Director and CEO, SAGE India.

Bulk Sales

SAGE India offers special discounts
for purchase of books in bulk.
We also make available special imprints
and excerpts from our books on demand.

For orders and enquiries, write to us at

Marketing Department
SAGE Publications India Pvt Ltd
B1/I-1, Mohan Cooperative Industrial Area
Mathura Road, Post Bag 7
New Delhi 110044, India

E-mail us at **marketing@sagepub.in**

Subscribe to our mailing list
Write to **marketing@sagepub.in**

This book is also available as an e-book.

TRANSLATIONAL RESEARCH AND APPLIED PSYCHOLOGY IN INDIA

Edited by
Kamlesh Singh
Suman Sigroha

Los Angeles | London | New Delhi
Singapore | Washington DC | Melbourne

First published in 2019 by

SAGE Publications India Pvt Ltd
B1/I-1 Mohan Cooperative Industrial Area
Mathura Road, New Delhi 110 044, India
www.sagepub.in

SAGE Publications Inc
2455 Teller Road
Thousand Oaks, California 91320, USA

SAGE Publications Ltd
1 Oliver's Yard, 55 City Road
London EC1Y 1SP, United Kingdom

SAGE Publications Asia-Pacific Pte Ltd
18 Cross Street #10-10/11/12
China Square Central
Singapore 048423

Published by Vivek Mehra for SAGE Publications India Pvt Ltd. Typeset in 10/13 pt Berkeley by Zaza Eunice, Hosur, Tamil Nadu, India.

Library of Congress Cataloging-in-Publication Data Available

ISBN: 978-93-532-8554-8 (HB)

SAGE Team: Abhijit Baroi, Safia Hassan and Rajinder Kaur

Contents

List of Figures

List of Tables

List of Abbreviations

AI	Appreciative Inquiry
APA	American Psychological Association
AR	Augmented Reality
BACP	British Association for Counselling and Psychotherapy
CBT	Cognitive Behavioural Therapy
CBPR	Community-based Participatory Research
CBSE	Central Board of Secondary Education
CIHR	Canadian Institute for Health Research
CTSA	Clinical Translational Science Award
D & I	Dissemination and Implementation
EGNH	Educating for Gross National Happiness
ERDS	Economic Rural Development Society
ESM	Experience Sampling Method
FGD	Focused Group Discussions
GNH	Gross National Happiness
IACP	Indian Association of Clinical Psychologists
IPA	Interpretive Phenomenological Analysis
IY	Incredible Years
JD-R	Job Demands–Resource
LSE	Life Skills Education
MBSR	Mindfulness-Based Stress Reduction
MHC-SF	Mental Health Continuum–Short Form
MHRD	Ministry for Human Resource Development
MRC	Medical Resource Council
NBCC	National Board for Certified Counselors
NIH	National Institute of Health
NIMH	National Institute of Mental Health
NIMHANS	National Institute of Mental Health and Neural Sciences
PANAS	Positive and Negative Affect Scale

PATHS	Promoting Alternative Thinking Strategies
PMR	Progressive Muscle Relaxation
POB	Positive Organizational Behaviour
POP	Penn Optimism Program
PP	Positive Psychology
PPIs	Positive Psychological Interventions
PPP	Positive Psychology Program
PRP	Penn Resilience Program
QoL	Quality of Life
R/S	Religious and Spiritual
R/S	Religious/Spiritual
RC	Resilience Curriculum
RC	Responsive Classroom
RCI	Rehabilitation Council of India
RCTs	Randomized Controlled Trials
RHCF	Rural Health Care Foundation
ROE	Roots of Empathy
RSSB	Radha Soami Satsang Beas
SBE	Scenic Beauty Estimation
SEAL	Social and Emotional Aspects of Learning
SEL	Social Emotional Learning
SMET	Self-Management of Excessive Tension
SMS	Short Messaging Service
SSRI	Selective Serotonin Reuptake Inhibitor
STEAM	Supporting Tempers, Emotions, and Anger Management
SWB	Subjective Well-Being
TD	Therapeutic Dina
TR	Translational Research
TR-KT	Translational Research–Knowledge Translation
UNPF	United Nations Population Fund
VISHRAM	Vidarbha Stress and Health Programme
VR	Virtual Reality
WHO	World Health Organization
YCDI	You Can Do It

Introduction
Laying the Groundwork—Translational Research and Its Role in Applied Psychology

Suman Sigroha and Kamlesh Singh

Translational research is an application-oriented research where the available scientific knowledge is implemented for the better quality of life (QoL). It endeavours to provide a pathway for ideas in basic research to reach product development, followed by their application or practical implementation. Already having a tradition in medical sciences, it is now being increasingly used in other areas as well, and it holds great potential for a similar framework for social sciences, especially applied psychology, where focused translational research is still rare. This chapter presents the current status of translational research in various fields with special focus on psychology. Furthermore, it describes relevant research methods in this area. For example, the community-based participatory research (CBPR) that has now developed as an important research model helps bridge the gap between science and practice through its emphasis on community engagement and social action, which in turn aids in balancing this disparity. Thus, it increases the potential for translational research to develop and implement effective interventions across varied communities, address the differences and reduce the gaps. The chapter presents how, within the Indian context, translational research can contribute significantly because of its panoptic vision to engage directly with the stakeholders and can provide a holistic understanding of basic sociocultural and behavioural processes that affect mental health, and indigenous approaches to culturally sustained intervention strategies that may lead to a sociocultural re-engineering.

TRANSLATIONAL RESEARCH: AN INTRODUCTION

'History has taught us that the path from basic discoveries to scientific and technological applications is seldom a straight line (Fang & Casadevall, 2010, p. 565).

The latest of the scientific disciplines to develop, translational research has its origin in the need to aid clinical research to catch up with basic research so as to reach the wider public, for whose betterment, after all, it is meant. In layman terms, one who does translational research translates or interprets research in one field to the practitioners in the other. Thus, there is a presupposition of an understanding of both the fields in such a translator. Additionally, as it deals with public, policies and health management, it is not merely transcribing of knowledge that happens in translational research. It requires a comprehensive, an all-encompassing perspective to public health management that comprises of awareness about diverse fields, such as medical science, laboratory studies, clinical trials, epidemiology, policy and economic as well as human aspects of all of it. Because of this panoptic vision, its interventions are also as widespread, taking as diverse approaches as scientific, politico-economic and sociocultural approaches.

Translational research appears to have a beginning in one of the most difficult challenges that the medical community appears to have faced in recent past, that is, finding a cure for HIV-AIDS (Perlstadt, 2009). By demonstrating the complex interplay of biomedical, economic and social factors in the development of the drug, its delivery and impact on health, this search paved the way for what is now known as translational research (Perlstadt, 2009). Despite being in vogue since the mid-1990s, when it was first used in the context of cancer research (Weremeychik & Eastman, 2015), the term 'translational research' has come to mean different things to different people. An application-oriented approach, whereby the available scientific knowledge is implemented for better QoL, it endeavours to provide a pathway for ideas in basic research to reach product development and on to their application or practical implementation. Very simply understood as 'bench-to-bedside' approach, the term is still not very well defined or very well understood. This perplexity aptly alluded to by Fang and Casadevall (2010) in the section's opening quote, is what this book sets out to address, particularly in the field of applied psychology in India.

SCHEME OF THE CHAPTER

To achieve this purpose of illustrating what translational research means for researchers, academicians and practitioners in applied psychology, through its different sections, this chapter charts the course of translational research from clinical and medical sciences to social and behavioural sciences, of which psychology is a part. Simultaneously, it traces the history of translational research from its beginning in the 1990s until the present time. Besides this historical understanding, this introduction also endeavours to present a brief spatial spread of translational research, including its status in India, for a comprehensive understanding of what it is and what makes it so crucial during contemporary times. The chapter then shifts its focus to research and implementation being done in psychology before coming to our motivation for writing this book. Although translational research may be creating a buzz in different circles, and various governments and funding agencies may be trying to prioritize it, it has its critics as well. We list their concerns after the review of the field. The last section briefly introduces our research in the area of applied psychology, the chapters that follow, and the chapter concludes by identifying areas of future research.

TRANSLATIONAL RESEARCH: A HISTORICAL PERSPECTIVE

The earlier-mentioned 'bench-to-bedside' approach in clinical research privileges the link between basic science research and the final product that can be a new treatment or commercially available drug or device (Woolf, 2008). The importance of translation of knowledge into novel methods for diagnosing, treating and preventing diseases, necessary to improve health (Fontanarosa & DeAngelis, 2002), cannot be emphasized enough. However, for others like health care professionals, translational research is meant to translate this research into practice, that is, an endeavour whereby the novel treatments, drugs or devices developed are delivered to the populace (Woolf, 2008). Thus, the endpoint of the former is the starting point for the latter, and they constitute the two blocks or phases within translational research, labelled as T1 and T2. While for T1, the laboratory setting in various fields of basic science or medicine constitute 'the bench', for T2, this 'bench' is the community or practice-based research networks (Mold & Peterson, 2005; Woolf, 2008), or, in simpler words, T2 seeks to bring T1 to public. Hence, though 'translational research means different things to different people, but it seems important to almost everyone' (Woolf, 2008). Its importance can be judged from the fact that the National Institutes of Health (NIH) in the United States of America constituted the Clinical and Translational Science Award (CTSA) in 2006.

Definitions

As translational research has a more robust beginning and background in basic clinical or medical sciences, it has been defined in those terms only. Narayan et al. (2000) defined it in the simplest of terms as 'comprehensive applied research that strives to translate the available knowledge and render it operational in clinical and public health practice' to 'facilitate optimal health care for as many people as possible rather than ideal health care for a few', when commenting on the lack of efficient treatment for diabetes patients despite available knowledge. Its aim is to 'assess implementation of standards of care, understand the barriers to their implementation, and intervene throughout all levels of health care delivery and public health to improve quality of care and health outcomes, including quality of life' (Narayan, Benjamin, Gregg, Norris, & Engelgau, 2004, p. 958).

Thus, while articulating the importance of bench-to-bedside approach in bringing the results of basic science research to the people as well as focusing on the hurdles faced during this process, they simultaneously focus on the people for whom basic research is meant. The spotlight shifts to the centrality of the people in the whole design, and improvement in their QoL becomes the ultimate aim of translational research. Similarly, NIH (2007) has come up with a definition of translational research that defines its scope:

Translational research includes two areas of translation. One is the process of applying discoveries generated during research in the laboratory, and in preclinical studies, to the development of trials and studies in humans. The second area of translation concerns research aimed at enhancing the adoption of best practices in the community. Cost-effectiveness of prevention and treatment strategies is also an important part of translational science.

This definition envisions translational research as a continuum, unidirectional in nature (Rubio et al., 2010) that again emphasizes its two-stage process, T1 (basic science to clinical trials) and T2 (clinical trials to practice in human population). So the ultimate aim of translational research can be understood as better and improved public health, of which mental health and well-being constitute an important part. It is something that Woolf (2008) and Rubio et al. (2010) have stressed upon no less. Both Sung et al. (2003) and Woolf (2008) have enunciated a knowledge of 'communication theory, behavioral science, public policy, financing, organizational theory, system redesign, informatics, and mixed methods/qualitative research' (Woolf, 2008, pp. 211–212) and co-option of 'economists, social scientists, epidemiologists, social workers' (Sung et al., 2003, p. 1283) imperative towards the achievement of this goal. However, despite this focus on the human element and ultimate aim of improving health and well-being, it is T1 that overshadows T2 in terms of funding (Kerner, 2006) and relative importance (Woolf, 2008). Sung et al. (2003) brought into focus the limitations of these two blocks in the application of science to betterment of human health because of their treatment as separate enterprises.

Another definition that has been given by Translational Research Working Group of the National Cancer Institute has incorporated the basic and clinical research in T1. According to it, translational research 'transforms scientific discoveries arising in the lab, clinic, or population into new clinical tools & applications that reduce cancer incidence, morbidity & mortality' (Hawk, 2006, slide 40). Rubio et al. (2010) are sceptical of this definition and purpose since, by clubbing together two very different areas of knowledge, it conceals the scope of multidisciplinary research that exists at their interface. More so because this multidisciplinarity is perceived to be an essential feature of translational research by

Sung et al. (2003) as well as Rubio et al. (2010). The latter have come up with their own definition that integrates this inter/multidisciplinarity. This leads to the third dimension added by Westfall, Mold and Fagnan (2007) to translational research by including clinical practice (T3) to the bench (T1) and bedside (T2). This T3 component is concerned with timely delivery to the patients and identifying issues with health care and pinpointing new clinical questions (Westfall et al., 2007). Rubio et al. (2010) build upon this model when they say that translational research fosters the multidirectional integration of basic research, patient-oriented research and population-based research, with the long-term aim of improving the health of the public. T1 research expedites the movement between basic research and patient-oriented research that leads to new or improved scientific understanding or standards of care. T2 research facilitates the movement between patient-oriented research and population-based research that leads to better patient outcomes, the implementation of best practices and improved health status in communities. T3 research promotes interaction between laboratory-based research and population-based research to stimulate a robust scientific understanding of human health and disease (Rubio et al., 2010).

By formulating and articulating a new paradigm, T3, that has always been there but not so clearly articulated until now as part of the continuum, Westfall et al. (2007) and Rubio et al. (2010) make the unidirectional continuum a dynamic 'bidirectional' circular model, where T3, with its results, can fuel further basic research by feeding into T1. Building upon this paradigm further, Dougherty and Conway (2008) have emphasized making T3 robust by quality improvement.

Khoury et al. (2007) added another dimension by including a T4 component to what they call the 'phases' (instead of the until now used 'types') of the bidirectional translational research continuum. It has been done to articulate and at the same time emphasize the need to focus on evidence-based applications (T3 and T4 phases), which are still rare in genomics (as well as in other disciplines) despite the increasing focus on translational research (Burke, Khoury, Stewart, & Zimmern, 2006; Khoury et al., 2007). So now the four phases of translational research are T1 research: from gene discovery to candidate health applications (translation to humans); T2 research: from health application to evidence-based guidelines (translation to patients); T3 research: from evidence-based guidelines to health practice (translation to practice); and T4 research: from practice to population health impact (translation to population health; Khoury et al., 2007; Miami CTSI, 2017). As per this model, a discovery at one level can foster research or provide 'feedback loops' in either direction of this two-way pathway. Developed in the context of genomics research, this clear-cut demarcation of the four phases of translational research with their essential overlaps widens their scope to include not only the population for which research is ultimately meant but also their feedback to make basic research more effective and efficient.

Translational Research and Clinical Sciences

A similar anxiety about this gap between research and actual benefits, that is, improved health care, is also present in other areas such as child health care and diabetes. Szilagyi (2009) asserts translational research's importance for improvement in child health in his review of translational research in paediatrics. Like others, he laments the slow translation of research and the long time that basic research takes to reach general population, if ever (Balas, 1998; Khoury et al., 2007; Westfall et al., 2007). Even when it does happen, these translations are not optimal and reveal disconnects between evidence-based research and practice (Halterman, Aligne, Auinger, McBride, & Szilagyi, 2000; Katon, Joan, Richardson, McCauley, & Lozano, 2008; Miller, Gergen, Honour, & Zhan, 2005; Szilagyi, 2009). Further, there is usually a gap between standard clinical practice and public health (Brownson, Kreuter, Arrington, & True, 2006; Glasgow, Fisher, Haire-Joshu, & Goldstein, 2007). Clearly, the benefits have not reached the children (like the rest of the population) for whom this research is eventually meant. The picture, however, is not completely bleak, given the case of rapid translation of immunization research and its successful delivery made visible through improved child health (Szilagyi, 2009). Interestingly, this has happened because basic research and strategies for delivery already exist within this domain (Szilagyi, 2009), a point to be noted if translational research is to be successfully delivered in other areas.

Diabetes is a chronic disease, a major public health issue for which effective treatments are available as a result of basic research. However, despite encouraging results, the quality of care is suboptimal (Narayan et al., 2000; Narayan et al., 2004; Vinicor, 1994) like in the case of child health care. Although treatments are available, their implementation is inadequate. Translational research, different due to its design orientation, is required to augment the clinical practice at the population level since efficacy of available treatments has not helped much (Narayan et al., 2000). Thus, treatment of diabetes also requires a zealous population-based perspective (Glasgow et al., 1999), which is provided by translational research (Narayan et al., 2000).

This historical review of the development of translational research reveals that there are wide gaps between translation of basic research and its clinical practice, and still wider gaps between clinical practice and delivery to the general populace, and resulting public health. These disconnects bring to light the importance of not only translational research but also its interdisciplinary nature. It also identifies the other important economic, social and cultural barriers to translation that have to do with disciplines such as social sciences, behavioural sciences, finance and management. Hitherto, the almost entire focus has been on the medical aspects of translation—basic research to clinical interventions—even in terms of funding (Fang et al., 2010; Pober, Neuhauser, & Pober, 2001; Sung et al., 2003), what is now needed for translational research to be effective in improving health and well-being, and fill the gap between clinical practice and public health, is to link it up with findings from social sciences (Schroeder, 2007; Szilagyi, 2008, 2009). Besides, the lack of funding in these areas of clinical practice, community and population health is another major barrier (Feinstein, 1999; Szilagyi, 2009).

From all of the above definitions given by those in medical or clinical sciences, and the review of the progress of translational research or rather barriers to it, besides gleaning a concurrence on the 'bench-to-bedside' approach, we can easily ascertain the importance of the human element in this endeavour. The urgency of making available the newly designed tools, methods of diagnosis and treatments does come across through them, as does the emphasis on health and well-being. There is also an apparent gravity about the gap that exists between research and availability of its benefits to the general public. The present book deals with this human element and filling this gap between research and practice. Having this tradition in medical sciences and its increasing use in its various fields like genomics, paediatrics, epidemiology, neuroscience, biosciences and so on, and given its interdisciplinary and multidisciplinary bent, translational research holds a great potential for a similar framework for social sciences, especially applied psychology where focused translational research is still rare (Tashiro & Mortensen, 2006). The review also brings to light the fact that social sciences and behavioural sciences are in fact a little late in climbing the translational research bandwagon, which the following section deals with.

TRANSLATIONAL RESEARCH AND SOCIAL SCIENCES

'[T]ranslational research represents a sustained commitment to an issue and a community' (Price & Will, 2015, p. 859).

Translational research is now increasingly attracting the practitioners of social sciences and behavioural sciences. The pressure to be part of the translational research bandwagon has been there from the beginning. In the present, when emphasis on QoL or achievement and propagation of good health has become a priority, the public health systems are also gearing towards or are responding to attainment of the same as reflected in their expenditure bent. One of the ways to achieve this QoL is via investment in health research that directly translates to investment in better delivery of health systems such as development of new or better diagnostic tools and treatments or organization of health services delivery (Keramaris, Kanakaris, Tzioupis, Kontakis, & Giannoudis, 2008). This is where translational research can help, by making available similar methods to both basic and applied researchers, which in turn should facilitate communication and collaboration across disciplines (Widiger, 2005; Zvolensky, Lejuez, Stuart, & Curtain, 2001).

In retrospect, it looks like social and behavioural sciences have been doing translational research for long (Perlstadt, 2009). As a result of translational research's multidisciplinary and interdisciplinary nature, and its acknowledged importance in applications and community-based research, the biomedical sciences, beginning with cancer and HIV-AIDS research, looked to behavioural sciences to translate their research into practice. The latter could help in delivery to the field, and thus lead to an improvement in public health and QoL that the biomedical sciences felt apprehensive about (Perlstadt, 2009) as a result of their respective differences in training (the former's with the humans and the latter's within the laboratory settings). Behavioural sciences had the perceived wherewithal to bridge the gap between basic science and clinical practice. It was in 1998 that push to translational research in socio-behavioural sciences was given with a comment by Thomas Wehr of National Institute of Mental Health (NIMH) that 'translational research—bench to bedside' was a buzzword at NIMH (Lamberg, 1998). NIMH also clarified what translational research's aim was in social and behavioural sciences thus, '[It] addresses how basic behavioral processes inform the diagnosis, prevention, treatment, and delivery of services for mental illness, and, conversely how knowledge of mental illness increases our understanding of basic behavioral processes' (NIMH, 2000, p. iii) and called to link it with CBPR. NIMH reorganized its divisions later to bolster translational research to advocate a better understanding of mental illness, promote collaborative efforts and come up with best practices in the field (Insel, 2004). However, further reorganizations after recommendations to strengthen basic research in social and behavioural sciences with respect to translational research led to dismantling NIMH's Basic Behavioral and Social Science branch to form three translational divisions that would work on translating basic science research into treatments for mentally ill (Dingfelder, 2005; Perlstadt, 2009). There was an exhortation to the sociologists to forge ahead with interdisciplinary teams and 're-engineering of the clinical enterprise' (Perlstadt, 2009), and to evolve basic questions related to scientific innovation and its usefulness.

Lemon et al. (2013) have mapped the phases of translational research with offerings from behavioural and social sciences, and thus provided an interesting guide map for those wanting to do translational research in these disciplines. According to them, identification of basic social and psychological processes of human functioning would be T1 research. T2 research would be testing of interventions in control groups and situations, that is, efficacy testing. Research in T3 phase would consist of generalizations from efficacy testing, that is, identifying programmes, policies and interventions for implementation in the population for health care. Evaluating the effectiveness of the intervention programmes upon dissemination would be T4 research. It would also evaluate communication tools, understanding or biases of and against it, and social environments that accept or reject those interventions, and would target improvement in health and QoL as well as inform policy for health care reform.

Sociology

Given the clarion call for translational research, let us look at how the researchers, academicians and the practitioners within social and behavioural sciences responded to it. Within the broader discipline of sociology, applied sociology is one area that appears ripe for the implementation of the aims of translational research (Nyden, Hossfeld, & Nyden, 2012; Perlstadt, 2007). It has, over the course of time, developed tools for data collection and has a tradition of producing descriptive and analytical reports. It would come up with results that can be translated into ideas, which can then be used by those working in the field (Perlstadt, 2007) or, in other words, those using community-based research applications. Wethington (2015) defines translational sociology as in 'an emerging style of sociology that applies sociological theory to addressing real-world problems using established scientific methods' (p. 1). She also highlights the interdisciplinary nature of translational sociology while drawing attention to its collaborative nature. It appears that some sociologists, particularly those working with aging populations, have been already doing translational research long before the calls for doing so came up in the beginning of the 21st century, although, like in other fields, it had not been termed 'translational research'. There, translational research is characterized by the application of theory to intervention design and development of programmes, and to the way the resultant findings are taken into account to make the theory robust (Pillemer, Czaja, Schulz, & Stahl, 2003; Pillemer, Suitor, & Wethington, 2003) or translate them into 'goals, objectives and action steps for groups, thereby making sociological research more useful' (Price & Will, 2015). Thus, sociological research appears to be bidirectional and dynamic in nature, the hallmark of any translational research. Translational sociology, with its greater engagement with other disciplines as well as better collaboration among the practitioners within the discipline or team science, as Wuchty, Jones, & Uzzi (2007) call it, use of scientific method to link research and theory to real-world social problems identified by general public, policymakers or practitioners, leads to innovative research besides communicating effectively with the public (Wethington, 2015). In addition, it encourages communication between the academia and the public or the universities and the communities (Wethington, 2015) and helps in alleviating major health issues that have a strong link with social conditions, like the aforementioned HIV-AIDS. Furthermore, as translational research is more about 'the issue of knowledge use', there can be a development of strategies to transform the root cause of this issue of knowledge used by 'social inventions' that are 'problem solutions created by the members of one social context to address problems in that context' (Krause, 2009, p. 39). Since it seeks to re-engineer the 'corroded social fabric' (p. 45) in order to boost knowledge use for public health, according to Krause (2009), 'de-siloing strategies like team science and community engagement in the translational research process' (p. 46) can not only do so but would also bring sociologists with different specializations on to a single platform.

Psychology

Similar concerns about psychology's place within the larger translational research map and related funding have plagued some in psychology as well. Psychology, which has a heterogeneous mix of clinical practitioners, appears to be even more poised for translational research than sociology. As is the case with applied sociology, some, like those working in academic health centres, appear to be doing translational research already by linking research with health and well-being interventions and making bridges between basic researchers and clinical practitioners within psychology. Despite this, Breckler (2008) did sound out a cautionary note by commenting that psychology is not perceived as conducive to translational research because of its varied specializations that have led to only a few psychologists working to link basic research with interventions in the field. However, it simultaneously points to the fact that there are already some psychologists doing so; as Tashiro and Mortensen (2006) assert, practising psychologists translate better, and perhaps the pace is increasing slowly but surely. This is why NIMH has prioritized funding for basic behavioural processes in mental illness, the functioning capabilities affected by the latter, and the influence of context for both illness and treatment (NIMH, 2000). In other words, how emotions, motivations and interactions affect social or professional behavioural outcomes within the family or in a sociocultural context, all fall under its purview. Alongside, there is a strong emphasis on an understanding of underlying biological processes, innovations in measurement and promoting interdisciplinary collaborations.

In fact, theories from behavioural science can be used to certify that intervention trials have an impact on individual behaviour (Wethington, 2015), and the findings can help in better implementation afterwards. Translational behavioural research model can act as a blueprint to expedite acceptance of these findings into practice, and thus impact individual health (Hommel, Modi, Piazza-Waggoner, & Myers, 2015). Since every phase of translational research can be used to provide feedback for the betterment of the previous as well as the next step, community partnership approaches may be utilized to check the effectiveness of evidence-based interventions (Warnecke et al., 2008). Evans (2012) suggests that social or behavioural researchers embrace the medical model to begin with and blend within it the intricacies of the social environment. Recent advances in the treatment of anxiety-related disorders illustrate this approach for which although unimodal therapy works as well as or better than a combination of psychological and medicinal approaches, researches in neuroscience have offered a novel combination of psychological and drug interventions to reduce fear. Exposure to fear resulting in its reduction is further facilitated by the drugs that target sites of extinction learning (Hofmann, 2007). Issues like health care policy can have substantial inputs from social, behavioural and psychological researches by offering data on a diverse range of social and psychological measures as well as by data collection and analysis techniques (Evans, 2012).

Psychological Interventions as Translational Research

Both Stanley Milgram's 'Behavioral Study of Obedience' (1963) and Zimbardo's Prison Experiment (1972; Haney, Banks, & Zimbardo, 1973) are classic examples of translational research in psychology, since both of them reveal the power structures inherent in the society as well as their effects on people who make that society. Bandura's (1997) social cognitive theory that started with a study of short manipulations and their outcomes in normal population has added the self-efficacy component to the CBT approaches. The findings that possess internal validity and are theoretically strong have been translated to understand the relation between graded stimuli exposure and its outcomes. This translation points to the individual's self-efficacy to engage with the intervention component of a treatment. Coyne (1999) also remarks upon the potential of an intervention component. Additionally, empirically attested principles of change can act as good translational bridges (Beutler, 2000; Rosen & Davison, 2003) since their focus is on how a particular component of the treatment affects the symptoms in psychotherapy, which helps in bolstering focused interventions thus bearing upon the overall performance of psychotherapy. Masten (2011) mentions the power of positivity in basic and applied research on resilience. There is a need felt to apply evidence-based interventions to translational techniques while working with prevention or recovery in children. Stakeholders are found to be keen if interventions are framed as positive goals, and morale improves with continuous rewards to strength-based approaches. However, the progress in the usage of interventions has been slow, although sustained. Despite the anecdotal nature of reportage, the effects of positive interventions have also been outlined extensively (Flynn, Dudding, & Barber, 2006). Holt and Jones (2008) talk about positive youth development by means of interventions as part of translational research. Interestingly, Greenwald and Cullen (1985) give a five-phase research framework that can be termed translational, for positive development. According to them, these five phases are basic research (generating models), development of methods (designing interventions, feasibility testing), followed by efficacy trials (validity testing) and effectiveness trials (intervention testing), and ending with dissemination in the field (evaluation of promoting or obstructing conditions and adoption of the intervention). Thus, translations in the form of psychotherapies, interventions and following best social practices in a community facilitate mental health, augment QoL and well-being, and consequently have positive effects on the overall public health.

The ever-increasing socio-economic differences and racial or ethnic disparities lead to widening gaps in access to various resources, health care among them. In psychology, CBPR that has now developed as an important research model helps bridge the gap between science and practice through its emphasis on community engagement and social action, which in turn aids in balancing this disparity. Thus, as a result of its community-specific focus, it increases the potential for translational research to develop and implement effective interventions across varied communities, and address the differences and reduce the gaps. It can help determine the relevance of data for policy inputs as well as channel information back to the community, thereby creating a sense of involvement in research and policy, something that is the hallmark of translational research.

Given the huge time lag between knowledge generation and its implementation for health (it requires 17 years for only 14% of new scientific discoveries to become incorporated into standard practice [Balas, 1998]), translational research, especially in mental health, can speed up this process of implementation and help build bridges between research and practice that will increase the clinical relevance of mental health research (Department of Health and Human Services, 2006). However, translation of social or behavioural research into practice is much more a complicated process than that of biomedical research, primarily because of the dynamics of interplay between people and groups, and communities. Community-based participatory models broaden this process, but they do require a framework for research and production of knowledge within these complex delivery systems (Brekke, Ell, & Palinkas, 2007). Having said that, applied psychology, like applied sociology, is ready to take on the translational research challenge. The inclusion of some well-thought-out practical action steps would help in designing intervention programmes and feedback mechanisms to evaluate and bolster further research.

TRANSLATIONAL RESEARCH: A BRIEF SPATIAL UNDERSTANDING

Before we move on to our interventions as part of translational research in applied psychology, having done a historical review of the development and acceptance of translation research, it would be pertinent to look at the attention being paid to translational research in some of the major regions or countries of the world, such as the United States of America, the United Kingdom, the European Union, Japan, Australia, China, Africa and India.

The United States of America: As discussed above, the United States of America has been leading the shift to translational research via NIH that has been pushing for it through its road maps and new pathways to discovery along with emphasis on research teams of the future, director's pioneer awards, CTSA, interdisciplinary research training initiatives, re-engineering the clinical research enterprise and so on.

The United Kingdom: The United Kingdom's Medical Research Council (MRC) came up with guidelines for expediting the translation of medical research in 2007. In a workshop (MRC, 2007) that gave rise to the guidelines, it emerged that along with the continuation of basic research, there was a need for change within the research community, and it should understand its role in translating and communicating research findings. Funding mechanisms and structural processes also needed to be framed to encourage the researchers. Industry partnership was also mooted for new initiatives. There was a need felt to have training programmes in the translational processes. The emphasis has been on 'best research for best health' (Research and Development Directorate Department of Health, UK, 2006).

The European Union: Translational research in the European Union has been based on the Lisbon strategy of 2000, which set the aim of investing 3 per cent of European GDP in it (European Communities, 2004). It has European Research Council and European Medical Research Council to encourage and strategize for translational research activities, while Karolinska Institutet, Sweden, is one of the leading centres of translational research.

Japan: In Japan, there has been a healthy allocation of human and financial resources to the promotion of basic medical research, but not so for the translational research. Feeling the urgency to do so, Translational Research Informatics centre was set up in 2002, with support from the Ministry of Education, Culture, Sports, Science and Technology. It is committed to facilitating the transfer of basic medical research findings to clinical practice and promotion and management of translational research. Its 'Research Revolution 2002' initiative has provided funding for translational research in the areas such as immuno-biology and cancer immuno-surveillance (Triendl, 2004).

Australia: Translational research in Australia is defined as an early phase of clinical research, including preclinical and Phases I and II clinical trials, much more broader in definition than the United States of America's, but with as clear concepts (Nakaya, Shimizu, Tanaka, & Asano, 2005). It has some global institutes such as Ludwig Institute for Cancer Research (for tissue banking, bioinformatics, etc.), Walter and Eliza Hall Institute of Medical Research (for haematology), Royal Melbourne Hospital (houses Cancer Trials Australia) and Peter MacCallum Institute (imaging with PET) that carry on major clinical trial programmes. Funding is provided by private donations with some governmental support. Australia's major strength is the emphasis on evidence-based care, supported by science as well as the connect between researchers and clinicians (Nakaya et al., 2005).

China: According to Dai, Yang and Gan (2013), although China began late in the translational research domain, it has already made inroads because of its determination. Beginning in 2009, institutions have been established to translate research in varied areas such as stem cells, musculoskeletal system, cancer, leukaemia, cardiovascular, paediatrics, diabetes, regenerative medicine and drug development. Academic conferences have also been held in various cities. The government is emphasizing translational research as a major strategy in the medical field, although it faces similar challenges as elsewhere, like a limited connection between laboratories and clinics, with no concrete results in practice. Clarity is also required on responsibility, work protocols, staff and evaluation systems.

Africa: Africa, which carries 24 per cent of world's disease burden, has the lowest research capacity, accounting for only 2 per cent of world's research (Kay, 2015). Recently, Wellcome Trust, an independent global charitable foundation, along with the Bill & Melinda Gates Foundation and the UK government's Department for International Development announced measures to address these challenges. Sub-Saharan African Network for TB/HIV Research Excellence is the multinational and multi-disciplinary organization that focuses on advancing quality of science in Africa, especially African-led research in HIV and TB. It provides research and training, emphasizes research in microbiology, immunology and epidemiology and clinical trials across all sites. Community engagement is a primary element in all of these activities.[1] The basic aim of both of these initiatives is to strengthen South–South partnerships for translational research.

India: Within the Indian context, the Indian Society of Translational Research[2] is leading the way for translational research. It is dedicated to applying discoveries from basic sciences for human health. It aims at identifying thrust areas in public health, family welfare, nutrition and innovative systems of medicine to apply these discoveries, besides gathering data pertaining to clinical evidence in order to offer innovative and personalized health care. Identification of barriers to translational research and production of trained manpower are its other goals. Translational Health Science and Technology Institute is a society set up by some leading science administrators that addresses issues of public health that are a national priority and plans to make innovations available to all. For this, it has formed some niche research centres that comprise of six intramural centres with interdisciplinary focus, two extramural centres and one partnership centre. The thrust areas are vaccine, infectious diseases, paediatric biology, bio-design and diagnostics, biomedical, drug discovery, human microbial ecology, in collaboration with population science. Indian Council of Medical Research[3] is also encouraging translational research by prioritizing such research while giving funds and has also taken some steps like making clusters of Regional Centre for Biotechnology and Translational Health Sciences and Technology Institute (Banerjee, 2016) for the purpose. Although a process has been initiated, a lot needs to be done.

This short review of the spatial scope of translational research also reveals a similar urgency as revealed by the earlier review section, for implementation of the programme to make available the fruits of basic research to the community at large. It simultaneously brings to light the vast differences in the allocation of resources as well as the level of priority given to translational research by various governments. However, without

---

[1] https://www.santheafrica.org
[2] http://www.istr.in
[3] http://www.icmr.nic.in

fail, all of them emphasize the need to make translation the priority for health care.

Translational research can contribute significantly towards accessible public health and well-being because of its panoptic vision to engage directly with the stakeholders in a country like India where the majority of the population does not have access to adequate health care. It can provide a holistic understanding of the following:

1. Basic sociocultural and behavioural processes that affect mental health
2. Abilities that are affected by an imbalance in mental health
3. Indigenous approaches to culturally sustained intervention strategies that may lead to a sociocultural re-engineering

Hence, the steps involved in the process would be developing research priorities in consultation with stakeholders (the general population), following up with pilot programmes and then launching outreach programmes (with the involvement of practitioners in the field) in the community. Since the success of translational research is dependent on evolving everyday practices and assumptions about ways of conducting research, it would be interesting to design programmes that would position the local within the broader research environment, and where these local resources would also be able to help in/form policy for further research and its implementation for health care.

CRITICISM OR CAUTIONARY NOTE

All said, critics of translational research see it merely as a fad, and, given the fact that it is difficult to understand and comprehend and has no clear-cut definition, it sometimes appears to be just so, a fad. Also, contrary to the assumption when discussing translational research that what needs to be translated and how is known to the practitioners, many a time this is not the case. Apart from this, the major criticism stems from the very premise of translational research that by focusing on translation of available basic research, it is directing the impetus away from basic research, which invariable has had practical benefits (O'Connor, 2013).

THE WAY AHEAD: WHY TRANSLATIONAL RESEARCH?

Despite these points of criticism, translational research perspective would be conducive in developing efficacious public health policies as a result of its focus on delivery within the resources present and with equitable distribution (Narayan et al., 2000). And, because of its multidisciplinary nature, it can also act as a strategizing space for policy advocacy, and can at the same time foster expansion beyond traditional health care systems (Franks & Fiscella, 2008). Another important element that makes it invaluable and challenging at the same time is the interplay of the global and the local knowledge because of its emphasis on evidence-based practices (Palinkas & Soydan, 2012). Whereas the researchers bring in the global elements based on evidence, community-based practitioners bring in the local elements based on experience (Palinkas et al., 2009), thus making translational research culturally sensitive, and thus more effective as well as efficient. Besides, it is an opportunity for the academia to meet their public service goals and for communities to make a difference within their own community spaces (Wethington, 2016).

Translational research can advance by means of a reorganization of academic and research groups in a translational manner as well as by creating translationally oriented positions within various academic disciplines (Keramaris et al., 2008). Since there is hardly any discussion on the ways in which behavioural science or psychology can unite with medical sciences, there is a need to find out such inclusive approaches to foster effective translation. Additionally, the review reveals a fragmented approach to translation, which again calls for a consolidation for effective health outcomes. This approach should go hand in hand with targeted training programmes for researchers, academicians, practitioners and staff so that they can understand and appreciate the fact that although translational research may not fulfil internal or external validity expectations, nevertheless it is necessary (Tashiro & Mortensen, 2006). There has been a growing framework of empirical studies about intervention strategies (e.g., within the resilience research; Masten, 2011), although without evaluation or standardized testing component. So it needs to be made accountable without breaking the pace, which can be attained by means of a fusion of theoretical and practical knowledge. This can happen by reformulating the aims as to develop knowledge of the processes or schemas that need intervention by means of theory-informed research.

ABOUT THE BOOK

The present book broadly deals with two aspects of translational research in the field of applied psychology in India—review of existing work in the domain and actual translational work being done now. Accordingly, the book has been divided into two corresponding parts. The objectives of this book are to describe the psychosocial screening of situations that necessitated intervention as part of translational research and to summarize that psychosocial data. It also presents the major initiatives that are underway to improve mental health care by the standardization of models and health management practices, including psychosocial assessment, as well as collection of data on individual characteristics, required interventions and outcomes thereon to add on to the emerging best practices in the field. The delivery of basic research findings in terms of health and other domains of human behaviour generally follow two approaches—existing intervention models are customized to cultural contexts or new interventions are developed based on constant feedback received from the end users (Palinkas, 2010). This study follows both the approaches in its pursuit of translation of available basic research for improving QoL. We have identified and implemented intervention strategies in diverse areas such as education, organizations and rural areas, and on varied populations such as children, adults and older people. We have focused on the identification of problems and intervention strategies to address these problems to improve health and QoL. These interventions are targeted to increase awareness about and knowledge of markers of health, situated in both behaviour and social environment, and these have been delivered in community settings. In our interventions, we follow what various social psychological theories and models propose—that intention implementation occurs at a different stage than intention formation and that processes in this phase are responsible for the extent of conversion of intentions to actions (Hagger & Chatzisarantis, 2014; Heckhausen & Gollwitzer, 1987; Rhodes & de Bruijn, 2013; Rhodes, Fiala, & Nasuti, 2012; Schwarzer, 2008). Action-control frameworks that were created in action phases model (Gollwitzer, 1990; Heckhausen &

Gollwitzer, 1987) propose that intention implementation occurs due to volitional processes functioning in a post-intentional manner. These frameworks have also been used in other approaches such as health action process (Schwarzer, 2008), the I-Change model (de Vries, Mesters, van de Steeg, & Honing, 2005) and others (see Fuchs, Seelig, Göhner, Burton, & Brown, 2012; Hagger & Chatzisarantis, 2014). The next section briefly introduces the chapters that follow.

AN INTRODUCTION TO THE CHAPTERS

As we know, translation or interpretation is central in translational research and text is the 'vehicle' with which meaning is ultimately transferred to the reader. In a few disciplines like psychology, which is mostly Western psychology, all the concepts and principles are available in the English language only. Hence, translation becomes the only way to communicate with non-English-speaking people. In 'Knowledge Translation and Translational Research', Shokeen and Singh explore gaps in knowledge translation and their impact on health care service delivery in both developed and developing countries. Besides, they deal with different strategies to address these gaps through knowledge translation.

They discuss the role of translation in translational research and highlight how translation can result in multiple language challenges and needs revisions to achieve 'equivalence' such that the items remain consistent, valid and meaningful in the new language for use in a different cultural milieu. In addition, they challenge the assumption that data translation is merely a technical task where the translator could 'objectively and faithfully' transfer the meaning of research data from source language to target language.

In Chapter 2, titled 'Research Methods in Applied Psychology: An Evaluation', Singh and Bandyopadhyay review the research methods that can be used in policy-relevant research such as translational research and knowledge translation. They delineate some of the research methods being used in applied psychology and also recommend certain trajectories for achieving greater progress in research on applied psychology in India.

With majority of India's population living in rural area, 'Applications of Psychology in Rural India' presents a holistic picture of all mental health development measures and initiatives undertaken by the Indian government, local bodies, NGOs, private organizations, etc., to help people lead more fulfilling lives. Kaur and Singh broadly document research and intervention programmes aimed at improving their well-being in this chapter. Moving on, happiness is a topic that has intrigued social scientists for long. Singh, Takahashi and Kaur deal with perceptions of happiness in 'Perceived Happiness and its Determinants'. The chapter focuses on how a layperson perceives happiness and life satisfaction with reference to the past, present and future. Their research is an important contribution to translational research as its findings can give a framework on how a layperson views happiness, and this framework may prompt other communities, cultures and nations to outline their mental health and other related policies in line with the interest of their people.

In the chapter titled 'Role of Religious and Spiritual Practices in Mental Health', Sharma and Singh look at the various ways in which religion and spirituality contribute to the promotion of overall well-being. It has been estimated that 68 per cent of the world's population (about 4.6 billion) believes religion to be an important part of its life. This chapter documents different spiritual practices, religious rituals and interventions promoting mental health in literature in the Indian setting. The chapter is a significant contribution to translational research as it offers a sampling of different scientific researches and indigenous practices that can be applied to communities to improve health and QoL. In a related manner, positive psychology contributes to the flourishing or optimal functioning of people, groups and institutions, and positive psychological interventions are an important means to this end. Globally, there has been an increasing focus on the assimilation of positive psychology within the school milieu. However, a lot remains to be done in the Indian school system which is still marked by neglect and a deficit-focused approach towards mental health. There is a need to contextualize and adapt programmes to best fit the needs of the key stakeholders. Khanna and Singh dwell on these issues and concerns in 'Applications of Positive Psychology in Indian School Setting'.

Next, Bandyopadhyay and Singh review the status of the existing documented programmes delivered through the Internet from India, and in other eastern and western countries, to improve the well-being and QoL in 'Web-based Interventions to Improve Quality of Life' and make recommendations about how online techniques could be used more robustly to deliver adoption of best practices to the masses. It is proposed that by bringing together translational research and web-based interventions, the ultimate goal of successfully enhancing QoL would be recognized. Shifting from cyber world to the workplace, Raina and Singh posit that despite its promise, programmatic translation research is still rare owing in part to the lack of familiarity with translational methods on part of the psychologists. In the corporate sector, employee well-being and efforts to increase the same are being focused upon only now. In 'Employee Well-Being in Organizations', they examine the efforts that are being carried out in India and internationally to promote the well-being of employees working across the spectrum of workplaces. One of the objectives of translational research is aimed at enhancing the adoption (of scientific findings) of the best practices in the community. Applications of social and behavioural sciences have noteworthy impact on individuals, families and communities.

We wrap up the book with the concluding chapter 'Conclusion: Psychology and Translational Research—The Way Ahead' that focuses on the retrospect and prospects of translational research in applied psychology in India. It discusses various directions in which translational research could grow, better ways in which psychological findings may be utilized to improve the overall QoL, and the need to relook at the existing sociocultural practices that may help in maintaining and increasing well-being, mental health and QoL. The chapter concludes with recommendations for future directions for the field.

An important element of the book, and its various chapters, is the inclusion of the role that other organizations, like NGOs, are playing in the translation of knowledge and research. Academicians and researchers would be better positioned to do translational research by taking a cue from the NGOs who have already devised different strategies, targeting different populations across the vast expanse of India, and have achieved commendable results. However, there is a need of standardized practices, which individual chapter calls for while discussing the respective sector/ issue.

FUTURE DIRECTIONS

This section provides our recommendations for future translational research in applied psychology as well as for the policymakers in India. Based on our interventions, we find that in order to address the long-term comprehensive goals of public health care, mental well-being and QoL, there is a need to root the future interventions in psychological theories of change as they contribute towards an understanding of required outcomes. A focus on these will help identify processes that bring a change and thus explain why certain interventions work while others do not. Theoretical frameworks such as cognitive behavioural framework, empowerment theory and resilience theory, among others, have already been used successfully to alleviate depression and post-traumatic stress, and increase positivity and resilience (Graham-Bermann & Miller, 2013; Iverson et al., 2011; Kubany et al., 2004; Masten 2001; Miller, Howell, & Graham-Bermann, 2014; Ungar, 2012). They can help in measuring the mechanisms of change that may affect elements like self-efficacy or social support, which make interventions fail or succeed. This can in turn help increase the effectiveness of interventions.

The reviews reveal the array of research available wherein most of the current frameworks of interventions are focused on the immediacy of needs, which leave certain sections like women, older adults or children unattended. There is a need to prioritize the health of these sections of population. New interventions should consider their individualized and systemic needs and should pursue more highly integrated health care frameworks, encompassing individual's needs, familial problems and systemic social issues. These interventions should be designed to help them understand the importance of personal health and should have ease of accessibility for successful implementation. Health care organizations or community health centres should have adequately trained staff along with sufficient resources to manage care. Since resources might pose a problem, at least for staffing, instead of opting for new appointments, local mental health centres can partner community health centres. A rethink on the tools used for intervention can also help—mobile and tele-health interventions (something that Kuhn et al. [2014] also point towards) or media such as television or video (Humphreys, Tsoh, Kohn, & Gerbert, 2011) could be effective in reaching out to the population living in rural or remote areas. Since translational research is still in its infancy in India, more so in applied psychology and its interventions, there is a need to recognize the importance of work being done, as well as caution in moving ahead. New components should be added after keeping the successful elements of already implemented interventions intact and keeping in mind the uniqueness of individual and community experiences. This will help foster self-efficacy and well-being, and lessen the stigma attached (if any).

REFERENCES

Balas, E. A. (1998). From appropriate care to evidence-based medicine. *Pediatric Annals*, 27(9), 581–584.

Bandura, A. (1997). *Self-efficacy: The exercise of control*. New York, NY: Freeman.

Banerjee, E. R. (2016). *Perspectives in translational research in life sciences and biomedicine*. Singapore: Springer.

Beutler, L. E. (2000). Empirically based decision making in clinical practice. *Prevention and Treatment*, 3(1), 1–17.

Breckler, S. J. (2008). The NIH roadmap: Are psychologists in or out? *Journal of Clinical Psychology in Medical Settings*, 15(1), 60–64.

Brekke, J. S., Ell, K., & Palinkas, L. A. (2007). Translational science at the National Institute of Mental Health: Can social work take its rightful place? *Research on Social Work Practice*, 17(1), 123–133.

Brownson, R. C., Kreuter, M. W., Arrington, B. A., & True, W. R. (2006). Translating scientific discoveries into public health action: How can schools of public health move us forward? *Public Health Reports*, 121(1), 97–103.

Burke, W., Khoury, M. J., Stewart, A., & Zimmern, R. L. (2006). The path from genome-based research to population health: Development of an international public health genomics network. *Genetics in Medicine*, 8(7), 451–458.

Coyne, J. C. (1999). Thinking interactionally about depression: A radical restatement. In T. Joiner & J. C. Coyne (Eds.), *The interactional nature of depression* (pp. 365–392). Washington, DC: American Psychological Association.

Dai, K. R., Yang, F., & Gan, Y. K. (2013). Development of translational medicine in China: Foam or feast? *Journal of Orthopaedic Translation*, 1(1), 6–10.

de Vries, H., Mesters, I., van de Steeg, H., & Honing, C. (2005). The general public's information needs and perceptions regarding hereditary cancer: An application of the integrated change model. *Patient Education and Counseling*, 56(2), 154–165.

Department of Health and Human Services. (2006). NIH roadmap for medical research. Retrieved from http://nihroadmap.nih.gov/

Dingfelder, S. F. (2005). Transitioning to 'translational' times: The funding climate for behavioral science research is changing. How can psychological scientists adapt? *APA Monitor on Psychology, 36*(3), 22.

Dougherty, D., & Conway, P. H. (2008). The '3T's' road map to transform US health care: The 'how' of high-quality care. *JAMA, 299*(19), 2319–2321.

European Communities. (2002). Facing the challenge: The Lisbon strategy for growth and employment. November 2004. Retrieved from http://ec.europa.eu/growthandjobs/pdf/kok_report_en.pdf

Evans, V. J. (2012). Translation in the social and behavioral sciences: Looking back and looking forward. In E. Wethington & R. E. Dunifon (Eds.), *Research for the public good: Applying the methods of translational research to improve human health and well-being.* Washington, DC: Magination Press (American Psychological Association), 23–31.

Fang, F. C., & Casadevall, A. (2010). Lost in translation—basic science in the era of translational research. *Infection and Immunity, 78*(2), 563–566.

Feinstein, A. R. (1999). Basic biomedical science and the destruction of the pathophysiologic bridge from bench to bedside. *The American Journal of Medicine, 107*(5), 461–467.

Flynn, R. J., Dudding, P. M., & Barber, J. G. (Eds.). (2006). *Promoting resilience in development: A general framework for systems of care.* Ottawa: University of Ottawa Press.

Fontanarosa, P. B., & DeAngelis, C. D. (2002). Basic science and translational research in JAMA. *JAMA, 287*(13), 1728.

Franks, P., & Fiscella, K. (2008). Reducing disparities downstream: Prospects and challenges. *Journal of General Internal Medicine, 23*(5), 672–677.

Fuchs, R., Seelig, H., Göhner, W., Burton, N. W., & Brown, W. J. (2012). Cognitive mediation of intervention effects on physical exercise: Causal models for the adoption and maintenance stage. *Psychology & Health, 27*(12), 1480–1499.

Glasgow, R. E., Fisher, E. B., Haire-Joshu, D., & Goldstein, M. G. (2007). National Institutes of Health science agenda: A public health perspective. *American Journal of Public Health, 97*(11), 1936–1938.

Glasgow, R. E., Wagner, E. H., Kaplan, R. M., Vinicor, F., Smith, L., & Norman, J. (1999). If diabetes is a public health problem, why not treat it as one? A population-based approach to chronic illness. *Annals of Behavioral Medicine, 21*(2), 159–170.

Gollwitzer, P. M. (1990). Action phases and mind-sets. In E. T. Higgins & R. M. Sorrentino (Eds.), *Handbook of motivation and cognition: Foundations of social behavior* (Vol. 2, pp. 53–92). New York, NY: Guildford Press.

Graham-Bermann, S. A., & Miller, L. E. (2013). Intervention to reduce traumatic stress following intimate partner violence: An efficacy trial of the Moms' Empowerment Program (MEP). *Psychodynamic Psychiatry, 41*(2), 329–349.

Greenwald, P., & Cullen, J. (1985). The new emphasis in cancer control. *Journal of the National Cancer Institute, 74*, 543–51.

Hagger, M. S., & Chatzisarantis, N. L. D. (2014). An integrated behavior change model for physical activity. *Exercise and Sport Sciences Reviews, 42*(2), 62–69.

Halterman, J. S., Aligne, C. A., Auinger, P., McBride, J. T., & Szilagyi, P. G. (2000). Inadequate therapy for asthma among children in the United States. *Pediatrics, 105*(1), 272–276.

Haney, C., Banks, C., & Zimbardo, P. (1973). Interpersonal dynamics in a simulated prison. *International Journal of Criminology & Penology, 1*(1), 69–97.

Hawk, E. (2006). National Cancer Institute, Translational Research Working Group, Roundtable II. Retrieved from https://www.cancer.gov/images/trwg/Hawk-RT-10-16-06.pdf

Heckhausen, H., & Gollwitzer, P. M. (1987). Thought contents and cognitive functioning in motivational and volitional states of mind. *Motivation and Emotion, 11*(2), 101–120.

Hofmann, S. G. (2007). Enhancing exposure-based therapy from a translational research perspective. *Behaviour Research and Therapy, 45*(9), 1987–2001.

Holt, N. L., & Jones, M. I. (2008). Future directions for positive youth development and sport research. In N. L. Holt (Ed.), *Positive youth development through sport* (pp. 122–132). Oxon: Routledge.

Hommel, K. A., Modi, A. C., Piazza-Waggoner, C., & Myers, J. D. (2015). Topical review: Translating translational research in behavioral science. *Journal of Pediatric Psychology, 40*(10), 1034–1040.

Humphreys, J., Tsoh, J. Y., Kohn, M. A., & Gerbert, B. (2011). Increasing discussions of intimate partner violence in prenatal care using video doctor plus provider cueing: A randomized, controlled trial. *Women's Health Issues, 21*(2), 136–144.

Insel, T. R. (2004). NIMH director's report to the National Advisory Mental Health Council September 2004. Retrieved from http://www.nimh.nih.gov/council/dirreportSept04.pdf

Iverson, K. M., Gradus, J. L., Resick, P. A., Suvak, M. K., Smith, K. F., & Monson, C. M. (2011). Cognitive–behavioral therapy for PTSD and depression symptoms reduces risk for future intimate partner violence among interpersonal trauma survivors. *Journal of Consulting and Clinical Psychology, 79*(2), 193–202.

Katon, W., Joan, R., Richardson, L., McCauley, E., & Lozano, P. (2008). Anxiety and depression screening for youth in a primary care population. *Ambulatory Pediatrics : The Official Journal of the Ambulatory Pediatric Association, 8*(3), 182–188.

Kay, S. (2015). Africa's leadership in biomedical research: Shifting the center of gravity. *Science Translational Medicine, 7*(314), 314ed13.

Keramaris, N. C., Kanakaris, N. K., Tzioupis, C., Kontakis, G., & Giannoudis, P. V. (2008). Translational research: From benchside to bedside. *Injury, 39*(6), 643–650.

Kerner, J. F. (2006). Knowledge translation versus knowledge integration: A 'funder's' perspective. *Journal of Continuing Education in the Health Professions*, 26(1), 72–80.

Khoury, M. J., Gwinn, M., Yoon, P. W., Dowling, N., Moore, C. A., & Bradley L. (2007). The continuum of translation research in genomic medicine: How can we accelerate the appropriate integration of human genome discoveries into health care and disease prevention? *Genetics in Medicine, 9*(10), 665–674.

Krause, J. D. (2009). Taking it into the interactional field: Toward translational applied sociology. *Humboldt Journal of Social Relations, 32*(1), 35–85.

Kubany, E. S., Hill, E. E., Owens, J. A., Iannce-Spencer, C., McCaig, M. A., Tremayne, K. J., & Williams, P. L. (2004). Cognitive trauma therapy for battered women with PTSD (CTT-BW). *Journal of Consulting and Clinical Psychology, 72*(1), 3.

Kuhn, E., Greene, C., Hoffman, J., Nguyen, T., Wald, L., Schmidt, J ... Ruzek, J. (2014). Preliminary evaluation of PTSD coach, a smartphone app for post-traumatic stress symptoms. *Military Medicine, 179*(1), 12–18.

Lamberg, Lynne. (1998). Dawn's early light to twilight's last gleaming... *JAMA, 280*(18), 1556–1558.

Lemon, S. C., Bowen, D., Rosal, M. C., Pagoto, S. L., Schneider, K., Pbert, L., ... Ockene, J. K. (2013). Translational research phases in the behavioral and social sciences: Adaptations from the biomedical sciences. In K. A. Riekert, J. K. Ockene, & L. Pbert (Eds.), *The handbook of health behavior change* (pp. 483–497). New York, NY: Springer.

Masten, A. S. (2001). Ordinary magic: Resilience processes in development. *American Psychologist, 56*(3), 227.

———. (2011). Special section article. Resilience in children threatened by extreme adversity: Frameworks for research, practice, and translational synergy. *Development and Psychopathology, 23*(2), 493–506.

Miami CTSI. University of Miami. (2017). What is translational research? Retrieved from http://miamictsi.org/about/translational-research

Milgram, S. (1963). Behavioral study of obedience. *Journal of Abnormal and Social Psychology, 67*(4), 371–378.

Miller, L. E., Howell, K. H., & Graham-Bermann, S. A. (2014). The effect of an evidence based intervention on women's exposure to intimate partner violence. *American Journal of Orthopsychiatry, 84*(4), 321–328.

Miller, M. R., Gergen, P., Honour, M., & Zhan, C. L. (2005). Burden of illness for children and where we stand in measuring the quality of this healthcare. *Ambulatory Pediatrics: The Official Journal of the Ambulatory Pediatric Association, 5*(5), 268–278.

Mold, J. W., & Peterson, K. A. (2005). Primary care practice-based research networks: Working at the interface between research and quality improvement. *Annals of Family Medicine, 3*(1, Suppl.), S12–S20.

MRC. (2007). Accelerating the translation of medical research. *MRC workshop*, 20–21 February 2007, 1–22.

Nakaya, J., Shimizu, T., Tanaka, H., & Asano, S. (2005). Current translational research in Australia and translational research supporting center in Japan. *Chem-Bio Informatics Journal, 5*(2), 27–38.

Narayan, K. M., Benjamin, E., Gregg, E. W., Norris, S. L., & Engelgau, M. M. (2004). Diabetes translation research: Where are we and where do we want to be? *Annals of Internal Medicine, 140*(11), 958–963.

Narayan, K. M., Gregg, E. W., Engelgau, M. M., Moore, B., Thompson, T., Williamson, D., & Vinicor, F. (2000). Translation research for chronic disease. *Diabetes Care, 23*(12), 1794–1798.

National Institute of Mental Health (NIMH). (2000). *Translating behavioral science into action* (NIMH Publication No. 00–4699). Washington, DC: US, Government Printing Office. Retrieved from http://www.ti-gr.com/Resources/Publication%20Materials/NIMH-Translating%20Behavioral%20Science%20into%20 Action.pdf

National Institutes of Health (NIH). (2007). *RFA-RM-07-007: Institutional Clinical and Translational Science Award (U54)*. Retrieved from https://grants.nih.gov/grants/guide/rfa-files/rfa-rm-07-007.html

Nyden, P., Hossfeld, L., & Nyden, G. (2012). *Public sociology: Research, action, and change*. Los Angeles, CA: SAGE Publications/Pine Forge.

O'Connor, T. (2013). Translational research in practice. *Journal of Child Psychology and Psychiatry, 54*(11), 1153–1154

Palinkas, L. A. (2010). Commentary: Cultural adaptation, collaboration, and exchange. *Research on Social Work Practice, 20*(5), 544–546.

Palinkas, L. A., Aarons, G. A., Chorpita, B. F., Hoagwood, K., Landsverk, J., & Weisz, J. R. (2009). Cultural exchange and the implementation of evidence-based practices: Two case studies. *Research on Social Work Practice, 19*(5), 602–612.

Palinkas, L. A., & Soydan, H. (2012). New horizons of translational research and research translation in social work. *Research on Social Work Practice, 22*(1), 85–92.

Perlstadt, H. (2007). Applied sociology. In C. D. Bryant & D. L. Peck (Eds.), *21st Century sociology: A reference handbook* (pp. 342–352). Thousand Oaks, CA: SAGE Publications.

———. (2009). Translational research: Enabling the biomedical and social behavioral sciences to benefit society. *Humboldt Journal of Social Relations, 32*(1), 4–34.

Pillemer, K. A., Suitor, J. J., & Wethington, E. (2003). Integrating theory, basic research, and intervention: Two case studies from caregiving research. *The Gerontologist, 43*(1), 19–28.

Pillemer, K., Czaja, S., Schulz, R., & Stahl, S. M. (2003). Finding the best ways to help: Opportunities and challenges of intervention research on aging. *The Gerontologist, 43*(1), 5–8.

Pober, J. S., Neuhauser, C. S., & Pober, J. M. (2001). Obstacles facing translational research in academic medical centers. *FASEB Journal, 15*(13), 2303–2313.

Price, J., & Will, J. (2015). Applied sociology. In James D. Wright (Ed.), *International encyclopedia of the social & behavioral sciences* (2nd ed., pp. 858–860). Oxford: Elsevier.

Research and Development Directorate Department of Health, UK. (2006). *Best research for best health: A new national health research strategy.* Retrieved from https://www.gov.uk/government/publications/best-research-for-best-health-a-new-national-health-research-strategy

Rhodes, R. E., & de Bruijn, G. J. (2013). How big is the physical activity intention behavior gap? A meta-analysis using the action control framework. *British Journal of Health Psychology, 18*(2), 296–309.

Rhodes, R. E., Fiala, B., & Nasuti, G. (2012). Action control of exercise behavior: Evaluation of social cognition, cross-behavioral regulation, and automaticity. *Behavioral Medicine, 38*(4), 121–128.

Rosen, G. M., & Davison, G. C. (2003). Psychology should list empirically supported principles of change (ESPs) and not credential trademarked therapies or other treatment packages. *Behavior Modification, 27*(3), 300–312.

Rubio, D. M., Schoenbaum, E. E., Lee, L. S., Schteingart, D. E., Marantz, P. R., Anderson, K. E., Platt, L. D., & Esposito, A. B. K. (2010). Defining translational research: Implications for training. *Academic Medicine, 85*(3), 470–475.

Schroeder, S. A. (2007). Shattuck lecture. We can do better—improving the health of the American people. *The New England Journal of Medicine, 357*(12), 1221–1228.

Schwarzer, R. (2008). Modeling health behaviour change: How to predict and modify the adoption and maintenance of health behaviors. *Applied Psychology: An International Review, 57*(1), 1–29.

Sung, N. S., Crowley, W. F., Jr., Genel, M., Salber, P., Sandy, L., Sherwood, L. M., … Rimoin, D. (2003). Central challenges facing the national clinical research enterprise. *Journal of the American Medical Association, 289*(10), 1278–1287.

Szilagyi, P. G. (2008). Academic Pediatric Association (APA) presidential address: Changing the world for children. *Ambulatory Pediatrics, 8*(5), 273–278.

———. (2009). Translational research and pediatrics. *Academic Pediatrics, 9*(2), 71–80.

Tashiro, T., & Mortensen, L. (2006). Translational research: How social psychology can improve psychotherapy. *American Psychologist, 61*(9), 959–966.

Triendl, R. (2004). Translational research in immunology: Japanese perspectives. *Nature Reviews Immunology, 4*(1), 72–77.

Ungar, M. (Ed.). (2012). *The social ecology of resilience: A handbook of theory and practice.* New York, NY: Springer.

Vinicor, F. (1994). Is diabetes a public-health disorder (review)? *Diabetes Care, 17*(1, Suppl.), 22–27.

Warnecke, R. B., Oh, A., Breen, N., Gehlert, S., Paskett, E., Tucker, K. L., Lurie, N., … Hiatt, R. A. (2008). Approaching health disparities from a population perspective: The National Institutes of Health Centers for population health and health disparities. *American Journal of Public Health*, *98*(9), 1608–1615.

Weremeychik, E., & P. Eastman. (2015). How do you define translational research? Labdesignnews.com. Retrieved from https://www.labdesignnews.com/article/2015/01/how-do-you-define-translational-research

Westfall, J. M., Mold, J., & Fagnan, L. (2007). Practice-based research—'Blue Highways' on the NIH roadmap. *JAMA*, *297*(4), 403–6.

Wethington, E. (2015). Translational sociology. In R. A. Scott & S. Kosslyn (Eds.), *Emerging trends in the social and behavioral sciences: An interdisciplinary, searchable, and linkable resource* (pp. 1–8). New York, NY: J. Wiley & Sons.

———. (2016). What is translational research? Retrieved from http://evidence-basedliving.human.cornell.edu/2010/08/18/what-is-translational-research/

Widiger, T. A. (2005). Five factor model of personality disorder: Integrating science and practice. *Journal of Research in Personality*, *39*(1), 67–83.

Woolf, S. H. (2008). The meaning of translational research and why it matters. *JAMA*, *299*(2), 211–213.

Wuchty, S., Jones, B. F., & Uzzi, B. (2007). The increasing dominance of teams in production of knowledge. *Science*, *316*(5827), 1036–1039.

Zimbardo, P. G. (1972). The pathology of imprisonment. *Society*, *9*(6), 4–8.

Zvolensky, M. J., Lejuez, C. W., Stuart, G. L., & Curtain, J. J. (2001). Experimental psychopathology in psychological science. *Review of General Psychology*, *5*, 371–381.

Chapter 1

Knowledge Translation and Translational Research

Bharti Shokeen and Kamlesh Singh

In the last few decades, unprecedented global investment has been made in the field of health care research. Despite having generated a substantial storehouse of knowledge, its translation in the form of refined health care services, products, outcomes and policies has been imperceptible. The concept of knowledge translation has developed against this backdrop. This chapter explores the various gaps and 'death valleys' in knowledge translation and their impact on health care service delivery in both developed and developing countries. It also looks at how these countries are trying to address and bridge these gaps through knowledge translation strategies. In India, among the various other barriers in knowledge translation, language and communication has emerged as a major issue because psychological research is primarily disseminated in English. In contrast, about 70 per cent of the population is rural and is conversant with Hindi and/or other vernacular languages. This raises the need for effective communication and interaction which has been emphasized in the knowledge translation literature worldwide. The chapter closes with a discussion of various strategies for effective health communication and suggests how effective and strategic communication can reduce this knowledge gap in psychological research.

It has been observed that communication between researchers about their current or forthcoming research is a common, smooth and expected occurrence (David, 2001; Haynes, 1990). On the other hand, communication between researchers and practitioners about research findings is not given much emphasis and is rare (Lavis, Robertson, Woodside, McLeod, & Abelson, 2003). Researchers tend to view research as 'decisions' whereas decision-makers, general public, patients and care providers view research as a purchasable product, which is, however, often found in the wrong size or one size fits all, requires altering, is in less demand or on back order. The path to well-informed researched decision-making depends on better communication, transmission and exchange between those who do research and the ones who implement and incorporate them (Lomas, 2000). This not only requires quality communication between researchers and practitioners but also a cognizance of the contexts in which they work (Landry, Amara, Pablos-Mendes, Shademani, & Gold, 2006). Herein lies the role of translation and effective communication to bridge the gap between researchers, practitioners, general public and policymakers. In this chapter, we emphasize the concept of 'knowledge translation' which has emerged recently and gained currency globally, particularly in Canada. While discussing the gaps in knowledge translation, we will see how effective and strategic communication can help reduce the gaps.

Every year, the National Institutes of Health makes huge investments in health care and biomedical research. Despite the financial and infrastructural resources provided to health sciences research, it has been observed that the translation of research findings into practice is a delayed process which is often of a disorganized nature (Agency for Health Research and Quality, 2001). It has been estimated by researchers that even in advanced countries such as United States of America and the Netherlands, 30–45 per cent of the patients receive care which is not based upon scientific evidence (Grol, 2001; Schuster, McGlynn, & Brook, 1998). Research findings also indicate that in the United States of America, less than 20 per cent of the medical treatment provided by physicians is grounded on strong scientific evidence (Kumar & Nash, 2011). Moreover, according to Schuster et al. (1998), approximately 20–30 per cent of the patients are made to undergo unnecessary diagnostic tests, receive unnecessary medications or other health damaging medical services.

The research and scientific world needs to seek new ways to meet these challenges and to ensure that discoveries, experiments and research findings reach the public and the patients as quickly and as efficiently as possible. To understand this process of dissemination of knowledge, a variety of models such as 'translational research', 'knowledge translation' and 'dissemination and implementation (D&I) research' have emerged. They help us understand the factors that are involved in the process of transformation of research findings into new implementable practices or enhancements in pre-existing practices. Research findings, particularly from an applicative field like psychology, should feature in policy briefs, augment new research and be implemented by practitioners wherever feasible. Translational research sees how best to translate research into practice while knowledge translation tackles specific gaps in translation (Davidson, 2011). In health research, there are two major gaps or valleys. The first gap exists between basic and clinical research; the second gap lies between clinical research and health care practice. Translational research 'bridges' the first gap whereas knowledge translation addresses the second gap. Sung et al. (2003) clarified the distinction between translational research and knowledge translation—two terms that often overlap and that are used alternatively. While translational research is the translation of basic research into clinical science and knowledge, knowledge translation is the translation of this new clinical science and knowledge into practice. Donabedian (1982) opines that the use of the terms translational research and knowledge translation in several different contexts, and often simultaneously, has resulted in confusion about their meanings. It has thereby led to their incorrect usage in some contexts.

The next few sections will focus on 'knowledge translation', the gaps in knowledge translation in developed and developing countries, and provide an overview of the effective and strategic communication that can reduce the exiting gaps in knowledge translation.

'DEATH VALLEYS': GAPS IN KNOWLEDGE TRANSLATION

The transformation of basic research into clinical knowledge and the translation of the clinical knowledge into practice are characterized by barriers and challenges. In scientific research, these barriers are named as 'valleys of death' which prevent the health research and innovations from reaching patients. Morris, Wooding and Grant (2011) observed that in health-related research, the 'valleys of death' lie in two arenas—the first lies between basic and clinical research, and the second lies between clinical research and health-related practices. The barriers and obstacles posed by these 'valleys of death' include lack of incentives, failure of technology to reach clinical implementation, transition from traditional funding and granting resources to other investor options (Bornstein, 2014; Butler, 2008), securing stable funding for research (Dorsey, Thompson, & Carrasco, 2009; Yusuf & Cairns, 2012), and managing and overcoming the other resource constraints associated with clinical practice.

In addition to that, there are several other interacting factors that result in this gap between health research and practice. Orlandi (1987) observed that for evidence-based practices, there is lack of feedback and incentives, insufficient infrastructural facilities, inadequate systems organization to support translation, limited resources of practitioners and insufficient training. Other factors include inaccessibility of peer-reviewed journals, need for greater specificity for catering to the requirements of individual clients or a specific patient population and concerns of practitioners regarding the possible lack of control over the therapeutic process (Glasgow, Lichtenstein, & Marcus, 2003; National Advisory Mental Health Council, 1999; Palinkas et al., 2008; Schoenwald & Hoagwood, 2001).

Terminology and Definition

There exists a variety of terminologies related to knowledge translation. For example, Graham, Tetroe, Robinso and Grimshaw (2005) conducted a study involving 9 different countries and 33 research-funding agencies, and identified around 29 different terms that are related to knowledge translation. In UK and Europe, this process is referred to as research utilization whereas in the United States of America, it is called research diffusion, dissemination or knowledge uptake. In Canada, on the other hand, knowledge translation, knowledge transfer and knowledge exchange are the commonly used terms. In Canada, the Canadian Institute for Health Research (CIHR) has major responsibility for funding as well as promoting and disseminating knowledge translation based health care research.

CIHR views knowledge translation as 'a dynamic and iterative process which involves synthesis, dissemination, exchange, and ethically-sound application of knowledge to enhance health care. Over the course of time, it helps to strengthen the health care system by providing effective health care services to the care recipients, which translates into better health outcomes' (Canadian Health Services Research Foundation, 2003).

Following the definition of the CIHR, the World Health Organization (WHO) has defined knowledge translation as 'the amalgamation, exchange and utilization of local and global research. Their definition also draws attention to the role of knowledge translation in innovation of the health care systems thereby strengthening the system itself, and improving the overall health of the population' (Oborn, Barret, & Racko, 2010).

The main objective of knowledge translation is to reduce the gap between the voluminous amount of research and its systematic review, application and execution by practitioners (Ohlsson, 2002). To bridge this gap and advance knowledge translation further, several international organizations and research agencies have set up centres which execute research and carry out developmental and dissemination activities related to knowledge translation. A multidisciplinary academic programme, Knowledge Translation Program, has been developed at the University of Toronto to bridge the existing gap between evidence-based research and clinical practice. It also addresses the need to develop innovative ways and processes by means of which knowledge can be efficaciously translated into health care practices. National Health Service, located in the United Kingdom, is another major organization that conducts systematic reviews of research, analyses the impact of health care interventions and disseminates research-based information. Another initiative for furthering knowledge translation is the Translating Research into Practice (TRIP) programme whose primary emphasis lies in translating and applying research findings to a variety of applied settings with the help of implementation techniques.

Dissemination and Implementation Research

An early research done by Archie Cochrane in the 1970s shows that many medical treatments use passive methods such as mass mailings or consensus statements and lack scientific rigour in their efforts at disseminating practical guidelines. Many practitioners have been found to indulge in medical practices that are based on personal experience rather than those which are based on sufficient scientific evidence (Brekke, Ell, & Palinkas, 2007).

In addition, doing research solely on the basis of passive dissemination practices, such as journal articles and conference presentations, without any consideration for its 'potential' translation, does not contribute to knowledge translation *or* translational research. Research shows that 90 per cent of publicly funded systems, such as mental health, juvenile justice, child welfare, among several others, do not utilize evidence-based practices (Hoagwood & Olin, 2002). This indicates the need for adequate dissemination activities for use by policymakers. D&I research tries to address this gap.

D&I research supports evidence-based health care services and prevention strategies, promotes the use of evidence-based interventions among practitioners and implementation of scientifically proven approaches to health care. In other words, it focuses on the transformation of evidence-based research and interventions into practice to improve health outcomes of population. Thus, D&I are the organizational processes through which new scientific research and advances can be translated and transferred to people, social settings and communities to improve public health and services (Rabin, Brownson, Haire-Joshu, Kreuter, & Weaver, 2008).

Knowledge Translation Gaps in Developed and Developing Countries

There is a high disparity between health research and implementation in those developing countries where evidence-based research is done scarcely (Lavis, 2009; Niessen, Grijseels, & Rutten, 2000). As per the recent United Nations (2010) update, in economically advanced countries, mostly all births are taken care of by skilled health personnel, whereas, in parts of the developing countries, less than half of the women have access to such health care amenities while giving birth. Similarly, it has been reported that the mortality rate of children under 5 years of age is also 18 times more in low- and middle-income nations than the economically advanced ones (Fay, Leipziger, Wodon, & Yepes, 2005). In addition, it has also been seen that child mortality rate and average life expectancy have improved more and are found to be much better in the higher income economies than their lower counterparts (United Nations, 2010).

Despite the large production and availability of scientific research and information, there is no change or decrease in the overall burden of disease in most low- and middle-income nations, pointing to a basic discrepancy between what was known and what was done with the available information and relevant knowledge. This failure to use the available research and knowledge effectively to address health disparities (the 'know do' gap) in low- and middle-income nations through strategic planning, professional practice and policy formulation, and implementation has gained the attention of various national and international research organizations, such as the National Institute of Health, the World Bank, the Alliance for Health Policy and Systems Research and the WHO.

Even in countries where health inequalities have improved, there is no reason for complacency since the differences in health across population groups remain substantial (e.g. child mortality in Colombia). (Welch, Euffing, & Tugwell, 2009, p. 1068)

The challenges encountered by the low- and middle-income economies in conducting and implementing health care research have been attributed to their limited resources. The Joint Learning Initiative, which is a consortium of over 100 global health leaders, has pointed out the scarcity of health care personnel in most low- and medium-income countries (Chen et al., 2004). Lavis and colleagues identified a few factors that may be hindering the implementation of evidence-based research in such nations. They include conflicts between the civil servants and the elected health officials, lack of financial resources, and an unstable and conflict-ridden political environment (Lavis et al., 2005).

In addition to these factors, Siddiqi, Newell and Robinson (2005) reviewed the literature and suggested that local factors also affect the success of these interventions. Haines, Kuruvilla and Borchert (2004) identified one such local factor. They found that the local public or the potential consumer may not have knowledge of the intervention, and they may be influenced by the culture, ideological beliefs and values. This may deter them from accepting the scientific evidence as it is incongruent with their social and cultural beliefs. This emphasizes the need of developing strategies and interventions that are perceived positively by the potential users and are congruent with their cultural and social setting.

KNOWLEDGE TRANSLATION IN INDIA

India is also considered as one of the lower-ranking countries in knowledge translation efforts globally, regionally and among the BRICS nations (Brazil, Russia, India, China and South Africa; Decoster, Appelmans, & Hill, 2012). Moreover, in India, evidence-informed policymaking is still in its nascent stages. However, with the launch of National Rural Health Mission, and establishment of the National Health Systems Resource Centre, the Public Health Foundation of India at the national level and the State Health Systems Resource Centres at the state level, there has been a more concerted effort on health systems research. However, it has been found that the bulk of the research potentiality is consolidated in a few research institutions and is focused on only a few select states and domains (Rao, Arora, & Ghaffar, 2014). Moreover, formal knowledge translation programmes that should systematically engage policymakers, researchers and social organizations to jointly discuss key policy issues and challenges and take note of the available research around those issues are very rare.

In addition to this, it has also been observed that researchers and practitioners often have differing notions of what constitutes actionable evidence, which evidence is more crucial or what is good evidence (Shrivastava & Mitroff, 1984). Sometimes they have distinctive policy priorities and constraints (Thomas & Tymon, 1982; Johns, 1993). It has been seen that the researchers and practitioners do not always trust each other which creates mutual suspicion and makes them more resistant to change (Ellen et al., 2014).

Knowledge Translation in Psychology

Psychology has immense value in promoting holistic well-being of the general population and in catering to the special needs of certain specific disciplines (Thompson, Boxall, Hodgins, & Patrick, 2013). Moreover, it has an invaluable role in resolving everyday problems in a wide variety of settings, and a substantial amount of its research findings has relevance in policymaking (Kenkel, 2015; Miller, 1969). Psychologists have the responsibility of translating psychological science for the public in order to raise public awareness about the ways psychological science can benefit individuals, families, societies, nations and the world. Psychologists must 'give psychology away' (Miller, 1969, p. 1074) by disseminating psychological science for public consumption (Thompson et al., 2013). Baron (2010) states that successful translation of psychology means conveying the psychological research to others in a way that resonates with them.

Language and Communication Issues in Dissemination of Psychological Knowledge in India

Knowledge dissemination of social sciences differs from other natural sciences. In these disciplines, the circulation of knowledge is characterized by linguistic diversity that requires the mediation of translation more than the natural sciences. Knowledge demands to be used by ordinary people, therefore communication in local languages is a condition for reaching the non-academic audience. Thus, translation becomes a medium and major vehicle for the dissemination of knowledge in a discipline like psychology. It requires not only training and experience but also a connection with the local cultures and society (Borchelt, 2001). Translating psychological science means conveying the message to the audience in a comprehensible and relevant manner so that the audience understands what it means and what difference the science makes. Psychological science needs to be translated to the general public, including individuals with different cultural and educational backgrounds and varying interests in the understanding and application of social sciences like psychology. Moreover, due to this linguistic diversity, greater emphasis has been given to written expressions and interpretive analysis than the standardized conceptual formulations.

THE DISCONNECT: ARE WE SPEAKING THE SAME LANGUAGE?

The process of translation of scientific discoveries and research findings into a usable form cannot be achieved without the use of language. Language serves as the basic link to achieve collaboration between scientists and practitioners, and academia, health care and industry. It is here that one encounters conflicts because of the different social, cultural and academic background of scientists and clinicians. In this context, the British scientist and novelist, Snow (2012) described 'the two cultures' and explained how intelligent people may differ greatly or may have different perspectives based on their backgrounds. In a similar way, pre-clinical and clinical work also differs in terms of their culture and work environment. Generally, very few researchers and scientists have experience of working in clinics and hospitals. Similarly, very few medical practitioners and physicians have actual experience of carrying out any 'wet' lab work.

Once again, if we shift our focus back to the importance of language in knowledge translation, we realize that its most fundamental role in knowledge translation lies in expressing the knowledge. Knowledge is produced through research that is available only in English whereas the society uses a language that is dissimilar to the language used by the researcher. Hence, language plays a vital role in dissemination of this knowledge and research. 'Science needs, and indeed has a global language, but such a language cannot flatten the world' (Montgomery. 2013, p. 186). The literature of the social science research can reach the population only if it is disseminated in a language intelligible to them.

Language Gaps in India

Despite the multiplicity of languages and dialects spoken in India, most of our scientific or research publications are in English. With regards to the global scenario, 60 per cent of the knowledge in all disciplines is produced in English, which can be accessed through translation from or into English. Redmann opines, 'English spans the divide between people and culture. It is not owned by Britain and America: now it belongs to everyone' (2000, p. 45). In the words of Lord Alan Watson, Chairman of the English-Speaking Union, 'English has become the working language of the global village' (Redmann, 2000, p. 45). Currently, English is the predominantly used language for trade and business communications and for disseminating the improvements that have been made in science and technology (Brutt-Griffler, 2002; Cronin, 2003).

There are 7,102 living languages in the world, and, as per a 2015 study by the British Council, 3 out of the 5 top languages in the world are Indian—Hindi, Bengali, and Urdu. Interestingly, India, as per the 1961 count, has more than 1,652 mother tongues. However, English and Hindi are the two main languages that are recognized by the central government as official languages of communication. With a huge number of 551 million speakers, Hindi is the most common language in India. On the other hand, only 12 per cent of India's population speaks English even if we consider people who speak English as a second language. Hence, translating the available research and knowledge content into Hindi will make it accessible to half or 53 per cent of the population.

In addition to that, nearly 70 per cent of the population (Rural and Urban distribution: 68.84% and 31.16%) lives in villages wherein, as Gandhi Ji remarked, lives the soul of India (Census of India, 2011). Of the total 1.21 billion Indian population, 833 million Indians reside in rural regions whereas 377 million of the population resides in urban regions (Census of India, 2011). Given the multiplicity of languages and dialects spoken and varying levels of literacy in India, translation becomes the most important tool for research and for reaching out to the masses in India.

Challenges in Disseminating Psychological Science

Psychologists often find it challenging to determine how to integrate their science culture with the culture of public engagement (Baron, 2010). In addition to that, some psychological scientists feel that the added responsibilities associated with science communication, such as preparing lay summaries, giving media interviews, communicating via social media, intensify the demands on their time and may reduce their academic productivity (Kuehne & Olden, 2015). They often lack the required knowledge, skills and attitudes for communicating information in a manner that would increase psychological science literacy (Pinker, 2014). The general public often has stereotypical images of psychologists, viewing them only as practitioners, not as scientists. Psychological scientists mostly avoid reaching out to the public due to the perception that the latter might not be knowledgeable or literate enough to respond to their efforts. Thus, unfortunately, psychological science is often communicated by psychologists neither with diverse backgrounds nor in a manner that takes the audience's diversity into account. Similarly, the audience's cultural backgrounds also influence their attitudes toward science, including psychological science, and how they understand and interpret findings.

Language Barriers in Health Care

Inappropriate communication leads to misunderstandings between a health care provider and the potential consumer and becomes a barrier in accessing health care services (Bischoff, 2003). Further, it has been observed that due to language problems, community health care lacks systematic cultural care assessment (Thyli, Athlin, & Hedelin, 2007). However, language barrier and its consequences can be overcome by making use of the service of interpreters and translators (Karliner, Jacobs, Chen, & Mutha, 2007). In the context of people with limited or no proficiency in English, the WA Health System Language Services Policy (Government of Western Australia, 2011) emphasizes the need to promote effective interaction between health care providers and recipients who need language assistance (Government of Western Australia, 2011). It clearly states that the interpreters must meet the criterion of minimum proficiency both in English and in the local community language. In a health care setting with multilingual or multicultural population, the Language Policy (WA Health System Language Services Policy) clearly delineates the situations in which the services of an accredited interpreter may be used. As per the WA Health System Language Services Policy in Australia, the translators and interpreters are accredited nationally, and, while in service, they are required to abide by the ethics of confidentiality, impartiality and accuracy (Centre for Culture Ethnicity and Health, 2008).

Professional interpreters, translators, bilingual health professionals, and social and community workers can help in approaching population with vernacular languages. They can also provide information about the cultural and social milieu, cultural codes and concepts of the population of interest to the researcher. Hence, it is not only language proficiency but also cultural knowledge that is provided by bilingual/bicultural workers

(Centre for Culture Ethnicity and Health, 2008). In contrast, translators perform the role of translating a text in written form from one language into another (Government of Western Australia, 2011).

Language Barriers in Multicultural & Multilingual Setting

In the social and medical sciences, survey questionnaires are often used for data collection. For a multicultural and multilingual country, it becomes necessary to translate the questionnaire into the local language of the particular population of research interest. Besides being time consuming and bearing extra monetary costs, translating questionnaires can have various other challenges. If the research questionnaire is too academic, it becomes difficult to understand the meaning for a majority of its intended audience, which may lead to concerns regarding the appropriate level of language (Hanna, Hunt, & Bhopal, 2006). Similarly, the informal expressions used in one language might not have an identical expression in another language, and translation becomes difficult. Sometimes, the translator also changes the meaning of a phrase unintentionally to convey the exact meaning (Culley & Rapport, 2007). In addition to that, there may be differences in language usage across countries even with regard to the same language. For example, Bengali that is spoken by Bengalis in India and Bangladesh has certain minute differences. Thus, translation does not necessarily help the speakers of a language (Flaskerud & Nyamathi, 2000). Hence, a back translation of the translated document is required to ensure its equivalency. Community members may also be involved in the process of translation; the questionnaires can be further refined based on their feedback (Small et al., 1999). Sometimes, there may be disagreement between the translators and community members regarding the choice of words. Under such circumstances, further communication will be needed to clarify and resolve these doubts.

Role of Language and Communication in Translating Knowledge to Action

Among the various challenges facing research translation, the research–practice gap is one of the biggest challenges. It was in 2006 that WHO emphasized for the first time the requirement to bridge this gap, referred to as the 'know–do gap'. Lee Jong-wook, the then Director-General of WHO (2005), highlighted the gap between the scientific advances being made and their implementation. In essence, he was referring to the gap between what is known and what is actually being done—if action without knowledge is wasted effort, then knowledge without action is a wasted resource.

In contemporary times, one of the crucial challenges being encountered in health research is bridging the 'know-do gap', and knowledge translation has emerged as the mechanism to achieve this. There are varieties of knowledge translation strategies that have emerged to bridge this gap (Orton, Lloyd-Williams, Taylor-Robinson, O'Flaherty, & Capewell, 2011). Among them, one strategy is that of dissemination through strategic communication (Jones et al., 2013). Strategic communication is 'the purposeful use of communication by an organization to fulfil its mission' (Hallahan, Holtzhausen, Van Ruler, Vercic, & Sriramesh, 2007, p. 3). In this regard, Lomas (2007, p. 131) says that knowledge translation plays a critical role in linking 'decision makers with researchers, facilitating their interaction so that they are able to better understand each other's goals and professional cultures, influence each other's work, forge new partnerships, and promote the use of research-based evidence in decision-making'.

In their ethnographic study, Gabbay and Le May (2004) report how communication and the development of social networks helped in translating clinical research and implementing them in the form of interventions in a community setting in England. Similarly, Greenhalgh and colleagues stated that 'knowledge depends for its circulation on interpersonal networks, and will only diffuse if these social features are taken into account and barriers overcome' (Greenhalgh, Robert, Macfarlane, Bate, & Kyriakidou, 2004, p. 607). All of these emphasize the significance of human interaction and communication in driving research into practice. In other words, it signifies the need of translation as a medium between the worlds of research and action. Similarly, Innvaer, Vist, Trommald and Oxman (2002, p. 241) believe that 'personal two-way communication between researchers and decision-makers should be used to facilitate the use of research. This can reduce mutual mistrust and promote a better understanding of policy-making by researchers and research by policy-makers'.

In health care, evidence reports are synchronized with scientific researches in related fields, thus ignoring the practitioners and the care receivers who ultimately take health-related decisions. Effective communication and easy dissemination of research findings to its audience in simple and comprehensible formats are crucial for creating greater awareness, promoting adoption and use of evidence. Communication strategies, also called health communication, help making evidence accessible, understandable, persuasive and useable. Scientists, researchers, organizations and government institutions should use various strategies to communicate the evidence effectively so that the target audience is motivated to process the information actively, can understand it, find it relevant and pay attention to the message conveyed. In Persuasive Communication Matrix, McGuire (1968) discusses five input variables for persuasive communication—the source of communication, the message, the channel of communication, the audience characteristics, and the setting and background in which the communication is received. Lasswell (1948, p. 216) describes persuasive communication: 'Who says what in what channels to whom with what effect'. Health communication is essential to health promotion and disease prevention. It involves the use of communication strategies for imparting information and influencing health-related decisions taken by individuals and the community at large. It highlights the importance of communication in health and integrates the field of communication and health. The field of health communication is currently being acknowledged as having a significant role in improving public health.

The market segmentation strategies that are prepared in the field of marketing and business also provide some critical inputs here. These strategies involve tailoring and developing materials for a specific audience. Similarly, in health research, specifying the target audience is a prerequisite for developing an individualized outreach programme or material (Kreuter & Wray, 2003). However, in health sciences, few researchers are able to target directly their ultimate end users who are the beneficiaries of research outputs. Generally, it has been observed that a more defined and specific audience requires simple, economic and more effective outreach that considers the cultural, geographic and demographic characteristics of the audience. Researchers can disseminate their message effectively by planning their communication strategy that aligns well with the cultural, geographic location and other demographic characteristics of the intended audience. There is no specific and written framework of communication strategies available to guide or follow. However, there are a few key communication strategies that are commonly applicable in all fields.

Tailoring the Message

Like other communication strategies, tailored communication or tailoring the message can be highly effective. It has the potential to make the communication more pertinent to the audience. Tailoring includes various steps and stages such as assessing the characteristics of audience, creating individualized messages, and then transferring the messages (Hawkins, Kreuter, & Resnicow, 2008; Kreuter & Wray, 2003). Rimer and Kreuter (2006) emphasized that a researcher will be able to elicit more nuanced responses and create a greater impact if s/he tailors the message based on the needs and interests of his/her audience. Targeting the message to audience segments, on the other hand, does not require specific details of audience. In this, a single approach or intervention is applied for a specific population subgroup, considering the characteristics of that population group such as age, sex, ethnicity and spoken language (Kreuter & Wray, 2003).

NARRATIVES TECHNIQUE

In the Narrative technique, messages are presented as 'story-like prose pieces that focus on elaborating one example of an event, and they provide appealing detail, characters, and some plot, presented in either the first or third person' (Winterbottom, Bekker, & Conner, 2008, p. 2080). The characters in such narratives act as role models for motivation and learning. Such narratives include case histories, personal experiences in the form of stories, anecdotes and testimonies.

Framing the Message

Messages related to health care should be created within a specific context as it helps make them more understandable. For example, gain- and loss-framed messages can be used to point out the positive or negative aspects of a particular behaviour, circumstance or product. Research shows that gain-framed messages have a more positive impact on behaviour change than loss-framed messages (Latimer, Brawley, & Bassett, 2010; O'Keefe & Jensen, 2007).

In fact, the most effective communication strategies are those which the target audience can relate to. Besides, the message should come from a source they trust, and should be related in some way to the people, places and media they communicate with on an everyday basis. Moreover, language also needs to be simple, easy, jargon free and relevant to their interests and 'conditions where people live, work and play' (Robert Wood Johnson Foundation, Carger, & Western, 2010).

The role of information technology cannot be ignored while discussing communication strategies. Researchers can now communicate findings to targeted audiences with the click of a button. With digital platforms, research findings can be transferred and disseminated to the audience in real-time conversations, and can also engage and involve the audiences through social media platforms such as live webinars, hangouts, etc.

ROLE OF NGOS IN DISSEMINATING RESEARCH IN INDIA

Along with researchers, social scientists and psychologists, many NGOs are doing substantial knowledge translation in India, and also disseminating psychological research to general public using strategic and persuasive communication. A few of these NGOs have been discussed as sample. However, a detailed and more elaborative setting-oriented discussion can be found in other chapters.

RACSHA[1]

Based in Kolkata, Rise Against Child Sexual Harm and Abuse (RACSHA) is a network of individuals and organizations working for the prevention, recognition, addressing and healing of victims and survivors of child sexual abuse. The group consists of teachers, lawyers, activists, doctors, social workers, special educators, corporates and others in the team. This NGO works for the under privileged children in the area of health and nutrition, education and emergencies. The NGO follows specifically tailored programmes and disseminating strategies such as involving local community members, mobile health units to take health care to the doorsteps of needy, counselling, and organizing various social events to sensitize people and make them aware of various preventive measures for the safety of children.

Anjali: Mental Health Rights Organization[2]

Anjali is another NGO that works in the area of mental illness. Anjali works for people who suffer from chronic mental illnesses and are living in State institutions for health care and treatment. The NGO disseminates appropriate physical, psychological and social therapies for the patients through its various well-organized programmes and activities such as life skills training programme, creation therapy, cognitive therapy, occupational therapy, psychotherapy, etc.

Sangath

Started in 1996 in Goa, one of the largest NGOs in the state, Sangath[3] is another NGO disseminating health care services in the area of developmental disabilities and mental health. Sangath developed various ways and strategies for disseminating mental health care and making it more accessible and affordable for the wider community. A few of them include utilizing 'lay counsellors' to deliver psychosocial interventions, use of

---

[1] http://www.mhfkolkata.com/racsha/
[2] http://www.anjalimentalhealth.org/
[3] http://www.sangath.in

technology, partnerships with government health services, department of education, schools and other NGOs, and organizing national events for sharing research.

Rural Health Care Foundation

Spread across various districts of West Bengal with a network of 10 clinics, Rural Health Care Foundation (RHCF)[4] is an organization that disseminates health care services to the lowest strata of the socio-economic pyramid in rural India. RHCF provides OPD facilities as well as medication to the low-income and hard-to-reach population in India. It disseminates health care research through various persuasive methods such as free medical camps on general health, dental hygiene and eye check-ups, door-to-door medicine collection drive, installing sanitary napkin vending machines, free medicines to patients, etc.

As a result of these strategic methods and use of persuasive communication techniques, the NGOs have been able to not only disseminate health care research but also contribute to improving the quality of living in various fields.

RECOMMENDATIONS FOR KNOWLEDGE TRANSLATION IN PSYCHOLOGY

Besides the above-mentioned communication strategies in knowledge translation, there are a few more recommendations and suggestions specific to psychological science.

With increased emphasis and global investment on disseminating science, including psychological science, a systematic culture change must occur within psychology. There is a need to realize that translational efforts are a constant endeavour and component of psychology's social contract with society. Social institutions must reward psychologists for engaging in public service-oriented applied research that can inform our

---

[4] http://www.ruralhealthcarefoundation.com

society's conceptualizations of and responses to complex social problems (Silver & Fischhoff, 2011).

Researchers in psychology must be trained in ethical communication, considering beneficence and non-maleficence; fidelity and responsibility; promoting accuracy, honesty, and truthfulness of communications; and competence, confidentiality and public statements, and informed consent (McGarrah, Alvord, Martin, & Haldeman, 2009). They should develop strategies such as knowing one's audience; developing individual messages; narrating a story and incorporating a take-home message for the audience; tailoring one's approach to the particular medium through which they are engaging with the public; communicating clearly using everyday language that is simple but not simplistic; and incorporating supporting information, including statistics (made personal when possible), visual depictions and anecdotes as relevant (Baron, 2010; Christensen, 2007; Feldman & Silvia, 2010; Kendall-Tackett, 2007). Psychologists need to be trained in dual dissemination so that they learn both 'public' speak and 'journal' speak, and can simultaneously share their science in scholarly journals and public fora (Sommer, 2006). They must be trained about how to tailor and present their materials for the scientific audience and for the public. This includes a consideration of the style of writing (academic versus informal), the level of detail according to the target audience, among several others. In addition to that, a few more suggestions may be incorporated:

1. Applied research, in India, should work in a holistic manner to get the optimum benefits from scientific research to translational research and further to knowledge translation for the benefit of people who differ linguistically. It is only then we can have happy, healthy and flourishing communities and societies.
2. In India, some NGOs are working on mental health issues and other behavioural aspects, but there is a lack of documentation and the right platform where this work can be cited in research.
3. There should be some more organizations that can help research travel from lab to field, and their work should be reinforced.
4. Students who will work in applied fields should have first-hand training and exposure, therefore more practical knowledge, along with theoretical know-how, should be provided in the classroom.

5. There is a need for platforms to translate such research in different Indian languages and dialects.

6. Special training and practice should be provided about these platforms to facilitate knowledge translation journey.

REFERENCES

Agency for Health Research and Quality. (2001). *Translating research into practice (TRIP - II)*. Washington, DC: Agency for Health Research and Quality. Retrieved from http://www.ahrq.gov/research/trip2fac.htm

Baron, N. (2010). *Escape from the ivory tower: A guide to making your science matter.* Washington, DC: Island Press.

Bischoff, A. (2003). *Caring for migrant and minority patients in European hospitals: A review of effective interventions.* Vienna: Institute for the Sociology of Health and Medicine.

Borchelt, R. E. (2001). Communicating the future: Report of the research roadmap panel for public communication of science and technology in the twenty-first century. *Science Communication, 23*(2), 194–211.

Bornstein, D. (2014). Helping new drugs out of research's 'valley of death'. *The New York Times.* Retrieved from https://opinionator.blogs.nytimes.com/2011/05/02/helping-new-drugs-out-of-academias-valley-of-death/

Brekke, J. S., Ell, K., & Palinkas, L. A. (2007). Translational science at the National Institute of Mental Health: Can social work take its rightful place? *Research on Social Work Practice, 17*(1), 123–133.

Brutt-Griffler, J. (2002). *World English: A study in its development.* Buffalo, NY: Multilingual Matters.

Butler, D. (2008). Translational research: Crossing the valley of death. *Nature, 453*(7197), 840–842.

Canadian Health Services Research Foundation. (2003). *The theory and practice of knowledge brokering in Canada's health system.* Ottawa: Canadian Health Services Research Foundation.

Census of India. (2011). Retrieved from http://censusindia.gov.in/2011-prov-results/paper2/data_ files/india/Rural_Urban_2011.pdf

Centre for Culture Ethnicity and Health. (2008). *Bilingual Staff: Research Project Report.* Melbourne: Author.

Chen, L., Evans, T., Anand, S., Boufford, J. I., Brown, H., & Chowdhury, M. (2004). Human resources for health: Overcoming the crisis. *Lancet, 364*(9449), 1984–1990.

Christensen, L. L. (2007). *The hands-on-guide for science communications: A step-by-step approach to public outreach.* New York, NY: Springer Science & Business Media.

Cronin, M. (2003). *Translation and globalization.* London: Routledge.

Culley, L., & Rapport, F. (2007). Using focus groups with minority ethnic communities: Researching infertility in British South Asian communities. *Qualitative Health Research*, 17(1), 102–112.

David, A. S. (2001). Wanted—more answers than questions: Literature review. *British Medical Journal*, 323(7327), 1462–1463.

Davidson, A. (2011). Translational research, what does it mean? *Anaesthesiology*, 115(5), 909–911.

Decoster, K., Appelmans, A., & Hill, P. (2012). *A health systems research mapping exercise in 26 low and middle-income countries: Narratives from health systems researchers, policy brokers and policy-makers* (Background paper commissioned by the Alliance for Health Policy and Systems Research to develop the WHO health systems research strategy).

Department of Health, Government of Western Australia. (2011). *WA Health System Language Services Policy*. Perth: Cultural Diversity Unit, Public Health Division, Government of Western Australia.

Donabedian, A. (1982). *Explorations in quality assessment and monitoring II: The criteria and standards of quality*. Ann Arbor, MI: Health Administration Press.

Dorsey, E. R., Thompson, J. P., & Carrasco, M. (2009). Financing of US biomedical research and new drug approvals across therapeutic areas. *PLoS One*, 4(9), e7015.

Ellen, M. E., Leon, G., Bouchard, G., Ouimet, M., Grimshaw, J. M., & Lavis, J. N. (2014). Barriers, facilitators and viewers about next steps to implementing supports for evidence-informed decision making in health systems: A qualitative study. *Implementation Science*, 9(1), 179.

Fay, M., Leipziger, D., Wodon, Q., & Yepes, T. (2005). Achieving child-health related Millennium Development Goals: The role of infrastructure. *World Development*, 33(8), 1267–1284.

Feldman, D. B., & Silvia, P. J. (2010). *Public speaking for psychologists: A light hearted guide to research presentations, job talks, and other opportunities to embarass yourself*. Washington, DC: American Psychological Association.

Flaskerud, J., & Nyamathi, A. M. (2000). Attaining gender and ethnic diversity in health intervention research: Cultural responsiveness versus resource provision. *Advances in Nursing Science*, 22(4), 1–15.

Gabbay, J., & Le May, A. (2004). Evidence based guidelines or collectively constructed 'mindlines?' Ethnographic study of knowledge management in primary care. *British Medical Journal*, 329(7473), 1013.

Glasgow, R. E., Lichtenstein, E., & Marcus, A. C. (2003). Why don't we see more translation of health promotion research to practice? Rethinking the efficacy-to-effectiveness transition. *American Journal of Public Health*, 93(8), 1261–1267.

Graham, I. D., Tetroe J., Robinson N., & Grimshaw, J. (2005). *An international study of health research funding agencies' support and promotion of knowledge translation.* Presented at the Academy Health Annual Research Meeting, Boston.

Greenhalgh, T., Robert, G., Macfarlane, F., Bate, P., & Kyriakidou, O. (2004). Diffusion of innovations in service organizations: Systematic review and recommendations. *Milbank Quarterly, 82*(4), 581–629.

Grol, R. (2001). Successes and failures in the implementation of evidence-based guidelines for clinical practice. *Medical Care, 39*(8), 1146–1154.

Haines, A., Kuruvilla, S., & Borchert, M. (2004). Bridging the implementation gap between knowledge and action for health. *Bulletin of World Health Organization, 82*(10), 724–731.

Hallahan, K., Holtzhausen, D., VanRuler, B., Vercic, D., & Sriramesh, K. (2007). Defining strategic communication. *International Journal of Strategic Communication, 1*(1), 3–35.

Hanna, L., Hunt, S., & Bhopal, R. (2006). Cross-cultural adaptation of a tobacco questionnaire for Punjabi, Cantonese, Urdu and Sylheti speakers: Qualitative research for better clinical practice, cessation service and research. *Journal of Epidemiology and Community Health, 60*(12), 1034–1039.

Hawkins, R. P., Kreuter, M., & Resnicow, K. (2008). Understanding tailoring in communicating about health. *Health Education Research, 23*(3), 454–66.

Haynes, R. B. (1990). Loose connections between peer-reviewed clinical journals and clinical practice. *Annals of Internal Medicine, 113*(9), 724–8.

Hoagwood, K., & Olin, S. S. (2002). The NIMH blueprint for change report: Research priorities in child and adolescent mental health. *Journal of the American Academy of Child & Adolescent Psychiatry, 41*(7), 760–767.

Innvaer, S., Vist, G., Trommald, M., & Oxman, A. (2002). A health policy-makers' perceptions of their use of evidence: A systematic review. *The Journal of Health Services Research & Policy, 7*(4), 239–44.

Johns, G. (1993). Constraints on the adoption of psychology-based personnel practices: Lessons from organizational innovation. *Personnel Psychology, 46*(3), 569–592.

Jones, K., Baker, P., Doyle, J., Armstrong, R., Pettman, T., & Waters, E. (2013). Increasing the utility of systematic review findings through strategic communication. *Journal of Public Health, 35*(2), 345–349.

Karliner, L., Jacobs, E., Chen, A., & Mutha, S. (2007). Do professional interpreters improve clinical care for patients with limited English proficiency? A systematic review of the literature. *Health Services Research, 42*(2), 727–754.

Kendall-Tackett, K. A. (2007). *How to write for a general audience: A guide for academics who wants to share their knowledge with the world and have fun doing it.* Washington, DC: American Psychological Association.

Kenkel, M. B. (2015). Bettering society and psychology: The two missions of TPS. *Translating Issues in Psychological Science, 1*, 1–2.

Kreuter, M. W., & Wray, R. J. (2003). Tailored and targeted health communication: Strategies for enhancing information relevance. *American Journal of Health Behavior, 27*(1), 227–32.

Kuehne, L. M., & Olden, J. D. (2015). Opinion: Lay summaries needed to enhance science communication. *PNAS Proceedings of the National Academy of Sciences of the United States of America, 112*(12), 3585–3586.

Kumar, S., & Nash, D. B. (2011). *Demand better! Revive our broken health care system in health care myth busters: Is there a high degree of scientific certainty in modern medicine?* Bozeman, MT: Second River Healthcare Press.

Landry, R., Amara, N., Pablos-Mendes, A., Shademani, R., & Gold, I. (2006). The knowledge-value chain: A conceptual framework for knowledge translation in health. *Bulletin of the World Health Organization, 84*(8), 597–602.

Lasswell, H. D. (1948). The structure and function of communication in society. In L. Bryson (Ed.), *Communication of Ideas* (pp. 37–51). New York, NY: Harper & Row.

Latimer, A. E., Brawley, L. R., & Bassett, R. L. (2010). A systematic review of three approaches for constructing physical activity messages: What messages work and what improvements are needed? *International Journal of Behavioral Nutrition and Physical Activity, 7*(1), 36.

Lavis, J. N. (2009). How can we support the use of systematic reviews in policymaking? *PLoS Medicine, 6*(11), e1000141.

Lavis, J., Davies, H., Oxman, A., Denis, J. L., Golden-Biddle, K., & Ferlie, E. (2005). Towards systematic reviews that inform health care management and policymaking. *Journal of Health Services Research and Policy, 10*(1, Suppl.), 35–48.

Lavis, J. N., Roberston, D., Woodside, J. M., McLeod, C. B., & Abelson, J. (2003). How can research organizations more effectively transfer research knowledge to decision makers? *The Milbank Quarterly, 81*(2), 221–48.

Lomas, J. (2000). Using linkage and exchange to move research into policy at a Canadian Foundation. *Health Affairs, 19*(3), 236–240.

———. (2007). The in-between world of knowledge brokering. *British Medical Journal, 334*(7585), 129–132

McGarrah, N. A., Alvord, M. K., Martin, J. N., & Haldeman, D. (2009). In the public eye: The ethical practice of media psychology. *Professional Psychology: Research and Practice, 40*(2), 172–180.

McGuire, W. J. (1968). Personality and attitude change: An information processing theory. In A. Greenwald, T. Brock, & T. Ostrom (Eds.), *Psychological foundations of attitudes* (pp. 171–196). New York, NY: Academic Press.

Miller, G. A. (1969). Psychology as a means of promoting human welfare. *American Psychologist, 24*(12), 1063–1075.

Montgomery, S. (2013). *Does science need a global language?* Chicago, IL: The University of Chicago Press.

Morris, Z. S., Wooding, S., & Grant, J. (2011). The answer is 17 years, what is the question: Understanding time lags in translational research. *Journal of the Royal Society of Medicine, 104*(12), 510–20.

National Advisory Mental Health Council. (1999). *Bridging science and service: A report by the National Advisory Mental Health Council's Clinical Treatment and*

Services Research Workgroup (NIH Publication No. 99-4353). Rockville, MD: National Institute of Mental Health.

Niessen, L. W., Grijseels, E. W., & Rutten, F. F. (2000). The evidence-based approach in health policy and health care delivery. *Social Science & Medicine, 51*(6), 859–69.

Oborn, E., Barret, M., & Racko, G. (2010). *Knowledge translation in healthcare: A review of the literature* (Working Paper Series). Cambridge Judge Business School, University of Cambridge.

Ohlsson, A. (2002). Knowledge translation and evidence-based perinatal/neonatal health care. *Neonatal Network, 21*(5), 69–67.

O'Keefe, D. J., & Jensen, J. D. (2007). The relative persuasiveness of gain-framed and loss-framed messages for encouraging disease prevention behaviors: A meta-analytic review. *Journal of Health Communication, 12*(7), 623–644.

Orlandi, M. A. (1987). Promoting health and preventing disease in health care settings: An analysis of barriers. *Preventive Medicine, 16*(1), 119–130.

Orton, L., Lloyd-Williams, F., Taylor-Robinson, D., O'Flaherty, M., & Capewell, S. (2011). The use of research evidence in public health decision making processes: Systematic review. *PloS One, 6*(7), e21704.

Palinkas, L. A., Schoenwald, S. K., Hoagwood, K., Landsverk, J., Chorpita, B. F., & Weisz, J. R. (2008). An ethnographic study of implementation of evidence-based treatments in child mental health: First steps. *Psychiatric Services, 59*(7), 738–746.

Pinker, S. (2014). *The sense of style: The thinking person's guide to writing in the 21st century.* New York, NY: Viking Books.

Rabin, B. A., Brownson, R. C., Haire-Joshu, D., Kreuter, M. W., & Weaver, N. L. (2008). A glossary for dissemination and implementation research in health. *Journal of Public Health Management and Practice, 14*(2), 117–123.

Rao, K. D., Arora, R., & Ghaffar, A. (2014). Health systems research in the time of health system reform in India: A review. *Health Research Policy and Systems, 12*(1), 12–37.

Redmann, C. (2000). Wanna speak English. *The American Prospect,* p. 45.

Rimer, B. K., & Kreuter, M. W. (2006). Advancing tailored health communication: A persuasion and message effects perspective. *Journal of Communication, 56*(1), 184–201.

Robert Wood Johnson Foundation, Carger, E., & Western, D. (2010). *A new way to talk about the social determinants of health.*
Retrieved from https://www.rwjf.org/en/library/research/2010/01/a-new-way-to-talk-about-the-social-determinants-of-health.html

Schoenwald, S. K., & Hoagwood, K. (2001). Effectiveness, transportability, and dissemination of interventions: What matters when? *Psychiatric Services, 52*(9), 1190–1197.

Schuster, M., McGlynn, E., & Brook, R. H. (1998). How good is the quality of health care in the United States? *The Milbank Quarterly, 76*(4), 517–563.

Shrivastava, P., & Mitroff, I. I. (1984). Enhancing organizational research utilization: The role of decision makers assumptions. *Academy of Management Review*, *9*(1), 18–26.

Siddiqi, K., Newell, J., & Robinson, M. (2005). Getting evidence into practice: What works in developing countries? *International Journal for Qualitative Health Care*, *17*(5), 447–454.

Silver, R. C., & Fischhoff, B. (2011). What should we expect after the next attack? *American Psychologist*, *66*(6), 567–572.

Small, R., Yelland, J., Lumley, J., Rice, P. L., Cotronei, V., & Warren, R. (1999). Cross-cultural research: Trying to do it better 2. Enhancing Data Quality. *Australian and New Zealand Journal of Public Health*, *23*(4), 390–395.

Snow, C. P. (2012). *The two cultures*. Cambridge, UK: Cambridge University Press.

Sommer, R. (2006). Dual dissemination: Writing for colleagues and the public. *American Psychologist*, *61*, 955–958.

Sung, N. S., Crowley, W. F., Genel, M., Salber, P., Sherwood, L., Johnson, S., ... Rimoin, D. (2003). Central challenges facing national clinical research enterprise. *Journal of the American Medical Association*, *289*(10), 1278–1287.

Thomas, K. W., & Tymon, W. G. (1982). Necessary properties of relevant research: Lessons from recent criticisms of the organizational sciences. *Academy of Management Review*, *7*(3), 345–352.

Thompson, A., Boxall, D., Hodgins, G., & Patrick, K. (2013). Best lessons for well-being from psychologists: Implications for the policy and for psychology. *Australian Psychologist*, *48*(6), 428–436.

Thyli, B., Athlin, E., & Hedelin, B. (2007). Challenges in community health nursing of old migrant patients in Norway—An exploratory study. *International Journal of Older People Nursing*, *2*(1), 45–51.

United Nations. (2010). *The millennium development goals report 2010*. New York, NY: United Nations.

Welch, V., Euffing, E., & Tugwell, P. (2009). Knowledge translation: An opportunity to reduce global health inequalities. *Journal of International Development*, *21*(8), 1066–1082.

Winterbottom, A., Bekker, H. L., & Conner, M. (2008). Does narrative information bias individual's decision making? A systematic review. *Social Science and Medicine*, *67*(12), 2079–2088.

Yusuf, S., & Cairns, J. (2012). The perilous state of independent randomized clinical trials and related applied research in Canada. *Canadian Medical Association Journal*, *184*(18), 1997–2002.

Chapter 2

Research Methods in Applied Psychology
An Evaluation

Kamlesh Singh and Shilpa Bandyopadhyay

Analogous to the advancement in applied psychology, equivalent advancement has been achieved in the research methods being used in the various branches of this field. The increasing appreciation of translational research and knowledge translation in the social and behavioural sciences, for instance, has increased the scope of research in applied psychology. This makes it essential to have an overview of the research methods which can be used in policy-relevant research such as translational research and knowledge translation. With this aim in mind, this chapter delineates some of the research methods being used in applied psychology. It also recommends certain trajectories for achieving greater progress in research on applied psychology in India.

INTRODUCTION

Research is a scientific inquiry into the nature of a new or an already existing phenomenon. It is based upon the use of research methods that enable the researcher to gather information systematically and logically about the subject of inquiry. Psychology, despite being a young science, has made progress in terms of both basic and applied researches. In this chapter, the emphasis will be on the field of applied psychology that endeavours to study both overt and covert human behaviour and mental processes in a variety of real-world settings. Its application has been observed in industrial and organizational settings, educational settings, the study of human response to environmental and health issues and concerns, and community-level intervention programmes for marginalized and socially disadvantaged sections of the society, among various other real life settings.

A distinct characteristic of applied psychological research is its practical utility in the solution of real-world issues. At the heart of such research lies the research method which is used for producing knowledge about the phenomenon of interest.

This chapter will begin with a discussion of the dominant paradigms and approaches to conducting research, followed by a brief overview of the traditional methods, which have been a part of psychology since its inception and thereafter the focus will be on quantitative and qualitative methods being used in the latest research in applied psychology. Some of these include experience sampling method (ESM), scenic beauty estimation (SBE) method, body mapping, listening guide, interpretive phenomenological analysis (IPA), protocol analysis, cognitive mapping and laddering technique. Besides these, a significant emphasis of this chapter will be on the research methods being used in translational research and knowledge translation.

DOMINANT PARADIGMS AND APPROACHES TO CONDUCTING RESEARCH

Western psychology, and thereafter the Oriental and the Indian traditions, have invariably been influenced by the experimental and the experiential paradigms. The research methods, which are a part of the former paradigm, adopt the model of the natural sciences in their investigation and analysis of human behaviour. They study human behaviour as a 'physical or biological phenomenon' (Krippner, 2015, p. 335). The research methods under the experiential paradigm, on the other hand, investigate and analyse 'the unique ontological characteristics of humans' (Krippner, 2015, p. 335).

Another distinction in research emerges from the use of two different methods of inquiry—qualitative or quantitative research methods—based on the nature of the data. Whereas, qualitative data can be in the form of written text, verbal language or images, numbers characterize quantitative data. Thus, quantitative methods involve the analysis of numerical data through the use of statistical techniques. The measurement of individual differences in intelligence, aptitude, achievement and personality through the use of psychometric tests is an example of the use of the quantitative method. Similarly, opinion polling or survey research through the use of questionnaires is also analysed through various quantitative methodologies. On the other hand, qualitative research is characterized by the analysis of qualitative data, such as narratives of participants, written documents and images.

Qualitative researchers stress the socially constructed nature of reality, the intimate relationship between the researcher and what is studied, and the situational constraints that shape inquiry. Such researchers emphasize the value-laden nature of inquiry. They seek answers to questions that stress how social experience is created and given meaning. Qualitative forms of inquiry are considered by many social and behavioral scientists to be as much a perspective on how to approach investigating a research problem as it is a method. (Norman & Lincoln, 2005, p. 10)

Both these approaches have their relative strengths and shortcomings. To speak of them briefly, the objective quality of the quantitative method makes it more valid, reliable and scientifically rigorous in the eyes of the quantitative researcher. However, the absence of the perspective of the participant and an account of their lived experience or their perception of social reality leads qualitative researchers to claim that it is inadequate in providing a holistic picture. Similarly, quantitative researchers opine that quantitative data being amenable to statistical analysis makes their methods more reliable as compared to the qualitative methods where the subjective bias of the researcher often impinges upon data analysis and interpretation. There are of course counterclaims to such an argument.

The currently prevalent approach, the eclectic methodology, combines both the methods, thus retaining the strengths of both while negating their weaknesses.

The first-, second- and third-person perspective is another way of viewing the research methods. The first-person perspective is considered to be subjective 'because it's based on, and directed at the epistemic subject's experience' whereas the third-person approach 'is based on objective evidence and gives access to all kinds of entities' and is in essence objective in nature. The second-person perspective, on the other hand, 'is inter-subjective because it is an epistemic relation between an epistemic subject and another sentient being's mental states' (Pauen, 2012, p. 2).

The third-person perspective is the dominant research paradigm in the physical sciences, for example, the experience of pain as being encountered by an individual is studied by the physical scientist by using physiological indicators of pain. 'The experience of pain when one is in pain' (Rao & Paranjpe, 2016, p. 25) on the other hand would be an example of a first-person observation. Third-person observations being amenable to experimental observation and manipulation are considered to be far more objective, generalizable, and hence, superior to first or second-person observation by the physical scientists.

Western psychologists in their attempt to be positivistic treat psychology like other positive sciences such as physics or biology. To them, the study of psychology should be value-neutral and objective. However, human experiences may be either external or internal. While external or shared experiences can be studied from the lens of the third-person perspective, internal experiences being experiential in nature are best viewed from the lens of the first-person perspective. In the case of the latter, the methods of natural sciences cannot help us to adequately study 'the full range of behavior and experience of man as a person' (Giorgi, 1970). Thus, this paradigm of research helps us recognize that although experimental method is an indispensable tool in psychology, a holistic study of human behavioural and mental processes calls for a study of the person from a first-, second- as well as third-person perspective. The first- and second-person perspectives require the use of other relevant methods which focus on the experience of the subject or the experience of the subject as viewed by the observer, respectively.

First-person observation acquires greater importance in the case of Indian psychology which does not limit itself to investigating biopsychosocial processes, unlike Western psychology. Instead, Indian psychology also includes the investigation of biopsychosocial-spiritual processes (Rao & Paranjpe, 2016). In this context, it is also important to elucidate the distinction between Indian psychology and psychology in India. Psychology in India, being the mainstream approach, has adopted the Western positivistic tradition of conducting research. It is characterized by the domination of the third-person perspective, which reflects the influence of the American and European psychology. 'The distinctive feature of Indian psychology', on the other hand 'is that its central tenets are rooted in native Indian practices and are derived from classical Indian thought' (Rao & Paranjpe, 2016, p. 5). Perhaps, the defining feature of Indian psychology is its appreciation of the first- and second-person approach in studying human behaviour, and its emphasis on the indigenous constructs grounded in the Indian sociocultural tradition.

The primary emphasis of Indian psychology is on the subject or the agent who is experiencing a particular event and on his/her experience of the event rather than the experience in isolation. The singular characteristic of the human subject being his/her consciousness makes it essential to study the internal event as experienced by him/her through a first-person perspective. The third-person perspective enables the observer to study the experience of the subject from an objective viewpoint, based on objective indicators of the experience. The inter-subjective element of the second-person perspective, on the other hand, allows the observer to engage with the subject's experience of the event. Hence, 'a pluralistic methodology is called for in dealing with the complexity of human nature' (Rao & Paranjpe, 2016, p. 26).

After having considered the dominant paradigms and approaches to conducting research, one is inclined to conclude that no one approach can claim to offer a holistic picture of the complex human nature and experience. Rather, an eclectic approach or pluralistic methodology seems to offer the befitting solution.

Having said that, we shall now shift our focus to the research methods used to study human behaviour and mental processes. A separate section will discuss the methods which are used in translational research and knowledge translation, and how translational research and knowledge translation are currently being used within the behavioural sciences.

RESEARCH METHODS

This section provides an overview of some of the research methods which fall under the purview of applied psychology. Among the methods that have traditionally been a part of psychological research are experimental, observational (naturalistic observation, and active or passive participant observation), cross-sectional, longitudinal and sequential methods, structured and unstructured interviews, the use of psychological tests, case studies, and field research (before and after field studies). Each of these methods has its own set of strengths and limitations. For example, while the experimental method yields highly objective results by minimizing the effects of the extraneous variables, it lacks ecological validity. Similarly, although the observational methods help the researcher take minute note of the behaviour of a group or individual in natural settings, it does not allow one to minimize the confounding effect of the extraneous variables. The use of psychological tests, on the other hand, leads to another set of shortcomings—the possibility of socially desirable responses on the part of the respondent. However, these instruments are indispensable for their role in helping to elicit latent variables which are otherwise not amenable to observation. Any method will have its own set of strengths and weaknesses; it is up to the researcher to select the method which is best suited to address his/her research question.

While each of the methods mentioned above is used to explore various dimensions of human behaviour, currently, researchers are effectively utilizing a wide range of research methods available to them, in addition to the traditional ones. We now look at those methods, along with a few of the traditional methods, which are enriching and furthering research in applied psychology. While providing an overview of these methods, the emphasis will initially be on the quantitative methods, next there will be a discussion of the qualitative methods, and finally there will be an elucidation of methods that can be used to analyse both qualitative and quantitative data.

Quantitative Research Methods

A quantitative method which has found large-scale application in applied psychology is the ESM which was developed by Csikszentmihalyi and Larson (1987). In this method, the participant has to record his feelings while in the moment or in 'real time'. In the initial years after the method was developed, pagers were used to signal the participants to record their feelings. Now, with the advancement in technology, there are various software programmes for signalling the participants. iHabit, for example, is a smartphone-based application which is used as a tool for collecting ESM data (Wong & Vallacher, 2017). The real-time capture of the subject's feeling is the key strength of this method because it limits the chances of recall bias. The ESM data which has been captured may be subjected to ordinary least squares statistical techniques or hierarchical linear modelling. Although it can be used to study various domains of human behaviour, it was initially developed for studying 'flow'. Thereafter, it has been particularly popular among positive psychologists.

Another method of quantitative inquiry, which has always been in vogue, is the 'use of psychological tests'. As defined by Freeman (1964, p. 46), '[It] is a standardized instrument designed to measure objectively one or more aspects of a total personality by means of samples of verbal or nonverbal responses, or by means of other behaviors'. Although the use of psychological tests is not new, there has been a shift from measuring constructs related to psychopathology (depression, anxiety, aggression) to measuring constructs related to positive aspects of human behaviour. These include the measurement of resilience, flow, flourishing, personal well-being, meaning in life, life satisfaction, values, mindfulness and personal strengths, among several others. Similarly, within the context of Indian psychology, psychometric tools measuring *vikaras* (Singh & Sharma, 2016), *sat-chit-ananda* (Singh, Chitra, Raj, Kumar, & Kumar, 2013) and *swadhayay* (Singh & Sahni, 2016) represent the changing paradigm of psychometric testing.

Before deciding upon a particular psychological test for one's research, the researcher should consider its psychometric properties including reliability, validity and norms. Also, before gathering data on a psychological test which has been developed on a sample that is culturally different, it is highly desirable to validate the test in the form of confirmatory factor analysis on an Indian sample. Test adaptation and translation may also be necessary if an Indian adaptation of the test has not already been developed.

With the advancement in health care technology, *neuropsychological methods* have also gained prominence in psychology, including single photon emission tomography, positron emission tomography and functional magnetic resonance (Lantz, 2004). These methods help to ascertain which brain areas are active during specific mental and emotional states. Their objectivity gives these methods an edge over other means of studying the cognitive processes. However, here again, one's research question is a key determinant of whether it will be more suitable for addressing one's research question, as compared to the other methods.

Similar to the neuropsychological methods, randomized controlled trials (RCTs) are also preferred for their objectivity. Its objectivity lies in its ability to minimize the effect of the extraneous variables through the technique of randomization. RCTs are used in clinical trials not only in behavioural science but also in medical science. They are used in evidence-based research and enable one to gauge the effectiveness of the intervention programme which one has designed and delivered. As the term suggests, research participants are randomly allocated to either the control group or the treatment group. The difference between the two groups lies in the latter receiving the intervention (or the independent variable) and the former not receiving it. The difference between the two groups is then analysed statistically and the intervention is ascertained to be either efficacious or inefficacious (Solomon, Cavanaugh, & Draine, 2009).

Another quantitative method, which is relatively less known due its specific application to the field of environmental psychology alone, is the SBE method. Although predominantly used in landscape planning and architecture studies, since the 1970s, it is currently being used in environmental psychology as well. This method is used for evaluating the visual quality and scenic beauty of any landscape as perceived by the general public. It is, in essence, psychophysical in nature and is classified as a picture elicitation method. The SBE method helps in determining the scenic beauty of any landscape, which is an important determinant of its tourist attraction. Hence, it has important implications for landscape planners and other stakeholders. It involves depicting the landscape using coloured slides, showing them to the observers and finally, arriving at the scenic beauty estimates of the landscape based upon the judgment of the observers. The evaluation of the observer's judgments is commonly done using the SBE computer programme (Boster & Ron, 1976).

Qualitative Research Methods

With regards to the qualitative methods, the *daily diary method* is often used in research, apart from being commonly used in therapeutic sessions. It requires the research participants to manually record significant and meaningful events of their daily life (Bolger, Davis, & Rafaeli, 2003). The events that are to be recorded depend upon the nature of the research question. Writing is considered therapeutic. Thus, the daily diary method not only serves as a form of data gathering technique but also has the potential to enhance the participant's positive mood state.

Another commonly used qualitative method is the *grounded theory* approach. It involves examining the patterns which emerge from one's empirical data to eventually generate a theory grounded in those patterns (Walsh et al., 2015). The theory, in turn, helps explain the pattern observed in the data.

As a method of qualitative inquiry, *confessional research* is usually employed in the study of spirituality. It is unique in that it is characterized by 'researchers who explicitly identify their own religious convictions as part of their investigative process'.

Phenomenology is another qualitative research method which focuses on studying an individual's experience of a particular event. For example, as a research method for the study of religion and spirituality, phenomenology takes note of the lived experience of individuals, such as their experience of transcendence (Nelson, 2009).

A variant of phenomenology is IPA. As we have already seen above, in phenomenological analysis, the focus lies on the participant's personal experience of a phenomenon rather than an objective analysis of the social reality. In IPA, there is a two-fold process of sense-making: first 'the participants are trying to make sense of their world' and second 'the researcher ... [is] trying to make sense of the participants' trying to make sense of their world' (Smith & Osborn, 2003, p. 53). It involves framing the interview questions; one may either choose to use a structured interview or an unstructured one; conducting the interview; analysing the data by looking for themes, connecting them and finally translating them into a narrative account. An example of a research which utilized this method was that of Flowers, Smith, Sheeran and Beail (1997) in which they analysed gay men's perception of unprotected sex and view regarding sexuality.

In the toolkit of qualitative research methods, *narrative analysis* has also found wide acceptance among researchers in our field. For example, in the context of health psychology, it involves a detailed examination and interpretation of stories narrated by individual patients. The onset of any acute or chronic illness is accompanied by a disturbance in the normal flow of one's life. Narrative analysis helps analyse how individuals make sense of such a disturbance and create order out of their disordered state (Murray, 2000).

The listening guide and body mapping are two other qualitative methods that have increased the access of a researcher to the internal psychological world of the subject. In the *listening guide method*, the emphasis lies on stories and various perspectives (the 'voice') present in the narratives of the participants. In essence, it is a relational voice-centred method which relies on narrative and thematic analysis, and incorporates certain key components from the grounded theory method. Carol Gilligan, the pioneer of the listening guide method, developed four questions to guide the 'listener' (i.e., the researcher) in relating to and analysing the *voice* of the participant. They are (Gilligan & Eddy, 2017, p. 77) 'Who is speaking and to whom? In what body or physical space? Telling what stories about which relationships? In what societal and cultural frameworks?' Thus, as conceptualized by Gilligan, Weinberg and Bertsch (2003), this method has four key steps, called *listening*: listening for the plot, constructing I poems, listening for contrapuntal voices and composing an analysis. It has found application in a wide range of research studies including that of eating disorders, depression, sexual decision-making, research on women combatants of the Israeli army (Jack, 1991), in analysing Supreme Court judgments and in family therapy sessions (Brown, 1999; Van, Loots, Grietens, & Jacquet, 2013).

The other qualitative method, *body mapping*, involves drawing a life-size—2-meter long—outline view of one's body on a chart using colours, pictures, symbols and words. It has three key components: a *testimonio* which is a brief story narrated by the participant, the body map and a key/legend which describes the visual elements present on the body map. Although the drawing serves as the primary source of data, a researcher may choose to develop a specific set of interview questions based upon his research inquiry and use that as a secondary source of data. Gastaldo, Magalhaes, Carrasco and Davy (2012) and Solomon (2002) have developed manuals for more detailed information, the former's is more suitable for the use of body mapping as a research technique whereas the latter's details body mapping as a form of art therapy. One can use the software NVivo 10 (QSR International) for coding, storing and analysing both the narratives and the body map per se (Charmaz, 2006). As enumerated by Gastaldo et al. (2012, p. 18), 'The purpose of the analysis is not to psychologically evaluate the participants through their art, but to gain insight into certain aspects of their logic, aspirations, desires, material circumstances and ways of handling particular issues'.

Body mapping recognizes the importance of art as a creative therapeutic tool, which helps in representing both inner and outer experiences of a person. Here, art is used as a form of qualitative inquiry to unravel the complex embodied experiences of the participant (Baerg, 2003). This technique has been used in research with individuals who have various forms of psychosomatic disorders. They were asked to represent their bodily pain through body maps. The use of body maps not only facilitated the psychiatrists in comprehending the client's problems but also facilitated rapport establishment between the client and the psychiatrist (Immadisetty, 2012). As a participatory qualitative research method, it has also found application in research studies which were examining sensitive issues such as sexual orientation (Oliveira, Meyers, & Vearey, 2016), the experience of victims of sexual abuse and trauma (Zoldbrod, 2015), the experience of migration (Gastaldo et al., 2012) and the likes.

Methods that Can Be Used to Analyse Both Qualitative and Quantitative Data

After having considered both qualitative and quantitative methods, we will now explore the basket of methods that can be used for analysing both qualitative and quantitative data. These include appreciative inquiry (AI), protocol analysis method, cognitive mapping, day reconstruction method, and laddering technique among various other such methods. AI is a form of action research commonly employed for organizational change and/ or development. It is characterized as an evolving process resulting in a positive change or outcome at both individual and organizational levels. The novelty of this method lies in its focus on the positive strengths of an organization rather than an emphasis on the existing organizational problems and deficits—a characteristic of other forms of organizational change and development initiatives, and also action research.

AI encompasses four phases—discovery, dream, design and destiny. This is the 4-D model (Cooperrider & Whitney, 2006) of AI. There are two other variants—one is the 5-D model (Mann, 1997; Watkins & Mohr, 2001) and the other is the 4-I model (Watkins & Mohr, 2001). Besides the four phases already stated, the 5-D model consists of an additional phase, 'definition', which forms the first phase. The four I's of the 4-I model are inquire, imagine, innovate and implement. Regardless of the model of AI one adheres to, its underlying principles and the key features remain the same: that every organization has a 'positive core' (Cooperrider, Whitney, & Stavros, 2008, p. vii), the characteristics which form the strength of the organization and give life to it. The AI initiative helps unearth and strengthen these unique strengths through dialogues with the organiza-tional members and brings to life 'what the organization looks like at its best' (Shendell-Falik, Feinson, & Mohr, 2007, p. 96).

AI begins with the selection of an affirmative topic that will be the focus of the intervention ('definition'); examples include happiness at the workplace, high quality of care for geriatric patients, high employee com-mitment and positive organizational climate. It helps the organizational members recognize their existing strengths, which may then be harnessed to realize the shared visions of all the stakeholders. It incorporates all the key stakeholders in the change and the development process, and encourages them to focus on their peak experiences as part of the organization. By promoting success-oriented and positive storytelling about the organization, it helps them discover the critical strengths of the organization ('discover') and envision a successful future ('dream') based on the past achievements of the organization. Since future success is envisioned through the stories of past successes, this vision is grounded in reality. Then, the stakeholders together 'design' the action plan considering the social architecture of the organization and other relevant factors. This culminates in its implementation in the 'destiny' phase, in the form of sustainable goals (Cooperrider et al., 2008).

Throughout the AI initiative, positively framed questions are asked which are designed to 'discover' the primary causes of success, the best practices and the most valued features of the organization (Neighborhood Centers Inc., 2009). This emphasis on the positives and its strengths-based orientation has led to its incorporation in the field of positive psychology as well. Although it developed within the framework of organizational behaviour, it does overlap with the basic tenet of positive psychology—that of a focus on human (/organizational) strengths rather than weaknesses, thereby enabling them to flourish (Whitney & Fredrickson, 2015). Although the method relies heavily on interviews, narratives and stories of the participants, it is also amenable to quantification through pre- and post-testing of the participants. Another way to capture AI through the quantitative methodology is by comparing participants of an AI intervention with non-participants. An example of the latter approach is demonstrated by Verleysen, Lambrechts and Van Acker (2015) in their study. They not only studied the role of AI in the development of psychological capital (PsyCap) among employees (AI group versus control group) but also investigated the mediating role of basic psychological need satisfaction (competence, autonomy and relatedness needs) in the development of PsyCap through AI intervention. Their findings revealed that the AI group had a greater satisfaction of all the three basic psychological needs as compared to the non-AI group. Furthermore, AI was found to be an effective way to develop PsyCap as well as fulfil the need for competency, autonomy and relatedness.

The *protocol analysis method*, characterized by recording and analysing the concurrent or retrospective verbal protocols of the participants, is in vogue in cognitive psychology. This method involves keeping a record of the verbalization of the participant's thoughts and sequential behaviours while they are engaged in the performance of a cognitive task such as a brainteaser, which becomes the data. The participants are first trained in the art of giving a verbal report—thinking out loud while performing the task (concurrent verbal protocol) or immediately after the task performance (retrospective verbal protocol). The first step of the protocol analysis method involves the collection and storage of the verbal reports of the participant in the form of recordings in the target task situation to be analysed later. The second step involves the preparation of the data for analysis. One needs to identify the general structure of the protocol and compartmentalize the material into meaningful phrases, infer the structure of the mental activities by combining the meaningful phrases into groups and finally apply a formal descriptive language to specify what is observed in the data. The third and final step is to analyse the content by using content analysis, or sequential analysis, diagrammatic modelling or computational modelling. Software such as MacSHAPA (Sanderson, 1993), EVA (MacKay, 1989) and VideoNoter (Roschelle & Goldman, 1991) are used for recording, encoding and analysing the verbal protocols.

Cognitive mapping is also being used in the field of applied cognitive psychology. Cognitive maps are 'internally represented schemas or mental models for particular problem-solving domains that are learned and encoded as a result of an individual's interaction with their environment' (Swan, 1997, p. 188). The method aids in understanding human cognitive processes and is currently in vogue in organizational and educational settings as a technique for stimulating creative thinking and enhancing problem-solving skills. We will briefly consider two cognitive mapping techniques—concept and mind mapping. A concept map shows the existing or the potential relationship between concepts. It is a conceptual diagram which has a tree-like structure, with several protruding branches. A mind map, on the other hand, has a radial structure and is used to depict one concept rather than multiple concepts and their linkages. It is hierarchical in nature and is employed in visually organizing information about a concept. The cognitive mapping techniques can be used for analysing both qualitative and quantitative data, thus making it a flexible tool (Frey, 2016).

The *day reconstruction method*, which was developed by Kanheman, Krueger, Schwartz and Stone (2004), is similar to maintaining a daily diary, except that it also provides quantitative data. Here, the participant has to provide an elaborate report of his entire day in the form of discrete events. The participant then rates each episode or event in terms of different adjectives, such as exhausting, happy, personally meaningful, on a 6-point rating scale (where 0 is not at all, 6 is very strongly).

The last method to be discussed is the *laddering technique*, which is a specific form of interviewing. Although commonly used in research on consumer behaviour, advertising and marketing (Gutman, 1982), it has application in other fields of psychology as well, and, in fact, emerged in the field of personality psychology (Allport & Ross, 1967). It includes three steps: eliciting attributes, the laddering interview and analysis (Miles & Rowe, 2004). The first step involves eliciting and selecting the attribute which is to be probed further through the laddering interview. These are elicited through various techniques such as triadic sorting, ranking, attribute list, free sorting and free/direct elicitation. The next step involves conducting the laddering interview by asking the participant why a particular attribute is important to him/her. The reason given in response is questioned thereafter, and the questions continue until the participant has no further response. Thus, a relatively lower order attribute is used to arrive at the higher order cognitive process (belief, attitude) that underlies the selection of lower order attributes by the participant. Depending upon the research question and the researcher's skill, either a hard or a soft laddering interview is used. For data analysis, generally, content analysis or a summary matrix is used.

A discussion of the laddering technique will remain incomplete without a mention of the Cantril Ladder. The Gallup World Poll, which collects the data for the *World Happiness Report* every year, uses the Cantril Ladder for data collection. 'It asks respondents to think of a ladder, with the best possible life for them being a 10, and the worst possible life being a 0. They are then asked to rate their own current lives on that 0 to 10 scale' (*World Happiness Report*, 2015, p. 1). Although it has gained popularity for its use in the *World Happiness Report*, the Cantril Ladder has been used in several researches on quality of life (Jaarsma et al., 1999), self-esteem (Carpenter, 1996), assessment of one's social status (Cramm & Nieboer, 2012) and so on.

As a concluding point to this section, it is important to emphasize that each of these methods has its own set of limitations and strengths. The choice of the method depends upon the researcher, which again depends upon its suitability for the research question she intends to address, practical considerations including time and financial resources, availability of participants and her skill in the method.

TRANSLATIONAL RESEARCH AND KNOWLEDGE TRANSLATION

As discussed in great detail in the first chapter, 'Translational research refers to translating research into practice; that is, ensuring that new treatments and research knowledge actually reach the patients or populations for whom they are intended and that they are implemented correctly' (Woolf, 2008, p. 211).

Traditionally, it has been the forte of medical sciences—applying the research-based findings to making new drugs, implementing new treatment options for those inflicted with disease and producing new health care devices. In fact, in the field of medical sciences, unless the research is 'translated' into practice, it does not accrue any benefits to our society. It is not enough to make a discovery; researchers need to find ways to 'translate' it in a form that can be meted out to the public. The potential of translational research has now been recognized in the fields of neuroscience, agriculture and even in the social and behavioural sciences (Woolf, 2008).

The translation of research from the researcher's laboratory (or 'bench', as it is commonly called) to the bedside of the patient, and the larger community takes place in two stages. Stage one involves the translation of knowledge and information from basic to clinical research. Stage two involves the application of research findings from clinical trials to real life settings. The success of stage two depends upon the inclusion of relevant findings from the 'sciences related to populations' (Rubio et al., 2010, p. 4) such as social and behavioural sciences in stage one (Woolf, 2008).

The application of translational research in the field of psychology would essentially aim at addressing the psychological health of both the clinical and non-clinical population. Akin to translational research in the medical sciences, translational research in psychology (and more specifically applied psychology) would similarly aim at interventions and strategies designed to improve mental well-being. These could be in the form of public awareness programmes with messages based on research findings, re-engineering indigenous practices in a form they will be accepted and practiced by the people, and unification of technology with mental well-being. In their attempt to undertake translational research, psychologists and other behavioural scientists are expected to follow the medical model of translational research. The core methodology of the medical model is the RCTs.

As a discipline, psychology offers a rich basket of research methods unlike the medical model, which limits itself to rigorous experimentation. In fact, while applying RCTs from the laboratory to real-life settings, some adaptations have to be made keeping in view the policies, health care practices, and existing infrastructural facilities. Hence, in the process of translation RCTs lose their rigor. Evans (2012) posits that the rich variety of qualitative and quantitative methods available to psychology researchers, coupled with RCTs, can help them develop a nuanced understanding of how to make the evidence-based research findings more policy-relevant and translational. Translation research methods in psychology should be characterized by the use of community-based participatory research, longitudinal research, observational techniques and the use of qualitative techniques which provide first-person accounts of the target population. Such a mixed methodology, according to Evans (2012), can be efficacious in generating policy-relevant research findings which will be in tune with the local community-level practices. Thus, mental health initiatives that are part of the 'adoption of best practices' framework within translational research must include the participation of the targeted community members, and a mixed research methodology if they are to yield significant positive outcomes.

While translational research aims to translate research findings into applicable real-world solutions, the primary focus of knowledge translation is to bridge the gap between knowledge and action. The World Health Organization defines it as, 'The synthesis, exchange, and application of knowledge by relevant stakeholders to accelerate the benefits of global and local innovation in strengthening health systems and improving people's health' (WHO, 2005, p. 2). It has been actively engaged in bridging the know–do gap by commissioning a report to develop programmes to address HIV, reproductive health, chronic diseases and the needs and problems of older persons.

There is ample scope for knowledge translation in psychology in general, and behavioural health in particular. Over the years, several intervention programmes have been developed which have aimed at enhancing well-being (Schotanus-Dijkstra et al., 2017), addressing drug abuse (Jhanjee, 2014), problem-gambling (Gainsbury & Blaszczynski, 2011), cigarette smoking (Yap, Lunn, Pang, Croft, & Stern, 2015), eating disorders (Roig, 2016), energy conservation (Prabhu, Nair, Ahmed, & Ganesh, 2013), capacity-building among slum dwellers (Boyd et al., 2001), employee motivation (Jungert, Van den Broeck, Schreurs, & Osterman, 2018), and reducing turnover rates in the corporate sector (Rickard et al., 2012). Currently, with the increasing importance being given to positive psychology, several positive psychology interventions (PPIs) covering a myriad of behavioural dimensions have been developed. Also, the previously designed PPIs are now being adapted to cultural settings before being delivered to the target population. For example, Khanna and Singh (2016) delivered a gratitude intervention to North Indian school students based on 'Nice Thinking! An educational intervention that teaches children to think gratefully' (Froh et al., 2014). They introduced required modifications to the intervention modules keeping in view the Indian sociocultural context. Their study gives an important direction to the adaptation of intervention programmes to the local setting. A careful consideration of the sociocultural setting and exploration of indigenous practices can provide researchers with significant information that may be incorporated in their intervention module. The inclusion of local practices may enhance the effectiveness of the intervention in bringing about the desired long-term change. For instance, Singh, Sigroha, Singh and Shokeen (2017) provide a detailed analysis of the indigenous practice of *satsang* among rural women in Haryana. In their previous research, Singh, Jain and Singh (2014) have hailed this indigenous practice that has an impact equivalent to that of music therapy, and also report their study as having the orientation of translational research. The incorporation of *satsang* in a well-being enhancement intervention for rural women in

Haryana, may, in fact, give it the orientation of knowledge translation as well, if it is found to have a positive outcome.

Other Indian studies have explored the role of *kundalini* yoga (Kumar & Ali, 2003), *vipassana* meditation (Purohit & Sudha, 1999), naturopathy (Jadhav & Havalappanavar, 2009), and other yogic sciences on well-being. Another study, a transnational comparison, documented the impact of Soka Gakkai International's Buddhist practice on well-being indicators (Sachar, 2013). Two other studies investigated the outcome of the spiritual practice of heartfulness cleaning and meditation (Arya, Singh, & Malik, 2017a; Arya, Singh, Malik, & Mehrotra, 2018), and a five-day spiritual practice in the Himalayan Ashram of Sahaj Marg on mental and physical health indicators (Arya, Singh, & Malik, 2017b). Singh, Singh, Mitra, Junnarkar and Dayal (2016) evaluated the effectiveness of a culturally tailored intervention and explored the differences between non-practitioner and practitioner groups of pre-existing religious/spiritual practices (Brahma Kumaris, Radha Soamis and *satsang* adherents) on health and well-being indicators. It is now time to translate these research findings from the 'laboratory' to the home of every community member and help bridge the gap between knowledge and action.

Apart from the cultural context and local practices, another important variable related to intervention programmes is their mode of delivery (Choubsia, 2011). Group- or individual-based traditional or web-based intervention modules are the two options at the disposal of the researcher. The traditional modules are the ones which are delivered in the field— either in a classroom setting or with the community members—in the physical presence of the research team and the target population. The web-based mode of delivery, on the other hand, does not require the physical presence of the target population and the research team within the same physical space. Since a separate chapter has been devoted to a discussion on web-based interventions, we will limit our discussion on the mode of intervention delivery in this chapter.

Moving back to the methods for use in knowledge translation, since the focus is on the development of an intervention to address the existing gap between research and practice, researchers should incorporate first-, second- as well as third-person perspectives to ensure the development of an efficacious intervention. Focus group discussions (FGDs), community-based participatory research methods, narrative analysis, IPA, the use of survey questionnaires or laddering interview to derive the immediate needs and problems of the community are a few of the methods which can yield relevant information that the researchers may use to conduct policy-relevant research. Finally, they would need to translate that research into a community-level intervention, thereby making it a part of the policy implementation phase.

Despite their relevance for policy and importance in mental health policy implementation respectively, the use of translational research and knowledge translation in behavioural sciences has remained at a nascent stage in India. The WHO (2012) has identified some of the factors that may hinder or facilitate the success of an intervention programme which has been designed to address a specific health care need (physical or psychological). These include the socioeconomic-political context, lack of proper communication between the various stakeholders (the researchers, policymakers, and the target population), lack of generalizability of the research findings to the local community and lack of evaluation of the intervention. Regarding evaluation of interventions, Santesso and Tugwell (2006) point out that the lack of resources and political will in the less developed countries results in the interventions not being evaluated. In fact, knowledge translation strategies have been a significant part of policy implementation in both developing and developed countries. However, they have achieved greater success in the latter countries due to periodic follow-up studies and evaluation schemes.

In India, apart from these factors, there are an insufficient number of psychologists, and probably a lack of willingness on the part of the existing researchers and practitioners to be knowledge brokers and policy advocates. Whichever the case may be, it remains the responsibility of the psychologists to efficiently utilize the varied qualitative and quantitative research methods that are available to them. The selection of the method should be based upon the research question and should help them translate their research findings from their bench-to-bedside of the individual and the community, as well as bridge the existing know–do gap.

At the end, we would like to bring to light the importance of methodo-logical triangulation while conducting research in psychology, regardless of whether it pertains to applied psychology, translational research or knowledge translation. Mathison (1988, p.13), for example, recommends researchers to 'triangulate' and explicitly states that it is a 'good research practice'. Triangulation refers to 'the use of multiple methods, theories, data and or investigators in the study of a common phenomenon(a)' (Duffy, 1987, p. 130). It was Webb, Campbell, Schwartz and Sechrest (1966) who coined the term 'triangulation'. Soon after, Denzin (1978) explicated the different types of triangulation, which are data, investigator, theoretical and methodological triangulation.

- In *data triangulation*, the researcher gathers data regarding the phe-nomenon being studied from various sources.
- *Investigator triangulation* involves multiple interviewers, coders, observ-ers and/or data analysts in the same study, all of whom focus on the same phenomenon and data. Having multiple investigators not only ascertains greater reliability in data collection and analysis but also minimizes the bias inherent in single investigator studies (Denzin, 1970).
- *Theoretical triangulation* is the utilization of different theoretical per-spectives or frames of reference in analysing the same dataset.
- The fourth and final type of triangulation is *methodological triangula-tion* in which the researcher uses two or more than two methods in his study (Mathison, 1988). It is the most commonly used form of triangulation and is referred to by different names including mixed methodology (Tashakkori & Teddlie, 1998), mixed method (Creswell, 2003), multi-strategy (Bryman, 2004), or multi-method (Brannen, 1992). Although the framework of methodological triangulation was explicitly stated by Denzin (1978), Campbell and Fiske (1959) were the first ones to introduce the notion of utilizing multiple research methods within the same study.

Within methodological triangulation, there are two forms—within-method and between-method. An example of within-method triangula-tion is the use of multiple psychometric tests to assess different aspects of intelligence. However, as compared to between-methods triangulation, the within-methods approach is methodologically inadequate because the latter includes only one method. Although between-method triangulation is more rigorous and provides evidence of convergent validity (Zelditch, 1962), it has also been criticized. This is because it advocates using both qualitative and quantitative methods in the same study, and several researchers (e.g., Hunt, 1991) have pointed out that 'these two paradigms differ epistemologically and ontologically' (Hussein, 2009, p. 4). However, one cannot deny that both these paradigms are designed with the same objective—that of understanding a particular phenomenon of interest to the investigator (Hussein, 2009). Moreover, as Denzin (1978, p. 302) rightly points out, 'the flaws of one method are often the strengths of another: and by combining methods, observers can achieve the best of each while over-coming their unique deficiencies'.

In addition to compensating for one another's weaknesses, the use of quantitative and qualitative methods to explore the same research question helps to bring methodological rigour to the research, facilitates data richness and enables the researcher to attain a greater depth of inquiry. It also allows one to examine the patterns of convergence and corroboration as well as dissonance in the data (Erzerberger & Prein, 1997; Lambert & Loiselle, 2008; Mays & Pope, 2000). However, as researchers, we must remember, 'There is no magic in triangulation. The evaluator using different methods to investigate the same programme should not expect that the findings generated by those different methods will automatically come together to produce some-nicely integrated whole' (Patton, 1980, p. 330). The objective of methodological triangulation is to help us 'study and understand when and why there are differences', and it is up to the researcher to recognize the similarities and differences, and to dig deeper into his data and develop a holistic understanding.

An example of methodological triangulation is the use of questionnaires, interviews and FGDs for gathering data. While the questionnaire provides information about specific, measurable aspects of the phenomena, the interviews help in exploring the views and experiences of the participants in great detail. The FGDs, on the other hand, provide additional insight and help test and refine the understanding gained through the individual interviews. Also, the conversational nature and interaction in the FGDs stimulate commentary that may not have been elicited from the one-on-one interviews. Methodological triangulation not only strengthens the credibility and reliability of the findings but also deepens one's understanding of the phenomena in question.

The study of Flick, Garms-Homolova´ and Röhnsch (2012) exemplifies the use of methodological triangulation. They investigated the differences in the perspectives regarding the use of sleep medications among health care providers and patients in a nursing home. Their study necessitated the use of triangulation as a methodological framework. First, because, quantitative data was required to understand the prevalence of sleep disorders for which sleep medications are generally prescribed to the patients. Second, the quantitative data so gathered would have been inadequate had it not been placed in the context of the health care providers' knowledge and attitude towards the treatment of sleep disorders, the patients' perceptions and beliefs about sleep disorders and their treatment. It was only through the use of a mixed methodology that the investigators could develop an in-depth and a holistic understanding of their research problem.

The use of methodological triangulation must, however, be guided by the following four principles, as stated by Mitchell (1986):

1. The investigators must frame a clear and specific research question.
2. They need to ensure that the methods being used complement each other's strengths and shortcomings.
3. The methods must be carefully selected depending upon the nature of the phenomenon being studied.
4. The investigators must continually evaluate their methodological approach to check whether they are adhering to the first three principles.

Such repeated monitoring will enable the researcher to keep track of how the various methods being used are playing against each other, and whether, if at all, they are maximizing the validity of the research being undertaken.

With this, we end our discourse on the research methods in applied psychology. In the next section, we will consider a few recommendations for achieving greater progress in research on applied psychology in India.

SUGGESTIONS FOR FUTURE RESEARCHERS WITH SPECIAL REFERENCE TO THE INDIAN CONTEXT

The domain of quantitative research is heavily dependent on the use of statistical tools and computer software programmes. Linear structural relations (LISREL), analysis of moment structures (AMOS), statistical package for the social sciences (SPSS), R programming, EQS—Structural Equation Modeling Software, M-Plus, statistical analysis system (SAS), WINMIRA, and latent variable analysis (LAVAAN) are among the various software that are available for research purposes. However, are all researchers in applied psychology sufficiently equipped to handle these diverse software programmes? The estimates could be obtained by surveying researchers and academicians. Such a survey could fetch information about the software programmes most researchers are comfortable using, the reasons behind their choice and the computer programmes in which they would like to gain further expertise. The results of this survey could be utilized by private enterprises specializing in the production of such computer software programmes. It would help them determine the training needs and organize and promote training programmes for interested clients (educational institutions, research firms, think tanks, etc.). Individuals receiving the training could then further impart this knowledge they have acquired through workshops in collaboration with the software companies.

However, competence in using such software will remain unutilized if researchers do not have adequate knowledge about statistical concepts. The courses designed at the graduate level should be such that they enable students to comprehend which statistical method is best suited to a particular research situation. Speaking from practical experience, we can undoubtedly say that this is perhaps the biggest challenge while doing quantitative research. For this, it is crucial for one to be aware of the diverse range of statistical techniques belonging to both the parametric and non-parametric domains. The median test, hotelling t-test, Mardia's test, hierarchical regression, quantile regression, Bonferreni-horn correction regression, hierarchical cluster analysis, and ward linkage method are examples of the few statistical concepts which are often not covered as part of the postgraduate coursework in psychology in Indian universities. However, we realize that it is not feasible to cover all the existing techniques as part of the coursework. One way through which both new concepts may be taught, and their practical application understood, would be by making available research papers from renowned journals—that have used new statistical techniques—to students and making them understand those techniques within the context of that specific research. After that, they may be demonstrated the use of those techniques via the appropriate computer software.

Another alternative at the disposal of researchers is to collaborate with statisticians. Such a collaboration would not only help them gain further clarity but also enhance their knowledge of those statistical concepts of which they are relatively less aware.

Similar to statistical techniques, test construction is another area which deserves attention. For researchers who intend to specialize in psychometrics, it is crucial to acquire knowledge about various facets of test construction. This includes but is not limited to factor analysis (exploratory and confirmatory), structural equation modelling, those measures of reliability and validity which are not generally covered as part of coursework at the undergraduate and postgraduate level such as omega as reliability coefficient, nomological and incremental validity, the use of item response theory for test validation, among many others.

Another recommendation relating to psychological tests includes incorporating open-ended questions as part of the tests, which would provide the scope of qualitative analysis, a model coming in vogue nowadays. Researchers should also, as a rule, attempt to conduct FGDs with a small sample of the target population before formulating questionnaire items.

There is also a need to construct tests which measure indigenous constructs that are associated with the Indian sociocultural context, instead of merely borrowing Western concepts and translating and adapting those tests to Indian conditions. It cannot be denied that some work is being done in this direction. Attempts have been made to capture concepts such as *anasakti* (Singh & Raina, 2015), *vikaras* (Singh & Sharma, 2016), *sukh–dukh* (Singh, Raina, & Sahni, 2016), and *ashtanga* yoga (Raina & Singh, 2018) through psychological tests. This work needs to be expanded and carried forward by Indian psychologists.

Apart from an appreciation of indigenous practices and constructs, psychologists also need to be wary of their sample. Picture elicitation methods may be more effective while collecting data from an illiterate rural sample, similarly, the likelihood terms in response categories of Likert type scales (sometimes, rarely, not very often) may not be understandable to all the participants. Under such circumstances, it is up to the researcher to use his/her judgment and introduce ways in which the response categories can be made comprehensible to the participants.

Overall, there needs to be a greater appreciation of programmatic research among psychologists in India. In conducting such long-term-oriented research, an eclectic methodology needs to be adopted. The use of both qualitative and quantitative methods may help compensate for one another's shortcomings and give us more valid and reliable results than the use of one approach alone (Black, 1994).

Now, if we look back at the factors which inhibit successful knowledge translation, we find that one of the key factors is the lack of evaluation of the developed interventions (WHO, 2012). This can be overcome by conducting longitudinal studies, follow-ups and both process and outcome evaluation of the mental health, social, environmental, workplace interventions to ensure their effectiveness in helping bring about the desired outcome.

Another recommendation would be for theorists and researchers to work in collaboration. Theorists are generally the ones to devise the new methods while researchers are the ones who use them. The former need to be well informed about the limitations of working in the field, for which there is an increased need for collaboration between the two. This can help bridge the gap between theory and research application.

Similarly, there is a need for active discourse and collaboration between psychologists and other social science researchers such as economists, sociologists and linguists. The field of economics has been instrumental in making behavioural economics (where psychology has a crucial role to play) an essential part of policymaking. The relative lack of importance given to other fields and research findings of psychology in policymaking bears testimony to the fact that either we have been unsuccessful research brokers or our findings do not possess sufficient ecological validity. Policy-relevant research findings will require the use of methods which are not restricted within laboratories and which follow an eclectic methodology. It is highly unlikely that policymakers will be sufficiently convinced of the application of research findings if they are merely based on laboratory studies amid highly controlled conditions. Economics has shown us the way, and it is only fair that psychologists try to forge their relationship with policymaking even further. Applied social psychology, health, and environmental psychology are all domains whose research findings have relevance for policymaking, provided they have ecological validity. The research method used is a crucial determinant of whether the research will have ecological validity. Sociology, and its research method of ethnography, which follows a participatory research paradigm in which the researcher spends time in the field, amidst his target population, trying to study a particular phenomenon or behaviour, has also found acceptance in our discipline, specifically in applied social psychology. Similarly, the strong quantitative orientation of linguistics calls for collaboration between the fields to share knowledge and learn from one another.

It cannot be over emphasized that psychologists need to actively collaborate and communicate with policymakers in order to make their research more policy-relevant and to disseminate their policy-relevant findings. Taking on the role of knowledge brokers is a good way forward. This could help promote the culture of translational research in India.

Also, when it comes to knowledge translation, we need to communicate the critical takeaway of our findings to the population for whom the intervention was developed in the first place. Conducting research and documenting and publishing its findings will not have much significance unless it is disseminated to the target public. It is we who need to place our findings on the bedside of the community. Perhaps one way of doing this would be to write more frequently in newspapers and health magazines. In doing this, we need to ensure that our message is crafted in a simple and clear form and is repeated often. We must avoid using jargons and should instead opt for simpler substitutes. Also, the structure and format of such presentations cannot be the same as that of scientific journals. While communicating with our peers, we start with the background information, then move on to the supporting details and finally talk about the key findings. Somerville and Hassol (2011) recommend inverting this pyramid when we are communicating with the general public. We must begin with the bottom-line, then answer the 'so what' question and finally talk about the supporting details. They opine that the 'so what' question is critical when we are communicating our findings to the general public because 'people want to know why they should care' (Somerville & Hassol, 2011, p. 50). They also suggest that we must avoid overstating the details because people can find it difficult to sort out the important points from the unimportant ones as a result, 'the more you say, the less they hear' (Somerville & Hassol, 2011, p. 50). Another recommendation provided by them is to use metaphors, analogies, imagery and narratives in our communication with the general public.

Finally, as a researcher, one should not lose sight of their ethical responsibility and professional obligations. Regardless of the research paradigm one adopts, there should be complete transparency to the ethical committee and the research participants. The researcher should not only acquire approval from the ethical committee of his or her institute but also acquire the consent of the participants before gathering data. The researcher needs to be sensitive to the issue of self-disclosure of the participants, especially with regards to the qualitative methods of data collection. In the case of minors, parental approval should be taken before collecting data. Moreover, regardless of the age of the participants, a debriefing session should be held at the end of the data collection process.

These are only a few recommendations for expanding the knowledge base of psychologists regarding research methods. It is but fair to acknowledge that no such list of recommendation can ever be exhaustive.

CONCLUSION

The advancement of research methods in applied psychology is indeed a step in the right direction considering that psychology as a discipline is a young science. However, without application and use in research, their development does not add much value to the discipline. This does not in any way imply that one should blindly opt for any one of the relatively novel and underutilized methods. Before deciding upon the use of a particular method, the researcher needs to ensure that it addresses his/ her research question and it can successfully tap the constructs which he/she is aiming to analyse. It requires the initiative of researchers— experienced and new entrants alike—to actively seek information about various research methods that can be used in a particular study. This can prevent them from relying on methods that have traditionally been a part of the toolkit for researchers because of their familiarity, without due consideration of whether any other method could have been more relevant.

REFERENCES

Allport, G. W., & Ross, J. M. (1967). Personal religious orientation and prejudice. *Journal of Personality and Social Psychology, 5*(4), 432–443.

Arya, N. K., Singh, K., & Malik, A. (2017a). Effect of heartfulness spiritual-based program on mental and physical health indicators. *International Journal of Research in Management & Social Science, 5*(3), 91–103.

———. (2017b). Impact of five days spiritual practice in Himalyan ashram of Sahaj Marg on well-being related parameters and selected physiological indicators. *The International Journal of Indian Psychology, 4*(2), 36–51.

Arya, N. K., Singh, K., Malik, A., & Mehrotra, R. (2018). Effect of heartfulness cleaning and meditation on heart rate variability. *Indian Heart Journal, 70*, 1–6.

Baerg, S. (2003). Sometimes there just aren't words. Using expressive therapy with adolescents living with cancer. *Canadian Journal of Counselling, 37*(1), 65–74.

Black, N. (1994). Why we need qualitative research. *Journal of Epidemiology & Community Health, 48*(5), 425–426.

Bolger, N., Davis, A., & Rafaeli, E. (2003). Diary methods: Capturing life as it is lived. *Annual Review of Psychology, 54*(1), 579–616.

Boster, D., & Ron, S. (1976). *Measuring landscape esthetics: The scenic beauty estimation method* (USDA Forest Service Research Paper). Colorado: USDA Forest Service.

Boyd, A., Geerling, T., Midgley, G., Murray, P., Walsh, M., & Kagan, C. (2001). *Capacity building for evaluation: A report on the HAZE Project to the Manchester, Salford and Trafford Health Action Zone.* Centre for Systems Studies, University of Hull.

Brannen, J. (1992). *Combining qualitative and quantitative approaches: An overview.* Aldershot: Avebury.

Brown, L. M. (1999). *Raising their voices: The politics of girls' anger.* Cambridge, MA: Harvard University Press.

Bryman, A. (2004). *Social research methods* (2nd ed.). Oxford: Oxford University Press.

Campbell, D. T., & Fiske, D. W. (1959). Convergent and discriminant validation by the multitrait-multimethod matrix. *Psychological Bulletin, 56*(2), 81–105.

Carpenter, J. S. (1996). Applying the Cantril methodology to study self-esteem: Psychometrics of the self-anchoring self-esteem scale. *Journal of Nursing Measurement, 4*(2), 171–189.

Charmaz, K. (2006). *Constructing grounded theory. A practical guide through qualitative analysis.* London, United Kingdom: SAGE Publications.

Choubsia, R. (2011). *Enhancing college students well-being through a web based intervention module: An empirical investigation* (Unpublished doctoral thesis). Retrieved from http://eprint.iitd.ac.in/bitstream/2074/5827/1/TH-4124.pdf

Cooperrider, D. L., & Whitney, D. (2006). Appreciative inquiry: A positive revolution in change. In P. Holman & T. Devane (Eds.), *The change handbook* (pp. 19–33). San Francisco, CA: Berrett-Koehler Publishers.

Cooperrider, D., Whitney, D., & Stavros, J. M. (2008). *Appreciative inquiry handbook: For leaders of change* (2nd ed.). Brunswick, OH; San Francisco, CA: Crown Custom Publishing; Berrett-Koehler Publishers.

Cramm, J. M., & Nieboer, A. P. (2012). Differences in the association of subjective well-being measures with health, socio-economic status and social conditions among residents of an Eastern Cape Township. *International Journal of Well-Being, 2*(1), 54–67.

Creswell, J. W. (2003). *Research design: Qualitative, quantitative, and mixed methods approaches.* Thousand Oaks, CA: SAGE Publications.

Csikszentmihaly, C., & Larson, R. (1987). Validity and reliability of the experience sampling method. *The Journal of Nervous and Mental Diseases, 175*(9), 526–536.

Denzin, N. K. (1970). *The research act: A theoretical introduction to sociological methods.* Chicago, IL: Adline Publishing.

———. (1978). *The research act: A theoretical introduction to sociological methods.* New York, NY: McGraw-Hill.

Duffy, M. E. (1987). Methodological triangulation: A vehicle for merging quantitative and qualitative research methods. *Journal of Nursing Scholarship, 19*(3), 130–133.

Erzerberger, C., & Prein, G. (1997). Triangulation: Validity and empirically based hypothesis construction. *Quality and Quantity, 31,* 141–154.

Evans, J. V. (2012). Translation in the social and behavioral sciences: Looking back and looking forward. In E. Wethington & R. E. Dunifon (Eds.), *Research for the public good: Applying the methods of translational research to improve human health and well-being* (pp. 23–31). Washington, DC: American Psychological Association.

Flick, U., Garms-Homolová, V., & Röhnsch, G. (2012). 'And mostly they have a need for sleeping pills': Physicians' views on treatment of sleep disorders with drugs in nursing homes. *Journal of Aging Studies, 26*(4), 484–494.

Flowers, P., Smith, J., Sheeran, P., & Beail, N. (1997). Health and romance: Understanding unprotected sex in relationships between gay men. *British Journal of Health Psychology, 2*(1), 73–86.

Freeman, F. S. (1964). *Theory and practice of psychological testing.* New Delhi: Oxford and IBH Publishing.

Frey, C. (2016). *Concept map vs. mind map.* Retrieved from http://mindmapping-softwareblog.com/concept-maps-vs-mind-maps/

Froh, J. J., Bono, G., Fan, J., Emmons, R. A., Henderson, K., Harris, C., ... Wood, A. (2014). Nice Thinking! An educational intervention that teaches children how to think gratefully. *School Psychology Review, 43*(2), 132–152.

Gainsbury, S., & Blaszczynski, A. (2011). Online self-guided interventions for the treatment of problem gambling. *International Gambling Studies, 11*(3), 289–308.

Gastaldo, D., Magalhaes, L., Carrasco, C., & Davy, C. (2012). *Body-map storytelling as research: Methodological considerations for telling the stories of undocumented workers through body mapping.* Toronto: Creative Commons. Retrieved from http://www.migrationhealth.ca/undocumented-workers-ontario/body-mapping

Gilligan, C., & Eddy, J. (2017). Listening as path to psychological discovery: An introduction to the listening guide. *Perspectives on Medical Education, 6*(2), 76–81.

Gilligan, C., Weinberg, M. K., & Bertsch, T. (2003). On the listening guide: A voice-centered relational method. In P. Camic, J. Rhodes, & L. Yardley (Eds.), *Qualitative research in psychology: Expanding perspectives in methodology and design.* Washington, DC: American Psychological Association.

Giorgi, A. (1970). *Psychology as a human science: A phenomenologically based approach.* New York, NY: Harper and Row.

Gutman, J. (1982). A means-end chain model based on consumer categorization processes. *Journal of Marketing, 46*(2), 60–72.

Hunt, S. D. (1991). *Modern marketing theory: Critical issues in the philosophy of marketing science.* Cincinnati, OH: South-Western Publishing.

Hussein, A. (2009). The use of triangulation in social sciences research: Can qualitative and quantitative methods be combined? *Journal of Comparative Social Work, 4*(1), 1–12.

Immadisetty, V. (2012). Body mapping: A novel tool for psychiatrists. *Andhra Pradesh Journal of Psychological Medicine, 13*(2), 115–118.

Jaarsma, T., Halfens, R., Abu-Saad, H. H., Dracup, K., Strappers, J., & van Ree, J. (1999). Quality of life in older patients with systolic and diastolic heart failure. *The European Journal of Heart Failure, 1*(2), 151–160.

Jack, D. C. (1991). *Silencing the self: Women and depression.* Cambridge, MA: Harvard University Press.

Jadhav, S. G., & Havalappanavar, N. B. (2009). Effect of yoga intervention on anxiety and subjective well-being. *Journal of the Indian Academy of Applied Psychology, 35*(1), 27–31.

Jhanjee, S. (2014). Evidence based psychosocial interventions in substance use. *Indian Journal of Psychological Medicine, 36*(2), 112–118.

Jungert, T., Van den Broeck, A., Schreurs, B., & Osterman, U. (2018). How colleagues can support each other's needs and motivation: An intervention on employee work motivation. *Applied Psychology, 67*(1), 3–29.

Kahneman, D., Krueger, A. B., Schkade, D., Schwarz, N., & Stone, A. A. (2004). A survey method for characterizing daily life experiences: The day reconstruction method. *Science, 306*(5702), 1776–1780.

Khanna, P., & Singh, K. (2016). Effect of gratitude educational intervention on well-being indicators among north Indian adolescents. *Contemporary School Psychology, 20*(4), 305–314.

Krippner, S. (2015). Research methodology in humanistic psychology in light of postmodernity. In K. J. Schneider, F. J. Pierson, & J. F. Bugental (Eds.), *The handbook of humanistic psychology: Theory, research, and practice* (pp. 335–350). London: SAGE Publications.

Kumar, K. G., & Ali, M. H. (2003). Meditation: A harbinger of subjective well-being. *Journal of Personality and Clinical Studies, 19*(1), 93–102.

Lambert, S. D., & Loiselle, C. G. (2008). Combining individual interviews and focus groups to enhance data richness. *Journal of Advanced Nursing, 62*(2), 228–237.

Lantz, J. (2004). Research and evaluation issues in existential psychotherapy. *Journal of Contemporary Psychotherapy, 34*(4), 331–339.

MacKay, W. E. (1989). EVA: An experimental video annotator for symbolic analysis of video data. *SIGCHI Bulletin, 21*(2), 68–71.

Mann, A. J. (1997). An appreciative inquiry model for building partnerships. Global social innovations. *Journal of GEM Initiative, 1*(2), 41–44.

Mathison, S. (1988). Why triangulate? *Educational Researcher, 17*(2), 13–17.

Mays, N., & Pope, C. (2000). Assessing quality in qualitative research. *British Medical Journal, 320*(50), 50–52.

Miles, S., & Rowe, G. (2004). The laddering technique. In G. M. Breakwell (Ed.), *Doing social psychology research* (pp. 305–343). Cornwall: BPS Blackwell.

Mitchell, E. S. (1986). Multiple triangulation: A methodology for nursing science. *Advances in Nursing Science, 8*(3), 18–26.

Murray, M. (2000). Levels of narrative analysis in health psychology. *Journal of Health Psychology, 5*(3), 337–347.

Neighborhood Centers Inc. (2009). *Appreciative inquiry and aging in place: Unlocking the strengths of our neighborhoods.* Houston, TX: Neigborhood Centers Inc.

Nelson, J. M. (2009). Phenomenological approaches to religion and spirituality. In J. M. Nelson (Ed.), *Psychology, religion and spirituality* (pp. 103–142). New York, NY: Springer.

Norman, D., & Lincoln, Y. (2005). *The SAGE handbook of qualitative research.* London: SAGE Publications.

Oliveira, E., Meyers, S. V., & Vearey, J. (Eds.). (2016). *Queer crossings: A participatory arts-based project.* Johannesburg, South Africa: MoVE and ACMS. Retrieved from https://issuu.com/move.methods.visual.explore/docs/queer_crossings_publication_v.2_-_f/27

Patton, M. Q. (1980). *Qualitative evaluation methods.* Beverly Hills, CA: SAGE Publications.

Pauen, M. (2012). The second-person perspective. *Inquiry, 55,* 33–49. doi:10.1080/0020174X.2012.643623

Prabhu, A. V., Nair, S. R., Ahmed, P. K., & Ganesh, C. (2013). Energy conservation in rural India: The impact of context and attitudes on behavior. *Journal of Asian and African Studies, 48*(4), 469–483.

Purohit, S., & Sudha, H. (1999). Effects of vipassana on adolescent's adjustment and preference of power bases. *Indian Journal of Clinical Psychology, 26,* 205–208.

Raina, M., & Singh, K. (2018). The Ashtanga Yoga Hindi scale: An assessment tool based on eastern philosophy of yoga. *Journal of Religion and Health, 57*(1), 12–25.

Rao, R. K., & Paranjpe, A. C. (2016). *Psychology in the Indian tradition.* New Delhi: Springer.

Rickard, G., Lenthall, S., Dollard, M., Opie, T., Knight, S., Dunn, S., … Brewster-Webb, D. (2012). Organisational intervention to reduce occupational stress and turnover in hospital nurses in the Northern Territory, Australia. *Collegian, 19*(4), 211–221.

Roig, A. E. (2016). *Efficacy of a positive psychological intervention in patients with eating disorders.* Retrieved from https://clinicaltrials.gov/ct2/show/NCT03003910

Roschelle, J., & Goldman, S. (1991). VideoNoter: A productivity tool for video data analysis. *Behavior Research Methods, Instruments & Computers, 23*(2), 219–224.

Rubio, D. M., Schoenbaum, E. E., Lee, L. S., Schteingart, D. E., Marantz, P. R., Anderson, K. E., … Esposito, K. (2010). Defining translational research: implications for training. *Academic Medicine, 85*(3), 470–475.

Sachar, R. (2013). *Impact of Buddhist practice on psychological well-being and related factors of positive psychology: A transnational comparison* (Unpublished doctoral thesis). Retrieved from http://eprint.iitd.ac.in/bitstream/2074/6761/1/TH-4476.pdf

Sanderson, P. M. (1993). Designing for simplicity of interference in observational studies of process control: ESDA and MacSHAPA. Proceedings of the *Fourth European Conference on Cognitive Science Approaches to Process Control (CSAPC'93): Designing for Simplicity,* Frederiksborg, Denmark.

Santesso, N., & Tugwell, P. (2006). Knowledge translation in developing countries. *The Journal of Continuing Education in the Health Professions, 26*(1), 87–96.

Schotanus-Dijkstra, M., Drossaert, C. H., Pieterse, M. E., Boon, B., Walburg, J. A., & Bohlmeijer, E. T. (2017). An early intervention to promote well-being and flourishing and reduce anxiety and depression: A randomized controlled trial. *Internet Interventions, 9,* 15–24.

Shendell-Falik, N., Feinson, M., & Mohr, B. J. (2007). Enhancing patient safety: Improving the patient handoff process through appreciative inquiry. *The Journal of Nursing Administration, 37*(2), 95–104.

Singh, K., Chitra, K., Raj, A., Kumar, A. N., & Kumar, K. S. (2013). Development and validation of a new scale: Sat-Chit-Ananda scale. *International Journal on Vedic Foundations of Management, 1*(2), 54–74.

Singh, K., Jain, A., & Singh, D. (2014). Satsang: A culture specific effective practice for well-being. In H. Agueda Marujo & L. M. Neto (Eds.), *Positive nations and communities: Collective, qualitative and culture-sensitive processes in positive psychology* (pp. 79–100). Dordrecht: Springer.

Singh, K., & Raina, M. (2015). Development and validation of a test on Anasakti (non-attachment): An Indian model of well-being. *Mental Health, Religion & Culture, 18*(9), 715–725.

Singh, K., Raina, M., & Sahni, P. (2016). The concept and measure of *sukha–dukha*: An Indian perspective on well-being. *Journal of Spirituality in Mental Health, 19*(2), 116–132.

Singh, K., & Sahni, P. (2016). Swadhyaya Scale: An Indian perspective. *The International Journal of Indian Psychology, 4*(1), 5–14.

Singh, K., & Sharma, S. (2016). Development and validation of Vikaras Hindi scale. *Mental Health, Religion & Culture, 19*(5), 420–432.

Singh, K., Sigroha, S., Singh, D., & Shokeen, B. (2017). Religious and spiritual messages in folk songs: A study of women from rural India. *Mental Health, Religion & Culture, 20*(5), 464–477.

Singh, K., Singh, D., Mitra, S., Junnarkar, M., & Dayal, P. (2016). Effect of well-being of spiritual practices among elderly rural women. Mid-year conference on *Psychology, Spirituality and Religion*, Society for the Psychology of Religion and Spirituality & St. Josephs' College, New York.

Smith, J., & Osborn, M. (2003). Interpretive phenomenological analysis. In J. A. Smith (Ed.), *Qualitative psychology: A practical guide to research methods* (pp. 53–80). London: SAGE Publications.

Solomon, J. (2002). *Living with X: A body mapping journey in time of HIV and AIDS. Facilitators Guide—Psychosocial well-being series.* Johannesburg: REPSSI.

Solomon, P., Cavanaugh, M. M., & Draine, J. (2009). *Randomized controlled trials: Design and implementation for community-based psychosocial interventions.* New York, NY: Oxford.

Somerville, R. C., & Hassol, S. J. (2011). Communicating the science of climate change. *Physics Today*, *64*(10), 48–53.

Swan, J. (1997). Using cognitive mapping in management research: Decisions about technical innovation. *British Journal of Management*, *8*(2), 183–198.

Tashakkori, A., & Teddlie, C. (1998). *Mixed methodology: Combining qualitative and quantitative approaches.* Thousand Oaks, CA: SAGE Publications.

Van, P. H., Loots, G., Grietens, H., & Jacquet, W. (2013). 'I just don't agree': A voice-oriented analysis of an IPS case of alleged child maltreatment. *Journal of Social Work Practice*, *28*(2), 173–192.

Verleysen, B., Lambrechts, F., & Van Acker, F. (2015). Building psychological capital with appreciative inquiry: Investigating the mediating role of basic psychological need satisfaction. *The Journal of Applied Behavioral Science*, *51*(1), 1–26.

Walsh, I., Holton, J. A., Bailyn, L., Fernandez, W., Levina, N., & Glaser, B. (2015). What grounded theory is … a critically reflective conversation among scholars. *Organizational Research Methods*, *18*(4), 620–628.

Watkins, J. M., & Mohr, B. J. (2001). *Appreciative inquiry: Change at the speed of imagination.* San Francisco, CA: Jossey-Bass.

Way, N. (1998). *Everyday courage: The lives and stories of urban teenagers.* New York, NY: NYC Press.

Webb, E. J., Campbell, D. T., Schwartz, R. D., & Sechrest, L. (1966). *Unobtrusive measures.* Chicago, IL: Rand McNally.

Whitney, D., & Fredrickson, B. L. (2015). Appreciative inquiry meets positive psychology: A dialogue between Diana Whitney and Barbara Fredrickson about organizational change, transformation and innovation. *AI Practitioner*, *17*(3), 18–26.

WHO. (2005). *Bridging the 'know-do' gap. Meeting on knowledge translation in global health.* Geneva, Switzerland: WHO Press. Retrieved from https://www.measureevaluation.org/resources/training/capacity-building-resources/high-impact-research-training-curricula/bridging-the-know-do-gap.pdf

———. (Ed.). (2012). *Knowledge translation framework for ageing and health.* Retrieved from http://www.who.int/ageing/publications/knowledge_translation/en/

Wong, A. E., & Vallacher, R. R. (2018). Reciprocal feedback between self-concept and goal pursuit in daily life. *Journal of Personality*, *86*(3), 543–554.

Woolf, S. H. (2008). The meaning of translational research and why it matters. *Journal of American Medical Association*, *299*(2), 211–213.

World Happiness Report 2015. Frequently asked questions. (2015). Retrieved from https://s3.amazonaws.com/happiness-report/2015/Ch2FAQ_final.pdf

Yap, S. Y., Lunn, S., Pang, E., Croft, C., & Stern, M. (2015). A psychological intervention for smoking cessation delivered as treatment for smokers with chronic obstructive pulmonary disease: Multiple needs of a complex group and recommendations for novel service development. *Chronic Respiratory Disease, 12*(3), 230–237.

Zelditch, M. (1962). Some methodological problems of field studies. *American Journal of Sociology, 67*(5), 566–576.

Żoldbrod, A. P. (2015). Sexual issues in treating trauma survivors. *Current Sexual Health Problems, 7*(1), 3–11.

Chapter 3

Applications of Psychology in Rural India

Jasleen Kaur and Kamlesh Singh

Communities are divided into urban and rural on the basis of criteria like location among others. While the 'urban' communities enjoy several amenities and are relatively free from routine struggles, the 'rural' communities face several challenges. From visible factors such as lack of proper health care and educational facilities, unemployment, problems related to infrastructure, etc., to invisible factors such as sociocultural issues, and obsolete customs and traditions, rural life is dictated by several parameters. Recognizing the threat thus posed to the well-being of rural people, psychologists and researchers are implementing psychology-based programmes to improve the well-being and overall quality of life of rural people, thereby also contributing to the area of translational research. Translational research is an important milestone in research as it reaches out to individuals and communities by translating findings from research to practice. This chapter presents a consolidated review of psychology-based translational researches/programmes undertaken across rural India (in the field of mental health, physical health, across different population groups, etc.), and also the different mediums used for the same. Additionally, it gives suggestions, ranging from effective use of technology to familiarity with local customs and traditions, etc., which may further ensure the success of interventions. However, it is going to take time as psychology-based translational research in rural India is still at its nascent stage. For translational research to achieve desired outcomes in rural India, collaboration between various agencies, starting from local NGOs and policymakers to psychologists and researchers, would be a step in the right direction. It is hoped that the review of past and ongoing translational research-based programmes in this chapter would also capture the attention of more applied psychologists and researchers to reach out to rural communities, and help them thrive.

INTRODUCTION

Given the complexities of human mind and behaviour, the field of psychology has been continuously evolving. It has seeped into almost all spheres of life and, to keep pace with the growing demand, has divided itself into a number of sub fields as per their focus on study of behaviour in particular settings, such as clinical, counselling, educational, forensic, industrial, sports, social, community, cross-cultural, urban, rural, etc. In recent times, increased interest is seen in studying communities, rural communities in particular and cross-cultural behaviour since these form the backbone of any nation. This attention may be due to the not-so-encouraging picture that emerges from the rural areas, be it in terms of health, infrastructure, education, sociocultural issues, etc., vis-à-vis their urban counterparts. Before proceeding further, it is important to understand what the term 'rural' actually entails.

RURAL COMMUNITIES

For a layman, the word 'rural' would mean a low-density population area with a small, close-knit community. Khattri, Riley and Kane (1997, p. 3) in their review paper drew attention to the four most utilized definitions of 'rural' based on geographical location. First, according to the US Census Bureau, if an area has a population of less than 2,500 people, it is defined as rural. Second, according to the Office of Management and Budget, this builds upon the Census definition and designates entire counties as 'metro' or 'non-metro'. If a county does not have a city with

50,000 or more inhabitants, or an urbanized area with at least 100,000, the county is designated 'non-metro'. Third, the US Department of Agriculture's Economic Research Service, uses rural–urban continuum codes to distinguish among metro counties, non-metro counties adjacent to metro areas and non-metro counties not adjacent to metro areas. Even non-metro counties not adjacent to metro areas, however, can have urban or rural populations. Parr and Philo (2003) distinguished between 'rural' and 'urban' in terms of physical and social proximity. According to them, rural communities are places where people are physically distant but socially proximate, in direct contrast to people who live in urban areas, while according to Wagenfeld (2003) 'rural' represented low population density areas. Malon and Werth Jr. (2014) highlighted certain characteristics such as the presence of complex, interrelated networks with deep historical, social, familial and political roots; strong family ties; avoiding conflict or discussing feelings; stoic attitudes toward life in general; and high involvement in religious activities in their communities, with rural residents.

As per the 2001 Census of India, 'rural sector' means any place that meets the following criteria:

- A population of less than 5,000
- Density of population less than 400 per sq. km. and
- More than '25 per cent of the male working population' is engaged in agricultural pursuits

RESEARCH FROM RURAL COMMUNITIES

Worldwide, rural communities in comparison with the urban communities are often at a disadvantage due to their location, size and infrastructure, which further hinders access to necessities and facilities. Studies have documented how living in rural areas can result in physical and social isolation, making access to stores, parks, medical care and other services a challenge (Rosenthal & Fox, 2000; Sharkey, Johnson, & Dean, 2010). Rural people, as compared to their urban counterparts, have fewer choices in social and economic terms. They face problems related to low income, unemployment, low quality of social services such as education and health care (Surchev, 2010). Adesiji, Dada and Komolafe (2012) investigated the problems faced by rural people in accessing health care facilities. The factors that acted as barriers were distance (far), road status (bad), cost of transportation (high), source of information (low) and gender (male dominated). Malon and Werth Jr. (2014) highlighted how daily life in rural areas is veiled by challenges such as poverty, unemployment, lack of transportation, lack of education, substance abuse, lack of health and mental health providers, which also create barriers in seeking physical and mental care. In a comparison between rural and non-rural areas, Anderson, Saman, Lipsky and Lutfiyya (2015) reported rural residents as more likely to have poorer health outcomes, along with significantly statistically lower scores on health behaviour, morbidity factors, clinical care and the physical environment. Limitations in infrastructure, socio-economic differences, insurance coverage deficiencies and higher rates of traffic fatalities and accidents were seen as the contributory factors. Silva et al. (2017) identified various factors acting as barriers to mental health services in rural areas. These were long waiting-times, inadequate patient rapport with referred professionals, and cost of treatment, transportation, geographical location, stigma and lack of education about available mental health services.

With rural people facing so many barriers, the effect is visible in their quality of lives too. Studies have reported a higher prevalence of mental health disorders in rural people as compared to the urban population (Diala & Muntaner, 2003; Probst et al., 2006). Lower help-seeking behaviour of rural people also plays a big role in their mental health status. This is due to several factors, such as lower available weekly budget not only for health care itself but also for transport to the health care facility. Hauenstein et al. (2007) documented several challenges faced by rural residents, ranging from poverty, stigma and lack of anonymity to culture of self-reliance, lack of culturally acceptable treatment and long travel times. Lambert, Ziller and Lenardson (2008) observed that rural children were less likely to receive mental health treatment in comparison to urban children. Families of children suffering from serious emotional problems in rural areas reported challenges related to rurality, including stigma, transportation, isolation, poverty and service availability in accessing appropriate care (Pullmann, VanHooser, Hoffman, & Heflinger,

2010). Another factor closely associated with low health care seeking for mental ailments in rural communities is the stigma associated with mental disorders; a fact documented in several studies (Aisbett, Boyd, Francis, Newnham, & Newnham, 2007; Atif et al., 2016; Parr & Philo, 2003; Parr, Philo, & Burns, 2004). Atif et al. (2016) provided intervention for perinatal depression in rural Pakistan through peer volunteers. However, several barriers were observed for this intervention. These were women's lack of autonomy, certain cultural beliefs, and stigma associated with depression, lack of some mothers' engagement and resistance from some families.

Rural people have to also deal with problems related to education of children, substance abuse and domestic violence. Roscigno and Crowle (2001) called attention to the fact that lower academic achievement and a higher rate of dropping out of school was more for rural adolescents in comparison to their non-rural peers. Adolescents growing up in rural areas face fewer curricular choices, fewer school activities, fewer employment prospects and isolation based on their geographical location (DeHaan & Boljevac, 2009). Binge drinking and alcohol dependence was found to be higher for rural areas in comparison to urban areas (Spence & Wallisch, 2007). Ziaaddini, Ziaaddini and Nakhaee (2013) investigated substance abuse in rural Iran over a 12-year period. While the authors reported increase in substance abuse due to easy availability, the study also reported that cigarette, opium and opium residue (9%) were the most frequent substances abused on a daily basis. Prevalence of domestic violence has also been found to be higher in rural regions in comparison to urban regions (Ajah, Iyoke, Nkwo, Nwakoby, & Ezeonu, 2014; Peek-Asa et al., 2011).

RESEARCH FROM RURAL INDIA

World over, barriers faced by rural residents affect their well-being as well as their quality of life, and India is no exception. India is as affected, or perhaps more, as it is primarily an agrarian society. To understand the picture of India in totality, it is important to revisit its past. When India gained independence seven decades ago, the government's obvious focus was nation-building by first providing shelter, livelihood and economic security to its people. This was by no means an easy task, as problems such as illiteracy, malnutrition, unemployment, poverty, etc., hampered the process. However, with its economic policies and focus on specific target sectors, India overcame the hurdles, and today it is one of the fastest growing economies in the world. While the overall progress demands appreciation, there are certain sectors that are still bearing the brunt of past neglect, rural India for example. The development of rural India, which is home to 68.84 per cent people, with an overall literacy rate of 68.9 per cent as compared to 85 per cent in urban India (Census of India, 2011) is still a challenge for the Indian government. To fast-track the development in rural areas, a large number of schemes were put in pipeline such as Community Development Programme (1952), Intensive Agriculture Development Programme (1960–61), Credit Authorization Scheme (1965), High Yielding Variety Programme (1966–1967), Crash Scheme for Rural Employment (1973), District Rural Development Agency (1993), Group Life Insurance Scheme for Rural Areas (1996), etc., to name a few. Indian government, keeping in mind the state of rural infrastructure, launched a time-bound business plan for action called Bharat Nirman in 2005. Under Bharat Nirman, action was proposed in the areas of water supply, housing, telecommunication and information technology, roads, electrification and irrigation. A national portal was also created to make every bit of information accessible to villagers, be it applying for loans or knowing how to protect crops or how to find the nearest hospital for health check-up or the nearest school for one's children; information about schemes for the promotion of rural industry; provision of basic infrastructure facilities in rural areas, for example, government assistance to individual families, and self-help groups living below poverty line, etc.

Although these various schemes and incentives by the government gave rural India the much-needed boost, there is a long way to go. Government has had to deal with several challenges. Nair (2014) highlighted multiple developmental challenges that rural India is facing: (a) increasing population, (b) depletion of natural resources, (c) pollution leading to shortage of drinking water and also adversely affecting agricultural production, (d) low access to education, thereby resulting in illiteracy and unemployment, which is adversely affecting their skills development, employment productivity, family welfare and education of their children, (e) poor health status due to lack of clean drinking water, and sanitation and drainage facilities, (f) globalization with which farmers are unable to keep pace and (g) problems of livelihood. Singh and Badaya (2014) highlighted the gap between the availability of primary health care facilities in rural India and the norms defined by the World Health Organization. Apart from the health scenario, status of women in rural India also faces several challenges. For example, Singh, Singh and Suman (2009) in their study documented how the sociocultural barriers (such as harmful traditional practices, conflicting situations, gender discrimination, etc.) were hampering the personal growth of the Indian rural adolescent girls. Rural women in India get less opportunity to even reach higher level of school education and therefore lack in knowledge and information about health and its perspectives (Bhargava, 2012). From among all the domains of quality of life, education has been reported as the most important predictor (Saxena, Misra, Vishwanath, Varma, & Soman, 2013). Similar finding was reported by Singh, Kaur, Singh and Junnarkar (2014) in their study on Indian rural women, where education emerged as a significant factor in determining the experience of well-being. Patel and Gandhi (2016) investigated the reasons for school dropouts in girls in rural Gujarat. From the first standard to seventh, the various reasons for dropping out of school were taking care of siblings and home (58.8%), social restrictions (such as menarche and marriage, 8.8%), more distance from school (11.7%), working with parents for financial reasons (5.8%) and unavailability of higher school nearby (11.7%). In a study of stress and coping among urban and rural youth, not only did the authors (Srivastava, Singh, & Srivastava, 2014) report higher stress for urban adolescents but also reported higher coping strategies in comparison to rural adolescents. The use of lower coping strategies by the rural adolescents was pinned down to several reasons, ranging from not having enough money to buy things to lack of electricity, drinking water, healthy academic atmosphere, etc., that directly or indirectly affect the personality of the adolescents. Prevalence of substance abuse is another issue facing rural communities in India. According to Mahi, Sharma, Sharma and Sidhu (2011), substance abuse in rural Punjab was found prevalent in more than one-third (39.3%) of the population, with illiterate population being the largest consumers. Kuberan et al. (2015) investigated the water and sanitation hygiene knowledge, attitude and practices in rural Chennai. Findings suggested that nearly more than one-third of the participants were not following any methods of water treatment, and, among them, half of the participants felt that water available to them was clean and did not require any additional treatment. About 17 per cent of the participants used plain water or water with ash to clean their hands. With regard to common mental disorders in rural areas, a recent cross-sectional study (Soni et al., 2016) among rural women of India associated the prevalence of common mental disorders with adverse health status and increasing health care costs.

RURAL INDIA AND TRANSLATIONAL RESEARCH

The overall development of the rural Indian society has been the focus of government's development agenda since long. However, Dalal, Kumar and Gokhale (2000) observed that the various efforts of the government failed to motivate rural communities to mobilize local resources for the developmental activities. People did not involve in the governance of even those development plans which intimately affected their lives. Community participation failed to materialize despite all planning and preparations. The apathy and alienation of people were held responsible for the failure of rural development programmes. Panchmukhi (2000) opined that unless economic development is supplemented by investment in social and human development, no sustainable change will take place.

It is time that psychology researches and findings are implemented in community to empower and enable rural people to deal with the fast-changing environment. Addressing the need to change theory into practice, Brekke, Ell and Palinkas (2007) highlighted the demand for translational science. The goal of translational science in mental health is to speed up the use of findings from our best science into usual-care settings and to build partnerships between research and practice constituencies that will increase the clinical relevance of mental health research (Department of Health and Human Services, 2006). There are two phases of translational research that would be helpful: Phase 1—moving knowledge from basic science to more applied clinical usage in human studies including efficacy and effectiveness trials of clinical interventions; and Phase 2—translation concerns research aimed at enhancing the adoption of best practices in the community.

This chapter reviews psychology-based translational research and intervention programmes in different areas of rural life in India across different domains—mental health, physical health—in rural people. Presently, psychology-based translational research in rural areas is at a very early stage, and the limited literature that is available is scattered. With this chapter, an effort has been made to review and consolidate the various past and ongoing psychology-based interventions and programmes in rural India.

ROLE OF NGOS IN PROMOTING INTERVENTIONS IN RURAL INDIA

In today's times, NGOs are looked upon as critical agents of change and empowerment in society. Right from human resource development programmes to agricultural to economic-based programmes, the role of NGOs in recent times have greatly diversified. It is difficult to ignore their presence during policy planning as they are critical to the success of any newly implemented programme, especially in rural areas. NGOs in India are involved at the grassroots level with the aim of improving the lives of rural people in various spheres. For example, a Barwani-based NGO (in Madhya Pradesh), Ashagram, works closely with rural people in various sectors, ranging from education and literacy to health and family welfare to women's development and empowerment, etc. However, its main area is different types of disabilities, with a special focus on mental health. Although it has a fully equipped and functional hospital, Ashagram prefers working in community-based rehabilitation mode. RUCHI (Rural Centre for Human Interests) is another NGO operating in a remote village in Chopal in the Shimla District. RUCHI transfers knowledge to village communities through education and empowerment and also generates the desire in the underprivileged to improve their own living conditions, thereby helping people to live a life of dignity and self-respect. Currently, operating in about 100 villages in Himachal, the focus areas of RUCHI are health care, promotion of rural technologies, education and awareness generation, sustainable management of natural resources and micro-credit for village projects. Operating in India since more than last six decades is CARE India, whose main focus is on alleviating poverty and social injustice. Their overall goal is ensuring the well-being of women and girls from poor and marginalized communities leading to improvement in their lives and livelihoods. In achieving their goals, CARE's key programming approaches include social analysis and action, gender transformative value chain approaches, leadership and life skills strengthening, building capacities and leadership roles at multiple levels, advocacy on national and international platforms, and facilitating links and dialogues between public, private and civil society.[1] Established in 1982 in West Bengal, Economic Rural Development Society (ERDS) was the culmination of hard work and dedication of Mr Madhu Basu. The primary objective of the organization is to engage in sustainable development techniques to empower the local rural communities, especially women and children.[2] Presently, ERDS has diversified into various other fields, ranging from children's education to rehabilitation of the elderly to disaster relief and rehabilitation, etc.

MENTAL HEALTH INTERVENTIONS IN RURAL COMMUNITIES

Mental health disorders in India are still associated with a lot of stigma and taboo which not only leads to delayed diagnosis but also delays the process of intervention and positive outcomes. The problem becomes more acute in rural communities where, due to a lack of education and prevalence of superstition, people prefer the services of a faith healer/tantric rather than visiting a mental health professional. Recently, as part of a SMART mental health project, Maulik et al. (2017) conducted a study to assess changes in knowledge, attitude and behaviour, and stigma related to help seeking among participants exposed to an anti-stigma campaign. Conducted across 42 villages in rural Andhra Pradesh, the campaign interviewed 1,576 and 2,100 people during pre- and post-intervention phases. Results proved the efficacy of this campaign by highlighting the improvement in the attitude and behaviour of participants related to mental health and reduction in stigma related to help seeking. Social contact was seen as the most effective intervention. Shidhaye et al. (2017) assessed the efficacy of a community-based mental health programme, Vidarbha Stress and Health Programme (VISHRAM), on 1887 participants. According to the authors, the aim of their study was to address the mental health risk factors for suicide in people from 30 villages in the Amravati district in Vidarbha, central

---

[1] https://www.careindia.org
[2] http://www.idrf.org/erds/

India. The authors looked into whether implementation of VISHRAM was associated with an increase in the proportion of people with depression who sought treatment (contact coverage). The findings reported a significant improvement in a range of mental health literacy indicators. Rural people conceptualized depression as a mental health problem and also showed intention to seek help for the same. Another mental health intervention with positive outcomes was documented by Sharma, Sinha and Sayeed (2016), wherein the authors conducted a mindfulness-based therapeutic programme for six weeks on rural adolescent girls diagnosed with dissociative disorder. Significant reduction in dissociative experiences and significant improvement in mindfulness was reported.

PHYSICAL HEALTH INTERVENTIONS IN RURAL COMMUNITIES

Mind and body share a close relationship, and, in case of physical health ailments, a mental health expert is often roped in to alleviate unhealthy attitudes and behaviours which may delay the recovery process. Mohan, Iyengar, Martines, Cousens and Sen (2004) investigated whether training doctors in counselling will have any effect on the care-seeking behaviour in families with sick children. The study was conducted in rural Rajasthan with 2,460 children (1,248 intervention, 1,212 control) and their mothers. The authors focused on three outcome measures: care-seeking behaviour of mothers for sick children; mothers' knowledge and perceptions of seeking care; counselling performance of doctors. A greater proportion of mothers in the intervention group than in the control group recalled having had at least one danger sign explained. It was observed that mothers' appreciation of the need to seek prompt and appropriate care for severe episodes of childhood illness increased, but their care-seeking behaviour did not improve significantly. Balagopal, Kamalamma, Patel and Misra (2008) investigated the efficacy of a 7-month community-based diabetes prevention programme. Programme components consisted of linguistically appropriate health education messages that addressed diet, physical activity and knowledge improvement. Intervention was successful in reducing some of the obesity parameters and improving dietary patterns of individuals with pre-diabetes and diabetes.

INTERVENTIONS ON RURAL WOMEN

Rao, Vanguri and Premchander (2011) undertook a community-based mental health intervention for economically underprivileged women in rural India. The intervention model consisted of group counselling and stress management. Majority of the women (86%) reported improved quality of sleep and felt unburdened after sharing their problems with a group. Singh, Jain and Singh (2014) studied the association of *satsang* (a culture specific indigenous practice in which women sing folksongs in a group) with well-being of rural women. Not only participants reported feeling more empowered and stress free but also were able to nurture healthier interpersonal relations and strengthen family and social support, a requirement for well-being. Dangi (2013) delivered an intervention module on rural migrant women that helped in raising the level of culture-related knowledge, affect, environmental mastery and quality of life of intervened migrant rural women. Roberts and Montgomery (2016) investigated the effectiveness of culturally adapted mindfulness-based intervention in rural women of Chhattisgarh, experiencing perinatal grief due to still births. Findings indicated significant reduction in perinatal grief and psychological symptoms; four of the five facets of mindfulness changed in the desired direction; and resilience scores indicated thriving.

INTERVENTIONS ON RURAL ADOLESCENTS

Pujar, Hunshal and Bailur (2014) provided life skills intervention to 328 rural adolescent girls. The authors provided intervention on five life skills—problem-solving, creative thinking, critical thinking, coping with stress and empathy. The intervention was spread over three months and was in the form of training through developed training module, guest lectures, brain-storming methods, working in small groups and role play to discuss and practice the skills. Post intervention, positive results were reported with majority of the participants scoring high on all five spheres. Jain (2015) in her research project on 44 Dalit rural girls assessed the impact of intervention on their level of achievement motivation, self-efficacy, academic performance, subjective well-being and self-esteem. Spread over a period of 10 months, the intervention programme consisted of effective time management, communication skills, career opportunities, leadership training, team building, goal setting, interpersonal skills, adolescent psychosocial issues, physiological development during adolescent, importance of nutrition during adolescence, dental hygiene, personal hygiene, public speaking, reading habits, memory skills, study habits, how to face exams, yoga training, women empowerment, group dynamics, life skills, self-esteem, English language training, civic sense, assertive training and self-defence. Apart from self-esteem, significant improvement was observed in the level of achievement motivation, self-efficacy, academic performance and subjective well-being. Leventhal et al. (2015) conducted a 5-month resilience-based programme (girls first resilience curriculum or RC) on more than 2,000 rural adolescent girls from Bihar. In comparison to controls, girls who received RC reported higher emotional resilience, self-efficacy, social–emotional assets, psychological well-being and social well-being. The authors also highlighted how psychosocial assets and well-being can be improved through a brief school day programme.

INTERVENTIONS FOR IMPROVING ACADEMIC PERFORMANCE

Narayanan undertook a project (2009–2011) wherein interventions were provided to rural students from low SES to foster academic resilience (Annalakshmi, 2015). The interventions were focused on certain psychological concepts such as conscientiousness, self-concept and creativity, locus of control, motivation and level of aspiration, study skills and academic attitudes. After three and a half months, post intervention, participants adopted more internal locus of control in dealing with their academic venture to improve their study skills and to adopt a more positive attitude towards education. Joseph, Easvaradoss and Solomon (2016) gave chess training to 100 sixth grade rural students coming from low socioeconomic status families. According to the authors,

> Chess playing focuses on developing cognitive skills like focusing, visualizing, thinking ahead, weighing options, analyzing concretely, thinking abstractly, planning, and juggling multiple considerations simultaneously, which would invariably have its effect on the academic performance of the students. Over time, chess helps develop patience and thoughtfulness. (Joseph et al., 2016, p. 23)

Chess intervention after one year showed significant improvement in academic scores in various subjects.

Religion-/Spirituality-Based Interventions

People in rural India regularly follow religious and spiritual practices that plausibly tend to contribute to well-being. Planning interventions, keeping in mind the religious and spiritual beliefs of rural people, will greatly contribute to the success of the programmes. Culture-specific interventions take into consideration the beliefs, values and language relevant to that culture (Singh, Jain et al., 2014). The researchers observed that participating in *satsang*, which principally involves 'group work', activities performed therein like active prosocial spending (group donations for welfare of the deprived), sharing with same age group, and participation in religious activities, all are found to enhance well-being collectively. They also found that participating in *satsang* led many rural women to feel more empowered, with healthier interpersonal relationships and more social and family support. Furthermore, the authors observed that messages embedded in *bhajans* (folk songs) in *satsang* promote human virtues, thereby increasing well-being. They also noted that repeated participation in groups and singing songs containing religious and positive virtues' messages can lead to an increase of well-being in the participants (Singh, Jain et al., 2014). Furthermore, *bhajans* in Satsang were observed broadly in three categories: praise of gods and goddesses, events from holy books such as the Bhagavad Gita, Mahabharata and Ramayana, and spiritual and religious messages (Singh, Sigroha, Singh, & Shokeen, 2017). Singh, Singh, Junnarkar, Mitra and Dayal (2016) reported on the association between religious/spiritual practices and well-being of women in rural India. Three groups of participants—field experimental group (FEG), practitioners of pre-existing S/R practices, and non-practitioners of S/R practices were recruited for the study. The FEG participants received an intervention encouraging them to practice *satsang* (singing S/R folk songs in a group), relaxation techniques and physiotherapy exercises daily for an hour for one and a month. The pre-existing S/R practitioners' groups were defined as participants engaged in S/R activities in a group for at least one and a half month, specifically *satsang*, Brahma Kumaris and Radha Soami, and non-practitioners group, who did not practice the pre-existing

S/R activities. Higher scores on indicators of health, quality of life and well-being were observed for practitioners of spiritual/religious practices in comparison to non-practitioners. A recent study by Power (2017) brought to fore the link between religiosity and prosocial behaviour in rural South India. The author reported that individuals who regularly indulged in religious acts were better able to call on support and have a greater likelihood of reciprocal relationships. According to the author of the study, religious practice is taken as a signal of trustworthiness, generosity and prosociality, leading village residents to establish supportive, often reciprocal relationships with such individuals.

Technology-Based Interventions

In this age of digitalization, technology has made the life of the people easier. It is now also being used to provide psychology-based interventions to people in rural areas, with the aim of improving their lives and hence their well-being. Garai (2011) highlighted the role of mobile phones as a dependable and effective intervention tool for health sector in rural India. He also brought to notice how in the state of Orissa in India mobile videos were instrumental in improving the quality of counselling among the community health workers. These messages have been successfully utilized in assisting the beneficiaries achieve their health behaviour goals. Shields-Zeeman, Pathare, Walters, Kapadia-Kundu and Joag (2017) recently implemented ATMIYATA programme in rural Maharastra. Started in 2013, ATMIYATA is a community-led intervention in rural India[3] for the detection, support and referral for persons with common and severe mental disorders. Volunteers are trained to detect and provide primary support and counselling to persons with common mental disorders. Volunteers are also provided with a smartphone that includes capacity development and community films. ATMIYATA intervention follows an integrated care approach: horizontal integration (integration of care between mental health and social care), vertical integration (integrating professionals working at the community level, primary care level and tertiary care level), and between preventive and curative services.

---

[3] http://www.mhinnovation.net/innovations/atmiyata-community-led-intervention-rural-india

ATMIYATA summary reports 80 per cent improved well-being outcome after intervention.

Folk Media Based Interventions

Chapke and Bhagat (2006) highlighted the role of traditional and folk media communication in rural Maharashtra. In three selected villages, they showed five most popular traditional media: *tamasha* (performance), *bhajan* (psalm), *kirtan* (devotional singing), *dhandhar* and *qawwali* (forms of Sufi devotional music). Majority of the rural people preferred *tamasha* (40.50%, due to lively performance) followed by *bhajan* (46.62%, due to content covering familiar religious themes). According to the researchers, traditional media programmes are effective and had good impact on rural masses. Naskar (2011), through her participatory awareness and mobilization programmes using the folk media, addressed the issue of child marriage in about 30 villages of rural Bengal. The intervention which was done in collaboration with District Social Welfare Department of Malda, UNICEF and a reputed NGO of Kolkata, banglanatak dot com (banglanatak.com), included several phases such as street theatre shows, workshops, meetings with adolescent girls, etc. The intervention which targeted about 3,300 villagers showed high acceptance of messages conveyed through dance dramas. Also, it reported sensitization and improved awareness on issues related to child marriage and rights of a girl child.

SUGGESTIONS FOR INCREASING EFFECTIVENESS OF INTERVENTIONS

While efforts by various sections of people are underway to provide psychological interventions in rural areas, this chapter, apart from the review of the interventions, provides suggestions which actively involve the role of applied psychologists. Applied psychologists, with their ability to translate psychological research into tools and interventions, will contribute greatly in improving the well-being and quality of life of rural people.

Some of the suggestions are as follows:

- *Effective use of technology*: Due to various factors, ranging from dearth of applied psychologists to lack of governmental focus, it at times becomes difficult to cover all rural areas in person and provide interventions. However, this can be overcome with the effective use of technology. Live video chats, several online forums, websites, etc., can be provided to rural people to get in touch with the right people to answer their queries even from a different city.

- *Training of people*: Effective use of technology warrants people who act as a bridge between rural people and the psychologists. For this, it is important to identify the local people (counsellors, NGOs workers, teachers, voluntary workers, etc.) who work at the grassroots level and are aware of their needs and the prevailing local conditions as well to facilitate the needed interventions.

- *TED talks*: TED (short form for technology, entertainment and design) started in 1984 with a view to spread ideas and make them accessible. TED talks are subtitled in over 100 languages, ranging from Hindi, Gujarati, Malay, Malayalam, Marathi, Tamil, Telugu, etc. In their short powerful speeches by experts and motivational speakers, they cover various topics from science to health to global issues, etc. They offer a lot on issues pertaining to rural areas as well. However, rural people have virtually no awareness of this forum and hence remain bereft of its benefits. Making TED talks available to rural people can go a long way in providing them the exposure and needed information which otherwise they may miss out on.

- *Mental health programmes for various sectors in rural areas*: Applied psychologists involved with delivering interventions in rural sectors need to keep in mind the needs of different segments and plan programmes accordingly. For example, while targeting mental health of children in rural areas, the best place to start is the schools in rural areas and working closely with school psychologist and/or teachers there. Kolkata-based Kishalay Foundation works closely with government primary schools in most remote rural villages (educationally backward blocks) in India. Their aim is to improve learning outcomes through mainly three types of intervention programmes – Sports Intervention Programs, Edutoys Intervention Programs, and IT Intervention Programs. Likewise, interventions programmes maybe planned according to the needs of different sections of rural society, such as women, adolescents, elderly, etc.

- *Translation in local language*: Given the number of languages and dialects spoken in India, it is important to ensure that all interventions being delivered to people, via technology or in person, are in native dialect of the place.
- *Community-based participatory research (CBPR)*: Rural areas will benefit greatly from CBPR. Israel, Schulz, Parker and Becker (1998, p. 184) defined CBPR as 'a collaborative approach to research that equitably involves, for example, community members, organizational representatives and researchers in all aspects of the research process'. CBPR was deemed to be highly effective in a recent study conducted in Hong Kong, highlighting the effectiveness of positive psychology interventions to target behaviours that enhance family relationships (Zhou et al., 2016). The researchers planned interventions based on three themes—gratitude, hope and open mindedness—and collaborated with 30 NGOs for the study. Taking a cue from this, similar researches can be carried out in rural areas which would go a long way in broadening the reach of such intervention programmes.
- *Understanding of local conditions*: While planning interventions in rural areas, it is important for researchers to have an understanding of the prevailing social customs, traditions and factors acting an inhibitors and facilitators of well-being. For example, in a study in rural Haryana, Singh, Kaur and Singh (2014) identified certain facilitators and inhibitors of well-being for rural women. Fulfilment of all basic needs, socialization and healthy interpersonal relationships, etc., emerged as the facilitators of well-being for rural women. On the other hand, factors such as little or no social support, ill-health, joblessness, etc., were inhibitors of well-being. Singh, Kaur and Singh (2014) also reported majority of the elderly rural women to be either suffering (41%) or struggling (41%), while just 18 per cent were flourishing. While reasons for suffering ranged from unemployment and alcoholism in the family to worrisome health conditions and/or poor housing conditions, the reasons for flourishing were joyful family circumstances and connection with the divine. Studies like these can go a long way in providing a pre-understanding of facilitators and inhibitors of well-being of rural people, which will help in planning the intervention programmes in a way that it provides maximum benefit to those in need.

- *Utilising the strengths of Indian rural communities to promote wellbeing:* Till now, the discussion has focused on how best the theoretical knowledge grounded in psychology can be implemented in rural areas to have desired outcomes. A lot of factors, ranging from understanding of social conditions to availability of resources (in terms of people and technology), etc., are important prerequisites. However, what can really prove beneficial is gaining an understanding as to what forms the backbone of the rural communities. Indian society, especially the rural community, strongly identifies itself with a collectivist culture. Found mostly in less developed and Eastern countries, Hofstede (2011, p. 11) defined collectivism 'as the degree to which people in a society are integrated into groups'. Some of the characteristics of collectivist culture that differentiates it from an individualist culture are stress on belonging, maintenance of harmony, extended families or clans that protect their members in exchange for loyalty, opinions and votes predetermined by in-group, transgression of norms lead to shame, etc. Psychologists and practitioners involved in providing interventions in rural areas need to take into account the collectivist nature of rural communities to ensure the success of interventions. For example, Letvak (2002) highlighted how social support in rural India directly affects the well-being of the mentally ill individuals and their families. An exploratory study (Balaji, Andrews, Andrew, & Patel, 2010) done on rural and urban youth of Goa evaluated the acceptability, feasibility and effectiveness of population-based interventions to promote youth health. Multi-component interventions (information materials, community peer education and educational institution-based components) were used. Amongst other findings reported, community peer education intervention was found to be more feasible and acceptable in the rural community in comparison to the urban community. In rural Tamil Nadu, community-based intervention coupled with supervised medical care was found to be more effective in managing people with moderate to severe psychosis as compared to medical care alone (Chatterjee et al., 2014). Efficacy of support group intervention programmes in caregivers of stroke patients was reported from rural South India (Malini, 2015).

The close-knit Indian rural communities/families can be a source of great physical and emotional support in times of need. Integrating community with intervention programmes may boost the desired outcomes. It is therefore recommended that translational professionals/researchers working in rural communities plan intervention programmes keeping in mind not just the individual but his/her family/core group and the community members to ensure success.

CONCLUSION

Successfully planned and implemented interventions may go a long way in improving the quality of life of people. This would not only benefit the individuals but also communities at large, and this is what makes them thrive. However, for individuals and communities to thrive, it is important to have the scientific understanding of the determinants of living of a particular community. For example, Craven at al. (2016) developed a model for thriving for the indigenous population of Australia by combining research methodologies with Western approaches. Known as the Reciprocal Research Partnership Model of Indigenous Thriving Futures, it focuses on the dynamic and interrelated characteristics—respect, responsibility, reciprocity and relationships—all underpinned by strengths-based approaches: educational, physical, psychological, and family and community thriving. One may also take cue from the framework (Rimmer, Vanderbom, & Graham, 2016) developed by National Centre on Health, Physical Activity and Disability which has successfully integrated knowledge to action sequence in four steps: knowledge, adaptation, translation and scale-up (N-KATS). Developed for people with disabilities, the rationale behind this framework was to not only motivate people with physical disabilities to engage in physical exercise but to also provide them with services and facilities and venues that make exercising a possibility.

This is the need of the hour—taking theoretical knowledge to the field, and implementing it through best possible mediums, especially in rural areas. However, simultaneously the complexity of rural life and sociocultural factors and diversity need to be paid attention to. Translational psychologists and researchers need to begin by assessing rural communities on various psychological and sociocultural parameters. This is possible by looking closely at the factors responsible for enhancing the quality of life in rural areas as well as factors responsible for its deterioration. Additionally, what is to be considered is the diversity in India due to which psychological parameters of a village in Punjab (North India) might be totally different from that of Maharashtra (West India) or Karnataka (South India). Only when the translational psychologists and those working at the ground level get familiar with these varying conditions and sociocultural factors can interventions be designed in practical and achievable ways.

REFERENCES

Adesiji, G., Dada, S., & Komolafe, S. (2012). Problems faced by rural people in accessing health care facilities in Akure north and Akure south local government areas of Ondo State, Nigeria. *Journal of Applied Sciences Research, 8*(4), 2260–2266.

Aisbett, D. L., Boyd, C. P., Francis, K. J., Newnham, K., & Newnham, K. (2007). Understanding barriers to mental health service utilization for adolescents in rural Australia. *Rural and Remote Health, 7*(624), 1–10.

Ajah, L. O., Iyoke, C. A., Nkwo, P. O., Nwakoby, B., & Ezeonu, P. (2014). Comparison of domestic violence against women in urban versus rural areas of southeast Nigeria. *International Journal of Women's Health, 6*, 865.

Anderson, T. J., Saman, D. M., Lipsky, M. S., & Lutfiyya, M. N. (2015). A cross-sectional study on health differences between rural and non-rural US counties using the County Health Rankings. *BMC Health Services Research, 15*(1), 441.

Annalakshmi, N. (2015). Fostering academic resilience among rural low socio-economic college students. In S. Subramanian, S. J. M. Raj, A. Velayudhan, & N. Annalakshmi (Eds.), *The recent trends in psychology* (pp. 106–119). Coimbatore: Garuda Publishers.

Atif, N., Lovell, K., Husain, N., Sikander, S., Patel, V., & Rahman, A. (2016). Barefoot therapists: Barriers and facilitators to delivering maternal mental health care through peer volunteers in Pakistan: A qualitative study. *International Journal of Mental Health Systems, 10*(1), 24.

Balagopal, P., Kamalamma, N., Patel, T. G., & Misra, R. (2008). A community-based diabetes prevention and management education program in a rural village in India. *Diabetes Care, 31*(6), 1097–1104.

Balaji, M., Andrews, T., Andrew, G., & Patel, V. (2011). The acceptability, feasibility, and effectiveness of a population-based intervention to promote youth health: An exploratory study in Goa, India. *Journal of Adolescent Health, 48*(5), 453–460.

Bhargava, A. (2012). *A regional analysis of perceived awareness of reproductive health infections (RTIs) among rural women in India.* National Seminar on Health, Regional Disparities and Social Development, IASSH, Mumbai, in collaboration with Jawaharlal Nehru University, New Delhi.

Brekke, J. S., Ell, K., & Palinkas, L. A. (2007). Translational science at the National Institute of Mental Health: Can social work take its rightful place? *Research on Social Work Practice, 17*(1), 123–133.

Census of India. (2011). Retrieved from http://censusindia.gov.in/2011-prov-results/paper2/data_ files/india/Rural_Urban_2011.pdf

Chapke, R., & Bhagat, R. (2006). Traditional folk media: A potentially effective communication tool in rural areas. In *Proceedings of the 22nd Annual Conference of the Association of International Agricultural Extension and Education, Florida, USA* (pp. 123–133).

Chatterjee, S., Naik, S., John, S., Dabholkar, H., Balaji, M., Koschorke, M., … McCrone, P. (2014). Effectiveness of a community-based intervention for people with schizophrenia and their caregivers in India (COPSI): A randomised controlled trial. *The Lancet, 383*(9926), 1385–1394.

Craven, R. G., Ryan, R. M., Mooney, J., Vallerand, R. J., Dillon, A., Blacklock, F., … Magson, N. (2016). Toward a positive psychology of indigenous thriving and reciprocal research partnership model. *Contemporary Educational Psychology, 47*, 32–43.

Dalal, A. K., Kumar, S., & Gokhale, D. (2000). *Participatory evaluation of community-based rehabilitation* (Project report). Allahabad: Department of Psychology, University of Allahabad.

Dangi, S. (2012). *Assessment and enhancement of well-being of married migrant women in selected villages of Haryana* (Doctoral dissertation). Delhi: Department of Humanities & Social Sciences, Indian Institute of Technology.

DeHaan, L., & Boljevac, T. (2009). Alcohol use among rural middle school students: Adolescents, parents, teachers, and community leaders' perceptions. *Journal of School Health, 79*(2), 58–66.

Department of Health and Human Services. (2006). *NIH roadmap for medical research.* Retrieved from http://nihroadmap.nih.gov/

Diala, C. C., & Muntaner, C. (2003). Mood and anxiety disorders among rural, urban, and metropolitan residents in the United States. *Community Mental Health Journal, 39*(3), 239–252.

Garai, A. (2011). Role of mHealth in rural health in India and opportunities for collaboration. New Delhi: Indira Gandhi National Open University.

Hauenstein, E. J., Peterson, S., Rovnyak, V., Merwin, E., Heise, B., & Wagner, D. (2007). Rurality and mental health treatment. *Administration and Policy in Mental Health, 34*(3), 255–267.

Hofstede, G. (2011). Dimensionalizing cultures: The Hofstede model in context. *Online Readings in Psychology and Culture, 2*(1), 8.

Israel, B. A., Schulz, A. J., Parker, E. A., & Becker, A. B. (1998). Review of community-based research: Assessing partnership approaches to improve public health. *Annual Review of Public Health, 19*(1), 173–202.

Jain, V. (2015). *Achievement motivation, self-efficacy, academic performance, subjective wellbeing and self-esteem among Dalit girl students*. Minor Research Project, University Grants Commission, New Delhi.

Joseph, E., Easvaradoss, V. V., & Solomon, N. J. (2016). Impact of chess training on academic performance of rural Indian school children. *Open Journal of Social Sciences, 4*(02), 20.

Khattri, N., Riley, K. W., & Kane, M. B. (1997). Students at risk in poor, rural areas: A review of the research. *Journal of Research in Rural Education, 13*(2), 79–100

Kuberan, A., Singh, A. K., Kasav, J. B., Prasad, S., Surapaneni, K. M., Upadhyay, V., ... Joshi, A. (2015). Water and sanitation hygiene knowledge, attitude, and practices among household members living in rural setting of India. *Journal of Natural Science, Biology, and Medicine, 6*(1, Suppl.), S69.

Lambert, D., Ziller, E. C., & Lenardson, J. D. (2008). *Use of mental health services by rural children*. Maine Rural Health Research Center, Institute for Health Policy, Muskie School of Public Service, University of Southern Maine.

Letvak, S. (2002). The importance of social support for rural mental health. *Issues in Mental Health Nursing, 23*(3), 249–261.

Leventhal, K. S., Gillham, J., DeMaria, L., Andrew, G., Peabody, J., & Leventhal, S. (2015). Building psychosocial assets and wellbeing among adolescent girls: A randomized controlled trial. *Journal of Adolescence, 45*, 284–295.

Mahi, R. K., Sharma, A., Sharma, K. C., & Sidhu, B. S. (2011). An epidemiological survey of alcohol and drug dependence in a village of district Sangrur, Punjab. *Delhi Psychiatry Journal, 14*(2), 314–322.

Malini, M. H. (2015). Impact of support group intervention on family system strengths of rural caregivers of stroke patients in India. *Australian Journal of Rural Health, 23*(2), 95–100.

Maulik, P. K., Devarapalli, S., Kallakuri, S., Tewari, A., Chilappagari, S., Koschorke, M., ... Thornicroft, G. (2017). Evaluation of an anti-stigma campaign related to common mental disorders in rural India: A mixed methods approach. *Psychological Medicine, 47*(3), 565–575.

Mohan, P., Iyengar, S. D., Martines, J., Cousens, S., & Sen, K. (2004). Impact of counselling on careseeking behaviour in families with sick children: Cluster randomised trial in rural India. *British Medical Journal, 329*(7460), 266.

Nair, I. (2014). Challenges of rural development and opportunities for providing sustainable livelihood. *International Journal of Research in Applied, Natural and Social Sciences (IMPACT: IJRANSS) ISSN (E), 2*(5), 2321–8851.

Naskar, R. (2011). The role of folk media and participatory communication in rural development: An exploratory case study of combating child marriage in Malda. *Global Media Journal, 2*(2), 1–9.

Panchmukhi, P. R. (2000). Social impacts of economic reforms in India. *Economic & Political Weekly*, 15(10), 836–847.

Parr, H., & Philo, C. (2003). Rural mental health and social geographies of caring. *Social & Cultural Geography*, 4(4), 471–488.

Parr, H., Philo, C., & Burns, N. (2004). Social geographies of rural mental health: Experiencing inclusions and exclusions. *Transactions of the Institute of British Geographers*, 29(4), 401–419.

Patel, B., & Gandhi, D. (2016). A study of girls school dropout in rural Gujarat. *International Journal of Scientific Research*, 5(5), 75–76.

Peek-Asa, C., Wallis, A., Harland, K., Beyer, K., Dickey, P., & Saftlas, A. (2011). Rural disparity in domestic violence prevalence and access to resources. *Journal of Women's Health*, 20(11), 1743–1749.

Power, E. A. (2017). Social support networks and religiosity in rural South India. *Nature Human Behaviour*, 1(3), 57.

Probst, J. C., Laditka, S. B., Moore, C. G., Harun, N., Powell, M. P., & Baxley, E. G. (2006). Rural–urban differences in depression prevalence: Implications for family medicine. *Family Medicine-Kansas City*, 38(9), 653.

Pujar, L., Hunshal, S. C., & Bailur, K. B. (2014). Impact of intervention on life skill development among adolescent girls. *Karnataka Journal of Agricultural Sciences*, 27(1).

Pullmann, M. D., VanHooser, S., Hoffman, C., & Heflinger, C. A. (2010). Barriers to and supports of family participation in a rural system of care for children with serious emotional problems. *Community Mental Health Journal*, 46(3), 211–220.

Rao, K., Vanguri, P., & Premchander, S. (2011). Community-based mental health intervention for underprivileged women in rural India: An experiential report. *International Journal of Family Medicine*, 1–7.

Riding-Malon, R., & Werth, J. L., Jr. (2014). Psychological practice in rural settings: At the cutting edge. *Professional Psychology: Research and Practice*, 45(2), 85.

Rimmer, J. H., Vanderbom, K. A., & Graham, I. D. (2016). A new framework and practice center for adapting, translating, and scaling evidence-based health/wellness programs for people with disabilities. *Journal of Neurologic Physical Therapy*, 40(2), 107–114.

Roberts, L. R., & Montgomery, S. B. (2016). Mindfulness-based intervention for perinatal grief in rural India: Improved mental health at 12 months follow-up. *Issues in Mental Health Nursing*, 37(12), 942–951.

Roscigno, V. J., & Crowle, M. L. (2001). Rurality, institutional disadvantage, and achievement/attainment. *Rural Sociology*, 66(2), 268–292.

Rosenthal, T. C., & Fox, C. (2000). Access to health care for the rural elderly. *JAMA*, 284(16), 2034–2036.

Saxena, S., Misra, P. J., Vishwanath, N. S., Varma, R. P., & Soman, B. (2013, April). Quality of life and its correlates in central India. *International Journal of Research & Development of Health*, 1(2), 85–96.

Sharkey, J. R., Johnson, C. M., & Dean, W. R. (2010). Food access and perceptions of the community and household food environment as correlates of fruit and vegetable intake among rural seniors. *BMC Geriatrics, 10*(1), 32.

Sharma, T., Sinha, V. K., & Sayeed, N. (2016). Role of mindfulness in dissociative disorders among adolescents. *Indian Journal of Psychiatry, 58*(3), 326.

Shidhaye, R., Murhar, V., Gangale, S., Aldridge, L., Shastri, R., Parikh, R., ... Patel, V. (2017). The effect of VISHRAM, a grass-roots community-based mental health programme, on the treatment gap for depression in rural communities in India: A population-based study. *The Lancet Psychiatry, 4*(2), 128–135.

Shields-Zeeman, L., Pathare, S., Walters, B. H., Kapadia-Kundu, N., & Joag, K. (2017). Promoting wellbeing and improving access to mental health care through community champions in rural India: The ATMIYATA intervention approach. *International Journal of Mental Health Systems, 11*(1), 6.

Silva, T., Prakash, A., Yarlagadda, S., Johns, M. D., Sandy, K., Hansen, V., ... Pit, S. (2017). General practitioners' experiences and perceptions of mild moderate depression management and factors influencing effective service delivery in rural Australian communities: A qualitative study. *International Journal of Mental Health Systems, 11*(1), 1–10.

Singh, K., Jain, A., & Singh, D. (2014). Satsang: A culture-specific effective practice for well-being. In *Positive Nations and Communities* (pp. 79–100). Dordrecht: Springer.

Singh, K., Kaur, J., & Singh, D. (2014). Well-being of rural women in North India. *Journal of Indian Academy of Applied Psychology, 40*(1), 129–137.

Singh, K., Kaur, J., Singh, D., & Junnarkar, M. (2014). Socio-demographic variables affecting well-being: A study on Indian rural women. *Psychological Studies, 59*(2), 197–206.

Singh, K., Sigroha, S., Singh, D., & Shokeen, B. (2017). Religious and spiritual messages in folk songs: A study of women from rural India. *Mental Health, Religion & Culture, 20*(5), 464–477.

Singh, K., Singh, D., Junnarkar, M. Mitra, S., & Dayal, P. (2016). *Effect on well-being of spiritual practices among elderly rural women.* Mid-Year Conference on Psychology, Spirituality and Religion, Society for the Psychology of Religion and Spirituality (APA Div. 36) and St. Joseph's College, New York, USA, March 11–12.

Singh, K., Singh, D., & Suman, S. (2009). Socio-cultural barriers in the personal growth of rural adolescent girls. *Indian Journal of Social Science Researches, 6*(3), 153–161.

Singh, S., & Badaya, S. (2014). Health care in rural India: A lack between need and feed. *South Asian Journal of Cancer, 3*(2), 143.

Soni, A., Fahey, N., Byatt, N., Prabhakaran, A., Simas, T. A. M., Vankar, J., ... Nimbalkar, S. (2016). Association of common mental disorder symptoms with health and healthcare factors among women in rural western India: Results of a cross-sectional survey. *BMJ Open, 6*(7), e010834.

Spence, R. T., & Wallisch, L. S. (2007). Alcohol and drug use in rural colonies and adjacent urban areas of the Texas border. *The Journal of Rural Health, 23*(s1), 55–60.

Srivastava, S., Singh, J. P., & Srivastava, O. P. (2014). Stress and coping style of urban and rural adolescents. *International Journal of Technical Research & Applications, 2*(5), 217–220.

Surchev, P. (2010). Rural areas—problems and opportunities for development. *Trakia Journal of Sciences, 8*(3), 234–239.

Wagenfeld, M. O. (2003). A snapshot of rural and frontier America. In B. H. Stamm (Ed.), *Rural behavioral health care: An interdisciplinary guide* (pp. 33–40). Washington, DC: American Psychological Association.

Zhou, Q., Chan, S. S. C., Stewart, S. M., Leung, C. S. C., Wan, A., & Lam, T. H. (2016). The effectiveness of positive psychology interventions in enhancing positive behaviors and family relationships in Hong Kong: A community-based participatory research project. *The Journal of Positive Psychology, 11*(1), 70–84.

Ziaaddini, H., Ziaaddini, T., & Nakhaee, N. (2013). Pattern and trend of substance abuse in eastern rural Iran: A household survey in a rural community. *Journal of Addiction*, 1–6.

Chapter 4

Perceived Happiness and Its Determinants

Kamlesh Singh, Yoshiaki Takahashi and Jasleen Kaur

Happiness has always been a topic of intrigue among the social scientists. While the Western connotation of happiness is explained with the help of modules such as subjective well-being (SWB), psychological well-being, social well-being and the PERMA model, the Eastern concept of happiness conforms to a focus on inner self such as inner harmony, peace of mind and *satchitanand* (inner source of happiness). The chapter begins with an introduction to happiness, followed by a review of happiness studies in the context of individual and cultural overtones as well as correlates and determinants of happiness. Additionally, it documents an empirical study on happiness from the state of Haryana (India) on 138 participants (mean age = 38.41 years, SD = 15.09). Voice recordings of face-to-face interviews were taken along with responses on data collection booklet. The study focuses on how a layperson perceives happiness and life satisfaction in reference to past, present and future. Five types of Likert scales of happiness, including Cantril Ladder (1965) and Interdependent Happiness Scale (IHS; Hitokoto & Uchida, 2015), and qualitative questions on happiness and life satisfaction, were used to capture the responses. The results are discussed in the light of both qualitative and quantitative data. Present research is an important contribution to translational research, as the findings from this chapter can give a framework to how a layperson views happiness, which may prompt other communities and countries to outline their mental health policies in line with the interest of its people.

INTRODUCTION

Rational thinking is what sets human beings apart from other creatures. As rational beings, we all strive to attain happiness through our choices and actions. While happiness is a universal goal of people and countries alike, it is thought provoking that as a concept, happiness has different meaning to different people. While Aristotle equated happiness with complete virtue and complete life (Ethics, 1100, a4–5), Socrates, along with good fortune, listed (Jones, 2013, p. 4) certain goods, the possession of which ensures happiness: goods of body (health, wealth, good looks), goods in relation to others (power and honour) and goods of the soul (justice, courage, etc.). Cassel (1954, p. 79) defined happiness as 'goal-setting and goal-striving with ego involvement present on the part of the individual'. A quick glance for synonyms of happiness in Oxford dictionary[1] yielded a list of following words: 'contentment, pleasure, satisfaction, well-being, enjoyment, joy, bliss, euphoria, exhilaration, cheerfulness, gladness, delight'. The multiple ways in which happiness can be defined has in fact made it a very elusive concept. However, this to some extent was taken care of with a scientific term for happiness, that is, SWB. According to Diener (1984), SWB refers to how people experience the quality of their lives and includes both emotional reactions and cognitive judgments. He also highlighted the fact that terms such as happiness, morale, satisfaction and positive affect were frequently used in studies pertaining to SWB. SWB consists of mainly three components—life satisfaction, presence of positive mood and absence of negative mood—together often summarized as happiness (Diener & Lucas, 1999). Similarly, Keyes (2002) conceptualized mental health as sum of positive emotions and psychological and social well-being. Psychological well-being encompasses six dimensions— purpose in life, self-acceptance, environmental mastery, personal growth, autonomy and positive relations—with others (Ryff, 1989), whereas social well-being (Keyes, 1998) consists of five domains—social growth, social

---

[1] https://en.oxforddictionaries.com/thesaurus/happiness

integration, social actualization, social acceptance and social coherence. Any discussion on well-being is incomplete without the mention of the PERMA theory of well-being, put forward by Seligman (2011).

PERMA theory of well-being: Seligman (2011) considered well-being to be comprised of five building blocks, namely, positive emotions, engagement, relationships, meaning and accomplishment, known as PERMA model. According to Seligman's (2011) model, *positive emotions* align with hedonic happiness and encompasses emotions such as gratitude, hope, optimism, forgiveness, etc. *Engagement* aligns itself with the experience of flow, wherein an individual's skills match with the challenging task at hand and where performing an activity is a reward in itself. *Relationships* refer to positive social connections that make an individual feel a part of a society and generate feelings of connectedness and belongingness with each other. *Meaning* refers to having a direction in life and feeling connected to a larger purpose in life. The last element *accomplishment* refers to making positive strides towards one's goal and achieving a sense of accomplishment and pride on its completion. Each of these five elements is independent of other, and each element in itself, is capable of contributing to well-being of an individual to varying degree. In a comparison of PERMA model of well-being with Diener's SWB, a latent correlation of 0.98 was reported (Goodman, Disabato, Kashdan, & Kauffman, 2017).

According to Suh and Koo (2003), seeking happiness is a global desire, and rightly so, as happiness has gradually found its way on national indexes as well. For example, the Gross National Happiness (GNH) Index, first coined by Bhutan in 1972, measures happiness across nine domains—psychological well-being, health, education, time use, cultural diversity and resilience, good governance, community vitality, ecological diversity and resilience, and living standards. Thailand has its own Green and Happiness Index (GHI), which it released first in 2007. GHI has six domains—physical and mental well-being, family, health, moral living, self-esteem, and perceived quality of neighbourhood. Japan also developed national well-being indicators including socioeconomic condition, health and relatedness (Commission on Measuring Well-being, Japan, 2011). The UN Sustainable Development Solution Network published its first *World Happiness Report* in 2012, ranking 156 countries on the basis of their happiness levels. The existing happiness journals (*Journal of Happiness Studies, Journal of Happiness and Well-Being,* and *International Journal of Happiness and Development*) are a proof of the interest it has garnered in the research community.

LAY DEFINITIONS OF HAPPINESS

The quest for happiness has prompted researches from several quarters; however, the fundamental question remains unanswered—what does happiness mean to a layperson? In an attempt to answer this, several studies have been undertaken. For example, Kamvar, Mogilner and Aaker (2009) explored the meaning of happiness across age groups. While younger people associated happiness with excitement, for older people happiness was synonymous with feeling at peace, stemming from increasing connectedness to others. In a review of happiness at workplace, Fisher (2010) listed work engagement, job satisfaction and affective organizational commitment as responsible for an individual's happiness. Datu and Valdez (2013) explored the meaning of happiness in Filipino adolescents. Happiness emerged as a multifaceted concept with participants' understanding centred on expression of positive emotions, absence of negative affect, relational needs fulfilment, wants, satisfaction and motivation. Happiness for primary age students in Australia was associated with friendship, belonging and optimism (O'Rourke & Cooper, 2010). A Polish study by Bojanowska and Zalewska (2016) also tried to answer this question by asking more than 700 participants the first word that comes to their mind on hearing 'happiness'. Health and relationships topped the list followed by knowledge, work, material goods and freedom.

Jaafar et al. (2012), in a qualitative study, attempted to find out the indicators of happiness in two Eastern countries—Malaysia and Indonesia. A total of 12 indicators emerged—family at the top, followed by career, interpersonal relationships, self-growth, wealth, recreation needs, education, and absence from negative feelings, national prosperity, health, religion and basic needs. Oishi, Graham, Kesebir and Galinha (2013) took a different route and analysed various definitions of happiness from 30 countries and definition of happiness in Webster's dictionaries from 1850 to the present day. They concluded that across time and cultures, happiness was defined as good luck and favourable external conditions.

In *World Happiness Report* (Helliwell, Layard, & Sachs, 2015), happiness was explored in reference to a country's GDP, social support, healthy life expectancy, and freedom to make life choices, generosity, and perception of corruption, positive affect and negative affect. Out of them, the three most important factors reported were differences in social support, income and healthy life expectancy. In a recent study, DelleFave et al. (2016) analysed people's understanding of happiness along psychological and contextual domains. Data from 12 countries with 2,799 participants was analysed. While inner harmony topped the list as psychological definition of happiness, family and social relationships were at the helm in contextual domain.

HAPPINESS: EAST AND WEST

This section looks at happiness in the context of culture. Culture plays a strong role in predicting happiness of individuals as well as societies. Uchida and Oishi (2016) summarized that people belonging to different cultures seek happiness in different ways. They further stated that individuals from independent cultures are more likely to seek happiness for themselves, and hence will make more efforts to maximize the experience of positive affect. Contrarily, individuals from East Asian countries with an interdependent culture view happiness as something that is experienced within shared relationships and cannot be pursued individually. On similar lines, Ye, Ng and Lian (2015) opined that prevalence of individualistic culture in European–American countries is responsible for higher happiness levels, given the fact that individualistic cultures promote individual freedom, individual achievement and pursuit of individual positive feelings. Eastern countries, on the other hand, promote collectivist culture that stresses interpersonal relationships. Happy feelings are affected relatively more due to evaluation by others, thereby lowering the happiness levels. While Western culture explores happiness in the context of well-being, Eastern culture studies the same in the context of harmony, peace of mind and inner well-being (Laungani, 2006; Lee, Lin, Huang, & Fredrickson, 2013).

In cross-cultural studies, Luo, Gilmour and Kao (2001) examined the relationship between cultural values and happiness in participants from

Eastern culture (Taiwan) and from Western culture (United Kingdom). Relationship between values and happiness was found to be stronger for the Eastern sample as compared to the sample from the West. Uchida, Norasakkunkit and Kitayama (2004) reported that happiness in European–American cultures is synonymous with personal achievement, whereas it is experienced as a realization of social harmony in East Asian cultures (Uchida & Ogihara, 2012). Joshanloo and Weijers (2014) documented that happiness is more valued in West and is also the guiding force of American people, while principles of harmony and conformity are at the forefront for the East Asians.

INDIAN VIEW ON HAPPINESS

Over centuries, the traditions and culture of India have been strongly affected by the presence of sages, seers and spiritual gurus. During this period, many concepts related to happiness existed but they all converged on the point that happiness is an internal state and that an individual should look for happiness from within rather than without. The Indian viewpoint on happiness exists within the realms of consciousness and transcendent self. Kumar (2003) reviewed and reported from the Hindu religious literature that emphasized the ultimate aim of human existence which was in knowing the ultimate truth that comes only by knowing the difference between what is eternal (*nitya*) and permanent (*satya*) and what is momentary (*kshanika*) and liable to decay (*kshara*). This same concept was applied while defining happiness. It is considered that *atma*—the transcendental self or the 'pure consciousness' as *nitya* and *satya*—should strive for *ananda* or bliss, the aim of all human beings, achieved only by attaining *moksha* or liberation from all kinds of sufferings (Kumar, 2003). He also brought to light different concepts of happiness (*sukha*) associated with different sheaths—*annamaya kosha* is associated with satisfaction of sensual pleasures (*trpti*); *pranamaya kosha* and *manomaya kosha* are associated with *harsha* (excitement associated with some events), *ullasa* (feelings of pleasantness associated with natural beauty) and *santosha* (being pleased by some interpersonal interaction); *vijnanamaya kosha* is associated with *ananda* (moments of bliss); and lastly *anandamaya kosha* which is associated with *anandamaya* sheath (pervaded by bliss). Srivastava and Misra (2011) suggested that according to ancient texts, humans seek their inner source of happiness or *satchitanand*, while Veeraiah (2015), employing the theory of non-dualism, believed that each human being is equipped with an innate quality of being (*sat*), consciousness (*chit*) and unalloyed happiness (*anand*), and has to look inward to find happiness.

In a study on happiness and productivity at workplace, 'state of mind' topped the list, where happiness was associated with peace of mind, feeling of contentment and satisfaction, and it was not related to a specific cause (Sharifzadeh & Almaraz, 2014). DeRobertis (2016), in his paper on phenomenology of happiness, highlighted Stephen Strasser's six manifestations of happiness. These were contentment, harmony, release, rapture, transcending anticipation and good fortune. Singh, Mitra and Khanna (2016) explored aspects of happiness in the context of Eastern culture. They reported a significant positive correlation between peace of mind, inner harmony and *satchitanand*. Furthermore, *satchitanand* was found to be significantly correlated with subjective happiness, life satisfaction, flourishing, and negatively correlated with negative feelings (Singh, Khanna, Khosla, Rapelly, & Soni, 2016; Singh, Khari, Amonkar, Arya, & Kasav, 2013). It reports that different modules of happiness are interconnected with each other.

From the above review, it is safe to conclude that meaning of 'happiness' varies across age groups, nations and cultures. 'Happiness', being subjective in nature, makes it difficult to provide a one-term meaning to it. Although we all know when we are happy, when it comes to defining this construct, we fall short of a common, formal definition. Hence, it has been rightly said that happiness is a word, the meaning of which is known to everybody but nobody can define it (Jones, 1953).

CORRELATES AND DETERMINANTS OF HAPPINESS

It is interesting to note that more the researchers try to delve into and explain happiness, the more complex it becomes due to the multitude of factors on which it depends. For example, Singh and Jha (2008) found grit, positive affect and life satisfaction to be positively correlated to happiness. In a study of Kuwaiti students, optimism, self-rating of happiness with a single item, self-esteem, satisfaction with life, positive affect, self-rating of mental health, hope, self-rating of both physical health and religiosity, and number of close friends were found positively correlated with happiness (Abdel-Khalek & Lester, 2010). Self-esteem and social support were significantly positively correlated with happiness in a study on adolescents living in socioeconomic hardships (Sharma & Gulati, 2014). In a study on Icelandic school students, Haraldsdóttir (2015) reported perception of financial status at home, physical health, emotional support from parents and emotional support from friends as determinants of happiness. Babin ák and Parkanská (2016) found existential well-being and experiential/phenomenological dimension as significant predictors of subjective happiness in Slovakian university students. Role of home and home setting was thoroughly investigated to see if it has any association with happiness. Corrigan-Doyle, Escobar-Tello and Lo (2016) identified several key elements as determinants of happier and sustainable homes. These were strong family bonds, facilitated by time relaxing, socializing and pursuing interests together.

Several studies have also highlighted a positive correlation between personality traits and happiness (Bakhshipour, Panahiyan, Hasanzadeh, & Tamaddoni, 2014; Okwaraji, Nduanya, Okorie, & Okechukwu, 2017; Pishva, Ghalehban, Moradi, & Hoseini, 2011). Prosocial behaviour was also seen to be correlated positively with happiness in an Indian study on 250 undergraduate students (Khanna, Sharma, Chauhan, & Pragyendu, 2017). In a study on determinants of happiness in rural Indian adults, good relationship with family members and neighbourhood and the absence of co-morbidities came to fore. The factors that seemed to threaten happiness were hospitalization, concerns about employment and marriage of their children (Rao et al., 2017). A recent Thai study (Senasu & Singhapakdi, 2018) associated various elements of quality of life (QoL)—quality of family life, quality of community life, and quality of work life—as determinants of happiness.

SOCIO-DEMOGRAPHIC FACTORS AND HAPPINESS

Happiness researchers have also explored this construct in the context of several socio-demographic variables. For example, with regard to marital status, a 17-nation study was undertaken to study the association between happiness and being married (Stack & Eshleman, 1998). Being married was found to be 3.4 times more closely tied to happiness in contrast to simple cohabitation. It was also thought to promote happiness by the promotion of financial satisfaction and improvement in health. Age and happiness are associated through a U-shaped relationship (Clark & Oswald, 1994). Baetschmann (2011) reported that happiness levels show a steady decline in 20–55 years of age, followed by a hump shape, and then increasing sharply until 70 years of age. Vera-Villarroel et al. (2012) looked at the association of socio-demographic variables with happiness. They reported age and socioeconomic status as main components of happiness. While higher age predicted lower levels of happiness, higher socioeconomic status was linked to greater happiness levels. In a Spanish study, Cunado and De Garcia (2012) reported that education level does not affect happiness directly whereas an Indian study (Singh, Kaur, Singh, & Junnarkar, 2014) reported level of education, apart from age, as a significant factor in determining the experience of well-being. In a study on determinants of happiness in Indonesian population, Rahayu (2016) showed that married, urban area residents and more religious people were happier than others. The author reported no differences in happiness level based on gender and ethnicity. Similarly, Malik and Sadia (2013) reported insignificant differences between male and female scores on happiness. However, various Indian studies reported higher scores on happiness for females in comparison to their male counterparts, (Sharma and Gulati, 2015; Singh & Junnarkar, 2014; Singh, Junnarkar, & Jain, 2017; Singh, Ruch, & Junnarkar, 2014). Similarly, Tiefenbach and Kohlbacher (2013) also documented that women in Japan were significantly happier than men. Contradictions in results convey that more research is needed to explore in depth the effect of socio-demographic variables on happiness levels.

SOCIOCULTURAL PRACTICES TO ENHANCE HAPPINESS

Taking a broader view on what determines happiness, Lyubomirsky, Sheldon and Schkade (2005) reported that a person's chronic happiness level is governed by three major factors: a genetically determined set point for happiness, happiness-relevant circumstantial factors, and happiness-relevant activities and practices. Relevant activities and practices are the deciding factors of happiness, as these are intentional and something that an individual voluntarily indulges in for his own good. Importance of intentional activities can be gauged from the study of Singh, Jain and Singh (2014), wherein the authors explored the significance of cultural indigenous practice, *satsang* (singing religious/spiritual songs in a group), which most of the Indian rural women regularly practise. Improvement in measures of well-being, prosocial behaviour and spiritual growth was reported along with decrease in stress and conflicts. Mehrotra (2013) studied the efficacy of an intervention-based programme 'Feeling Good and Doing Well' in Indian youth. The programme was based on the application of strengths, goal pursuit and emotional regulation. Significant increase in well-being and self-efficacy was observed with a decline in psychological distress. Encouraging results have been reported from intervention-based studies in the West and Europe, designed specially to enhance happiness (Bolier et al., 2013; Gander, Proyer, Ruch, & Wyss, 2013; Proyer, Wellenzohn, Gander, & Ruch, 2015). Lyubomirsky and Layous (2013) suggested a positive activity model to increase happiness, and emphasized two factors—features of positive activities (e.g., their dosage and variety), and features of persons (e.g., their motivation and effort)—to enhance happiness. Singh, Singh, Junnarkar, Mitra and Dayal (2016) highlighted the positive impact of spiritual practices on elderly rural women across several parameters such as happiness, global physical health and global mental health.

NEED OF THE STUDY

The present study is an attempt to contribute to the ever-expanding field of happiness. While a lot of research has been ongoing in understanding 'happiness' in its entirety, the answer still eludes most of us. The study has been undertaken with a twofold objective: (a) to explore how a layperson perceives happiness and (b) to study the correlation between subjective happiness (by Cantril Ladder) and interdependent happiness (based on interpersonal harmony, ordinariness and quiescence; Hitokoto & Uchida, 2015). It is hypothesized that these two modules of happiness would be positively correlated.

METHOD

Study area: The study was conducted in a northern state (Haryana) of India which has a strong agrarian character with 65.21 per cent of its population residing in rural areas (Census of India, 2011) by the JICA Research Institute under the project of Re-examination of Development policy from happiness study. Haryana is one of the economically sound states of India and is home to several key industries such as automotive, agro-based industry, information technology, oil refining, petrochemicals, etc. In 1970s, Haryana contributed significantly to the Green Revolution, thereby making the country self-sufficient in food production. One of the leading states in agriculture and dairy farming in India, Haryana scores high on economic indices. It is primarily a Hindu state (87.46%) with an overall literacy rate of 76.64 per cent (Census of India, 2011), men outnumbering women with a big margin (85.38% vs. 66.77%). However, data from the state presents a picture steeped in orthodox culture and traditions, and strong patriarchy. Haryana is also infamous for its low sex ratio (877 per 1000 males; Census of India, 2011), early child marriages, strong son preference, selective abortions and domestic violence.

Participants: A total of 138 participants (69 males and 69 females) with a mean age of 38.41 years (SD = 15.09) were recruited from about 15 random villages of Haryana and Chandigarh (capital of Punjab and Haryana). Demographic information about the participants' is presented in Table 4.1.

Procedure: A booklet containing consent form, demographic informa-tion sheet, two questionnaires—Cantril Ladder (Cantril, 1965) and IHS (Hitokoto & Uchida, 2015)—and open-ended questions on happiness were prepared for data collection. The demographic information sheet, apart from information on their education, age, gender, etc., also required participants to answer closed-ended questions on aspects of their daily lives, facilities, housing, perception of their living standard, etc.

Measures used: The Cantril Ladder (Cantril, 1965), also known as Cantril's Self-Anchoring or Ladder of Life Satisfaction, was used. The scale requires respondents to select an option on Likert scale ranging from 0 to 10 via following question: Please imagine a ladder with steps numbered from 0 at the bottom to 10 at the top. The top of the ladder represents the best

Table 4.1 *Demographic Profile of Participants*

Demographic Characteristics of Participants (N=138)			
Religion	**N (%)**	**Number of Children**	**N (%)**
Hindu	125 (90.6)	No child	30 (21.7)
Sikh	5 (3.6)	Only child or up to 2 children	49 (35.5)
Muslim	7 (5.1)	>2 children	59 (42.8)
Missing values	1 (0.7)	Missing values	None
Level of Education		**Employment Status**	
Illiterate	22 (15.9)	Working	28 (20.3)
<10th standard	47 (34.1)	Housewife/not working	12 (8.7)
10th–12th standard	29 (21.0)	Retired	3 (2.2)
Graduate & above	38 (27.5)	Student	9 (6.5)
Missing values	2 (1.4)	Missing values	86 (62.3)
Marital Status		**Income (per annum)**	
Unmarried	34 (24.6)	Up to 10,000	9 (6.5)
Married	95 (68.8)	10,001–50,000	33 (23.9)
Widowed	7 (5.1)	50,001–100,000	25 (18.1)
Separated/ Divorced	None	>100,000	46 (33.3)
Missing values	2 (1.4)	Missing values	25 (18.1)
House Ownership		**Sibling**	
Own Accommodation	89 (64.5)	No	70 (50.7)
Rented Accommodation	11 (8)	Yes	67 (48.6)
Missing values	38 (27.5)	Missing values	1 (0.7)

possible life for you and the bottom of the ladder represents the worst possible life for you. On which step of the ladder would you say you personally feel you stand at this time?

By following Cantril Ladder, these questions have been used to capture past, present and future status of happiness from the respondent.

Happiness: This measure has been used since long in large-sample social surveys such as European Social Survey[2] and the Cabinet Office of Japan National Survey on Lifestyle Preferences.[3] For example, participants are required to select an option on Likert scale ranging from 0 to 10: 'Taking all things together, how happy would you say you are? Please mark a 10 on a scale if you are very happy and 0 if you are very unhappy'. The questionnaire also requires each response to be elaborated by the participant.

Ideal happiness: This is a question about ideal happiness. Do you believe that all persons should be happy? If so, to what extent should we be happy? If you chose 0, it would mean that your ideal happiness condition is 'only when we feel unhappy'; a score of 5 would mean that your ideal happiness is 'the situation where happiness is 50 per cent and unhappiness is 50 per cent'; and a score of 10 would mean that your ideal happiness is 'a state in which we feel only happiness'. Please rate yourself on a 0–10 scale. Takahashi (2015) showed that the ideal happiness is very useful to ask some Asian countries, in order to know cultural difference affecting happiness.

Future Happiness: This measure was proposed by the Commission on Measuring Well-being, Japan (2011) since happiness could be understood as the status of future. If the scale 0–10 is used, cultural difference of happiness may affect its result. Therefore, participants are required to select an option on Likert scale not as level but as direction ranging from −5 to 5: Taking all things together, how happy would you say you will be in the future, say about *five years* from now? If you choose 0, it would mean that your happiness is same as now, a score of 1–5 would mean that you

---

[2] http://www.europeansocialsurvey.org
[3] http://www5.cao.go.jp/seikatsu/senkoudo/senkoudo.html

would be happier than now, and a score of from −1 to −5 would mean that you would be unhappier than now.

Life satisfaction: Participants are required to select an option on Likert scale ranging from 0 to 10: All things considered, how satisfied are you with your life as a whole these days? Using a scale on which 0 means you are 'completely dissatisfied' and 10 means you are 'completely satisfied'. OECD (2013) reported that this would serve as the primary measure of SWB. This question is also often used in large-sample social surveys such as the World Values Survey and the British Household Panel Study.

Every question had a second open-ended section to it—'Please give us the reason why you have chosen the response'—for qualitative data. The advantage of the Cantril Ladder is that it results in a continuous and theoretically equal-interval measure (Palmore & Luikart, 1972) and takes into account past, present and future status from the respondent. Cantril Ladder has been adapted in the *Gallup World Poll* and used in the *World Happiness Report*. It is deemed as a reliable and valid tool for measuring life satisfaction (Levin & Currie, 2014).

Additionally, in the present study, responses on happiness and satisfaction were further probed by the researchers. Participants were also interviewed on a set of seven qualitative questions designed by the researchers. The questions required participants to answer on (a) difference between the meaning of 'happiness' and satisfaction', (b) their 'happiest' and 'unhappiest' moment in the past, (c) their most 'satisfied' and 'dissatisfied' moment in the past, (d) the 'happiest' and the 'unhappiest' person they know, (e) the meaning of 'best possible life' and 'worst possible life', (f) the source of their 'happiness' in their daily life, and (g) policies that can be used to enhance happiness.

IHS: IHS (Hitokoto & Uchida, 2015) is a 9-item scale, based on interpersonal harmony, ordinariness and quiescence. According to Uchida & Ogihara (2012), IHS is based on Japanese idea of happiness, which revolves around 'relational harmony' (Uchida & Kitayama, 2009). Participants are required to answer on a 5-point Likert scale with responses ranging from 'strongly disagree' to 'strongly agree', and the total score is the sum of all responses. The authors have shown IHS to be valid in various countries such as Japan, the United States of America, Germany and Korea.

Data collection: Participation in the study was voluntary. Since data collection was done on individual basis, prior time was fixed with each participant. The purpose of the study was explained in detail and confidentiality of their responses was assured to each participant. The questionnaire booklet was prepared in Hindi. Bilingual expert translated the questionnaires into Hindi, which were back translated to English by another bilingual expert to verify the content similarity. The discrepancies were corrected and the tests were once again verified by the experts and authors. The study employed a mixed methodology approach. In order to get a better understanding, participants were required to answer a set of questions as well as explain their responses. Responses were marked in the data collection booklet and then face-to-face interviews were conducted and were live recorded (voice recording with participants' consent). In case where the participants showed an inability to write the quantitative questions' response due to low education level, responses were noted down by the interviewer. All interviews were conducted in Hindi and last 1–1.5 hour.

RESULTS

Results have been presented in four sections. Section I—results based on demographic data; Section II—Cantril Ladder based qualitative and quantitative results; Section III—the seven questions on happiness and life satisfaction designed by researchers; Section IV—correlation between two selected scales of happiness.

Section I

Section I presents information gathered from the participants on the demographic sheet. To reiterate, participants answered on housing aspects of their daily lives (Figure 4.1), material deprivation (Figure 4.2) and their perceived standard of living (Figure 4.3). It should be noted that the displayed results are from the participants who have responded, and he remaining percentage on each response is missing data.

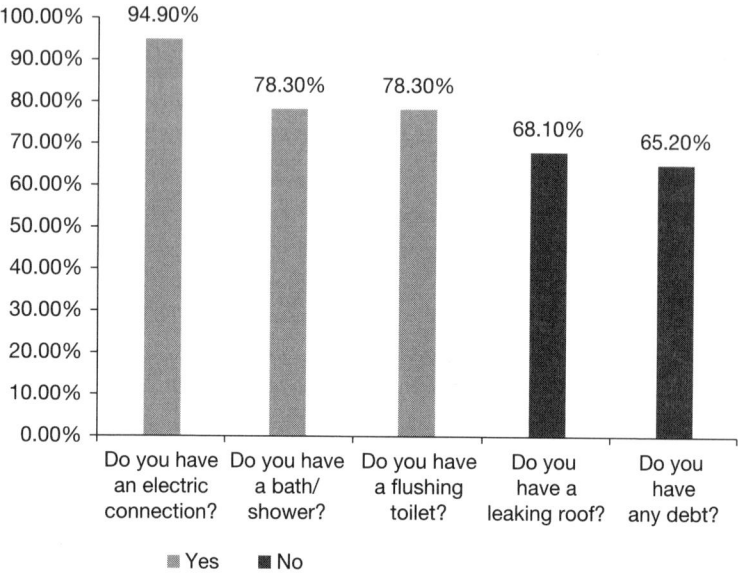

Figure 4.1 *Responses on Various Aspects of Housing*

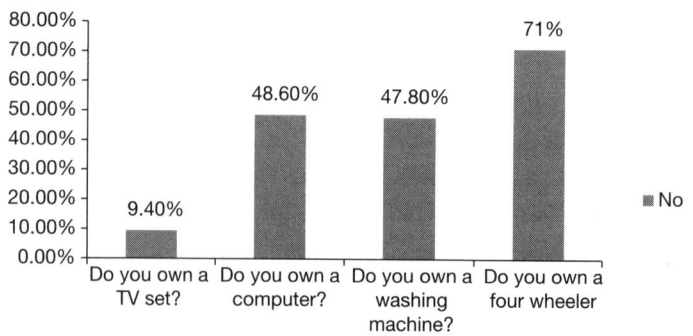

Figure 4.2 *Participants' Responses on Material Deprivation*

Information on the housing aspects of participants revealed that majority of the participants had access to basic amenities. This was evident from the statistics which revealed that a substantial number of participants had an electric connection at home (94.9%), access to shower (78.3%) and a flushing toilet (78.3%). Majority of the participants also lived in houses with no leaking roofs (68.1%) and were debt free (65.2%).

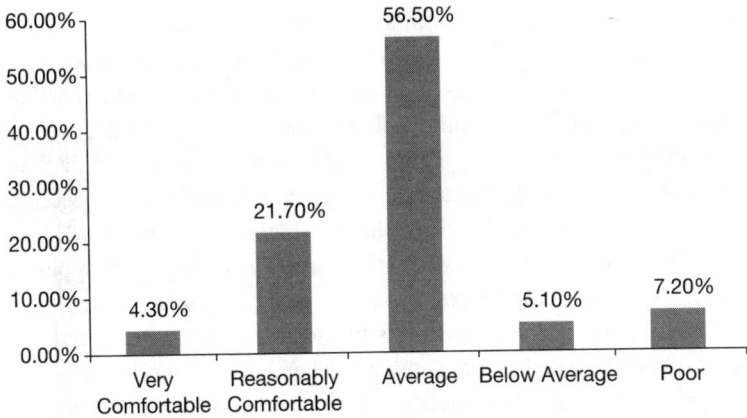

Figure 4.3 *Participants' Response on Their Perceived Standard of Living*

Questions pertaining to material durables possessed by participants were also put forth. The responses revealed that more than one-third of the sample (48.6% and 47.8%) did not own either a computer set or a washing machine, respectively. Majority (71%) did not have a four-wheeler, while only a small percentage (9.4%) did not have a television at home. However, when it came to their standard of living, most of the participants perceived it as average (56.5%) or reasonably comfortable (21.7%).

Data analysis: SPSS–21 was used for the analysis of the quantitative data. Means, standard deviations and frequencies were calculated for the data. Correlation analysis was undertaken for IHS and Cantril Ladder scale. Content analysis was done for audio recordings and written qualitative responses, and later categorized. Both types of responses (written and recorded) were collated and exhaustive content analysis was performed.

Section II

Results in this section are presented question wise. To reiterate, the happiness measures used in the study require individuals to answer questions on both quantitative and qualitative formats, and hence each question has two parts. For quantitative analysis, SPSS was used and percentages were calculated and presented in form of bar graphs for each question. For qualitative results, content analysis was applied and responses were categorized in broad themes. For each theme/category, percentage of responses was calculated. Number of responses against each category was divided by the total number of participants (N = 138) and multiplied by 100 to get the percentage of responses. This was followed for all categories. Furthermore, direction of the result for each category was also noted. For example, in 'family' category, where the reason for participant's happiness was the positive circumstances within the family such as wellness of parents, love among all family members and so on, this was categorized as a positive response (P). On the other hand, where reasons of being unhappy were negative family circumstances (conflicts among family members, ill health of any member, etc.), this was categorized as a negative response (N). However, the bifurcation of responses into positive and negative direction was required for only some categories and not in all. Analysis for the seven qualitative questions designed to explore responses on the Likert scale of happiness were analysed in the same way.

Question 1 (i). Taking all things together, how happy would you say you are? Please mark a 10 on a scale if you are very happy and 0 if you are very unhappy.

Gallup (2009) classified individuals who rated their present lives a 7 or higher, and their future lives an 8 or higher as 'thriving'. Individuals who rated their current lives a 4 or lower and their future lives a 4 or lower were classified as 'suffering'. Individuals who met neither of these criteria were classified as 'struggling' (e.g., rated their current lives as 5 and future lives as 6). This criterion has been followed throughout in the study.

Accordingly, on happiness ladder (Figure 4.4), about 59.5 per cent people were thriving (7+ score) and 12.3 per cent (4 or lower score) suffering, whereas 28.2 per cent (5 and 6 score) people were struggling. As per *Gallup World Poll, 2016* (Lyons, 2016), countries with highest suffering in the world were South Sudan, Haiti and Ukraine, where more than 4 in 10 people rated their current and future lives poorly enough to be categorized as suffering. Mean and SD scores on this question were 7.09 and 2.46.

(ii). Please give the reason why you chose the response.

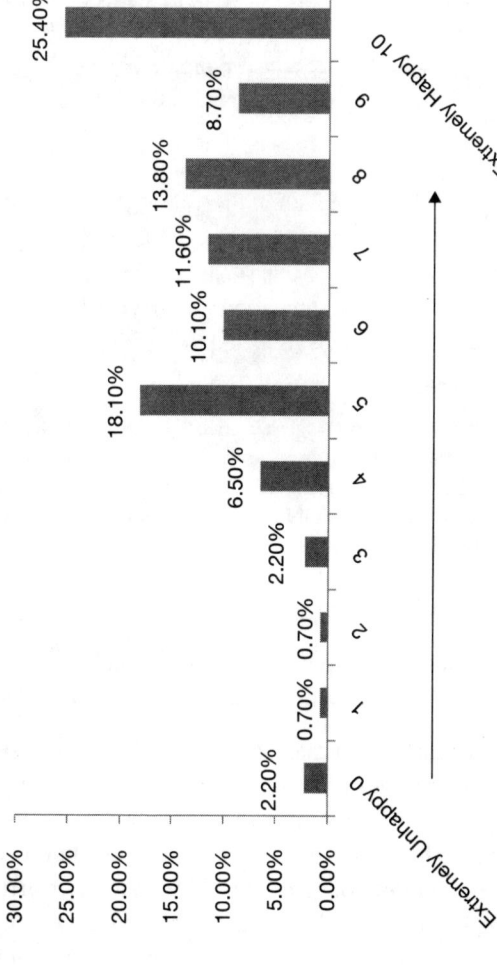

Figure 4.4 *Participants' Response on Happiness Ladder*

Table 4.2 *Direction, Number and Percentage of Participants' Responses on Reason for Their Happiness*

S. No.	Response Category	Direction of Response (n/%)	n (%)[a]
1.	Interpersonal relationships	P (60/43.48) N (19/13.77)	79 (57.25)
2.	Happiness centric	P (42/30.43) N (8/5.80)	50 (36.23)
3.	Work oriented	P (35/25.36) N (15/10.87)	50 (36.23)
4.	Money oriented	P (16/11.60) N (15/10.87)	30 (22.47)
5.	Health oriented	Ill Health (14/10.14) Good Health (1/0.72)	15 (10.86)
6.	Indifferent	–	13 (9.42)
7.	Loss oriented	–	7 (5.07)
8.	Miscellaneous (spiritual and time oriented)	–	5 (3.62)

Note: [a] Percentage of responses = {Number of responses (n)/Total number of participants (N = 138)} × 100

The content analysis of responses yielded several broad categories, all of which reflected the reason for participants' happiness (Table 4.2).

Interpersonal relationships: This category contained responses pertaining to the interpersonal relationships (family/friends/relatives) of the participants. Here, there were two subcategories. First subcategory talked about the positive aspect as happiness or wellness of parents, spouse, children, siblings or growth and development of children (studies/marriage/job), doing something for family, etc. The responses were also about happiness or wellness of others (friends, neighbourhood, and community) or maintaining friendship. The second subcategory talked about the negative aspect, for example, quarrels in the family, unhappiness, and dissatisfaction, unhappiness due to awful interpersonal relationship or lack of interpersonal relationship (loneliness). As far as the present data is concerned, 57.25 per cent (79 responses out of 138 responses) responses were elicited under this category, out of which majority of the participants (43.48%) highlighted the positive aspects of the interpersonal relationships, while only 13.77 per cent participants answered in the negative manner.

Overall happiness: The responses which did not reflect any specific reason but the participants had given a global response were kept under this category. Nearly 36.23 per cent responses were elicited under this category, of which majority were positive (30.43%) and belonged to overall happiness, and nearly 5.80% participants seemed to be unhappy overall. Positive responses were those where the participants said they were happy because their life was overall good and there was no additional problem, who responded globally saying 'everything is normal' or 'everything is good/fine', etc. While negative responses were those where participants were not happy at all but they did not give any specific reason and responded globally in a negative sense such as 'nothing is good', 'I am not happy because there is tension and struggle in my life' (did not specify the reason of his tension and struggle).

Work (job/work/business/career/education): The responses about participant's job, work, career, occupation and education (in case of those participants who were students) were assigned to this category. The responses stating about getting a new job, satisfaction with job, satisfaction with workplace, etc., were considered as positive (25.36%). The negative responses (10.87%) were about fear of unemployment, dissatisfaction with job, uncertainty about future, loss in business, failure in class (for students), etc.

Money: Nearly 22.47 per cent responses were found under this category, of which 11.60 per cent were positive and 10.87 per cent responses were negative. The responses in which the participants considered the monetary aspect to explain their happiness were put into this category. Earning good, good financial status, regular income, having property or facilities, good living standard, etc., were positive responses whereas 'my income is less than my expenses', 'I don't have money', etc., were negative responses.

Health/illness: This category included the responses in which participants mentioned their health-related issues or any other person's, who may be the reason for their happiness. Overall 10.86 per cent responses were found under this category, of which only 0.72 per cent were positive and while majority (10.14%) were negative. Positive responses corresponded to 'my health is good', while negative responses corresponded to 'but I have some illness'", 'I have diabetes and anxiety', etc.

Indifferent: Responses (9.42%) that showed an indifferent attitude towards the question, such as 'neither happy nor sad', 'don't know the reasons', 'can't tell', etc., were placed in this category.

Loss oriented: This category has a negative orientation in itself, and hence direction-based responses were not required. The responses (5.07%) stating about the unhappiness of the participant due to loss of someone close (death of parents, spouse, children, siblings, and any other member in the family or death of a friend or a known person), were kept in this category.

Miscellaneous: A total of five responses (3.62%) were seen for this category which included spiritual/religious belief and time-/punctuality-oriented responses. For spiritual category, no bifurcation of responses was observed, and responses such as 'praying to God', 'God is with me' and the religious beliefs were included here. It was also observed that for some participants, time factor is important for their happiness. They were happy if they got things on time (positive responses) and vice versa if they didn't get things on time or were unable to finish their work on time.

Question 2 (i). How would you rate the ideal condition of happiness for yourself on 0–10 scale? If you chose 0, it would mean that your ideal happiness condition is 'only when you feel unhappy'; a score of 5 would mean that your ideal happiness is 'the situation where happiness is 50 per cent and unhappiness is 50 per cent'; and a score of 10 would mean that your ideal happiness is 'a state in which you feel only happiness'. Please rate yourself on a 0–10 scale.

It was seen that 67.5 per cent people were thriving (7+ score) and 3.5 per cent (4 or lower score) suffering whereas 29 per cent (5 and 6 score) people were struggling when they considered ideal happiness (Figure 4.5). Mean and SD scores on this question were 7.61 and 2.24.

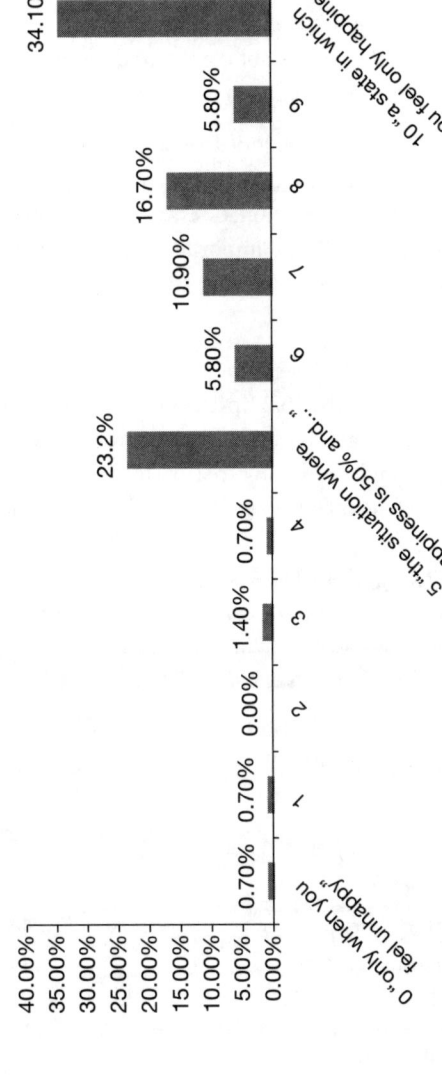

Figure 4.5 *Responses on Ideal Conditions for Happiness*

(ii). Please give the reason why you chose the response.

For this question responses were coded under 11 categories (Table 4.3). Unlike the previous question, where results were bifurcated in positive and negative direction, the nature of this question did not require result categories to be direction based, except for one category—life- or death-oriented responses. Responses not corresponding to any of the 11 categories were placed under 'miscellaneous' category.

Happiness and sorrow: This category included responses (39.86%) in which participants held the view that happiness and sorrow both are important in life. Some of the participants mentioned terms such as 'sorrow', 'sadness', 'problems', 'tension', which are important in life along with happiness. Participants also mentioned 'no one can be happy always' and 'sorrow as well is a part of life'.

Global view: Under this response category, participants had expressed a global view on happiness. Nearly 36.23 per cent responses such as 'one should be happy because it is good to be happy', 'life is good when person is happy', 'because one should be happy (reason for the response)', 'one should be happy as much as one can' were noted for this category. The

Table 4.3 *Direction, Number and Percentage of Responses for What Participants Believed Lead to Ideal Conditions of Happiness*

S. No.	Response Category	n (%)[a]
1.	Happiness and sorrow both are important	55 (39.86)
2.	Global responses	50 (36.23)
3.	Work oriented	32 (23.19)
4.	Interpersonal relationships oriented	30 (21.74)
5.	Health oriented	19 (13.77)
6.	Life/death oriented	16 (11.59)
7.	Miscellaneous[b]	11 (7.97)

Notes: [a] Percentage of responses={Number of responses/Total number of participants (N=138) × 100}

[b] Motivational, spiritual, social issues, indifferent and good habits-oriented responses.

responses having key words such as 'everyone', 'always', etc., were also placed under this category.

Work: The responses that corresponded to the participants' job, work or business as well as the food, other facilities, money or wealth, and education (in case of those participants who are students) were assigned to this category. Overall 23.19 per cent responses were noted under this category.

Interpersonal relationships: In this category only those responses were included which revolved around about interpersonal relationships (with family, friends or other people in society). In the present study, 21.74 per cent responses were found under this category.

Health: In this category, a total of 13.77 per cent responses were noted. As the name suggests, responses corresponded to physical or mental health issues of the participant or any other person close to them.

Life and/or death: Responses in which participants spoke about life or death were retained in this category. Out of 11.59 per cent, 10.87 per cent responses were positive, that is, which pertained to life, responses, such as 'only happy people can live', 'happiness is a must to live', 'there is no life without happiness', etc. The other pole of this category had response (0.72%) related to 'death' or 'dying' included responses such as 'one will die if not happy' or 'it is better to die if can't be happy'.

Miscellaneous category: This included responses (7.97%) pertaining to individual motivation, spiritual beliefs, social issues, good habits and indifferent responses. Motivation-oriented responses included statements such as 'happiness gives strength to live well', 'happiness give motivation for success', while responses referring to God, fate, luck, destiny, fortune and religious beliefs were categorized as spiritual responses. Out of a total of 138 participants, only two participants (1.45%) spoke about social issues such as corruption and increasing crime in society. Good habits and/or not having any bad habits as the reason for happiness were given by just one participant (0.72%). An indifferent attitude such as 'can't say', 'do not know the reasons', 'can't tell' was categorized as 'indifferent response' and was seen for only one participant (0.72%).

Question 3 (i). Taking all things together, how happy would you say you will be in the future, say about five years from now?

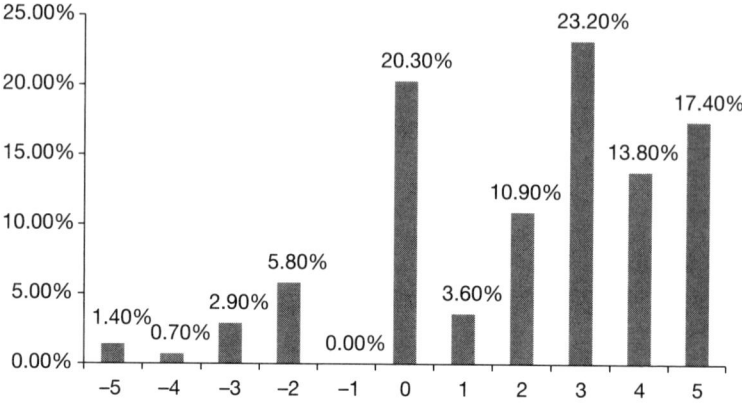

Figure 4.6 *Responses on Happiness Continuum in 5 Years*

Broadly, 68.9 per cent responded as much happier (1–5), 10.8 per cent responded as much unhappier (from –5 to –1), and remaining 20.3 per cent same as now (0). Mean and SD scores were 7.10 and 2.43, respectively (Figure 4.6).

(ii) Please give us the reason why you chose this response.

Content analysis revealed seven broad categories (Table 4.4). The only response category which was further bifurcated on the basis of the direction of responses (positive and negative) was the 'Global' response category.

Interpersonal relationships: This category included responses in which the participants considered their parents, spouse, children or friends to be a reason for their happiness after five years. In other words, they will remain happy after five years because of their relations with their family or friends. In the present data, 42.03 per cent (58 responses out of 138 participants) responses were elicited under this category.

Work: The responses in which the participants were hopeful to be happy after five years because of their work were taken under this category. This category included the participant's job, work, career, occupation and/or education-related responses (in case of those participants who are students). Nearly 34.06 per cent (47 responses for 138 participants) responses were found under this category. Responses such as 'will get a

Table 4.4 *Direction, Number and Percentage of Participants' Responses on the Reason for Their Happiness in Future*

S. No.	Response Category	n (%)[a]
1.	Interpersonal relationships oriented	58 (42.03)
2.	Work oriented	47 (34.06)
3.	Global oriented	29 (21.02)
4.	Money oriented	22 (15.94)
5.	Indifferent	19 (13.77)
6.	Health oriented	11 (7.97)
7.	Spirituality oriented	1 (0.72)

Note: [a] Percentage of responses = {number of responses/total number of responses (N = 138)} × 100

job by then', 'will start working', 'will get a promotion in job', 'will work hard', 'will get success', etc., were placed in this category.

Global response: In this category, those responses in which participants have expressed a global view on happiness after five years were placed. Mostly positive responses (21.02%) that corresponded to statements such as 'everything will be good', 'things will be fine', 'if I try then only life can be good', 'I think may be my situation will be better than now', etc., except one neutral statement—'nothing will change'—were received in this category.

Money: This category was defined by the responses in which the participants considered the money or property or facilities for the reason of their happiness in future. Responses such as 'pay increases every year so in five year, pay will be increased satisfactory', 'make a house of own', 'I will build my own house and facilities will increase', 'I will collect money after five years', 'we will start getting money', etc., were kept in this category. About 15.94 per cent responses (22 responses for 138 participants) were found.

Indifferent: Those responses were considered under this category which showed an indifferent attitude towards the question, such as 'can't say', 'depends on God', 'depend on luck or time' or any other uncertain response. Of 138 participants, 19 responses (13.77%) were elicited under this category.

Health: This category included responses (7.97%) where participants mentioned their health-related issues or any other person's (family member or friend) who may be the reason for their happiness after five years.

Spiritual: In this category, those responses were kept in which participants have mentioned God like 'depends on god'. Only one response (0.72%) fell under this category.

Question 4 (i). All things considered, how satisfied are you with your life as a whole nowadays? Please mark 10 if you are very satisfied and 0 if you are very dissatisfied.

As displayed in Figure 4.7 below, 62.3 per cent people were thriving (7+ score) and 12.3 per cent (4 or lower score) suffering whereas 25.4 per cent (5 and 6 score) people were struggling. Mean and SD scores on this question were 7.10 and 2.54, respectively.

(ii). Please give the reason for your response

Content analysis yielded eight categories (Table 4.5). Some of the categories were also further bifurcated into two categories on the basis of the direction or nature of the responses (positive and negative) under the same major category.

Satisfaction-centric (global) response: In the study, the satisfaction-centric (global) responses referred to those responses wherein the participants did not give a specific reason for their responses but defined it as a whole. For example, 'everything is fine' or 'I am happy with what I have', etc. This category was further divided into two categories: positive and negative responses. Positive responses were those where the participants said they were satisfied with their life, or things in life are overall satisfactory without any additional problem; responses such as 'I have everything', 'everything is OK', 'everything is fine', 'I am happy with what I have', etc. Negative responses were wherein the participants were not satisfied with their present life but did not give any specific reason and responded globally in a negative sense such as 'I have some wishes which I cannot complete', etc. In the present set of data, 50 per cent (69 responses for

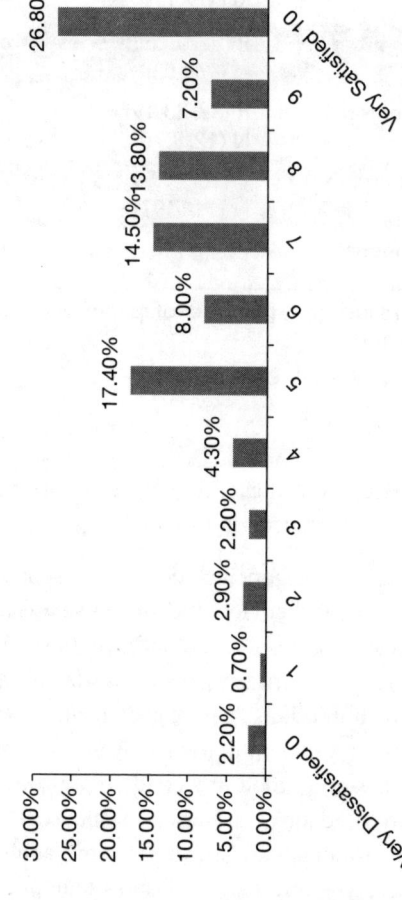

Figure 4.7 *Responses on Overall Satisfaction with Life*

Table 4.5 *Direction, Number and Percentage of Participants' Responses for Their Reason of Satisfaction with Life*

S. No.	Response Category	Direction of Response (n/%)	n (%)[a]
1.	Satisfaction centric	P (66/47.83) N (3/2.17)	69 (50.00)
2.	Family oriented	P (52/37.68) N (9/6.52)	61 (44.20)
3.	Work oriented	P (32/23.19) N (12/8.70)	44 (31.89)
4.	Money oriented	P (16/11.59) N (11/7.97)	27 (19.56)
5.	Miscellaneous[b]		16 (11.59)

Notes: [a] Percentage of responses = {Number of responses/Total number of responses (N = 138) × 100}

[b] Health (9), personal freedom (4), society (3)

138 participants) responses were elicited under this category, of which 47.83 per cent and 2.17 per cent were positive and negative, respectively.

Interpersonal relationships: This category included those responses wherein a participant's family/family member/close friend/relative was responsible for their present state. Positive (37.68%) and negative (6.52%) responses were assessed. Positive responses corresponded to 'my family is good and children obey me', 'I don't hurt others', 'I have good relations with almost everyone I know', 'I have no problem in my family', 'I am happy due to my good family', 'my husband is good, my children are good', 'kids are happily married and have good job', etc. Negative responses elicited were 'my girlfriend got married to someone else', 'due to some family problems and joint family, I have some tension', 'husband's temporary job and problem of alcohol', etc.

Work: The category revolved around satisfaction in life derived from one's occupation and overall career. In case of students, responses related to education were also assigned to this category. With an overall response rate of 31.89 per cent, 23.19 per cent were positive responses as compared to 8.70 per cent negative responses. In the present study, positive responses ranged from 'I am satisfied because I have started work', 'have good occupation' to 'work is going good', etc. The negative responses such as 'I have no job', 'I don't have a good job', etc., stated dissatisfaction with life due to job, work or business, more specifically, loss in business, failure in class (for students), etc.

Money: The responses in which the participants mentioned monetary aspect for satisfaction in their present life were put into this category. In this data, 19.56 per cent (27 responses for 138 participants) responses were found under this category, of which 11.59 per cent were positive and 7.97 per cent responses were negative. Positive responses included aspects such as good earning, good financial status, regular income, having property, facilities, good living standard, etc. The responses such as 'I am satisfied because I've made a house and took animals', 'I have enough money', 'not having any loan or debts', etc., were considered under this subcategory. The second subcategory was with negative responses such as 'my income is less than my expenses', 'I don't have money', 'I am not satisfied because I have to buy a house but do not have enough money for it', etc.

Miscellaneous: This included responses pertaining to health (6.52%), personal freedom (2.90%), and society (2.17%). In health category, participants responded to health-related issues of their own self or any of their family members or any person close to them. Responses such as 'I am satisfied because I am healthy', 'my health is good' and 'I have no illness' were considered positive whereas negative responses, such as 'my mood remains sad and unsatisfied due to illness', 'I am not satisfied from my life due to my illness', were dissatisfaction due to ill health or sickness. Personal freedom category reflected satisfaction primarily derived from having a sense of freedom and exercising free will. For example, 'I have no obligations and I wear clothes that I want to and I have full freedom to go out anywhere and anytime I want to', 'I am satisfied, I have freedom', etc. Society-oriented responses were those wherein the participants were observed relating their satisfaction (particularly dissatisfaction for the present data) from present life with social issues, such as corruption, government policies or any other. Responses taken under this independent category, for example, were 'I am not satisfied because government doesn't do anything for us' and 'poor children can't get admission to schools'.

Question 5 (i). Please imagine a ladder, with steps numbered from 0 at the bottom to 10 at the top. The top of the ladder represents the best possible life for you and the bottom of the ladder represents the worst possible life for you. On which step of the ladder would you say you personally feel you stand at this time?

As displayed in Figure 4.8, 55.7 per cent people were thriving (7+ score) and 7.2 per cent (4 or lower score) suffering whereas 37 per cent (5 and 6 score) people were struggling when they considered ideal happiness. Mean and SD scores on this question were 7.08 and 2.23.

(ii) Please give the reason for your response.

Content analysis yielded seven broad categories as shown in Table 4.6. Similar to prior questions, responses were calculated based on direction, except for two categories, that is, interpersonal relationship oriented response and indifferent responses.

Global response: The responses under this category were those in which no specific reason was mentioned but a generalized response was given. This category was further divided into two categories: positive and negative responses. Positive responses were those where the participants said

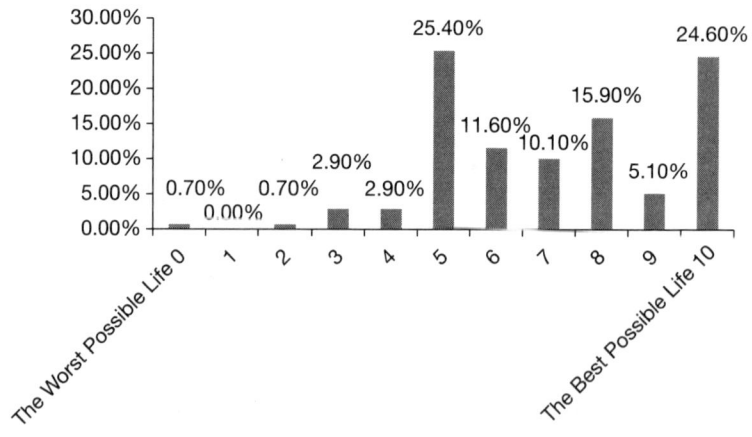

Figure 4.8 *Participants on Overall Perception of Their Lives*

Table 4.6 Direction, Number and Percentage of Responses on Reason for Participants' Position on Top or Bottom of Life Ladder

S. No.	Response Category	Direction of Response (n/%)	n (%)[a]
1.	Global response	P (69/50.00) N (12/8.70)	81 (58.70)
2.	Interpersonal relationships	P (48/34.78) N (12/8.70)	60 (43.48)
3.	Money oriented	P (17/12.32) N (14/10.14)	31 (22.46)
4.	Work oriented	P (21/15.22) N (9/6.52)	30 (21.74)
5.	Indifferent oriented	–	17 (12.31)
6.	Health oriented	–	8 (5.80)

Note: [a] Percentage of responses={Number of responses/Total number of responses (N=138) × 100}

they are happy with their life and responded globally saying 'everything is normal' or 'everything is good/fine' or 'my life is on the top because I have everything that I want', etc. Negative responses were those wherein the participants were not happy with their life, such as 'nothing is good', 'I am sad and have some problems in my life'. In the present set of data, 58.70 per cent (81 responses for 138 participants) responded under this category, of which 50 per cent responses were positive while the remaining 8.70 per cent were negative.

Interpersonal relationships: This category included those responses in which participants mentioned about their family/family member while thinking about their present QoL. Bifurcation of responses (43.48%) yielded 34.78 per cent positive and 8.70 per cent negative responses. Positive responses were 'my life is good because I have everything I wanted—my husband has a good job and now my son also has a job and I have no lacuna', 'all are good and my village is also good', 'I have good friends and relatives' to 'my village mates respect me', 'my family is very good', 'I have good family and my in laws are good', 'I have support of family members', etc. On the other hand, family-oriented negative responses were 'my life will be good if my son gets job and gets married', 'my life is not good because children are not earning', etc.

Money: Under this category, those responses were included in which participants spoke about their financial status. Positive responses (12.32%) included statements reflecting financial stability and facilities to lead a comfortable life. For example, 'I have all facilities and these are provided to me by my father', 'good family, good fields and have income from animals', etc. Similarly, in the negative subcategory (10.14%), participants lamented about problems faced in life due to financial instability, as reflected from statements such as 'now my life is not good, children are not earning and expenditure is more', 'lack of money and don't have a good life', etc.

Work: The responses under this category were related to work (job, studies or business) of the participants. Work-oriented positive (15.22%) responses corresponded to statements such as 'my studies are well and I think in future will get a job', 'I have a government job and I am happy', 'my studies are going good'. While the negative (6.52%) responses were 'right now I am not doing any job', 'I am unemployed now', etc.

Indifferent: Those responses were scored in this category in which the participants showed an indifferent attitude towards the question, such as 'I don't know', 'can't say', 'nothing', 'neither happy nor sad'. A total of 12.31 per cent (17 responses for 138 participants) responses were elicited for this question.

Health oriented: This category included responses pertaining to health (5.80%). In health category, the participants responses ranged from 'I have tension due to my illness', 'have back pain', 'I have some illness' to 'I am not satisfied due to illness' and 'my life is bad because I remain ill, do work but on medications'.

Section III

The last segment of the questionnaire dealt with open-ended questions related to happiness and satisfaction. Participants were encouraged to respond to what according to them is happiness and satisfaction. They were also asked about their happiest and unhappiest moments, most satisfied and dissatisfied moments, and so on. Responses were analysed using content analysis and result reporting followed the same pattern of preceding questions.

Question 1. What according to you is meant by happiness and satisfaction? Do you think they are the same or different? Give reason for your response.

Out of a total of 138 participants in the study, 125 participants responded to this question. While majority of participants (82) opined that happiness and satisfaction were two different entities, 30 participants believed that both were same. The rest 13 participants had no clear-cut opinion and their responses were hence categorized as indifferent responses.

Happiness and satisfaction are different: Majority of the participants (82) aligned to the view that happiness and satisfaction differ. Further, two types of responses were received on this category. In the first category, a total of 49 participants gave reasons why they thought happiness and satisfaction differ. Statements such as 'happiness gets through will and satisfaction is internal feeling', 'happiness is outer and satisfaction is an internal thing', 'happiness gets by own and satisfaction if we want it', 'happiness is for a short moments but satisfaction long lived', 'happiness is related to good work at home and satisfaction is good work related to village, state and country', etc., highlighted the difference between happiness and satisfaction. In the second category, 33 participants opined that happiness and satisfaction differ but could not however give any reason for the same.

Satisfaction and happiness are same: A total of 30 participants corresponded to the view that both happiness and satisfaction are same. This was evident from statements such as 'satisfaction is happiness', 'happiness and satisfaction are same', 'happiness and satisfaction both are same thing', 'no difference', etc.

Indifferent: A subset of 13 participants could not tell the difference between happiness and satisfaction. Responses such as 'can't say', 'don't know', 'can't specify', etc., were included in this subcategory.

Participants who had stated that happiness and satisfaction differ were further encouraged to elaborate upon their responses. The responses were then analysed to pick broad themes. For example, where the participants believed that their family was the reason for their happiness or their satisfaction, the response was categorized as 'family oriented' and so on. Likewise, three broad categories were formed: family, job and spirituality. A total of 20 responses were seen for 'family', out of which 13 participants believed that family is the reason for their happiness, while according to the remaining 7, family emerged as the reason for their satisfaction. Responses such as 'I have happiness because my parents gave me everything', 'satisfaction is for ourselves and happiness is for family', 'everything is good in my family than its happiness', 'if there is no problem in family then its happiness', etc., were included in this category. Likewise, 8 responses emerged for 'job', wherein 5 participants linked their jobs with their happiness, while for the rest, it was a reason for their satisfaction. Responses such as 'happiness is from income and job', 'I will be satisfied once I get a job', 'I get happiness from my occupation', 'satisfaction is from farming, animals and whatever we have', 'when occupation is going good then its happiness', etc., were included in this category. 'Spirituality', with 5 responses, was seen more as a source of satisfaction (4 responses) than happiness (one response). Example responses for spirituality are 'if we can live as life given by god then its satisfaction', 'from spiritual things I am satisfied', 'satisfaction came from doing *dharma*".

Question 2. What was the happiest moment of your life?

Content analysis on *happiest moments* yielded several broad categories (Figure 4.9). For example, if happiest moment was related to family, it was categorized as 'family oriented' and so on. For 138 participants, responses in each category and percentages were calculated.

Table 4.7 presents in detail the broad categories, the direction of response (i.e., any subcategory) and the number of responses along with the percentage against each category.

Interpersonal relationships: The response rate was highest in this category (51.45%), that is, for most of the participants their happiest moment was associated with their families and/or forming new interpersonal bonds. For example, 'marriage of my daughter', 'when my sister gave birth to baby boy', 'when my son got job and got married', 'in the marriage of my brother, he is handicapped by hand, at that time I was very happy

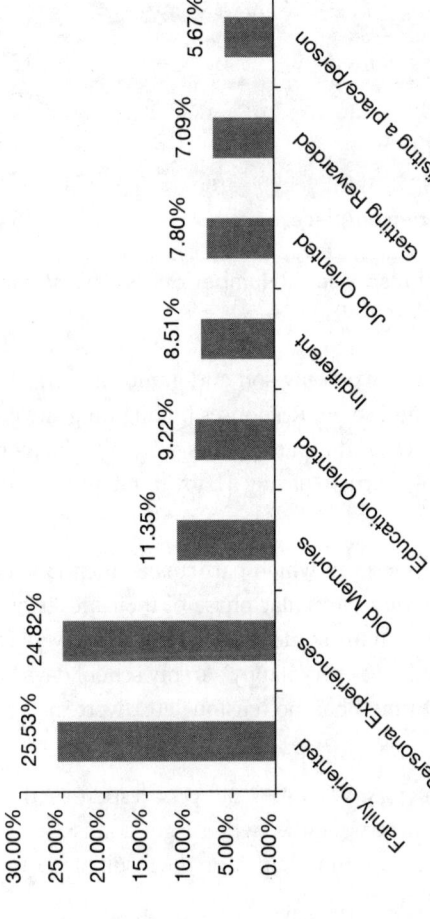

Figure 4.9 *Participants' Responses on Happiest Moment in Their Lives*

Table 4.7 *Direction, Number and Percentage of Participants'*
Responses on Happiest Moment in Their Lives

S. No.	Response Category	Direction of Response (n/%)	n (%)[a]
1.	Family oriented	–	71 (51.45%)
2.	Old memories	–	16 (11.59%)
3.	Education oriented	–	13 (9.42%)
4.	Indifferent	–	12 (8.70%)
5.	Work oriented	–	11 (7.97%)
6.	Getting rewarded	–	10 (7.25%)
7.	Visiting a person/place	–	8 (5.80%)

Note: [a] Percentage of responses={Number of responses/Total number of participants (N = 138) × 100}

that he also got partner', 'when my son and grandson born then I get a new status in my life', and so on. Responses highlighting any memorable interpersonal experience of the participants were also included in this category such as getting married, having a baby or finding a special person or a spiritual guru.

Old memories: The responses in which participants mentioned a specific date or a span of time or a particular phase of their life such as 'during college I had lot of fun', 'in my student days because we were free at that time', 'in my childhood I was very happy', 'in my school days I was more happy because at that time I had no tension', etc., were included in this category.

Education-oriented responses: With 9.42 per cent responses, this category corresponded to statements such as 'when I got admission in Haryana agriculture university', 'I was most happy on the result of my 1st semester in which I topped the class', etc.

Indifferent response: Similar to some of the earlier described items, this item also has an indifferent response category, wherein the participants displayed an indifferent attitude to the question asked or could not come up with an appropriate response. These were categorized as 'indifferent' and included statements such as 'I am always happy', 'don't remember', 'can't tell', 'don't know', etc.

Work-oriented response: In this category, job-oriented responses (7.97%) were included in which the happiest moment of the participant's life was found to be associated with his/her job or work. For example, 'I was very happy when I got a job', 'when I joined navy', 'I was very happy when I retired from the army; I took all the promotions', 'when I started earning', 'my happiest moment was when I got a job in *anganwadi* (government centres in Indian villages)'.

Getting rewarded: This category included responses wherein the participants expressed their happiness about getting a reward or a prize. Responses pertaining to personal achievements were also considered in this category. For example, 'when I made my own house', 'when I won in election, at that time I was happy', 'when my father gave me cell phone', 'when my team won in kabaddi match'.

Visiting a place or person: For some participants, their happiest moment was when they visited a long-desired place or met a special person after a long time. This was confirmed by statements such as 'when I went to Dehradun for three months', 'when I went to village with my friend', 'when I went to Goa', 'three years ago when I went to village there I did everything whatever I want', etc.

Question 3. What was the unhappiest moment of your life?

On the unhappiest moment of participants' lives, a total of 138 responses were elicited. Responses were categorized into broad themes as shown in Figure 4.10. The direction and number of responses along with the percentage for each category is shown in Table 4.8.

Loss-oriented response: In this category, the unhappiest moment of participants lives was associated with a loss associated with death or a loss associated with inability to marry the desirable person. Responses such as 'when my father died at that time I was very unhappy', 'my sad moment was when my mother in law died', 'I have a girlfriend from last 10 years and she get married on 9th April 2013, I couldn't marry her that's a sad moment for me' were analysed in this category.

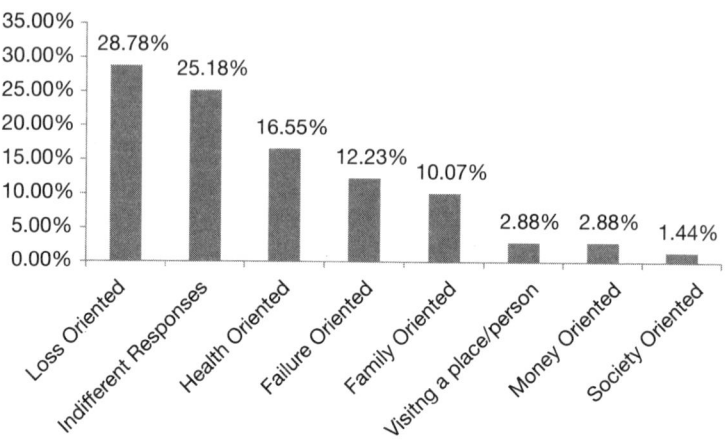

Figure 4.10 *Unhappiest Moment in Participants' Lives*

Table 4.8 *Direction, Number and Percentage of Participants' Responses on Unhappiest Moment in Their Lives*

S. No.	Response Category	Direction of Response (n/%)	n (%)[a]
1.	Loss oriented	Death (38/27.54) Unable to marry the person you loved (2/1.45)	40 (28.99)
2.	Indifferent responses	–	35 (25.36)
3.	Health oriented	Self (15/10.90) Other (8/5.80)	23 (16.7)
4.	Failure oriented	Personal (8/5.80) Education (5/3.62) Job (4/2.90)	17 (12.32)
5.	Interpersonal relationships	–	14 (10.14)
6.	Miscellaneous[b]	–	10 (7.25)

Notes: [a] Percentage of responses={Number of responses/Total number of participants (N = 138) × 100}

[b] Visiting a person/place, money and society oriented

Indifferent responses: Some participants could not recall any unhappiest moment or just chose to remain quiet about it. This was evident from responses such as 'can't tell', 'don't know'. However, some of them denied having experienced anything like that, and this was evident from responses such as 'I have never had a sad moment', 'no incident in my life where I was so sad', etc.

Health-oriented responses: With a response rate of 16.70 per cent, for some participants, their unhappiest moment was related either to their own health or health of a close family member/relative. This category corresponded to responses such as 'from my illness, I have headache (migraine) and illness of my body', 'my sad moment was when I admitted in hospital due to illness', 'when I knew about my throat cancer', 'when my back bone injured', 'the bad day of my life is in 1956 when I have an accident with truck', 'when my brother in law (*devar*) had an accident and in that accident he lost one of his leg', 'when my father had a heart attack', 'when my husband had an accident that a bad time for me', etc.

Failure-oriented responses: In this category, those responses were included in which participants spoke about facing failure in their lives. This was further subcategorized as failure in personal live (5.80%), failure in education (3.62%) and failure on professional front (2.90%). Responses such as 'when in failed in 11th standard', 'can't complete my studies', 'when I am not in job', 'I am sad due to my work' were included in this category. Personal failure corresponded to statements such 'I was sad on the talk of my marriage with my boyfriend due to other caste', 'after my marriage', 'they are all related to my personal life' were included.

Interpersonal relationships: With a response rate of 10.14 per cent, family-oriented responses were those where the unhappiest moments of one's life was due to their own family. Responses such as 'because I got separated from my parents', 'when my son went to his aunt's house for a long time due to his work, his absence was a very tough time for me', 'my grandson can't speak and my daughter in law is disabled and my son fell from the roof', 'when I came to my in-laws house after my marriage, and even now I feel bad by seeing the environment of this house'.

Miscellaneous: Some response categories saw few responses, and were termed as miscellaneous responses (7.25%). These included meeting up a poor person or visiting a place that left the participant with a bad memory, or financial issues or general prevailing conditions in society related to poverty.

Question 4. What was the most satisfying moment in your life?

Analysis on the *most satisfying* moment yielded (Table 4.9) responses with various categories (Figure 4.11).

Indifferent: This category includes, similar to the earlier questions, those responses in which participants (34.78%) were not able to mention/recall any specific most satisfying moment of their lives. The responses such as none/don't know/can't say/never/always were included. More specifically, the responses with an indifferent attitude such as 'I am not fully satisfied yet', 'we never get satisfied', 'I am always satisfied', 'can't remember', 'life is going good', 'no incident in which I get satisfaction', 'now I am little bit satisfied', etc., were included in this category.

Interpersonal relationships: This category contains those responses wherein the participants (33.33%) mentioned a person from family or family as a whole or any friend because of whom s/he experienced the most satisfying moment. It includes responses such as 'by seeing happiness of my children', 'I am satisfied till my family is with me', 'when I am with friends',

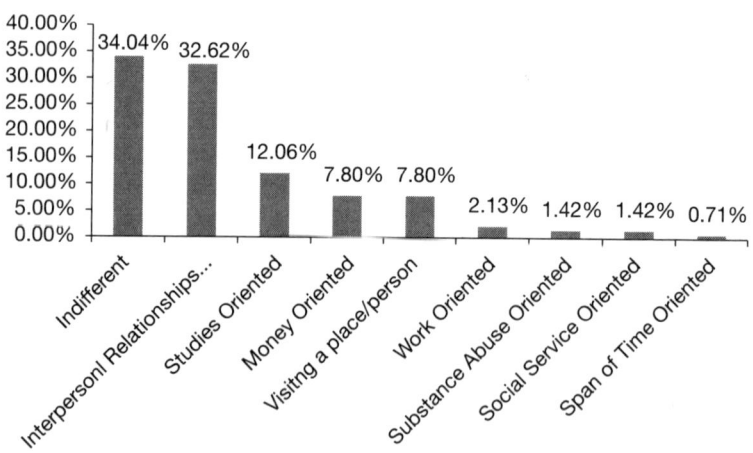

Figure 4.11. *Participants' Most Satisfying Moment*

Table 4.9 *Number and Percentage of Responses on Participants Most Satisfying Moments in Life*

S. No.	Response Category	n (%)[a]
1.	Indifferent responses	48 (34.78)
2.	Interpersonal Relationships	46 (33.33)
3.	Education oriented	17 (12.32)
4.	Money oriented	11 (7.97)
5.	Visiting a place or meet a person	11 (7.97)
6.	Miscellaneous[b]	8 (5.80)

Notes: [a] Percentage of responses = {Number of responses/Total number of responses (N = 138) × 100}

[b] work, substance abuse, social service and time oriented.

'I feel satisfied by seeing my family well settled', 'when my mother gave birth to my brother', 'when my son got permanent job after contractual job', '3 years ago, I did marriage of my children that was satisfied moment for me', 'when I became grandfather'.

Education-oriented: In this category, responses (12.32%) corresponded to achieving satisfaction through studies such as 'when I got admission in a city university', 'by studying … I get satisfaction', 'after my exams get over', 'when I got admission in MBA and MA English', 'in school, when I complete my work on time', 'when I topped in the 10th standard', etc.

Money: The responses, where participants gave money-oriented responses, (7.97%) as reason for their satisfaction, or mentioned having a property or any other such thing, were included under this category. For example, 'when I constructed my house with my own earnings', 'when we will have enough money', 'when I got my first salary', 'when my husband gifted me a piece of jewellery', etc.

Visiting a place or person: This category included responses (7.97%) where satisfaction was derived from meeting a desired person or visiting a long-desired place. This was evident from statements such as 'when I went to Delhi', 'when I met my spiritual guru', 'when I went to the destination of my choice and had a lot of fun', etc.

Miscellaneous: In this category, the responses corresponded to deriving satisfaction through one's work ('when I got my job'), by intake of substance ('when I took alcohol with friends'), social service ('once I helped a stranger felt satisfied') and remembering good times in the past ('in my childhood when I was 5–6 year old and had no tension and lived happily').

Question 5. What was the most dissatisfying moment in your life?

On the 'most dissatisfying' moments (Table 4.10), content analysis revealed broad categories (Figure 4.12).

Indifferent responses: This category included responses in which participants were not able to mention any specific moment they remembered as the most dissatisfying moment of their lives. Responses such as 'never happened', 'I didn't face anything like that', 'can't remember', 'I didn't face any unsatisfied moment', etc., were included in this category.

Failure-oriented responses: This category included responses in which participants spoke about their failure as responsible for their dissatisfaction. Three types of failures were cited, on the basis of which three response categories were formed. Failure in education, failure in job and personal life related failures. Failure in education such as 'left my studies', 'when I failed in 12th standard', 'when I had a compartment in 12th standard', 'I was

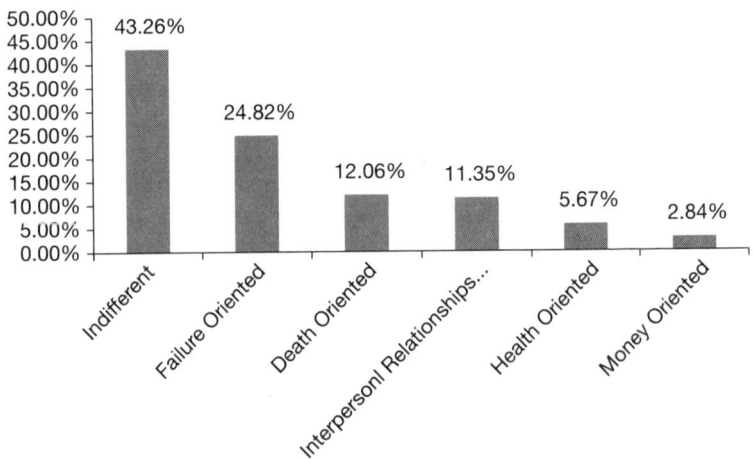

Figure 4.12 *Participants' Response on Most Dissatisfying Moments*

Table 4.10 *Direction, Number and Percentage of Participants' Responses on the Most Dissatisfying Moments in Their Lives*

S. No.	Response Category	Direction of Response (n/%)	n (%)[a]
1.	Indifferent	–	61 (44.20)
2.	Failure oriented	Education (15/10.87) Job (12/8.70) Personal (8/5.80)	35 (25.37)
3.	Loss oriented	–	17 (12.32)
4.	Interpersonal Relationships	–	16 (11.59)
5.	Miscellaneous (health and money oriented)		12 (8.69)

Notes: [a] Percentage of responses = {Number of responses/Total number of participants (N = 138) × 100}

dissatisfied when I didn't do well to get admission into a top engineering college', 'when my admission got cancelled for a dental course' responses. Failure in job such as 'when I left my job, and then they started some campaign against me', 'when I tried for army after 10+2, I cleared physical, medical and other test and due to approach system I was not selected', 'when I didn't get job' responses were seen. While talking about personal failures responses such as 'when my husband left me that's unsatisfied moment for me', 'when I had a break up with my girlfriend', 'when I heard that my girlfriend is getting married' were included. In this data-set, there was a sum of 25.37 per cent (35 responses) responses in this category, of which, 10.87 per cent, 8.70 per cent and 5.80 per cent responses were found for education, job and personal life related failure, respectively.

Loss-oriented: This category included responses in which participant's most dissatisfied moment was related to the loss of a significant person in participant's life. Responses such as 'the most dissatisfying moments was when my father died', 'when my sons died suddenly, one due to heart attack and one by falling from roof', 'in childhood death of father and death of father in law and mother in law' were assigned to this category. In this data 12.32 per cent responses (17 responses for 138 participants) were found in this category.

Interpersonal relationships: This category contained (11.59%) responses in which participants mentioned a person from family or family as a whole or any friend because of whom s/he experienced the most dissatisfying moment. This category includes responses such as 'when I beat my family members', 'domestic problem', 'everyone in family get involved in their own work and I remain alone', 'having no son is dissatisfaction', 'when I don't meet my friends', 'when my parents are not feeling well'.

Miscellaneous: This included responses related to health and money. Health category included responses in which participants mentioned their health-related issues such as any injury, accident and/or illness or someone else's which was the reason for their dissatisfaction. Responses such as 'when I worked in factory, and my leg fractured at that time', 'illness of brother', 'my unsatisfied moment was when my daughter went under an operation', 'I am ill so I am unsatisfied', 'when my father in law became ill due to blockage of nerve', etc., were elicited. Responses in which the participants considered money- or property-related issues when recalling the most dissatisfying moment were included in 'money' category. Responses such as 'I was dissatisfied at the time when we did not have our own house' and 'I think that I get money and pay all my debts and no money is coming' were assigned to this category.

Question 6. Who is the happiest person you know? What is the reason for your answer?

On the 'happiest' person known to participants (Table 4.11), a total of 138 responses were calculated and 7 categories were formed (Figure 4.13). Answers ranged from participants naming a person in the family, a famous personality, someone who was financially well-off as the happiest person and so on.

Indifferent responses: This category contained responses in which participants did not mention anything specific and responded using phrases such as 'none/don't know/can't say/can't specify/all/everyone', etc. In this data, there were 36.23 per cent responses under this category.

Interpersonal relationships: In this category, participants have mentioned their family and a person other than family, such as friends, neighbours or a person from community they think to be the happiest. Responses such as 'my elder son', 'my mother', 'my younger sister', 'the happiest person

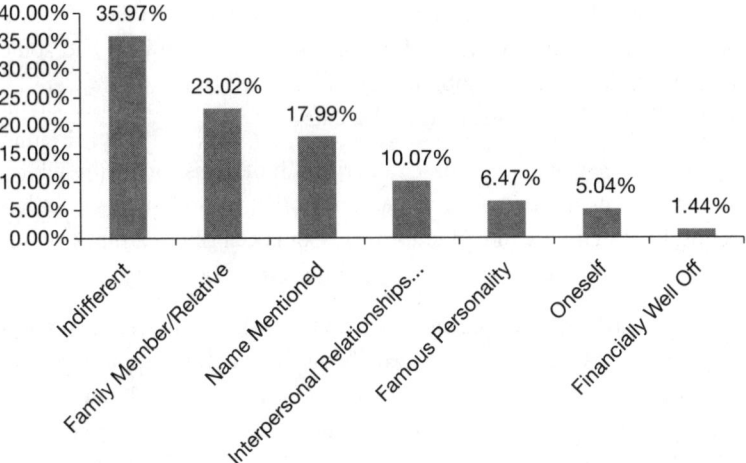

Figure 4.13 *Participants' Responses on the Happiest Person They Know*

Table 4.11 *Number and Percentage of Responses on Happiest Person Known to Participants*

S. No.	Response Category	n (%)[a]
1.	Indifferent	50 (36.23)
2.	Interpersonal relationships	46 (33.33)
3.	Name mentioned	25 (18.12)
4.	Any famous personality	9 (6.52)
5.	Miscellaneous (Self and finances oriented)	9 (6.52)

Note: [a] Percentage of responses={Number of responses/Total number of participants (N=138) × 100}

are my parents' were included. 'My neighbours', 'people of my village', 'one of my friend Usha is the happiest, because she get everything' were kept in this category.

A name: Responses wherein the participants simply named the person they know is happiest, without specifying the relationship with him/her were added to this category. For example, 'Sandeep Chaudhary', 'Kishanlal is very much happy', 'Surender is the happiest person', 'Raju is happiest person', etc. They mentioned people known to them who had some special achievements like job, money, etc. In this dataset, there were 25 responses which were assigned to this category.

Any famous personality: This category included responses in which participants mentioned a renowned and a rich person such as 'Sachin Tendulkar (a famous Indian cricketer)', 'Sonia Gandhi (a famous politician)', 'Amitabh Bachchan (a renowned Bollywood actor)'.

Miscellaneous: The first category in this was 'self-oriented' category, wherein the participants perceived themselves as the happiest person they know. For example, 'I am the happiest one', 'myself' and 'myself because I am happier than my other friends'. The second category under miscellaneous was wherein the participants mentioned someone to be happiest because of his higher financial status. This included just two responses: 'our state minister is the happiest person because he has lots of money' and 'he earns good amount of money and it is sufficient for their expenditure'.

Question 7. Who is the unhappiest person you know? What is the reason for your answer?

Analysis on 'unhappiest' person (Table 4.12) yielded a total of 10 categories (Figure 4.14).

Indifferent: In this category, responses in which participants did not mention anything specific and responded with an indifferent phrase such as 'none/don't know/can't say/can't specify/all/everyone', etc., were included. In this data, there were 21.74 per cent responses (30 responses for 138 participants).

Unfavourable life circumstances: This category included responses in which participants mentioned a lack of something, like money or job. For example, 'who are not in job', 'who have lack of money', 'who have no opportunity for job and have unmarried girls at home', 'poor people are sad', 'whom economic condition is bad', 'an unhappiest person who have lacuna of money'. In this data, 28 responses (20.29%) were retained in this category.

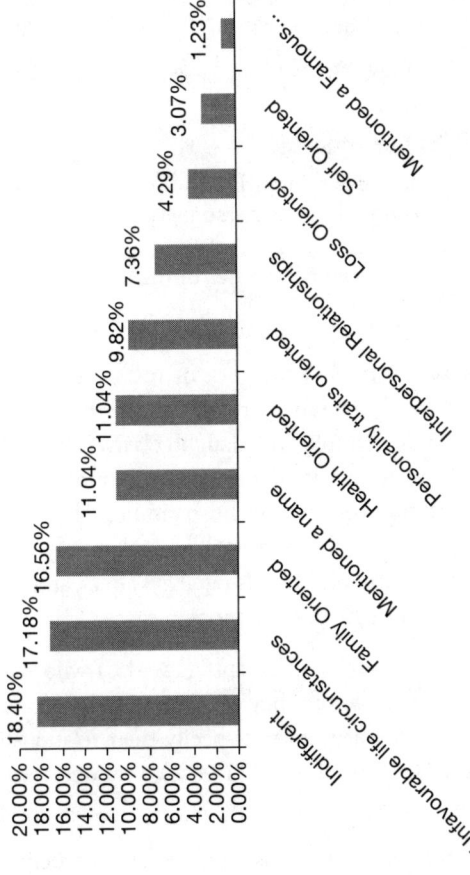

Figure 4.14. *Participants' Response on the 'Unhappiest' Person Known to Them*

Table 4.12 *Number and Percentage of Responses on the 'Unhappiest' Person Known to Participants*

S. No.	Response Category	n (%)[a]
1.	Indifferent	30 (21.74)
2.	Unfavourable life circumstances	28 (20.29)
3.	Interpersonal Relationships	39 (28.26)
4.	Mentioned a name	18 (13.04)
5.	Health oriented	18 (13.04)
6.	Personality traits oriented	16 (11.59)
7.	Miscellaneous(Loss oriented, self-oriented and mentioning a famous personality)	14 (10.14)

Note: [a] Percentage of responses={Number of responses/Total number of participants (N=138)×100}

Interpersonal-relationships: In this category of responses, participants (28.26%) mentioned family members/friend/relative they perceived as being most unhappy. For example, 'my daughter', 'my mother in law is always sad', 'it's my brother because my mother is no more', 'my daughter is not in good condition because her husband beats her', 'my friend because he has less family support and have no job', 'in my neighbourhood', 'one in my neighbourhood, she has paralysis attack and she is very sad', 'my neighbour, because he has less money'.

Mentioning a name: There were participants (13.04%) who mentioned only the name of the person whom they considered to be very unhappy with his/her life. However, they did not specify their relationship with that person. In this data, 18 responses (11.04%) were observed for this category.

Health: This category contained responses wherein the participants considered those unhappy who were having any health-related issues. For example, 'who is unhappy due to her illness', 'she also remains ill', 'a sweeper in our office as he is handicapped'. In this data, there were 18 responses (13.04%) of this type.

Personality traits: In this response category, participants mentioned a trait or a habit that can make a man unhappy. Responses such as 'one is sad, who have bad habits', 'cunning people', 'who are short tempered and always quarrel with others', 'who don't do good work and disobey parents', 'the one who has more wishes is more sad' were assigned to this category. In this dataset, there were 16 responses (11.59%) found under this category.

Miscellaneous: This included responses pertaining to three different categories—loss oriented, self and wherein the participants mentioned a famous personality whom they thought was unhappy. In loss-oriented category, those responses were taken in which participants have mentioned about any loss that has made them sad. For example, 'because his parents died in his childhood', 'who lost his everything in gamble and alcohol', 'whose husband and son died ... and have debt', 'her husband expired'. The second category included those responses in which participants believed themselves to be the saddest. Responses such as 'me', 'myself', with or without reason, were included. The last category included responses in which participants mentioned a renowned person who is most unhappy. Responses such as 'minister of Hyderabad', 'Afzal Guru as he could not complete his diploma' were considered in this category.

Question 8. What according to you is the meaning of 'the best possible life'?

A total of seven categories emerged on probing the meaning of the 'best possible life' (Figure 4.15).

Indifferent responses: With a response rate of 31.89 per cent, this category included responses in which the participants did not mention anything specific and responded with indifferent statements such as 'having everything/nothing', 'can't say/don't know', 'be happy/enjoy', 'my present life/all wishes fulfilled', etc. (Table 4.13).

Interpersonal-relationships: In this category of responses (20.26%), participants' idea of best possible life was aligned to their close interpersonal bonds. This was evident from responses such as 'a good life is having good family', 'when my all family member remain with me', 'best life is to make his family happy', 'there is peace at home and have good family'.

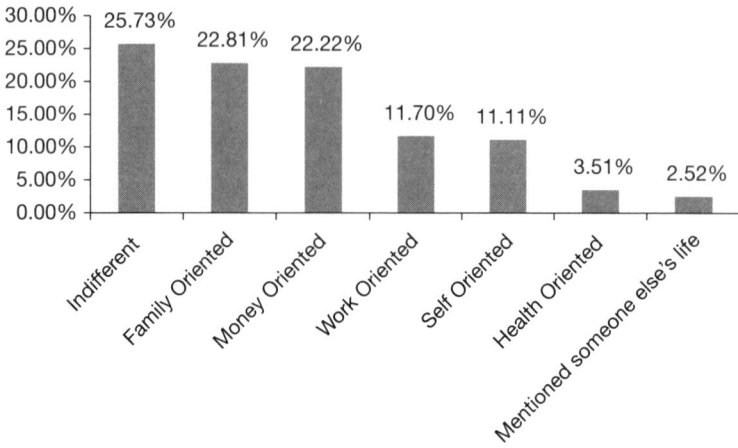

Figure 4.15. *Participants' Responses on What Categorizes the 'Best Possible Life'*

Table 4.13 *Number and Percentage of Participants' Responses on What Constitutes the Best Possible Life*

S. No.	Response Category	n (%)[a]
1.	Indifferent responses	44 (31.89)
2.	Interpersonal relationships	39 (20.26)
3.	Money oriented	38 (27.54)
4.	Work oriented	20 (14.50)
5.	Self-oriented	19 (13.77)
6.	Miscellaneous (health oriented, and mentioning someone else's life)	11 (7.97)

Notes: [a] Percentage of Responses={number of responses/total number of participants (N = 138) × 100}

Money-oriented responses: About 27.54 per cent responses mentioned money as an important element of leading a good life. Responses such as 'having lot of money', 'having enough money to get what you want', 'good financial status', 'lot of money to spend on your family', etc., were included in this category.

Work-oriented responses: This category contains the responses (14.50%) in which work, job, career or business were considered an important aspect of 'best life'. Responses such as 'be honest and do work with honesty', 'a good life is enjoyment of your own work', 'a good life is when get a job after study', 'who have good occupation', 'a good life is if anyone get a good job' were taken in this category.

Self: This category included responses (13.77%) in which the participants either believed that the life s/he is living currently was the best possible life, or were found talking about themselves or some personality characteristics. In this category, responses such as 'the best possible life's meaning is that you believe in your inner self, strengths and you give happiness to others, if you fulfilled all responsibilities to parents, friends and family', 'simple living high thinking', 'who have good character and good behaviour they have good life', 'which I am living' were included.

Miscellaneous: This included two types of response categories. The first was related to health, included responses that considered health important for leading a best possible life. Responses such as 'a good life is when you have a healthy body', 'according to me a good life is having healthy body', 'a good life is when you have no illness', 'a good life is when a person happy with health', etc., were considered for this category. The second category was wherein the participants named another person—a person in their social circle, in their close family or a famous personality, whose life they perceived as a best possible life.

Question 9. What according to you is the meaning of 'the worst possible life'?

On the meaning of *worst possible life* (Table 4.14), a total of seven categories were formed (Figure 4.16).

Indifferent responses: This category included responses in which the participants did not mention anything specific and responded with an indifferent phrase such as 'having nothing', 'Can't say/don't know', 'all wishes fulfilled', 'always sad', 'can't have/get something'. In this data, there were 35 responses (25.36%).

Money-oriented: This category included responses (24.64%) that mentioned lack of money as the single factor in one's life going downhill. Participants were forthcoming, and believed that lack of money was

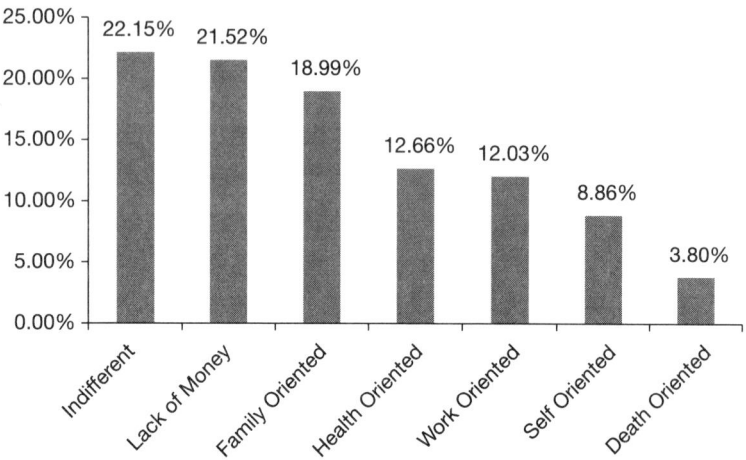

Figure 4.16 *Participants' Responses on What Categorizes a 'Worst Life'*

Table 4.14 *Number and Percentage of Participants' Responses on What Constitutes the Worst Possible Life*

S. No.	Response Category	n (%)[a]
1.	Indifferent responses	35 (25.36)
2.	Money oriented	34 (24.64)
3.	Interpersonal relationships	30 (21.74)
4.	Health oriented	20 (14.50)
5.	Work oriented	19 (13.77)
6.	Self-oriented	14 (10.15)
7.	Loss oriented	6 (4.35)

Note: [a] Percentage of responses={Number of responses/Total number of participants (N = 138) × 100}

further responsible for food shortage, lack of basic things, lack of one's own house to live, etc. Money-oriented responses were 'people who don't have money for daily needs', 'when a person has problem in getting food for himself or his family', 'being poor is equivalent to a bad life', 'when the facilities of medical treatment and water supply are inaccessible due to money shortage', 'when an individual has problem for food and shelter due to lack of money', 'when there is no money', 'beggars have worst life as they have no money at all and are on mercy of others for their survival', etc.

Interpersonal relationships: This category included responses in which the participants believed that family and/or relationship with others are contributing factors for life at its worst. This was forthcoming through statements such as 'personal relationships and not money are needed for good life', 'a woman in my relation whose husband and son died and she has no one to take care of her now', 'bad interpersonal relationships', 'conflicts within family members', etc. In this data, 21.74 per cent responses (30 responses) were assigned to this category.

Health-oriented responses: In this category, health-related responses were clubbed together. Such as 'who have illness', 'who have some mental illness', 'drink alcohol, abuse parents and have illness whose children took alcohol and use abusive language to his parents and a ill body', 'who have illness has a worst life'. In the data, there were 20 responses (14.50%) in this category.

Work-oriented responses: The responses of this category were mostly about the participant's job, work or business. For example, 'when a person have no job', 'who don't get job and have life full of tension', 'life of unemployed is a bad life', 'who don't work they have bad life'. Overall 19 responses (13.77%) were observed under this category in the data.

Self-oriented: The responses kept in this category were either related to the participants or they mentioned any personality characteristics. For example, 'a bad life is who is tensed due to himself', 'who fell in drug abusing habits and do commits theft', 'who have no respect in society', 'who are self-centred', etc. In this data, there were 10.15 per cent responses (14 responses).

Loss oriented: This category included responses in which participants mentioned about death, such as 'family member's death', 'life is ruined when someone close to you dies', 'my neighbour whose husband and son died and she now has no one to take care of the family', etc. In this data, only six responses (4.35%) were elicited.

Question 10. From which things do you get happiness in your daily life?

This question asks the participants how they derive happiness in their ordinary daily lives. Content analysis revealed six broad categories (Figure 4.17). Further quantitative analysis also revealed the number and percentage of responses against each category (Table 4.15).

Work-oriented response: This category included responses (45.65%) in which the source of participants' happiness was related to their daily work, be it household chores or their chosen profession. Responses that found place in this category ranged from 'when I finish my work', 'by finishing my work in office', 'I feel happiness by doing my work', 'by doing household work and by learning new things', 'for me happiness in making food', 'I feel happiness by finishing my work on time', etc.

Interpersonal relationships: In this category, those responses (25.36%) were considered where an interpersonal relationship of participant was seen as a source of his happiness. For example, 'spending time with my son', 'playing with my niece', 'by taking care of my family members', 'I feel happiness by talking to my friends', 'by sending children school and taking care of in laws', 'in my happiness I also think of my family members'.

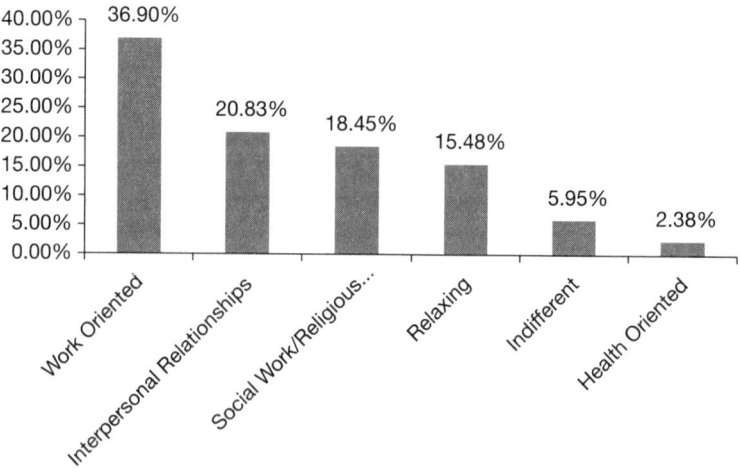

Figure 4.17 *Participants' Responses on the Source of Happiness in Their Daily Lives*

Table 4.15 *Number and Percentage of Participants' Responses on How They Derive Happiness in Their Daily Lives*

S. No.	Response Category	n (%)[a]
1.	Work oriented	62 (45.65)
2.	Interpersonal relationships	35 (25.36)
3.	Social work/religious activities oriented	31 (22.46)
4.	Relaxing	26 (18.84)
5.	Miscellaneous (indifferent and health oriented)	14 (10.14)

Note: [a] Percentage of responses = {Number of responses/Total number of participants (N = 138) × 100}

Social work/Religious activities: The responses (22.46%) where the source of participant's happiness was related to any social work or religious activity were put under this category. Statements such as 'when I pray in mandir', 'people come to me and share their problems', 'when some good work occurs from my hand', 'I enjoy reading Quran', 'I am involved in social activities, which gives happiness', 'I feel happy by helping others and from the social activities', etc., were considered in this category.

Relax (doing nothing): Some of the participants mentioned that for them happiness is taking rest, sleeping, playing, enjoying or simply doing nothing. Responses (18.48%) such as 'by sleeping', 'I feel happy by sleeping and taking rest', 'I get happiness from taking food, sleeping and watching serials on zee TV', etc., were included in this category.

Miscellaneous: Many participants had no opinion on the question asked or simply showed a disinterest, which was evident from their responses such as 'everything/can't say/don't know/nothing', etc. These responses were later categorized as 'indifferent'. Substance abuse-oriented responses such as 'I feel happiness by playing cards and by drinking alcohol', 'by smoking cigarette', etc., were included in this category.

Question 11. Which policies according to you should be followed by the government to make people happy?

This question tries to relate the happiness of common people with governmental policies. A total of nine categories were formed, based on the content analysis of the responses (Figure 4.18, Table 4.16).

Unemployment: Nearly 34.78 per cent responses were about unemployment while answering this question. Responses such as 'government should provide jobs', 'should increase job opportunities', 'give me job', 'should provide job opportunities to everyone' were included.

Basic amenities: About 26.09 per cent responses were about the availability of the basic amenities such as water, electricity, education, medical, security, etc., on this question. The responses included 'should increase arrangement of water supply', 'government should gave basic facilities', 'government should provide facilities like toilets', 'should give pension to old people', 'government should provide security for girls'.

Cost inflation: There were 30 responses (21.74%) where participants have mentioned the problem of cost inflation. For example, 'everything should be on cheap prices', 'decrease the cost of petrol and diesel', 'government should decrease costs', *'mehngai kam karni chahiye* (inflation should be decreased)', 'decrease inflation and should think also about middle class people'.

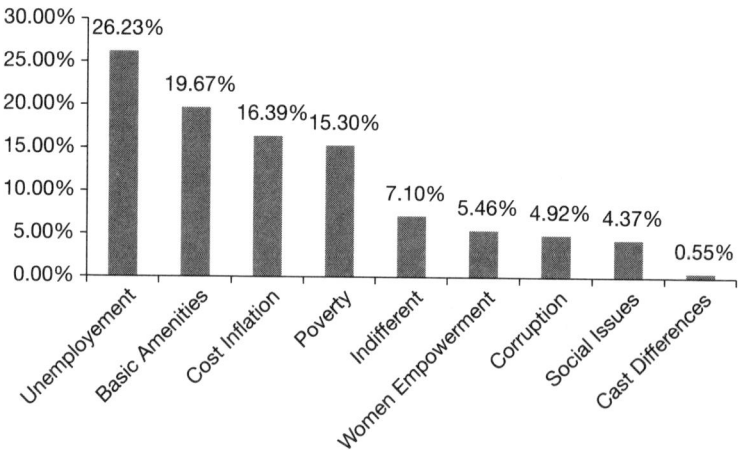

Figure 4.18 *Participants' Responses on Government Policies which May Enhance Happiness in People*

Table 4.16 Number and Percentage of Responses on Government Policies Which May Enhance Happiness

S. No.	Response Category	n (%)[a]
1.	Unemployment	48 (34.78)
2.	Basic amenities	36 (26.09)
3.	Cost inflation	30 (21.74)
4.	Poverty	28 (20.29)
5.	Indifferent	13 (9.42)
6.	Women empowerment	10 (7.25)
7.	Corruption	9 (6.52)
8.	Social issues	8 (5.80)
9.	Caste differences	1 (0.72)

Note: [a] Percentage of responses={Number of responses/Total number of participants (N=138)×100}

Poverty: This category included responses (20.29%) in which the participants spoke about dealing with poverty. For example, 'stop poorness of country', 'should care about poor people', 'should help poor people'.

Indifferent: Nearly 9.42 per cent responses on this question were categorized as 'indifferent' where participants had no interest in answering the question or gave vague replies or were not able to form an opinion regarding the same. Statements such as 'government should do as people want', 'nothing', 'government can't make any plan for happiness of all' and 'I have no opinion' were included in this category.

Women empowerment: This category accommodated responses (7.25%) where participants mentioned women empowerment or safety as their main concern. Statements such as 'make strict laws for rape', 'give good facilities to females and take them to front', 'make good laws for girls and take action on rape cases', 'government should provide security for girls', 'increase safety of girls', etc., were considered in this category.

Corruption: Responses (6.52%) such as 'should stop corruption and do care of all', 'government should finish corruption', etc., were included in this category.

Social issues: In about 5.80 per cent of responses, (8 responses) participants spoke about social issues like dowry, substance abuse and theft/robbery. For example, 'people are bad in the society, government should stop crime and ban alcohol', 'stop dowry system', 'government should take action on socially bad activities such as murder, theft and rapes'.

Caste differences: Only one response (0.72%) was found in this category, where the participant conveyed how government should do something about the prevailing caste system in society: 'put all castes in same position and make something that all castes have same profit'.

Section IV

Pearson's correlation analysis was conducted to find out the correlation between the scores on 0–10 Likert scale of Cantril Ladder patterned five questions on happiness and life satisfaction and the total score of IHS. IHS, which is based on 'relational harmony', was found to be significantly positively correlated with happiness (0.33, $p < 0.01$), life satisfaction (0.46, $p < 0.01$), and best possible life (0.35, $p < 0.01$; see Table 4.15). Happiness was found to be significantly correlated with future happiness (0.18, $p < 0.05$), life satisfaction (0.52, $p < 0.01$) and best possible life (0.39, $p < 0.01$). However, ideal happiness was not found to be correlated with these selected variables, except with life satisfaction (0.18, $p < 0.05$). Interestingly, life satisfaction and best possible life were found significantly correlated (0.60, $p < 0.01$) with each other (Table 4.17).

DISCUSSION

The present study explores how a layperson perceives happiness and life satisfaction with reference to his past, present and future. To reiterate, the study was divided into four sections, and likewise the results were discussed. The first section explored the participants' living and housing conditions, and how in general they perceive their standard of living. The second section explored participants' perception about happiness from various angles. The third section looked at differences between happiness and satisfaction (if any), while the fourth section of the study dealt with correlation among different measures used in the study.

Table 4.17 *Pearson's Correlation between the Questions on Happiness and Satisfaction (H) and IHS*

	H1	H2	H3	H4	H5	IHS Total
H1 (Happiness)	1	–	–	–	–	–
H2 (Ideal happiness)	0.13	1	–	–	–	–
H3 (Future happiness (after 5 years)	0.18[a]	–0.06	1	–	–	–
H4 (Life satisfaction)	0.52[b]	0.18[a]	0.09	1	–	–
H5 (best possible life)	0.39[b]	0.08	0.12	0.60[b]	1	–
IHS (Total)	0.33[b]	0.12	0.07	0.46[b]	0.35[b]	1
Mean	7.09	7.61	7.10	7.10	7.08	27.16
SD	2.46	2.24	2.43	2.54	2.23	7.23
N	138	138	136	138	138	128

Notes: [a] Correlation is significant at the 0.05 level (2-tailed)
[b] 0.01 level (2-tailed). N=range (128–138), and missing values were not replaced.

It was encouraging to find out that more than half (56.5%) of the participants in the study perceived their standard of living as average, and nearly 26 per cent perceived it to be reasonably or very comfortable. Only 12 per cent of the participants perceived it to be either below average or poor. Considering that majority of the participants were living in houses with basic necessities such as access to electricity (94.9%), flushing toilet and shower (78.3%), no leaking roof (68.1%) and were also debt free (65.2%), the results seem justified. Singh (2011) analysed the QoL in 21 districts of Haryana, based on seven indicators of housing and household amenities. Census of India (2011) was the data source for the study. Barring five districts, the remaining reported a high level of development with most of the residents having own house, tap water, electricity, a separate kitchen, closed drainage, LPG for cooking fuel, good bathroom (with roof and slab) and toilets (piped sewer system and septic tank). Kaur and Meenakshi (2015) studied the housing and household amenities in Haryana. According to their report, more than 90 per cent of households in Haryana in 2011 had access to electricity, more than 50 per cent had access to safe drinking water, while around 66.78 per cent had toilet facility at home, etc. Hence, results are broadly supported by the existing data.

The second section of the study dealt with happiness and satisfaction of participants in reference to their past, current and future life. As mentioned previously in the study, Gallup (2009) criteria of thriving, suffering and struggling was used for analysing responses on Cantril Scale. More than half of the participants were seen to be thriving with averages in all domains (happiness, ideal happiness, future happiness and life satisfaction) above seven. The top five happiness and satisfaction supporting factors that emerged in the study were (a) family, (b) work, (c) financial security, (d) health of self and family members and (e) positive interpersonal relationships. Apart from these, personal freedom and spirituality were also cited as reasons for being happy. The results of the study are in stark contrast to the findings of *World Happiness Report* (2016) where India ranked 118th out of 155 countries, and further slipped four notches at 122 as per *World Happiness Report* (2017). The present study was conducted in 15 villages of one of the 29 states of India (Haryana, which alone has 81 cities and towns and 6,759 villages; Census of India [2011]). Therefore, these findings cannot be compared to the findings of the *World Happiness Reports*. However, ample evidence exists that support the top five determinants of happiness and satisfaction that emerged in this study. For example, Shin, Suh, Eom and Kim (2017) explored Korean and American perception on happiness. Participants were prompted to give three words that their mind associated with happiness. For Koreans, 'family' was the most associated word for happiness, while it was 'friend' for Americans, thus underscoring the importance of healthy interpersonal relationships as a source of happiness. Another recent study from Brazil reported health, social support and economic situation as important predictors of happiness (Amorin, Franca, & Valentini, 2017). Anggraeny, Yuniarti, Moordiningsih and Kim (2016) enlisted several factors that contribute to happiness in their study on adolescents. These factors were family, achievement, love and be loved, spirituality, friendship and leisure time. Family and relationships were hailed as important elements in a study by DelleFave et al. (2016) pertaining to lay people's understanding of happiness. Antecedents of life satisfaction in Chilean workers revealed satisfaction with one's financial situation as the most important predictor, others being satisfaction with health, social relationships, one's self-worth, leisure-time, family and work (Loewe et al., 2014). Agyar (2013) reported a significant and positive correlation between perceived freedom for leisure and life satisfaction, while perceived good health was positively correlated with happiness (Sabatini, 2014). Llobet, Ávila, Farràs and Canut (2011) studied QoL, happiness and satisfaction in geriatric population cared for by a home health care service. Nearly 76.9 per cent of the people reported their QoL as good, with health, family and social relationships, and the ability to adapt emerging as the main reasons. In Japan National Survey on Lifestyle Preferences (2009), among many questions, participants' were asked to respond on factors they consider while judging their own happiness. In descending order, the following factors were reported: health, family relations, financial security, free time and leisure, job security, friends, a sense of purpose and social contribution/engagement, relationship with colleagues, community relations and others. Froh et el. (2007) examined the association among interpersonal relationships, irrational beliefs, and life satisfaction. Among many findings, interpersonal relationships were seen as the predictors of life satisfaction. In a review of various relevant studies from 1990 onwards, Dolan, Peasgood and White (2007) concluded poor health, separation, unemployment and lack of social support negatively correlate with SWB.

The study further explored a layperson's perception of happiness and satisfaction. Those who believed that the two differed considered happiness as external and short lived, while satisfaction was thought to be internal and long lived. Participants' reasons for not being satisfied with their lives again revolved around their family, work, health and interpersonal relationships. The study also explored the perception of people regarding government's role in influencing happiness of its people. Participants strongly believed that governmental policies strongly influence happiness in their day-to-day lives and that of community as a whole. They further believed that government intervention can lead to increased happiness by eradicating unemployment, providing people with basic amenities, controlling cost inflation, poverty, working towards women empowerment, decreasing corruption, addressing social issues and casteism. This sentiment has been found to be prevailing in previous studies as well. For example, Ott (2010) reported strong correlation between quality of governance and average happiness of citizens based on a comparison of 127 countries. Pankaj and Dorji (2004) looked at the happiness of Bhutanese individuals on several Gross National Health parameters. Among many factors, good governance also emerged as being responsible for people's happiness. In his study pertaining to cities' happiness, Ballas (2013), among other indicators, highlighted the impact of social and spatial inequalities and social justice on a city's well-being and happiness. In the latest *World Happiness Report* (2017), good governance among other factors such as caring, freedom, generosity, honesty, health and income was found as a cause of happiness for the top four countries.

Furthermore, the present study also found significant positive correlation between the measures of happiness and satisfaction used in the study (Cantril Ladder and IHS). In the past too, several studies have reported significant correlations between different modules of well-being. For example, Singh, Junnarkar and Jaswal (2016) reported significant and positive correlation of flourishing (Diener et al., 2010) and positive and negative feelings (SPANE; Diener et al., 2010) with mental health, which is composed of emotional, psychological and social well-being (Keyes, 2005). In another study, Perugini, Iglesia, Solano and Keyes (2017) reported a significant correlation of emotional well-being with satisfaction with life (SWLS; Diener, Emmons, Larsen, & Griffin, 1985), and the Positive and Negative Affect Scale (PANAS; Watson, Clark, & Tellegen, 1988). Further, a positive association of psychological well-being and Meaning in Life Questionnaire (MLQ; Steger, Frazier, Oishi, & Kaler, 2006) was also reported. The SWB subscale of Mental Health Continuum–Short Form (MHC-SF) showed a positive and significant correlation with the Well Being Index (WBI; Cummins, Eckersley, Pallant, & Davern, 2001). Singh, Kaur and Singh (2014) in their study on well being of rural women of Haryana reported a significant correlation between SWB and psychological well-being. Singh and Junnarkar (2015) in their study on predictors of positive mental health in children reported a significant and positive correlation of MHC-SF with SPANE P (Scale of Positive and Negative Experiences [Positive Feelings]), life satisfaction, personal well-being, flourishing and all four domains of QoL (physical health, psychological well-being, social relationships and environmental health). Hence, correlation between different modules of happiness is well supported in the research.

STRENGTHS, LIMITATIONS AND FUTURE DIRECTIONS

The strength of the present study lies in its implementation, mixed methodology approach and reporting. However, the study reports result as a whole, and not in the light of socio-demographic variables. It would be interesting if future studies may address this limitation and study the perception of people regarding happiness and satisfaction accordingly. While the results of this study were in stark contradiction to the *World Happiness Report*, it will not be surprising if notions of happiness also differ from one Indian state to another, as India is known for its cultural diversity and vast urban–rural divide. So, replicating this study within India or outside India might yield interesting results, and also encourage translational research. The study further highlights the role of government in affecting happiness of its people. Taking it as a pointer, further research and planning may be carried out in this direction as it may be of immense help to government and policymakers, if they have prior knowledge on what makes its citizens happy.

REFERENCES

Abdel-Khalek, A. M., & Lester, D. (2010). Personal and psychological correlates of happiness among a sample of Kuwaiti Muslim students. *Journal of Muslim Mental Health, 5*(2), 194–209.

Agyar, E. (2013). Life satisfaction, perceived freedom in leisure and self-esteem: The case of physical education and sport students. *Procedia—Social and Behavioral Sciences, 93,* 2186–2193.

Amorim, S. M., de FP França, L. H., & Valentini, F. (2017). Predictors of happiness among retired from urban and rural areas in Brazil. *Psicologia: Reflexão e Crítica, 30*(1), 2.

Anggraeny, A., Yuniarti, K., Moordiningsih, M., & Kim, U. (2016). Happiness orientations among adolescents raised in urban and rural areas. *Indigenous: Jurnal Ilmiah Psikologi, 13*(1). doi:10.23917/indigenous.v13i1.2312

Babinčák, P., & Parkanská, A. (2016). Religiosity and spirituality as predictors of subjectively perceived happiness in university students in Slovakia. *IAFOR Journal of Psychology & the Behavioral Sciences, 2*(1) 33–43.

Baetschmann, G. (2011). *Heterogeneity in the relationship between happiness and age: Evidence from the German socio-economic panel* (11 November). Retrieved from http://dx.doi.org/10.2139/ssrn.2021969

Bakhshipour, B., Panahiyan, S., Hasanzadeh, R., & Tamaddoni, A. (2013). Relationship between personality traits and happiness in patients with thalassemia. *Zahedan Journal of Research in Medical Sciences, 16*(11), 28–32.

Ballas, D. (2013). What makes a 'happy city'? *Cities, 32*, S39–S50.

Bojanowska, A., & Zalewska, A. M. (2016). Lay understanding of happiness and the experience of well-being: Are some conceptions of happiness more beneficial than others? *Journal of Happiness Studies, 17*(2), 793–815.

Bolier, L., Haverman, M., Westerhof, G. J., Riper, H., Smit, F., & Bohlmeijer, E. (2013). Positive psychology interventions: A meta-analysis of randomized controlled studies. *BMC Public Health, 13*(1), 119.

Cantril, H. (1965). *The pattern of human concerns*. New Brunswick, NJ: Rutgers University Press.

Cassel, R. N. (1954). Psychological aspects of happiness. *Peabody Journal of Education, 32*(2), 73–82.

Census of India. (2011). Retrieved from http://censusindia.gov.in/2011-prov-results/paper2/data_ files/india/Rural_Urban_2011.pdf

Clark, A. E., & Oswald, A. J. (1994). Unhappiness and unemployment. *The Economic Journal, 104*(424), 648–659.

Commission on Measuring Well-Being, Japan. (2011). *Measuring national well-being-proposed well-being indicators*. Retrieved from http://www5.cao.go.jp/keizai2/koufukudo/pdf/koufukudosia _english.pdf

Corrigan Doyle, E., Escobar-Tello, M., & Lo, K. P. Y. (2016). Exploring design for happiness in the home and implications for future domestic living. Paper presented at the 50th Anniversary DRS Conference 2016: Future-focused Thinking, Brighton, 27–30 June.

Cummins, R., Eckersley, J., Pallant, J., & Davern, M. (2001). *Australian Unity Wellbeing Index, Survey 2: Report 1*. Melbourne: Australian Centre on Quality of Life/Deakin University.

Cunado, J., & De Garcia, F. P. (2012). Does education affect happiness? Evidence for Spain. *Social Indicators Research, 108*(1), 1–12.

Datu, J. A. D., & Valdez, J. P. M. (2013). Exploring Filipino adolescents' conception of happiness. *International Journal of Research Studies in Psychology, 1*, 21–29. doi:10.5861/ijrsp.2012.251

DelleFave, A., Brdar, I., Wissing, M. P., Araujo, U., Solano, A. C., Freire, T., … Nakamura, J. (2016). Lay definitions of happiness across nations: The primacy of inner harmony and relational connectedness. *Frontiers in Psychology, 7*, 30.

DeRobertis, E. M. (2016). The phenomenology of happiness: Stephen Strasser's eidetic explication. *The Humanistic Psychologist, 44*(1), 72.

Diener, E. (1984). Subjective well-being. *Psychological Bulletin, 95*(3), 542–575.

Diener, E., Emmons, R. A., Larsen, R. J., & Griffin, S. (1985). The satisfaction with life scale. *Journal of Personality Assessment, 49*, 71–75.

Diener, E., & Lucas, R. E. (1999). Personality and subjective wellbeing. In D. Kahneman, E. Diener, & N. Schwarz (Eds.), *Wellbeing: The foundations of hedonic psychology* (pp. 213–229). New York, NY: Russell Sage Foundation.

Diener, E., Wirtz, D., Tov, W., Kim-Prieto, C., Choi, D. W., Oishi, S., … Biswas-Diener, R. (2010). New well-being measures: Short scales to assess flourishing and positive and negative feelings. *Social Indicators Research, 97*(2), 143–156.

Dolan, P., Peasgood, T., & White, M. (2008). Do we really know what makes us happy? A review of the economic literature on the factors associated with subjective well-being. *Journal of Economic Psychology, 29*(1), 94–122.

Fisher, C. D. (2010). Happiness at work. *International journal of management reviews, 12*(4), 384–412.

Froh, J. J., Fives, C. J., Fuller, J. R., Jacofsky, M. D., Terjesen, M. D., & Yurkewicz, C. (2007). Interpersonal relationships and irrationality as predictors of life satisfaction. *The Journal of Positive Psychology, 2*(1), 29–39.

Gallup. (2009). *World poll methodology* (Technical Report). Washington, DC: Gallup World Headquarters.

Gander, F., Proyer, R. T., Ruch, W., & Wyss, T. (2013). Strength-based positive interventions: Further evidence for their potential in enhancing well-being and alleviating depression. *Journal of Happiness Studies, 14*(4), 1241–1259.

Goodman, F. R., Disabato, D. J., Kashdan, T. B., & Kauffman, S. B. (2018). Measuring well-being: A comparison of subjective well-being and PERMA. *The Journal of Positive Psychology, 13*(4), 321–332.

Haraldsdóttir, K. T. (2015). *Determinants of happiness among secondary school students in Iceland.* Retrieved from http://hdl.handle.net/1946/22568

Helliwell, J., Layard, R., & Sachs, J. (2015). *World happiness report, 2015.* New York, NY: Sustainable Development Solutions Network.

Hitokoto, H., & Uchida, Y. (2015). Interdependent happiness: Theoretical importance and measurement validity. *Journal of Happiness Studies, 16*(1), 211–239.

Jaafar, J. L., Idris, M. A., Ismuni, J., Fei, Y., Jaafar, S., Ahmad, Z., … Sugandi, Y. S. (2012). The sources of happiness to the Malaysians and Indonesians: Data from a smaller nation. *Procedia—Social and Behavioral Sciences, 65*, 549–556.

Jones, H. M. (1953). *The pursuit of happiness.* Cambridge, MA: Harvard University Press.

Jones, R. E. (2013). Wisdom and happiness in *Euthydemus* 278–282. *Philosophers' Imprint, 13*(14), 1–21.

Joshanloo, M., & Weijers, D. (2014). Aversion to happiness across cultures: A review of where and why people are averse to happiness. *Journal of Happiness Studies, 15*, 717–735.

Kamvar, S., Mogilner, C., & Aaker, J. L. (2009). *The meaning(s) of happiness.* Stanford, CA: Graduate School of Business, Stanford University.

Kaur, S., & Meenakshi. (2015). Spatio-temporal study of housing and household amenities in Haryana. *SSARSC International Journal of Geo Science and Geo Informatics, 2*(1), 1–9.

Keyes, C. L. (2002). The mental health continuum: From languishing to flourishing in life. *Journal of Health and Social Behavior, 43*(2), 207–222.

Keyes, C. L. M. (1998). Social well-being. *Social Psychology Quarterly, 61*(2), 121–140.

———. (2005). Mental illness and/or mental health? Investigating axioms of the complete state model of health. *Journal of Consulting and Clinical Psychology, 73*, 539–548.

188 | Singh et al.

Khanna, V., Sharma, E., Chauhan, S., & Pragyendu. (2017). Effects of prosocial behavior on happiness and well-being. *The International Journal of Indian Psychology, 4*(2), 76–86.

Kumar, K. K. (2003). An Indian conception of well-being. In J. Henry (Ed.), *European positive psychology proceedings 2002.* Leicester, UK: British Psychological Society.

Laungani, P. D. (2006). *Understanding cross-cultural psychology: Eastern and Western perspectives.* London, UK: SAGE Publications.

Lee, Y. C., Lin, Y. C., Huang, C. L., & Fredrickson, B. L. (2013). The construct and measurement of peace of mind. *Journal of Happiness Studies, 14*(2), 571–590.

Levin, K. A., & Currie, C. (2014). Reliability and validity of an adapted version of the Cantril Ladder for use with adolescent samples. *Social Indicators Research, 119*(2), 1047–1063.

Llobet, M. P., Ávila, N. R., Farràs Farràs, J., & Canut, M. T. L. (2011). Quality of life, happiness and satisfaction with life of individuals 75 years old or older cared for by a home health care program. *Revista Latino-Americana de Enfermagem, 19*(3), 467–475.

Loewe, N., Bagherzadeh, M., Araya-Castillo, L., Thieme, C., & Batista-Foguet, J. M. (2014). Life domain satisfactions as predictors of overall life satisfaction among workers: Evidence from Chile. *Social Indicators Research, 118*(1), 71–86.

Luo, L., Gilmour, R., & Kao, S. F. (2001). Cultural values and happiness: An East–West dialogue. *The Journal of Social Psychology, 141*(4), 477–493.

Lyons, L. (2016). South Sudan, Haiti and Ukraine lead world in suffering. *Gallup World Poll, 2016.* Retrieved from http://www.gallup.com/poll/206891/south-sudan-haiti-ukraine-lead-world-suffering.aspx

Lyubomirsky, S., & Layous, K. (2013). How do simple positive activities increase well-being? *Current Directions in Psychological Science, 22*(1), 57–62.

Lyubomirsky, S., Sheldon, K. M., & Schkade, D. (2005). Pursuing happiness: The architecture of sustainable change. *Review of General Psychology, 9*(2), 111–131.

Malik, S., & Sadia. (2013). Gender differences in self-esteem and happiness among university students. *International Journal of Development and Sustainability, 2*(1), 445–454.

Mehrotra, S. (2013). Feeling good and doing well? Testing efficacy of a mental health promotive intervention program for Indian youth. *International Journal of Psychological Studies, 5*(3), 28.

O'Rourke, J., & Cooper, M. (2010). Lucky to be happy: A study of happiness in Australian primary students. *Australian Journal of Educational & Developmental Psychology, 10,* 94–107.

OECD. (2013). *Guidelines on measuring subjective well-being.* Paris: OECD Publishing. Retrieved from http://dx.doi.org/10.1787/9789264191655-en

Oishi, S., Graham, J., Kesebir, S., & Galinha, I. C. (2013). Concepts of happiness across time and cultures. *Personality and Social Psychology Bulletin, 39*(5), 559–577.

Okwaraji, F. E., Nduanya, C. U., Okorie, A., & Okechukwu, H. E. (2017). Personality traits, happiness and life satisfaction, in a sample of Nigerian adolescents. *JMR, 3*(6), 284–289.

Ott, J. (2010). Greater happiness for a greater number: Some non-controversial options for governments. *Journal of Happiness Studies, 11*(5), 631–647.

Palmore, E. B., & Luikart, C. (1972). Health and social factors related to life satisfaction. *Journal of Health and Social Behavior, 13*, 68–80.

Pankaj, P., & Dorji, T. (2004). Measuring individual happiness in relation to Gross National Happiness in Bhutan: Some preliminary results from survey data. 375–389. Retrieved from http://www.bhutanstudies.org.bt/publicationFiles/ConferenceProceedings/GNHandDevelopment/19.GNH&development.pdf

Perugini, M. L. L., de la Iglesia, G., Solano, A. C., & Keyes, C. L. M. (2017). The mental health continuum–short form (MHC–SF) in the Argentinean context: Confirmatory factor analysis and measurement invariance. *Europe's Journal of Psychology, 13*(1), 93.

Pishva, N., Ghalehban, M., Moradi, A., & Hoseini, L. (2011). Personality and happiness. *Procedia—Social and Behavioral Sciences, 30*, 429–432.

Proyer, R. T., Wellenzohn, S., Gander, F., & Ruch, W. (2015). Toward a better understanding of what makes positive psychology interventions work: Predicting happiness and depression from the person×intervention fit in a follow up after 3.5 years. *Applied Psychology: Health and Well Being, 7*(1), 108–128.

Rahayu, T. P. (2016). The determinants of happiness in Indonesia. *Mediterranean Journal of Social Sciences, 7*(2), 393.

Rao, C. R., Soans, S. J., Anjum, Z., Kumar, M., Kamath, A., & Shetty, A. (2017). Are rural adults happy? An observational study of happiness and its determinants. *International Journal of Community Medicine and Public Health, 4*(8), 2810–2815.

Ryff, C. D. (1989). Happiness is everything, or is it? Explorations on the meaning of psychological well-being. *Journal of Personality and Social Psychology, 57*(6), 1069.

Sabatini, F. (2014). The relationship between happiness and health: Evidence from Italy. *Social Science & Medicine, 114*, 178–187.

Seligman, M. E. P. 2011. *Flourish: A visionary new understanding of happiness and well-being.* New York, NY: Free Press.

Senasu, K., & Singhapakdi, A. (2018). Quality-of-life determinants of happiness in Thailand: The moderating roles of mental and moral capacities. *Applied Research in Quality of Life, 13*(1), 59–87.

Sharifzadeh, M., & Almaraz, J. (2014). Happiness and productivity in the workplace. *American Journal of Management, 14*(4), 19.

Sharma, N., & Gulati, J. K. (2014). Self-esteem and social support as predictors of happiness among adolescents living in socio-economic hardship. *Asian Journal of Home Science, 9*(2), 402–408.

———. (2015). Gender differences in happiness, self-esteem and personality traits in adolescents living in socio-economic hardship. *Adolescence, 54*(78), 75.

Shin, J. E., Suh, E. M., Eom, K., & Kim, H. S. (2017). What does 'happiness' prompt in your mind? Culture, word choice, and experienced happiness. *Journal of Happiness Studies, 19*(3), 1–14.

Singh, I. (2011). Pattern of availability of household amenities in Haryana 2011. *International Journal of Social Science and Humanities Research, 3*(1), 317–322.

Singh, K., Jain, A., & Singh, D. (2014). Satsang: A culture specific effective practice for well-being. In H. A. Marujo & L. M. Neto (Eds.), *Positive nations and communities: Collective, qualitative and cultural-sensitive processes in positive psychology* (pp. 79–100). Dordrecht: Springer.

Singh, K., & Jha, S. D. (2008). Positive and negative affect, and grit as predictors of happiness and life satisfaction. *Journal of the Indian Academy of Applied Psychology, 34*(2), 40–45.

Singh, K., & Junnarkar, M. (2014). Validation and effect of demographic variables on perceived quality of life by adolescents. *Asian Journal of Psychiatry, 12*, 88–94.

———. (2015). Correlates and predictors of positive mental health for school going children. *Personality and Individual Differences, 76*, 82–87.

Singh, K., Junnarkar, M., & Jain, A. (2017) Factors affecting mental health of North Indian adolescents. *Psychological Studies, 62*, 168–177. doi:10.1007/s12646-017-0398-6

Singh, K., Junnarkar, M., & Jaswal, S. (2016). Validating the Flourishing Scale and the scale of positive and negative experience in India. *Mental Health, Religion & Culture, 19*(8), 943–954.

Singh, K., Kaur, J., & Singh, D. (2014). Well-being of rural women in North India. *Journal of Indian Academy of Applied Psychology, 40*(1), 129–137.

Singh, K., Kaur, J., Singh, D., & Junnarkar, M. (2014). Socio-demographic variables affecting well-being: A study on Indian rural women. *Psychological Studies, 59*(2), 197–206.

Singh, K., Khanna, P., Khosla, M., Rapelly, M., & Soni, A. (2016). Revalidation of the Sat-Chit-Ananda Scale. *Journal of Religion and Health, 55*(6), 1–10.

Singh, K., Khari, C., Amonkar, R. S., Arya, N. K., & Kasav, S. (2013). Development and validation of a new scale: Sat-Chit-Ananda Scale. *International Journal on Vedic Foundations of Management, 1*(2), 102–122.

Singh, K., Mitra, S., & Khanna, P. (2016). Psychometric properties of Hindi version of peace of mind, harmony in life and Sat-Chit-Ananda Scales. *Indian Journal of Clinical Psychology, 43*(1), 58–64.

Singh, K., Ruch, W., & Junnarkar, M. (2014). Effect of the demographic variables and psychometric properties of the personal well-being index for school children in India. *Child Indicators Research, 7*(3), 1–15.

Singh, K., Singh, D., Junnarkar, M., Mitra, S., & Dayal, P. (2016). *Effect on well-being of spiritual practices among Elderly Rural Women.* Mid-Year Conference on Psychology, Spirituality and Religion, Society for the Psychology of Religion and Spirituality (APA Div. 36) and St. Joseph's College, New York, USA, 11–12 March.

Srivastava, A. K., & Misra, G. (2011). Cultural perspectives on nature and experience of happiness. In A. K. Dalal & G. Misra (Eds.), *New directions in health psychology* (pp. 109–131). New Delhi: SAGE Publications.

Stack, S., & Eshleman, J. R. (1998). Marital status and happiness: A 17-nation study. *Journal of Marriage and the Family, 60*(2), 527–536.

Steger, M. F., Frazier, P., Oishi, S., & Kaler, M. (2006). The meaning in life questionnaire: Assessing the presence of and search for meaning in life. *Journal of Counseling Psychology, 53*(1), 80–93.

Suh, E., & Koo, J. (2003). Comparing subjective well-being across cultures and nations. In S. J. Lopez & C. R. Snyder (Eds.), *Positive psychological assessment: A handbook of models and measures* (pp. 219–220). Washington, DC: American Psychological Association.

Takahashi, Y. (2015). Is happiness measurable across countries? *Mita Hyoron, 1189,* 26–31.

The Commission on Measuring Well-Being, Japan. (2011). *Measuring national well-being: Proposed well-being indicators.* Retrieved from http://www5.cao.go.jp/keizai2/koufukudo/pdf/koufukudosian_english.pdf

Tiefenbach, T., & Kohlbacher, F. (2013). *Happiness and life satisfaction in Japan by gender and age* (Working paper 13/2). German Institute for Japanese Studies (DIJ).

Uchida, Y., & Kitayama, S. (2009). Happiness and unhappiness in East and West: Themes and variations. *Emotion, 9*(4), 441.

Uchida, Y., Norasakkunkit, V., & Kitayama, S. (2004). Cultural constructions of happiness: Theory and empirical evidence. *Journal of Happiness Studies, 5*(3), 223–239.

Uchida, Y., & Ogihara, Y. (2012). Personal or interpersonal construal of happiness: A cultural psychological perspective. *International Journal of Wellbeing, 2*(4), 354–369.

Uchida, Y., & Oishi, S. (2016). The happiness of individuals and the collective. *Japanese Psychological Research, 58*(1), 125–141.

Veeraiah, C. (2015, February). The pursuit of happiness: An Advaita Vedanta perspective. Paper presented at the *Happiness and Hope1*, At Lisbon, Portugal. Retrieved from https://www.researchgate.net/publication/305703294_The_pursuit_of_happiness_An_Advaita_Vedanta_perspective

Vera-Villarroel, P., Celis-Atenas, K., Pavez, P., Lillo, S., Bello, F., Díaz, N., … López, W. (2012). Money, age and happiness: Association of subjective well-being with socio-demographic variables. *Revista Latinoamericana de Psicología, 44*(2), 155–163.

Watson, D., Clark, I. A., & Tellegen, A. (1988). Development and validation of brief measures of positive and negative affect: The PANAS scales. *Journal of Personality and Social Psychology, 54*(6), 1063–1070.

Ye, D., Ng, Y. K., & Lian, Y. (2015). Culture and happiness. *Social Indicators Research, 123*(2), 519–547.

Chapter 5

Role of Religious and Spiritual Practices in Mental Health

Swati Sharma and Kamlesh Singh

Indian culture is deeply rooted in religious and spiritual (R/S) practices wherein these practices play an important role in improving followers' health and quality of life. This chapter addresses the various ways in which religion and spirituality contribute to the promotion of overall well-being. It offers a sampling of different scientific researches that integrate psychology of religion and well-being with the individual having cultural overtones. It documents the role of different R/S practices, rituals, teachings, R/S leaders and related organizations in mental health. The gap between the scientific research and practice and suggestions for better accommodation of advocacy to science have also been discussed, along with an original qualitative investigation into the role of R/S practices in mental health of adherents.

INTRODUCTION

India is recognized for its rich and varied R/S climate. It is the birthplace of four major religions, namely, Hinduism, Sikhism, Buddhism and Jainism, and a home to many more such as Islam, Christianity, etc. (for national and world population distribution, see Table 5.1). It is also a birthplace of

Table 5.1 *Population Distribution Based on Six Major Religions in India*

Religion	World Population	Population in the India
Hinduism	1150 million (15.1%)	966 million (79.80%)
Sikhism	27 million (0.39%)	20.8 million (1.72%)
Buddhism	495 million (7%)	8.4 million (0.7%)
Jainism	10 million approx. (0.01%)	4.45 million (0.37%)
Islam	1800 million (24%)	172 million (14.23%)
Christianity	2200 million (31%)	27.8 million (2.30%)

Source: CIA: The World Factbook; Census of India (2011).

many spiritual organizations, such as Radha Soami Satsang Beas (RSSB), Art of Living Foundation, Osho Foundation, Brahma Kumaris and many others, that have strong following in the country. Hence, it should come as no surprise that Indians are rooted in rich ancient ethnic traditions and spiritual practices (Singh, Jain, & Singh, 2014), even more so, when it comes to mental health and related issues. Since ancient times, R/S leaders have held a very important position in shaping Indian society and influencing their followers' well-being. It was only with the arrival of British that establishment of mental asylums and hospitals occurred in India and that too mostly for the colonial rulers (Chadda, Patra, & Gupta, 2015). Even today, majority of people in India depend on alternative health care practices such as religion- and faith-based healing. Presence of such practices holds special importance in the context of a Third World nation like India, which still faces a considerable shortage of mental health care professionals; around 1 for over 200,000 (Thirunavukarasu & Thirunavukarasu, 2010); does not have a national health scheme for the citizens; and whose large share of the population falls in the low income bracket for whom indigenous healers are the primary help (Khandelwal, Jhingan, Ramesh, Gupta & Srivastava, 2009; Neki, 1979). Additionally, the exponentially rising costs of modern medicines and mental health services is making it increasingly more difficult for common people even in the developed countries (Gautam & Bansal, 2014). It is during these times of rapid change that the importance of community-based practices and traditional interventions is being recognized more than ever (Vedamurthachar, 2010).

Yet, there is relatively little understanding and inclusion of these practices in the scientific and clinical work. Among the many reasons for this is the focus of the discipline that until the last few decades was on mainstream psychology whereby comparatively less relevance was given to areas like religion and spirituality, which rested outside this domain. But lately, there is an emerging consensus on the importance of under-standing an individual's religious beliefs/faith and practices, especially in clinical and counselling settings because of the development in the fields of translational and indigenous research. Juthani (1998, p. 271) states, 'Just as one cannot treat the body without closely examining the mind, one cannot treat the disorders of the mind without understanding its spiritual dimension'. Researchers are beginning to explore the role of the therapist's understanding of a patient's R/S beliefs on therapeutic alliance and positive output of the therapy (Henderson, 2018). The role of religious advisors in mental health care was also recently examined (Kovess-Masfety et al., 2017). It has been stated that religion may play a role in transformation of patients who are explicitly religious, from a state of meaninglessness to one of meaningfulness (Mitra, 1994). Moreover, reli-gion and spirituality may form underlying dimensions of certain problems such as anxiety related to conflicting religious values, depression due to feelings of alienation from one's religion, etc., for which clients are seeking therapy (Singh & Madan, 2017). Thus, addressing client's R/S beliefs and providing services accordingly may be an important step in this direction.

In religiously diverse Indian society (Table 5.1), where people seek life guidance through different religious faiths, mental health professionals are likely to come across many people for whom religion is an integral part of their daily life. Therefore, it becomes imperative for researchers and practitioners to understand the intricate relationship between religion and mental health, and scientifically integrate this knowledge in clinical practice. The present chapter hence first addresses various ways in which religion and spirituality contribute to the promotion of human well-being, and then states how this knowledge can be integrated in modern mental health care divisions. It also documents scientific literature on spiritual practices, religious rituals and interventions promoting mental health, especially in the Indian setting, and the ways to integrate fine research with clinical and conventional practices in our mental health care divisions. We begin by defining the terms religion and spirituality, and briefly addressing the debate of religion vs. spirituality in order to offer a better perspective for the later parts of the chapter.

RELIGION AND SPIRITUALITY

Several theorists have attempted to define religion and spirituality; yet, until date, there is no single definition that has been widely accepted. Therefore, in our effort to understand the constructs, and define them within the purview of our chapter, we present certain past and present definitions of religion and spirituality (Table 5.2) in sequential order from the year 1938–2018.

Traditionally in psychology, religion was defined as a broad construct, which constituted all personal and social, objective and subjective, and good and bad elements. Then came a shift in meanings during the 1990s. As noted by Zinnbauer and Pargament (2005, p. 24), modern emphasis at their most extreme 'place a substantive, static, institutional, objective, belief-based, "bad" religiousness in opposition to a functional, dynamic, personal, subjective, experience-based, "good" spirituality". This can be well contrasted in the definitions provided.

Religion on one hand was viewed as involving rituals, beliefs, experiences and customs of groups connected to the perceived transcendent entity such as God or Allah (Koenig, 2012), and was quantified primarily through social and doctrinal perspective (Miller, 1998). Spirituality, on the other hand, was related to the individual and was considered lacking the institutionalized aspect of religion (Saroglou, 2014). This change has been associated with a broader cultural shift towards increased individualism and hostility towards traditional authority and organizations (e.g., Hood, 2003).

It was noted though that polarization of these constructs does not fit well with the experience of most people (Pargament, 2007; Zinnbauer & Pargament, 2005). Most people do not see any conflict between religion and spirituality. As noted by Bowen (2018), there is ample diversity in the world when it comes to the concept of religion and spirituality, and most people make sense of it through their own experiences and commitments.

Table 5.2 *Definitions of Religion and Spirituality*

Author	Definitions
Jung (1938, p. 8)	Religion is 'the attitude peculiar to a consciousness which has been altered by the experience of the numinosum'.
Clark (1958, p. 22)	Religion is defined as 'The inner experience of the individual when he senses a Beyond, especially as evidenced by the effect of this experience on his behavior when he actively attempts to harmonize his life with the Beyond'.
Argyle and Beit-Hallahmi (1975, p. 1)	Religion is 'a system of beliefs in a divine or superhuman power, and practices of worship or other rituals directed towards such a power'.
Vaughan (1991, p. 105)	Spirituality is said to be 'a subjective experience of the sacred'.
Doyle (1992, p. 303)	Religion is defined as concrete 'practices carried out by those who profess a faith'.
	Spirituality is defined as 'the search for existential meaning'.
Emblen (1992, p. 42)	Religiousness is 'a system of organized beliefs and worship which a person practices'.
	Spirituality is 'a personal life principle which animates a transcendent quality of relationship with God'.
Pargament, 1997, p. 32).	Religion is the 'search for significance in ways related to the sacred'.
	Spirituality is the 'search for sacred'.
Streib and Hood (2013, pp. 141, 146)	Religion is the symbolic and ritual, thus social construction of experiences of 'great' transcendences in terms of ultimate concern.
	Spirituality 'is essentially an unchurched mysticism'.
Bowen (2018)	Religion from a practitioners' point of view is a combination of common modern experience and their own particular commitments. There is. so far, no definition broad enough to work for the wide range societies

Source: Authors.

Thus, it brings back the conversation to unified R/S construct. Especially in pluralistic cultures, where religion is practiced in many different forms. Copland, Mabbett, Roy, Brittlebank and Bowles (2012) stated that religion and spirituality are equated. Religion, as they state, is defined as 'local customs', 'quest for salvation' and 'code for social morality' (p. 42).

Rao and Paranjpe (2016) also noted that in Indian tradition, there is no absolute divide between *saṁsāra* (the secular) and spirituality. Indian religious teachings explain human journey as one from the ordinary to the exceptional, from transactional excellence in observation and thinking to transcendental experience of pure conscious states. Further, they don't strictly segregate the outcomes based on different paths. Rigveda, one of the holy books of Hinduism, states, 'Truth is one, but the wise speak of it in different ways' (*ekam sad viprā bahudhā vadanti*).

Taking all of this into consideration, we believe religion and spirituality (R/S) cannot be considered as separate constructs, especially in the Indian setting. Rather, spirituality is one of the outcomes of religion. Spirituality can exist outside the domains of religion, but it nevertheless forms a significant part of religions and religious practices.

RELIGION, SPIRITUALITY AND MENTAL HEALTH: EXISTING PRACTICES AND SCIENTIFIC LITERATURE

Religion and spirituality are known to play a vital role in adherents' well-being and overall mental health. They are said to be associated with various positive mental health facets such as well-being, hope, optimism (Koenig, 2012), positive coping skills (Mohr et al., 2011; Zenkert, Brabender, & Slater, 2014), meaning in life (Park, 2005), and decrease in depression and anxiety (Smith, Bartz, & Richards, 2007). This relationship between R/S and different mental health outcomes are mediated by social, emotional and cognitive resources (Krause & Hayward, 2014; Van Cappellen, Toth-Gauthier, Saroglou, & Fredrickson, 2016). It was noted that participation in R/S activities and related social externalities positively impact well-being of adherents; association with a religion endorses purpose in life; people coping with issues such as aging, health shocks and adverse circumstances among others find psychological assurance in R/S faiths (Graham & Crown, 2014). The following sections present

different ways in which religion and spirituality influences mental health
of adherents, and how this knowledge can be integrated with the mainstream psychology of mental health care.

TRADITIONAL HEALING IN INDIA

India is a country of healers (Kakkar, 2012), where people still prefer to
approach traditional healers such as gurus, shamans, tantrics, and *ojhas*
for a variety of social, mental and personal problems (Chadda et al., 2001;
Dabi, 2017). The rapid progress in modern medicine has little affected
the popularity of these traditional systems (Sen & Chakraborty, 2017).
There is also a presence of religious institutions such as Balaji Mandir and
Teen Pahadi Mandir (temples in Rajasthan, a state in the north-west of
India), and Hazrat Nizamuddin Dargah (shrine of a Sufi saint) which are
dedicated to faith healing. Faith healing is a form of traditional healing that
refers to a 'concept that religious belie for faith can bring about healing—
either through prayers or rituals that, according to adherents, evokes
a divine presence and power towards correcting disease and disability'
(Bathna, Chandna, Bathna, & Kaloiya, 2015, p. 48). Devotees visit these
places along with their family members to get rid of a *sankat* (crisis/danger)
that they believe is encircling them (Siddiqui, Lacroix, & Dhar, 2014).

It is important to understand that people still believe in supernatural
causes of mental illness, and what works for faith healers is that they often
base their practice on the mediating role of emotions between religion and
well-being. It has also been reported that clients are more satisfied with
traditional healers as they spend much more time with them (Sharma,
Das, & Deshpande, 2006). The authors found no comparative study of
the cost of mental health care in traditional versus modern setting. Even
with the Mental Health Care Bill, 2013 and other ambitious plans to
bring down the cost of mental health care for people who cannot afford
it, there is still a long way to go in making it free of cost (Chadda et al.,
2015; Kala, 2013). Due to high demand and limited numbers of doctors
in government facilities, mainly visited by low-income population, time
given by health care professionals per patient is extremely less; moreover,
private facilities are beyond their financial reach. What makes matters
worse is the absence of government mental health divisions in rural areas,

making it inaccessible to 70 per cent of the population living in rural areas (Census of India, 2011).

COMMUNAL RITUALS AND FESTIVALS

Culturally embedded religious traditions and spiritual practices are found to play a significant role in elevating human strengths and well-being. They enhance the sense of community (Sohi, Singh, & Bopanna, 2017) and establish social order (dharma), which enhances social well-being of the participants. Dharma, in Indian context, plays an important role, and it is integrated in religion by various scholars (Copland et al., 2012).

Most festivals such as Diwali, Holi, Eid, Christmas are relatively small to modest size gatherings (Young & Sarin, 2014), wherein people perform a puja or socially exchange gifts and sweets which brings a family and community together. Social involvement in one's community has been previously associated with enhancement of social well-being (Cicognani et al. 2008; Sohi et al., 2017).

Festivals such as Karva Chauth (Hindu festival where married women in northern India fast from sunrise to moonrise for the safety and longevity of their husbands) and Raksha Bandhan (Indian festival where typically female siblings tie a holy thread called *rakhi* on the wrist of a male sibling as a form of ritual protection) strengthen interpersonal relationships.

Kshama Divas (forgiveness day), celebrated in Jainism, promotes forgiveness; region-specific harvest festivals such as Lohri and Makar Sankranti (traditionally honour family elders by giving them presents and distribute a portion of the harvest) celebrated in the northern states of India, Punjab and Haryana, respectively, and many more promote values such as gratitude and love. Sharma and Singh (2018) state that the virtues such as gratitude, forgiveness and altruism mediate the positive relationship between R/S and well-being.

Participation in *satsang*—an Indian practice of listening to *pravachan* (virtuous messages) as part of a group—develops a sense of community among the listeners/followers. Singing of folk songs (*bhajans*) in *satsang* (Singh et al., 2014; Singh, Sigroha, Singh, & Shokeen, 2017) enhances well-being. A study conducted on rural women of India (Singh et al.,

2014) participating as a group to sing songs carrying religious messages and positive virtues found that this practice not only liberates them from their day-to-day stressors but also leads to enhancement of well-being in the participants. Elderly women in rural settings are found to especially benefit from participation in pre-existing R/S practices in their society (e.g., *satsang*, Radha Soami and Brahma Kumari; Singh et al., 2016). It is said that social participation in the community and communal rituals enhances a sense of community, shared identity and relationality, which further benefits an individual by providing her with a sense of belonging and social inclusion (Cicognani et al., 2008; Derrett, 2003; Khan et al., 2014; Sohi et al., 2017).

R/S LEADERS AND ORGANIZATIONS

R/S organizations work on the same principles as that of institutionalized religion. Just as religious affiliation and endorsement offers one social support from the fellow followers, a positive sense of self, a sense of shared values with a socially valued community and a sense of belonging (Brodsky, 2000; Krause & Hayward, 2013), by being associated with a R/S organization or leader, most people benefit from enhanced social integration and social support from the leaders and associated group members (Krause & Hayward 2013; Strawbridge, Shema, Cohen, & Kaplan, 2001).

Most R/S gurus (teachers/leaders) and organizations work on the same philosophy. The Sant Nirankari Mission identifies itself as an all-embracing spiritual movement dedicated to human welfare. The Art of Living foundation recognizes itself as a humanitarian movement dedicated towards world peace. Such organizations inculcate a sense of shared values with a socially relevant community and a sense of meaning and purpose in life among its adherents, which in turn are linked to positive functioning (Kim-Prieto, 2014; Steger & Frazier, 2005) and perceived control (Levin, 2010). Sense of belonging, meaning and purpose shield the followers against the adverse effects of discrimination and other undesirable life circumstances (e.g., Jasperse, Ward, & Jose, 2012; Lechner, Tomasik, Silbereisen, & Wasilewski, 2013).

RSSB is an organization that identifies itself as a systematic method of god realization and a school of practical training in right living

(Radha Soami Satsang Beas, 2019). They propagate teachings of saints (*sant mat*), importance of service (*sewa*, e.g., offering physical, monetary or intellectual help to others) and spirituality (Mitra, 2012). A routine involving eating simplest and purest nourishments (vegetarian diet), earning an honest living and following high ethical and moral life is also fostered (Radha Soami Satsang Beas, 2019).

Brahma Kumaris is another such organization dedicated to personal transformation. It is spread over 110 countries, in all continents, and imparts lessons on positive thinking, stress management and higher goals of transcendence, focusing less on the material world and more on spirituality. It also teaches Raj yoga—a form of meditation—which has been correlated with various positive health outcomes (Kiran et al., 2017; Sharma et al., 2018).

Another practice from Sahaj Marg, Heartfulness Meditation, is a unique heart-based system with key practices such as cleaning and meditation, which is aided by yogic transmission. Arya, Singh and Malik (2017a, 2017b) reported that after five days of Heartfulness Meditation sessions, there were significant positive changes in various mental health indicators such as mental health, flourishing, positive experiences *sat-chit-ananda* (truthful–consciousness–bliss) and significant reduction in depression and negative emotions.

R/S TEXTS AND TEACHINGS

The Indian perspective uses the Sanskrit word, *swastha*, for health that means 'established in oneself' or 'self-abiding'. *Swastha* does not dichotomize the material and spiritual (Dalal & Misra, 2006). Therefore, it indicates the relevance of R/S in enhancing well-being especially in Indian culture which focuses on lifeworld (Jha, 2011; Joshi, Kumari, & Jain, 2008).

Concepts of personality and emotions are present in Indian religious and philosophical texts, in forms such as *vikaras* (vices), for example, *kama* (lust), *krodha* (anger), *moha* (attachment), *lobha* (greed) and *ahankara* (pride/ego), *sat-chit-ananda* (Sat meaning being truthful; chit refers to being aware and ananda being the bliss), *trigunas* (three traits), for example, *sattva* (goodness), *rajas* (passion), *tamas* (darkness), etc. They play an important role in a person's health and behaviour. Sharma and Singh (2016) found *vikaras* (vices) as negatively correlated in well-being. Sat-chit-ananda and its factors were found to be significantly positively correlated with flourishing and positive experiences and were negatively correlated with negative experiences (Singh, Khanna, Khosla, Rapelly, & Soni, 2016).

With the recent advancements in development and validation of psychometric assessments for these indigenous constructs (e.g., Raina & Singh, 2015; Sharma & Singh, 2016; Singh, Khari, Amonkar, Arya, & Kumar, 2013), the Indian perspective of health and related constructs can now be used for advancement in health psychology. With the growth in indigenous psychology, Asian researchers are exploring various community-based practices that can be standardized from a research and clinical application perspective. Varied perspectives in health are being considered for more holistic approach towards mental health.

YOGA AND MENTAL HEALTH

Yoga is an ancient discipline designed to bring balance and health to the physical, mental, emotional and spiritual dimensions of the individual (Sengupta, 2012). It is derived from the Sanskrit root '*yuj*', which means to connect, join or balance. It symbolizes union of a person's consciousness with the universal divine consciousness. This state of enlightened consciousness is referred to as *samadhi*.

Yoga has been practiced in India since centuries and is probably the most famous Hindu philosophical system in the world. There are various forms of yoga, such as *ashtanga yoga, hatha yoga, bikram yoga, kundalini yoga,* etc. *Ashtanga yoga* is one of the most popular forms of yoga. It is known for its eight branches *yama* (universal ethics), *niyama* (individual ethics), *asana* (body postures), *pranayama* (breathing exercises), *pratyahara* (control of the senses), *dharana* (concentration), *dhyana* (meditation) and *samadhi* (bliss). *Pranayama* (breathing exercises) is practiced by the people of all age groups as a part of their daily routine. Its practice is found to positively influence multiple systems in the body, including respiratory system, autonomic nervous system, stress, anxiety level, over all emotional status of the practitioner, etc. (Kuppusamy, Kamaldeen, Pitani, Amaldas,

& Shanmugam, 2017; Sengupta, 2012). *Iyengar Yoga* is a form of *Hatha Yoga*, which also places emphasis on *pranayama* (breathing exercises). Its practice requires detail, precision and alignment in *pranayama* and *asanas* (the performance of posture) for the development of strength and stability. Intervention of Iyengar Yoga and coherent breathing is said to decline depressive symptoms in patients suffering from major depressive disorder (Streeter et al., 2017).

Yoga is also said to benefit patients with hypertension (Misra et al., 2018; Murugesan, Govindarajalu, & Bera, 2000), heart failure (Mahajan, Reddy, & Sachdeva, 1999), mood disorders (Lavey et al., 2005) and diabetes (Chimkode, Kumaran, Kanhere, & Shivanna, 2015; Muthuselvi, Dhanalakshmi, & Abhishek, 2017). Especially when it comes to senior citizens, yoga interventions have been found to impact both health-related quality of life and mental well-being (Tulloch, Bombell, Dean, & Tiedemann, 2018). It has been concluded by various researchers that yoga and yogic breathing exercises may form additional non-pharmacological resources to improve health-related issues (Domingues, 2018; Misra et al., 2018). Based on this, many practicing organizations and professionals have devised integrated yoga therapies to help people of different age groups and professions deal with stress and enhance mental functioning. An example of one such technique is integrated stress management programme called Self-Management of Excessive Tension (SMET), offered at Swami Vivekananda Yoga Anusandhana Samsthana University, Bangalore. They aim at combating modern lifestyle problems related to race against time, technology and target stress, anxiety and depression, thereby help create a holistic way of living in health, harmony and happiness. Impact of SMET on improvement in mental health and possibly on 'executive efficiency' has been reported recently by Ganpat and Nagendra (2011) in their study on 72 managers. Positive associations of such lifestyle interventions based on yoga with an individual's subjective well-being has also been reported by other researchers (Sharma, Gupta, & Bijlani, 2008). *Sudarshan kriya*, a breathing exercise routine developed by Art of Living, has been found to positively improve different health-related outcomes, including depression, anxiety, substance abuse, insomnia and PTSD (Vedamurthachar, 2010; Zope & Zope, 2013). Scientific researches in the past have associated yoga and transcendental meditation to reduced aggression and violence (Hunnicutt & Rhodes, 2015), improved academic performance (Kauts & Sharma, 2009), treatment of drug abuse and alcoholism (Gryczynski et al., 2018; O'Connell & Alexander, 2014), and improvement in self-efficacy and perceived stress (Goldstein, Nidich, Goodman, & Goodman, 2018; Satyapriya, Nagendra, Nagarathna, & Padmalatha, 2008). Fleischman (2013) reported that *vipassana* meditation can also be utilized as an effective therapeutic tool in psychological and psychosomatic illnesses.

The advantage and reason of popularity of such practices is their cost-effectiveness and secularity. They are easy to integrate in diverse community care models (Gautam & Jain, 2010). Probably this is the reason that it is common for even allopathic doctors in India to prescribe such exercises for holistic well-being.

Ayurveda and Unani in combination with yoga and breathing exercises are also said to improve individual well-being (Behere, Das, Yadav, & Behere, 2013). Ayurveda is an ancient system of Indian medicine, which literally means science of life. It is a complete system of medicine that deals with holistic health of an individual. Unani is a Greek system of medicine which got incorporated in the Indian system of medicine with the rule of the Mughal. Although not directly related to R/S, they have their roots in ancient traditions and hence attract population that has a deep-seated connection to indigenous medicine. Health, in this Indian system of medicine, is not considered merely as an absence of physical or mental illness rather is outlined as a pursuit of achieving physical, mental and spiritual well-being (Manohar, 2013). Furthermore, mental health and quality of life are considered as outcomes of individual as well as group effort, thus, resonating more with the Indian psyche, which is collectivist in nature. They are also comparatively easily accessible in remote areas, and hence more popular among the masses. Many researchers have reported their relevance in promoting positive mental health. Gautam and Jain (2010) reported that certain Ayurvedic combinations such as *vacha* (*Acorus calamus*) and jyotishmati (*Celastrus panniculatus*) are used in treatment of anxiety and depression, reports of which they state can be availed from National Institute of Ayurveda, Jaipur. They further stated, 'Unmad Bhanjan Ras a combination of 24 compounds was found to have anti-psychotic effect equivalent to chlorpromazine' (p. S312). Moreover, simple home remedies, such as milk, head and foot massage, and sleep hygiene propositions like *shirodhara*, have been found to have indirect evidences of their effectiveness in management of sleep disorders (Vinjamury, Vinjamury, Martirosian, & Miller, 2014). A thorough review for the possible integration of the alternative schools of medicine with mainstream medicine has been demanded by scholars in translational research (Rastogi, 2018).

GAP BETWEEN SCIENTIFIC RESEARCH AND PRACTICE

With the widespread discontentment in the Western psychology and modern psychotherapies, there is now more than ever a resurgence of interest in understanding and acknowledging the contributions of alternative health care systems in combating physical and mental illness. Being the land of folk wisdom and traditional knowledge, India has much to offer in this respect. Deciphering this knowledge and examining its import to enhance therapeutic services can contribute a lot. All we need is to develop methodologies and mindsets to learn from this rich heritage.

Currently, practitioners are known to rely on either age-old set standard therapies or using common knowledge. This impacts the quality of psychological aid available to people in both prevention and therapeutic strategies. Like other sciences, psychology faces the problem of a huge gap between empirical research and conventional practice.

One of the reasons for this is that despite extensive literature assessing correlations or associations between R/S and mental health, few studies have investigated the clinical applicability of this evidence through controlled clinical trials (Gonçalves, Lucchetti, Menezes, & Vallada, 2015). And even these studies suffer from various irregularities. For example, Paukert, Phillips, Cully, Romero and Stanley (2011) noted there was inconsistency in how religion was incorporated into therapy in one of the researches. The sample characteristics were restricted (e.g., most participants were females from university or hospital psychiatric clinics), limiting generalization of results to broader populations. Various scholars have also identified a lack of scientific rigor in the research in this domain

(Aten & Worthington Jr, 2009; Bonelli & Koenig, 2013). The sample sizes of studies tend to be small, and there is a lack diversity of populations. Most researches are centred on Christian traditions and Western cultures (Richards, 2012; Watts, 2012). It is imperative to consider the cultural wisdom and indigenous traditions of the East to broaden and strengthen literature in this field.

It is also important to investigate the role of cultural factors such as types of stresses confronted by different racial and ethnic groups, whether they seek help, what types of help they seek, and what types of coping styles and social support they possess (Brekke, Ell, & Palinkas, 2007). It is more so relevant in India where caste-based discrimination is still prevalent. The road to optimizing mental health care in the country cannot be paved by a single discipline. It is, hence, vital for sociologists, economists, policy researchers, social workers and psychologists to make concerted efforts to bridge the gap between science and practice in mental health care in India.

The following research is a small attempt in this area to explore the role of religion and religious practices in adherents' well-being from psychological point of view.

R/S PRACTICES AND MENTAL HEALTH: A QUALITATIVE INVESTIGATION

A qualitative study was conducted to explore perceptions of followers about role of religion and spirituality in promoting virtues and well-being.

Participants

The sample consisted of 30 adult participants aged 30–60 years (M = 40.97, SD = 9.61), residing in Delhi–NCR region. The participants belonged to six major religions found in India (5 per religion, namely, Hinduism, Islam, Christianity, Sikhism, Buddhism and Jainism). Data was collected using focused group discussions (FGDs). Participants were briefed about the nature of the study, and there was voluntary participation in the study.

Measure

FGD schedule: FGD was conducted on the following questions: 'What are the positive virtues promoted by your religion (any spiritual saying, text, festival, ritual, commandment, duty, etc.) and how?' 'What are the positive virtues promoted by different religions (any spiritual saying, text, festival, ritual, commandment, duty, etc.)? Kindly name the virtues, religions and practices?' 'What is it about religion and religious practices that contribute to your positive mental health and happiness?'

Procedure

A group of five participants belonging to same religion participated in an FGD. Six FGDs were conducted at six different locations, mostly a community centre or a place of worship (or equivalent). After initial rapport formation, participants were asked to express their views on the three different questions in FGD schedule.

Results

Content analysis revealed different virtues perceived as being promoted by different religion in India. The themes/virtues are presented in Figure 5.1.

Hindu participants reported different festivals such as Nirjala Ikadashi (a festival in summers where water and cold water-based drinks are distributed among people on the streets), Makar Sakranti (a festival where cereals and clothes are donated among other rituals), Dussehra (the festival occurs twice a year; in summers, it is a ritual to donate hand fans, fruits and cold water-based drinks), which promote *daan* (charity). Sikhs reported a religious practice of a 24-hour *langar* (a communal free meal) in *gurudwaras* (the Sikh place of worship). People also indulge in *sewa* (selfless service) wherein they voluntarily offer their services to *gurudwaras*, for example, cooking and serving food at *langar* (communal free meal).

Participants reported feeling and expressing gratitude towards god everyday via daily prayers and weekly fasts. Gratitude towards girls/females was reported in Hinduism as being expressed via festivals like Navratri (nine days of fasting) and rituals like Kanjak Pujan (worshiping young

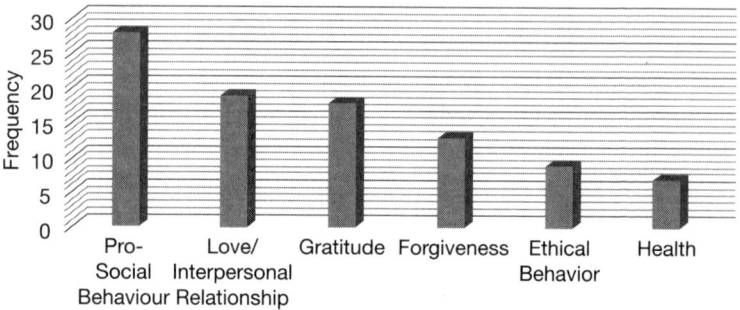

Figure 5.1 *Perceived Impact of Religion among Adherents*
Source: Authors.

girls as symbolic goddesses). It was also reported that during festivals like Sakat Chauth, gratitude is expressed towards elders of the family. *Sakat Chauth mein puja karke unko khana aur bayena dete hai, ya kuch cheez la kar dete hai* (In Sakat Chauth, we worship the almighty and present delicacies and a small token like money or gift as a gesture of respect and gratitude to our elders).

Some religion-oriented festivities, such as Makar Sakranti (Hinduism) where participants reported '*apne ruthe saas sasur ko manate hai aur kuch taufa dete hai*' (In Makar Sakranti, we seek forgiveness and conciliate our in-laws with gifts), Shab-e-Barat (Islam) where it was expressed that '*Allah se apne gunahon ki maafi maangte hai*' (seek forgiveness from Allah, the Almighty, for any wrongdoing) and Kshama Divas (Jainism) in which people seek forgiveness from others they might have intentionally or unintentionally wronged or caused pain, promote seeking forgiveness as a virtue.

Gratitude was reported as a parent virtue at many different instances during the discussion. For example, while talking about *sewa* and charity, one of the Sikh participants said, '*humare pass jo kuch bhi hai babaji ki kripa se hai. Toh unke liye humko wapis karna chahiye*', (whatever we have today is given by the almighty and hence we should do something for him as well).

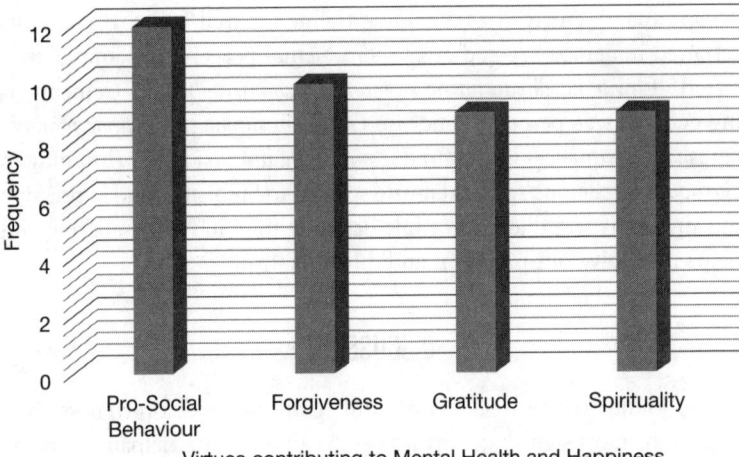

Figure 5.2 *Perceived Virtues Contribute to Mental Health and Happiness*

Source: Authors.

Thematic analysis further revealed the virtues that participants perceived as contributing to their positive mental health and happiness. The themes along with frequency are presented in Figure 5.2.

Participants reported prosocial behaviour as a major contributor to their positive mental health and happiness. When one of the participants said, '*Sewa bhav se mann ko shanti militi hai*' (the feeling of selfless service leads to mental peace), it met with other participants' affirmation as well. It was also conveyed that religious community practices such as praying for others, providing for the needy and charity for the poor enhanced their well-being.

Forgiving someone and seeking forgiveness was also expressed as contributing to their mental health positively.

Expressing gratitude towards others in the weekly ritual of expressing thanks in church and in general was also reported as enhancing well-being.

Spirituality emerged as a guiding theme for well-being. Participants reported remembering god gives them mental peace. For example, they stated, *'Ishwar ka dhyan karne se mann ko shanti militi hai'* (remembering god gives us peace of mind) or *'Gurubani sun'ne se aur apne mann ki pareshani dhyan mein vyakt karne se pareshani dur ho jati hai'* (listening to Gurubani—religious/spiritual music specific to Sikhism—and expressing our problems and dilemmas while listening to it and remembering god helps us resolve our problems and dilemmas).

DISCUSSION

It was found that prosocial behaviour, gratitude and forgiveness were among the most significant virtues perceived by the participants as being promoted by different religions. It was also found that the three virtues along with spirituality were considered as major contributors to their positive mental health by the participants. Past researchers have noted that the relationship of R/S with well-being strengthens and weakens depending on the cultural context (Bond, Lun, & Li, 2012; Diener, Tay, & Myers, 2011). The cultures where socialization of religious faith is more common, this relationship thrives more (Lun & Bond, 2013). Indian culture celebrates different socially embedded religious traditions that promote positive virtues such as prosocial behaviour, altruism, forgiveness and oneness, as also stated by the participants. This further strengthens the relationship between religion and positive mental health of participants. It can also be said that the ability to find answers through religion acts as an important support to an individual's well-being and happiness. Spirituality induced by various religious rituals and practices plays a central role in further promoting positive virtues in individuals. Interestingly, in India, rarely do we find a community without any folk or traditional beliefs.

This research is hence useful in integrating the common practices promoting mental health with mainstream research. It has been realized that practising psychologists do not have sufficient knowledge to alleviate a client's psychological suffering (Tashiro & Mortensen, 2006). Meaningful programmes for the community, which also have necessary scientific merit, are much needed. The present research explores how participants' well-being is impacted by different R/S practices, and how various rituals and traditions impact their psyche. Positive emotions form an important mediator in religion and well-being relationship (Van Cappellen et al., 2016), and should be taken into consideration in both scientific researches and client-centred therapies.

Although recent advancements have begun highlighting such research areas, there is a scope for much more work. The concluding section presents further suggestions for integration of R/S practices in clinical work and translational research.

From Advocacy to Science

1. Many mental health professionals and psychotherapists have started accommodating secular treatments to R/S perspectives in the wake of evidence suggesting that some clients highly value their R/S commitments. R/S interventions and exercises relevant to clients' beliefs and practices have also been used and studied in discussions related to faith, purpose and meaning (Pargament & Saunders, 2007). For example, relaxation exercises involving imagery consistent with a client's beliefs were studied by Barrera, Zeno, Bush, Barber and Stanley (2012). The role of spirituality-based interventions for therapists, involving alternate practices such as prayer, music therapy, etc., have also been discussed (Dyer & Hagedorn, 2013, Nyer et al., 2013). Religion-accommodative cognitive therapy is the new area of exploration for both researchers and practitioners. The shortcomings of these woks as discussed previously are that they need to expand the horizon to include the Eastern perspectives. It is also essential that practitioners in the Eastern settings focus on the lifeworld along with textbook guidelines. Based on the same, we enlist following suggestions for accommodating religion and spirituality in clinical practice.
   Suggestions for practice: There is a need to teach religious–spiritual issues to psychological trainees and mental health practitioners. Religion and spirituality are nearly ubiquitous in human life, and mental illness afflicts approximately 300 million people globally (WHO, 2017). There is no country where religion or mental illness does not exist. Besides, mental illnesses are also influenced by cultural and religious manifestations (Avasthi, Kate, & Grover, 2013). An interesting aspect

of neurosis in India is higher prevalence of possession states, trance states, fugues and hysterical fits compared to the West. On the other hand, multiple personality disorders, a common problem in the West, is rarely seen in our patients (Adityanjee, Raju, & Khandelwal, 1989; Varma, Bouri, & Wig, 1981). It is also suggested that ideas of guilt in depression, when present, are often attributed to karma or to the deeds of a previous birth, which in turn may render them less distressing (Varma, 1986). The same influences may explain more common delusions of persecution and reference in Indian patients than hypochondriacal, guilt, and nihilistic delusions (Rao & Begum, 1993). Thus, the education of mental health professionals must address treatment of illnesses in people of all faiths. It is vital to understand religious inclination of clients to provide the best-suited therapy.

2. Modern medical practitioners hesitate to discuss faith healing with patients, since there is a fundamental difference in modern medicine's approach to health as compared to traditional healing (Gopichandran, 2015). This intentional ignorance does not diminish the importance that these values may hold for the client. Thereby, it is suggested that the value of religion and spirituality for the client should be proactively enquired and understood. Researchers have found 94 per cent of patients who considered spirituality as important desired that their physicians discuss their spiritual beliefs. Even 50 per cent of those for whom spirituality was not important felt that doctors should at least inquire about spiritual beliefs in cases of serious illness (Ehman, Ott, Short, Ciamp, & Hansen-Flaschen, 1999). If psychotherapy is considered an interpersonal process, the psychotherapeutic relationship between therapist and client needs to be based on openness and trust which would help the patient become more accepting towards the change, and thereby improve the efficacy of the therapy. By taking into account the cultural concepts and the prevailing belief system, a better understanding of the clients can be formed by therapist (Gauam & Jain, 2010), thereby giving them space to be more comfortable, feel accepted and be open.

3. The principles of existing R/S practices in the non-Western societies, such as *satsang*, *dhyan*, etc., should be integrated in clinical trials and therapies. More complementary treatments such as yoga, meditation and spiritual exercises have been found to be effective in treatment

of people suffering from chronic diseases, by minimizing symptoms and improving quality of life (Macy, Jones, Graham, & Roach, 2018). Therapists should introduce tailored spirituality-related activities and rituals to be incorporated into their daily management of their illness. These activities should be based on the understanding of faith and symptoms of the client. For example, in the competitive modern world, in which stress and anxiety are part of everyday life, adding time-honoured, self-managed, evidence-based yogic practices and breathing exercises such as Surya Namaskar, Sudarshan Kriya and Pranayama may facilitate a healthy life (Chandra, Jaiswal, Singh, Jha, & Mittal, 2017; Srivastava, Goyal, Tiwari, & Patel, 2017).

4. A better understanding and integration of R/S resources can be gained through collaboration with R/S gurus/leaders. Psychologists rarely consider R/S leaders and gurus as potential collaborators, in spite of the fact that reliance upon religious and traditional healing systems is a culturally accepted source of support. The social and cultural power experienced by R/S leaders has a potential to influence behaviours, attitudes, decisions, approaches to services and strategies for support (Chadda et al., 2015; Sen & Chakraborty, 2017). It is, hence, advised that a psychologist consult R/S leaders to understand beneficial views and practices (Kovess-Masfety, 2017). It is also suggested that consultation may facilitate familiarity with the faith communities in which their clients are involved (Sperry & Shafranske, 2005).

5. Additionally, most traditional healers and R/S providers who counsel people have not received any formal training in clinical care, thus, making them insufficiently equipped to deal with serious mental illnesses. Since a large proportion of population in a developing country approaches traditional healers before resorting to modern health care, it is important to provide professional development training around mental health to such R/S practitioners. Collaborating with religious advisors would help provide such primary mental health advisors of rural population access to advanced training in counselling and mental health care, thereby facilitating better health care across the country.

6. It has been argued that the Asian traditions focus on advanced stages of development and states of well-being, and the Western systems provide details of psychopathology and early development (Dalal & Misra, 2012). To gain a better understanding of health, causes of

illness, recovery and maintenance of good health through stages of growth and enlightenment, practitioners should integrate the two perspectives. The knowledge of Ayurveda and other systems of Indian medicine may enhance speed and effectiveness of recovery and rehabilitation (Rastogi, 2018).

Suggestions for Research

1. There is a need for more rigor in R/S studies in the field of translational research. Controlled and randomized clinical trials of alternative therapies are found lacking in empirical literature.
2. Translational research in this field should focus on empirical evaluation of the question, whether incorporation of R/S in existing psychotherapy for R/S clients improves efficacy. There is scarcity of researchers who address this question in scientific fashion by using control groups.
3. For integrating R/S in clinical practice, its assessment is important. Therefore, more research should be conducted on understanding and measurement of concepts of personality and emotions found outside the domains of the Western psychology. It will help in establishing clear relationships with criterion variables.
4. As present literature suggested in this chapter, various measures of Indian R/S constructs have been constructed and validated. However, a series of researches should be promoted to confirm and revalidate them, in order to establish them in the mainstream psychology.
5. Greater specialization with respect to the measurement of R/S and R/S practices might lead to greater understanding of how their individual components might influence mental health status of the client. For example, what is the impact of Bhramari Pranayama—a type of breathing exercise that involves humming—specifically on anxiety disorders.

REFERENCES

Adityanjee, R. G. S., & Khandelwal, S. K. (1989) Current status of multiple personality disorder in India. *American Journal of Psychiatry, 146*, 1607–1610.

Argyle, M., & Beit-Hallahmi, B. (1975). *The social psychology of religion*. London and Boston: Routledge and Kegan Paul.

Arya, N. K., Singh, K., & Malik, A. (2017a). Effect of Heartfulness spiritual practice based program on mental and physical health indicators. *International Journal of Research in Management & Social Science, 5*(3), 91–103.

———. (2017b). Impact of five days spiritual practice in Himalayan Ashram of Sahaj Marg on well-being related parameters and selected physiological indicators. *The International Journal of Indian Psychology, 4*(2), 36–51.

Aten, J. D., & Worthington, E. L., Jr. (2009). Next steps for clinicians in religious and spiritual therapy: An end piece. *Journal of Clinical Psychology, 65,* 224–229. doi:10.1002/jclp.20562

Avasthi, A., Kate, N., & Grover, S. (2013). Indianization of psychiatry utilizing Indian mental concepts. *Indian Journal of Psychiatry, 55*(S2), 136–144.

Barrera, T. L., Zeno, D., Bush, A. L., Barber, C. R., & Stanley, M. A. (2012). Integrating religion and spirituality into treatment for late-life anxiety: Three case studies. *Cognitive and Behavioural Practice, 19*(2), 346–358.

Bathla, M., Chandna, S., Bathla, J., & Kaloiya, G. S. (2015). Faith healers in modern psychiatric practice: Results of a 4 years study. *Delhi Psychiatry Journal, 18*(1), 48–53.

Behere, P. B., Das, A., Yadav, R., & Behere, A. P. (2013). Religion and mental health. *Indian Journal of Psychiatry, 55*(S2), 187–194.

Bond, M. H., Lun, V. M.-C., & Li, L. M. W. (2012). The roles of secularism in values and engagement in religious practices for the life Satisfaction of young people: The moderating role of national-societal factors. In G. Trommsdorff & X. Y. Chen (Eds.), *Values, religion and culture in adolescent development* (pp. 123–145). New York, NY: Cambridge University Press.

Bonelli, R. M., & Koenig, H. G. (2013). Mental disorders, religion and spirituality 1990 to 2010: A systematic evidence-based review. *Journal of Religion and Health, 52,* 657–673. doi:10.1007/s10943-013-9691-4

Bowen, J. R. (2018). *Religions in practice: An approach to the anthropology of religion.* New York, NY: Routledge.

Brekke, J., Ell, K., & Palinkas, L. (2006). Translational science at the National Institute of Mental Health: Can social work take its rightful place? *Research on Social Work Practice, 17*(1), 123–133. http://dx.doi.org/10.1177/1049731506293693

Brodsky, A. E. (2000). The role of religion in the lives of resilient, urban, African American, single mothers. *Journal of Community Psychology, 28*(2), 199–219.

Chadda, R. K., Patra, B. N., & Gupta, N. (2015). Recent developments in community mental health: Relevance and relationship with the mental health care bill. *Indian Journal of Social Psychiatry, 31,* 153–60.

Chandra, S., Jaiswal, A. K., Singh, R., Jha, D., & Mittal, A. P. (2017). Mental stress: Neurophysiology and its regulation by Sudarshan Kriya Yoga. *International Journal of Yoga, 10*(2), 67–72.

Chimkode, S. M., Kumaran, S. D., Kanhere, V. V., Shivanna, R. (2015). Effect of yoga on blood glucose levels in patients with type 2 diabetes mellitus. *Journal of Clinical and Diagnostic Research, 9,* CC01–3. doi:10.7860/JCDR/2015/12666.5744

Cicognani, E., Pirini, C., Keyes, C., Joshanloo, M., Rostami, R., & Nosratabadi, M. (2007). Social participation, sense of community and social well being: A study on American, Italian and Iranian university students. *Social Indicators Research, 89,* 97–112. doi:10.1007/s11205-007-9222-3

Clark, W. H. (1958). *The psychology of religion.* Oxford, England: Macmillan.

Copland, I., Mabbett, I., Roy, A., Brittlebank, K., & Bowles, A. (2012). *A history of state and religion in India.* London: Routledge.

Dabi, T. (2017). A priests' chant: Healing traditions amongst the Galo tribe, Arunachal Pradesh, India. *Saudi Journal of Humanities and Social Sciences, 2*(11A), 1058–1061.

Dalal, A. K., & Misra, G. (2006). Psychology of health and well-being: Some emerging perspectives. *Psychological Studies, 51*(2–3), 91–104.

———. (Eds.). (2012). *New directions in health psychology.* New Delhi: SAGE Publications.

Derrett, R. (2003). Making sense of how festivals demonstrate a community's sense of place. *Event Management, 8*(1), 49–58.

Diener, E., Tay, L., & Myers, D. (2011). The religion paradox: If religion makes people happy, why are so many dropping out? *Journal of Personality and Social Psychology, 101,* 1278–1290. doi:10.1037/a0024402

Domingues, R. B. (2018). Modern postural yoga as a mental health promoting tool: A systematic review. *Complementary Therapies in Clinical Practice, 31,* 248–255. doi:10.1016/j.ctcp.2018.03.002

Doyle, D. (1992). Have we looked beyond the physical and psychosocial? *Journal of Pain and Symptom Management, 7,* 302–311.

Dyer, J. E. T., & Hagedorn, W. B. (2013). Navigating bereavement with spirituality-based interventions: Implications for non-faith-based Counselors. *Counseling and Values, 58,* 69–84. doi:10.1002/j.2161-007X.2013.00026.x

Ehman, J. W., Ott, B. B., Short, T. H., Ciampa. R. C., & Hansen-Flaschen, J. (1999). Do patients want physicians to inquire about their spiritual or religious beliefs if they become gravely ill? *Archives of Internal Medicine, 159*(15), 1803–1806.

Emblen, J. D. (1992). Religion and spirituality defined according to current use in nursing literature. *Journal of Professional Nursing, 8*(1), 41–47.

Fleischman, P. R. (2013). *Karma and chaos: New and collected essays on vipassana meditation.* Onalaska, WA: Pariyatti Publishing.

Ganpat, T. S., & Nagendra, H. R. (2011). Integrated yoga therapy for improving mental health in managers. *Industrial Psychiatry Journal, 20*(1), 45–48.

Gautam, A., & Bansal, S. (2014). Community-based approach as an innovation in mental health care in India. *Andhra Pradesh Journal of Psychological Medicine, 15*(1), 19–23.

Gautam, S., & Jain, N. (2010). Indian culture and psychiatry. *Indian Journal of Psychiatry, 52*(Suppl. 1), S309–S313.

Goldstein, L., Nidich, S. I., Goodman, R., & Goodman, D. (2018). The effect of transcendental meditation on self-efficacy, perceived stress, and quality of life in mothers in Uganda. *Health Care for Women International, 39*(7), 734–754. doi:10.1080/07399332.2018.1445254

Gonçalves, J., Lucchetti, G., Menezes, P., & Vallada, H. (2015). Religious and spiritual interventions in mental health care: A systematic review and meta-analysis of randomized controlled clinical trials. *Psychological Medicine, 45*(14), 2937–2949. http://dx.doi.org/10.1017/s0033291715001166

Gopichandran, V. (2015). Faith healing and faith in healing. *Indian Journal of Medical Ethics, 12*(4), 238–240.

Graham, C., & Crown, S. (2014). Religion and wellbeing around the world: Social purpose, social time, or social insurance? *International Journal of Wellbeing, 4*, 1–27. doi:10.5502/ijw.v4i1.1

Gryczynski, J., Schwartz, R. P., Fishman, M. J., Nordeck, C. D., Grant, J., Nidich, S., … O'Grady, K. E. (2018). Integration of transcendental meditation® (TM) into alcohol use disorder (AUD) treatment. *Journal of Substance Abuse Treatment, 87*, 23–30. doi:10.1016/j.jsat.2018.01.009

Henderson, T. E. (2018). The influence of therapist-patient religious/spiritual congruence on satisfaction with therapy: A review of research. *Theses and Dissertations.* 2553. Retrieved from https://rdw.rowan.edu/etd/2553

Hood, R. W. (2003). The relationship between religion and spirituality. In A. L. Greil & D. Bromley (Eds.), *Defining religion: Investigating the boundaries between the sacred and the secular: Vol. 10. Religion and the social order.* Amsterdam: Elsevier Science.

Hunnicutt, G., & Rhodes, D. (2015). Meditation practices and the reduction of aggression and violence: Towards a gender-sensitive, humanitarian, healing-based intervention. In J. Joseph & W. Crichlow (Eds.), *Alternative offender rehabilitation and social justice* (pp. 15–31). London: Palgrave Macmillan.

Jasperse, M., Ward, C., & Jose, P. E. (2012). Identity, perceived religious discrimination, and psychological well-being in Muslim immigrant women. *Applied Psychology: An International Review, 61*(2), 250–271.

Jha, S. (2011). *Wellbeing and religion in India: A preliminary literature review* (Working paper 68). Birmingham: Religions and Development Research Programme, University of Birmingham.

Joshi, S., Kumari, S., & Jain, M. (2008). Religious belief and its relation to psychological well-being. *Journal of the Indian Academy of Applied Psychology, 34*(2), 345–354.

Jung, C. J. (1938). *Psychology and religion.* Yale University Press. Retrieved from http://r.4dt.org/text/jung/Psychology%20and%20Religion%20(1938).pdf

Juthani, N. V. (1998). Understanding and treating Hindu patients. In H. G. Koenig (Ed.), *Handbook of religion and mental health.* San Diego, CA: Academic Press.

Kakkar, S. (2012). *Shamans, mystics, and doctors.* New Delhi: Oxford.

Kala, A. (2013). Time to face new realities: Mental Health Care Bill, 2013. *Indian Journal of Psychiatry, 55*, 216. doi:10.4103/0019-5545.117129

Kauts, A., & Sharma, N. (2009). Effect of yoga on academic performance in relation to stress. *International Journal of Yoga, 2*(1), 39–43.

Khan, S. S., Hopkins, N., Reicher, S., Tewari, S., Srinivasan, N., & Stevenson, C. (2014). Shared identity predicts enhanced health at a mass gathering. *Group Processes and Intergroup Relations.* doi:10.1177/1368430214556703

Khandelwal, S. K., Jhingan, H. P., Ramesh, S., Gupta, R. K., & Srivastava, V. K. (2004). India mental health country profile. *International Review of Psychiatry, 16*(1–2), 126–141.

Kim-Prieto, C. (2014). *Religion and spirituality across cultures.* Dordrecht: Springer.

Kiran, U., Ladha, S., Makhija, N., Kapoor, P., Choudhury, M., ... Balram, A. (2017). The role of Rajyoga meditation for modulation of anxiety and serum cortisol in patients undergoing coronary artery bypass surgery: A prospective randomized control study. *Annals of Cardiac Anaesthesia, 20*(2), 158.

Koenig, H. (2012). Religion, spirituality, and health: The research and clinical implications. *ISRN Psychiatry,* 1–33. http://dx.doi.org/10.5402/2012/278730

Kovess-Masfety, V., Evans-Lacko, S., Williams, D., Andrade, L. H., Benjet, C., Ten Have, M., ... Gureje, O. (2017). The role of religious advisors in mental health care in the World Mental Health surveys. *Social Psychiatry and Psychiatric Epidemiology, 52,* 353–367. doi:10.1007/s00127-016-1290-8

Krause, N., & Hayward, R. (2013). Religious involvement and feelings of connectedness with others among older Americans. *Archive for the Psychology of Religion, 35*(2), 259–282. http://dx.doi.org/10.1163/15736121-12341266

Kuppusamy, M., Kamaldeen, D., Pitani, R., Amaldas, J., & Shanmugam, P. (2018). Effects of Bhramari Pranayama on health: A systematic review. *Journal of Traditional and Complementary Medicine, 8*(1), 11–16. http://dx.doi.org/10.1016/j.jtcme.2017.02.003

Lavey, R., Sherman, T., Mueser, K., Osborne, D., Currier, M., & Wolfe, R. (2005). The effects of yoga on mood in psychiatric inpatients. *Psychiatric Rehabilitation Journal, 28*(4), 399–402. http://dx.doi.org/10.2975/28.2005.399.402

Lechner, C. M., Tomasik, M. J., Silbereisen, R. K., & Wasilewski, J. (2013). Exploring the stress-buffering effects of religiousness in relation to social and economic change: Evidence from Poland. *Psychology of Religion and Spirituality, 5*(3), 145–156.

Levin, J. (2010). Religion and mental health: Theory and research. *International Journal of Applied Psychoanalytic Studies, 7,* 102–115. doi:10.1002/aps.240

Lun, V., & Bond, M. H. (2013). Examining the relation of religion and spirituality to subjective well-being across national cultures. *Psychology of Religion and Spirituality, 5*(4), 304–315. http://dx.doi.org/10.1037/a0033641

Macy, R. J., Jones, E., Graham, L. M., & Roach, L. (2015). Yoga for trauma and related mental health problems: A meta-review with clinical and service recommendations. *Trauma, Violence, & Abuse, 19,* 35–57. doi:10.1177/1524838015620834

Mahajan, A. S., Reddy, K. S., & Sachdeva, U. (1999). Lipid profile of coronary risk subjects following yogic lifestyle intervention. *Indian Heart Journal, 51*(1), 37–40.

Manohar, P. R. (2013). Subjective well-being and health: A potential field for scientific enquiry into the foundational concepts of Ayurveda. *Ancient Science of Life, 33*(2), 79–80.

Miller, W. (1998). Researching the spiritual dimensions of alcohol and other drug problems. *Addiction, 93*(7), 979–990.

Misra, S., Smith, J., Wareg, N., Hodges, K., Gandhi, M., & McElroy, J. A. (2018). Take a deep breath: A randomized control trial of Pranayama breathing on uncontrolled hypertension. *Advances in Integrative Medicine.* doi:10.1016/j.aimed.2018.08.002

Mitra, K. M. (1994). *The role of religion in transformation: Its implication for counselling* (Master's Thesis). The University of British Columbia, Vancouver, Canada.

Mitra, M. (2012, 27 March). Radha Soami [Blog Post]. Retrieved from https://www.speakingtree.in/blog/radha-soami

Mohr, S., Perroud, N., Gillieron, C., Brandt, P., Rieben, I., Borras, L., … Huguelet, P. (2011). Spirituality and religiousness as predictive factors of outcome in schizophrenia and schizo-affective disorders. *Psychiatry Research, 186*(2–3), 177–182. http://dx.doi.org/10.1016/j.psychres.2010.08.012

Murugesan, R., Govindarajalu, N., & Bera, T. K. (2000). Effect of selected yogic practices on the management of hypertension. *Indian Journal of Physiological Pharmocology, 44*(2), 207–210.

Muthuselvi, K., Dhanalakshmi, S., & Abhishek, G. (2017). Effect of yoga on glycosylated hemoglobin levels in diabetic subjects. *Indian Journal of Clinical Anatomy and Physiology, 4*, 238–240. doi:10.18231/2394-2126.2017.0059

Neki, J. S. (1979). Psychotherapy in India. *Indian Journal of Psychiatry, 19*, 1.

Nyer, M., Doorley, J., Durham, K., Yeung, A., Freeman, M., & Mischoulon, D. (2013). What is the role of alternative treatments in late-life depression? *Psychiatric Clinics of North America, 36*(4), 577–596. http://dx.doi.org/10.1016/j.psc.2013.08.012

O'Connell, D. F., & Alexander, C. N. (2014). *Self-recovery: Treating addictions using transcendental meditation and maharishi Ayur-Veda.* London: Routledge.

Pargament, K. I. (1997). *The psychology of religion and coping.* New York: Guilford Press.

———. (2007). *Spiritually integrated psychotherapy: Understanding and addressing the sacred.* New York, NY: Guilford.

Pargament, K. I., & Saunders, S. M. (2007). Introduction to the special issue on spirituality and psychotherapy. *Journal of Clinical Psychology, 63*(10), 903–907. doi:10.1002/jclp.20405

Park, C. L. (2005). Religion and meaning. In R. F. Paloutzian & C. L. Park (Eds.), *Handbook of the psychology of religion and spirituality* (pp. 295–314). New York, NY: Guilford.

Paukert, A., Phillips, L., Cully, J., Romero, C., & Stanley, M. (2011). Systematic review of the effects of religion-accommodative psychotherapy for depression and anxiety. *Journal of Contemporary Psychotherapy, 41*(2), 99–108. doi: 10.1007/s10879-010-9154-0

Radha Soami Satsang Beas. (2019). The Radha Soami way of God realisation. RSSB newspaper articles. Retrieved from https://www.rssb.org/news20.html#

Raina, M., & Singh, K. (2015). The Ashtanga Yoga Hindi Scale: An assessment tool based on eastern philosophy of yoga. *Journal of Religion and Health, 57*(1), 12–25.

Rao, K. M., & Begum, S. (1993). A phenomenological study of delusions in depression. *Indian Journal of Psychiatry, 35*(1), 40–42.

Rao, K. R., & Paranjpe, A. C. (2016). *Psychology in the Indian tradition*. New Delhi: Springer.

Rastogi, S. (2018). *Translational Ayurveda*. Singapore: Springer.

Richards, P. S. (2012). Honoring religious diversity and universal spirituality in psychotherapy. In L. J. Miller (Ed.), *The Oxford handbook of psychology and spirituality* (pp. 237–254). New York, NY: Oxford University Press.

Saroglou, V. (2014). Introduction: Studying religion in personality and social psychology. In V. Saroglou (Ed.), *Religion, personality, and social behavior* (pp. 1–28). New York, NY: Psychology Press.

Satyapriya, M., Nagendra, H. R., Nagarathna, R., & Padmalatha, V. (2008). Effect of integrated yoga on stress and heart rate variability in pregnant women. *International Journal of Gynecology & Obstetrics, 104*, 218–222. doi:10.1016/j.ijgo.2008.11.013

Sen, S., & Chakraborty, R. (2017). Revival, modernization and integration of Indian traditional herbal medicine in clinical practice: Importance, challenges and future. *Journal of Traditional and Complementary Medicine, 7*(2), 234–244. doi:10.1016/j.jtcme.2016.05.006

Sengupta, P. (2012). Health impacts of yoga and pranayama: A state-of-the-art review. *International Journal of Preventive Medicine, 3*(7), 444–458.

Sharma, K., Trivedi, R., Chandra, S., Kaur, P., Kumar, P., Singh, K., Dubey, A. K. & Khushu, S. (2018). Enhanced white matter integrity in corpus callosum of long-term Brahmakumaris Rajayoga meditators. *Brain Connectivity, 8*(1), 49–55.

Sharma, P., Das, S. K., & Deshpande, S. N. (2006). An estimate of the monthly cost of two major mental disorders in an Indian metropolis. *Indian Journal of Psychiatry, 48*(3), 143–148.

Sharma, R., Gupta, N., & Bijlani, R. L. (2008). Effect of yoga-based lifestyle intervention on subjective well-being. *Indian Journal of Physiological Pharmacology, 52*(2), 123–131.

Sharma, S., & Singh, K. (2016). Development and validation of Vikaras Hindi scale. *Mental Health, Religion & Culture, 19*(5), 420–432.

———. (2018). Religion and well being: The mediating role of positive virtues. *Journal of Religion and Health, 58*, 119–131. doi:10.1007/s10943-018-0559-5

Siddiqui, S., Lacroix, K., & Dhar, A. (2014). Faith healing in India: The cultural quotient of the critical. *Disability and the Global South, 1*(2), 285–301.

Singh, D. C., & Madan, A. (2017). Religious coping in the process of counseling/ psychotherapy. *Biomedical Journal of Scientific and Technical Research, 1*, 340–347. doi:10.26717/BJSTR.2017.01.000191

Singh K., Jain A., & Singh D. (2014) Satsang: A culture-specific effective practice for well-being. In H. Á. Marujo & L. Neto (Eds.), *Positive nations and communities: Cross-cultural advancements in positive psychology* (Vol. 6). Dordrecht: Springer.

Singh, K., Khanna, P., Khosla, M., Rapelly, M., & Soni, A. (2016). Revalidation of the Sat-Chit-Ananda Scale. *Journal of Religion and Health, 57*(4), 1392–1401.

Singh, K., Khari, C., Amonkar, R., Arya, N. K., & Kumar, K. S. (2013). Development and validation of a new scale: Sat-Chit-Ananda Scale. *International Journal on Vedic Foundations of Management, 1*(2), 54–74.

Singh, K., Sigroha, S., Singh, D., & Shokeen, B. (2017). Religious and spiritual messages in folk songs: A study of women from rural India. *Mental Health, Religion & Culture, 20*(5), 464–477. http://dx.doi.org/10.1080/13674676.2 017.1356812

Singh K., Singh D., Mitra S., Junnarkar M. & Dayal P. (2016). *Effect on well-being of spiritual practices among elderly rural women.* Paper presented at Mid-Year Conference on Psychology, Spirituality and Religion, by Society for the Psychology of Religion and Spirituality (APA Div. 36) and St. Joseph's College, New York, USA, 11–12 March 2016.

Smith, T. B., Bartz J., & Richards, S. (2007). Outcomes of religious and spiritual adaptations to psychotherapy: A meta-analytic review. *Psychotherapy Research, 17*(6), 643–655.

Sohi, K. K., Singh, P., & Bopanna, K. (2017). Ritual participation, sense of community, and social well-being: A study of seva in the Sikh community. *Journal of Religion and Health, 57*(6), 2066–2078. https://doi.org/10.1007/ s10943-017-0424-y

Sperry, L., & Shafranske, E. P. (Eds.). (2005). *Spiritually oriented psychotherapy.* Washington, DC: American Psychological Association.

Srivastava, A., Goyal, P., Tiwari, S. K., & Patel, A. K. (2017). Interventional effect of Bhramari Pranayama on mental health among college students. *The International Journal of Indian Psychology, 4*(2), 87.

Steger, M. F., & Frazier, P. (2005). Meaning in life: One link in the chain from religiousness to well-being. *Journal of Counseling Psychology, 52*, 574–582. doi:10.1037/0022-0167.52.4.574

Strawbridge, W., Shema, S., Cohen, R., & Kaplan, G. (2001). Religious attendance increases survival by improving and maintaining good health behaviors, mental health, and social relationships. *Annals of Behavioral Medicine, 23*, 68–74. doi:10.1207/S15324796ABM2-301_10

Streeter, C. C., Gerbarg, P. L., Whitfield, T. H., Owen, L., Johnston, J., Silveri, M. M., ... Jensen, J. E. (2017). Treatment of major depressive disorder with iyengar yoga and coherent breathing: A randomized controlled dosing study. *Journal of Alternative and Complementary Medicine, 23*(3), 201–207. http://doi.org/10.1089/acm.2016.0140

Streib, H., & Hood, R. W. (2013). Modeling the religious field: Religion, spirituality, mysticism and related world views. *Implicit Religion, 16,* 137–155. doi:10.1558/imre.v16i2.133

Tashiro, T., & Mortensen, L. (2006). Translational research: How social psychology can improve psychotherapy. *American Psychologist, 61*(9), 959–966. http://dx.doi.org/10.1037/0003-066x.61.9.959

Thirunavukarasu, M., & Thirunavukarasu, P. (2010). Training and national deficit of psychiatrists in India: A critical analysis. *Indian Journal Psychiatry, 52* (S3), 83–88.

Tulloch, A., Bombell, H., Dean, C., & Tiedemann, A. (2018). Yoga-based exercise improves health-related quality of life and mental well-being in older people: A systematic review of randomised controlled trials. *Age and Ageing, 47,* 537–544. doi:10.1093/ageing/afy044

Van Cappellen, P., Toth-Gauthier, M., Saroglou, V., & Fredrickson, B. (2016). Religion and well-being: The mediating role of positive emotions. *Journal of Happiness Studies, 17,* 485–505. doi:10.1007/s10902-014-9605-5

Varma, K. V. (1986). Cultural psychodynamics in health and illness. *Indian Journal of Psychiatry, 28*(1), 13–34.

Varma, V. K., Bouri, M., & Wig, N. N. (1981). Multiple personality in India: Comparison with hysterical possession state. *American Journal of Psychotherapy, 35*(1), 113–120.

Vaughan, F. (1991). Spiritual issues in psychotherapy. *Journal of Transpersonal Psychology, 23*(2), 105–119.

Vedamurthachar, A. (2010). *The role of sudarshan kriya on mental health.* Paper presented at International Symposium on Yogism, December 2010. Retrieved from http://www.aeyt.org/resources

Vinjamury, S. P., Vinjamury, M., Der Martirosian, C., & Miller, J. (2014). Ayurvedic therapy (shirodhara) for insomnia: A case series. *Global Advances in Health and Medicine, 3,* 75–80. doi:10.7453/gahmj.2012.086

Watts, F. N. (2012). Parameters and limitations of current conceptualisations. In L. J. Miller (Ed.). *The Oxford handbook of psychology and spirituality* (pp. 36–46). New York, NY: Oxford University Press.

WHO (2017). *Depression.* Retrieved from https://www.who.int/news-room/fact-sheets

Young M. J., & Sarin, R. (2014). Fostering meaning, social connection, and well-being through Hindu beliefs and practices. In C. Kim-Prieto (Ed), *Religion and spirituality across cultures: Cross-cultural advancements in positive psychology* (Vol. 9). Dordrecht: Springer.

Zenkert, R., Brabender, V., & Slater, C. (2014). Therapists' responses to religious/spiritual discussions with trauma versus non-trauma clients. *Journal of Contemporary Psychotherapy, 44*(3), 213–221. doi:10.1007/s10879-014-9264-1

Zinnbauer, B. J., & Pargament, K. I. (2005). Religiousness and spirituality. In R. F. Paloutzian & C. L. Park (Eds.), *Handbook of the psychology of religion and spirituality* (pp. 21–42). New York, NY: Guilford Press.

Zope, S. A., & Zope, R. A. (2013). Sudarshan kriya yoga: Breathing for health. *International Journal of Yoga, 6*(1), 4–10.

Chapter 6

Applications of Positive Psychology in Indian School Setting

Pulkit Khanna and Kamlesh Singh

The main objective of positive psychology (PP) is to contribute to the flourishing or optimal functioning of individuals and communities. This chapter focuses on positive psychological interventions (PPIs) as an important approach to translate the gains from scientific and academic research into benefits for the community. Drawing on the heightened need of such interventions for children who are the future of any society, the chapter outlines the mental health status and problems faced by children in India. In the course of the discussion, the school is examined as an appropriate setting to promote mental health and well-being of children. It then moves on to review school-based PPIs from across the world, followed by the emerging status of PP in Indian schools. Following this detailed review, the chapter concludes with some recommendations for the way forward to apply the available knowledge in PP towards well-being promotion in Indian school setting.

POSITIVE PSYCHOLOGY AND ITS APPLICATION TO PROMOTE WELL-BEING

Psychology as a discipline studies behaviour and cognitive processes, and has a dual focus, to fulfil deficits (as a healing discipline) as well as to nurture wellness. Traditionally, it studied human problems, and searched for relevant solutions. However, it has seen an emerging focus on the positive aspects of human existence, thereby widening its application horizon. This development may in part be attributed to the rise and development of the branch of PP. It is pertinent to understand that given the increasing prevalence of mental health concerns, the importance of the traditional remedial function of psychology is undeniable. At the same time, prevention and promotion initiatives to ensure awareness, early intervention as well as enhanced well-being are the need of the hour. PP can contribute meaningfully to both these aims.

Review of literature substantiates that for every article examining positive constructs, relatively much greater focus is committed to work examining problems in people (psychological, physical and educational disorders), and the required repair and rectification (Lopez et al., 2006; Myers, 2000). Such preponderance of a problem rectification approach often leads to the misconception that alleviating psychological distress equals to ensuring optimal well-being. However, the absence of psychopathological symptoms is not essentially the same as optimal functioning (e.g., Keyes & Westerhof, 2012). This is where the holistic discipline of PP comes into the picture. PP aims to 'understand, test, discover and promote the factors that allow individuals and communities to thrive' (Sheldon, Fredrickson, Rathunde, Csikszentmihalyi, & Haidt, 2000, p. 2). Fredrickson (2001, p. 218) states, 'The mission of PP is to understand and foster the factors that allow individuals, communities, and societies to flourish'. Towards this end, what actually determines one's well-being and happiness needs to be understood.

An individual's happiness levels are understood to be determined by a combination of factors as explained by Lyubomirsky, Sheldon and Schkade's (2005) set-point model. According to this model, one's happiness level is partly determined by chronic set point (50%) comprising heritable and immutable personality traits, incidental yet fairly stable circumstantial factors (10%) and 'intentional activity' (40%) that has the potential to enhance one's happiness and well-being (Lyubomirsky et al., 2005). This last factor— 'intentional activity'—offers a promising approach in the form of deliberate interventions that promote sustainable well-being. Research suggests that more often sustainable happiness may be attained through changes in intentional activity than through changes in circumstances (Hosie & Sevastos, 2010; Sheldon & Lyubomirsky, 2006). Consequently, there is tremendous scope for translational research (TR) in the form of intervention work in this area.

When applied in educational settings, PP can help to offer 'a wellness focus that has the potential to expand conceptualizations of schooling, students, and educational processes' (Huebner, Gilman, Reschly, & Hall, 2009, p. 566). Positive education has been understood as 'the application of well-being science into an educational setting aimed at increasing the resilience and well-being of students, staff, and whole school community' (Green, 2014, p. 402). Applying PP in schools is an attempt to transcend beyond 'normal' levels of personal and academic attainment and strive for optimal performance for individuals and groups. In this context, school-based PPIs entail packaged programmes usually implemented through delivery of a defined curriculum at a stipulated time of the school day, spread over a fixed time period (Huebner, Hills, Siddall, & Gilman, 2014).

It must be noted that such interventions work to complement and by no means substitute traditional educational reforms (Yeager, Walton, & Cohen, 2013). There is widespread need for such applications of PP to promote the mental health and well-being of youth, the future of any society. The next section examines the status of children and youth in India, focusing on challenges and causes of concern.

CHILDREN IN INDIAN SCENARIO: PRESENT STATUS AND CONCERNS

About a third of the world's population consists of children and adolescents. Globally, 10–20 per cent of them are affected by mental health problems (Kieling et al., 2011). According to government data (Ministry of Statistics and Programme Implementation, 2012), children (0–14 years) account for one-third of the total population of India. Further, India is considered as a 'young nation', being home to 356 million 10–24-year olds, accounting for the world's largest youth population (United Nations, 2013). Research suggests that India alone is home to nearly 20 million adolescents with severe mental health concerns (Shastri, 2009). The concern may be even greater because the absence of mental illness doesn't necessarily imply mental health (Keyes & Cartwright, 2013). Given that 'the youth of the nation are the trustees of prosperity' (Ministry of Statistics and Programme Implementation, 2017), this data definitely builds a strong case for working to nurture the holistic well-being, and consequent prosperity of young people. Then it comes as no surprise that India, as also other nations globally, is increasingly concerned about the mental health status of its youth. In developing countries (like India), there are burgeoning concerns owing to relatively higher representation of youth in the population, a high load of health problems and paucity of resources (Fatusi & Hindin, 2010). Moreover, health research is skewed towards health problems rather than issues of normal development which significantly influences well-being and quality of life among young people (Fatusi & Hindin, 2010).

It may be pragmatic to consider the possibility that Indian children and youth's mental health has not received sufficient attention due to preoccupation with matters concerning physical health. Moreover, as children are usually presumed to be physically healthy, lower priority is given to issues of their mental health (Kumar & Reshmi, 2014). Another perilous issue within the Indian context is that many children grow in miserable circumstances of poverty, disease, illiteracy and crime. The enormous population, and expanse of India, further hinders the proper delivery of government as well as voluntary programmes in this area.

Over the past few decades, there has been increasing incidence of school-going children and adolescents experiencing social, emotional and behavioural difficulties that hamper normal growth and functioning. Abraham and Neogi (1997) reported a disturbing trend wherein the age of children visiting psychiatrists and psychologists in India is falling steadily and the number of those who need treatment is rising. An extremely competitive environment leads to school children being burdened with homework, tuitions and examinations (Jain, 1996). Urban school-going adolescents face the challenge of immense (often unhealthy) peer competition. Nearly two-thirds of the students in a study by Deb, Strodl and Sun (2015) reported stress on account of academic pressure, which was further found to be positively correlated with psychiatric cases. High school students in India have been reported to suffer from psychological concerns including depression and anxiety (Pushkarna & Veeraraghavan, 2014), and consequent pressure takes a toll on their health and well-being.

In another Indian study, Mohanraj, Subbhiah and Watson (2010) examined various risk and protective factors for depressive symptoms among school-going adolescents. While daily hassles and stressful life events came up as risk factors, self-esteem, social support and peer acceptance were identified as protective factors. Based on these findings, Mohanraj et al. (2010) recommended the need for school-based interventions to build the protective factors among children and adolescents.

A recent study of adolescents from the National Capital Region, India, found that nearly 51 per cent youth had 'moderate' mental health, 46.4 per cent were 'flourishing' and 2.4 per cent were languishing (Singh, Bassi, Junnarkar, & Negri, 2015). Singh and colleagues also found that 'flourishing youth' reported lower incidence of depression and adjustment difficulties besides more prosocial behaviour, when compared to their 'non-flourishing' counterparts. After exploring the factors affecting mental health of North Indian adolescents, Singh, Junnarkar and Jain (2015) proposed school interventions to boost well-being, especially to nurture children's family ties and social support.

Present times are characterized by social challenges, dual income families with busy schedules and a barrage of commercial forces vying to influence impressionable young minds. Research also reflects this and other concerns pertaining to mental health of children in India. To make the matters worse, the prevalent Indian education system often places tremendous focus on achievement, leaving much to be desired in terms of empowering students to deal with life challenges including academic stress and violence among others (Bharath & Kishore, 2010). Among the most adverse outcomes of this situation are the rising suicides among Indian students, especially on account of academic pressure. Mukherjee (2011) put forth a cogent argument for educational reforms, citing an alarming 26 per cent rise in student suicides in India from 2006–2010. It is common knowledge that such cases go up every year during the time following examinations and results. This points at a very horrific reality of the Indian education system, and calls for urgent and widespread action. In fact, the National Council of Educational Research and Training (NCERT, 2015) has spelled out the need to focus on psychosocial development and life skills education (LSE) of Indian school students. But clearly, much more needs to be done in view of the magnitude of the concerns at hand.

Given this scenario, translating academic knowledge into practice in order to promote youth mental health and well-being seems to be the need of the hour. While such programmes could be situated in diverse settings, schools emerge as a particularly appropriate setting due to various factors discussed hereafter.

School as an Appropriate Setting for TR to Promote Well-Being

Schools emerge as a very relevant backdrop to develop, nurture and reinforce psychological assets and strengths of young people. Assimilating evidence-based interventions into the school setting can prove very beneficial in addressing the larger public health goal of bridging the gap between those who need intervention and the availability of actual services (Warner & Fox, 2012).

At the outset, it appears almost commonsensical that school-going children are at a developmental stage where they are more 'malleable' in terms of being amenable to meaningful change as compared to adults who may be more set in their ways and also biologically 'limited' in various developmental aspects. Research shows that positive early experiences enable children to develop stronger biological systems, thereby setting the foundation for their growth into healthy and thriving adults (Center on the Developing Child, 2010). Further, positive early experiences are considered as building blocks for subsequent success in various life areas including school, workplace and community (Kasprzak, Jones, & Marshall,

2011). It is noteworthy that the onset of most mental health disorders in adults occurs during childhood and adolescence (Noggle, Steiner, Minami, & Khalsa, 2012). Consequently, early interventions implemented before the onset of negative processes are important in improving student-related outcomes in the long run (Garcia & Cohen, 2012).

It then seems only logical to work in schools to provide interventions in order to promote well-being. Schools have, in fact been regarded as 'privileged avenues of positive youth development' (Moreira et al., 2015, p. 13), in view of their potential to facilitate healthy coping skills, socio-emotional skills and well-being among children (Tran, Gueldner, & Smith, 2014). In the Indian context, schools emerge as a particularly suitable setting to translate research gains into youth focused well-being initiatives, given that most students usually spend over 30 hours per week at school (Pushkarna & Veeraraghavan, 2014).

Schools have a wide reach, play a pivotal role in the lives of children and their families, and are a location where initial concerns can arise and be addressed effectively (Greenberg, 2010). Multitudes of young people attend school where their daily interactions with teachers and peers become important determinants of their well-being. Furthermore, social stigma attached with utilizing mental health services continues to be an unfortunate reality, whereby schools offer a conducive setting to work with children.

Promotion of overall well-being of students is a key goal of education. According to Seligman, Ernst, Gillham, Reivich and Linkins (2009, p. 294), 'More well-being is synergistic with better learning'. There is growing acknowledgement of the link between the academic and emotional functioning of children and adolescents, encouraging focus on their strengths, resilience and socio-emotional skills that would hold them in good stead in school and beyond (Kranzler, Hoffman, Parks, & Gillham, 2014). Towards the overarching aim of promoting well-being, schools offer 'ready-made populations of students that can be targeted for general, as well as specific, mental health promotion initiatives' (Collaborative for Academic Social and Emotional Learning [CASEL], 2008).

On the whole, research suggests that school-based programmes to foster positive values and character strengths in students reap benefits for students, teachers and whole school communities (Benninga, Berkowitz, Kuehn, & Smith, 2006; Lovat, Toomey, & Clement, 2010). However, it is equally important to consider some practical constraints of working in school settings. Research posits practical concerns such as pre-determined schedules, difficulties of maintaining communication with parents and time and resource constraints of school professionals (Millar, Lean, Sweet, Moraes, & Nelson, 2013). Support from school authorities and staff, access to adequate resources, ensuring intervention fidelity, and alignment of intervention goals with the school goals and policies have also been identified as major issues. Nevertheless, the promising potential of PPIs in the school setting is undeniable. This is also reflected in the rich evidence base of school-based interventions across the world that are reviewed in the following section.

POSITIVE PSYCHOLOGY INTERVENTIONS IN SCHOOLS: A GLOBAL REVIEW

Research in the area of PPI in the Indian school setting is still in its early stages. It is therefore worthwhile to develop greater insight into the subject by reviewing existing research from other countries. The following sections of this chapter offer a detailed review of well documented studies in this field, emphasizing on classroom-based interventions across all stages of school.

Different parts of the world are at varied levels of progress in the area of TR. As if mirroring this trend, different countries exhibit varied levels of work in the field of PPIs, with majority of documented literature situated in the Western countries. At the centre of the present review are PPI studies from the turn of this century, that is, 2000 onwards, with the rationale of emphasizing recent and emerging trends, culminating in recommendations and thoughts about the way forward.

Within this frame of reference, school-based interventions across diverse themes have been included within the purview of this chapter. For coherent presentation, these studies have been organized by themes that should not be taken as indicative of any watertight compartments by which such interventions may be categorized. Within each theme, studies are presented chronologically, and summed up with meta-analytic findings wherever possible. The review begins with the theme of 'character strengths' as a whole, moving on to programmes focused on discrete aspects like 'gratitude,' 'hope' and 'resilience'. Studies pertaining to 'stress management, relaxation and mindfulness training' have been considered under one umbrella for the purpose of this review. The category of 'multi-component programmes' is a basket of studies encompassing comprehensive psychological wellness curricula or multiple themes simultaneously. The last category in this section summarizes research in the field of 'social emotional learning' (SEL). While literature usually reports SEL programmes as distinct from PPIs in general, the former have also been considered here in view of their shared goal of student well-being. In fact, new strains of academic scholarship have recommended a move to integrate approaches like SEL and positive youth development owing to considerable overlap in their goals (Taylor, Oberle, Durlak, & Weissberg, 2017). It must be reiterated that this categorization across themes is simply for ease of understanding, not representative of any rigid classification.

Character Strengths

Strengths in youth and adolescence have been conceptualized as behavioural and emotional attributes that generate 'a sense of personal accomplishment; contribute to satisfying relationships with family members, peers, and adults; enhance one's ability to deal with adversity and stress; and promote one's personal, social, and academic development' (Epstein, 2004, p. 4). Character strengths are strongly associated with well-being. Strengths such as love of learning, zest, gratitude, hope and perseverance have been found to be positively correlated with school achievement while others such as prudence and self-regulation are strongly correlated with positive classroom behaviour (Wagner & Ruch, 2015). Strengths-based interventions basically aim to enhance well-being or personal achievement by enabling identification, and subsequent development of strengths. While such interventions previously relied on participants' self-identification and labelling of strengths (Forster, 1991), subsequently strengths classifications have been developed to facilitate the process of recognizing strengths (Linley, Joseph, Maltby, Harrington, & Wood, 2009; Peterson & Seligman, 2004; Popov, 2000; Rath, 2007). Ever since the advent of the VIA classification and the VIA-Youth (Park & Peterson,

2006), numerous studies emanating from different cultures have reported meaningful links between character strengths and children and adolescents' well-being (Gillham et al., 2011; Ruch, Weber, Park, & Peterson, 2014; Van Eeden, Wissing, Dreyer, Park, & Peterson, 2008). Intentional activities that focus on signature strengths, and their use in new ways, have been found to be highly effective (Proyer, Gander, Wellenzohn, & Ruch, 2015). A few prominent strength-based interventions that have been used in the classroom settings are discussed next.

Turner (2004) evaluated a strengths-based programme for high school children using a quasi-experimental pre-test–post-test non-equivalent control group design. Programme participants engaged in weekly sessions of 45 minutes spread over two semesters, where they undertook strengths-based learning activities in small groups. At this time, control group participants were trained in computer word processing. After post-testing, Turner (2004) reported that the intervention group had significantly higher grades, was better disciplined and less likely to be late for class as compared to the control group.

Gillum (2005) researched the impact of a strengths intervention on mathematics performance among high school students. Participants (underperformers in state wide math tests) were enrolled in four math classes, and each class received a different strengths treatment. Qualitative data through semi-structured interviews was also collected from a purposive sample of five students from one of the treatment groups. Best results were obtained in case of groups who received specific instructions on how to use their strengths (Gillum, 2005).

Austin (2005) evaluated a six-week-long school-based strengths programme rooted in the Gallup strengths framework. In this controlled experimental study, participants were randomly allocated to the intervention or control condition. Intervention participants identified their top five strengths, shared these with friends and family and also maintained strengths diaries. Austin (2005) reported that these students had significantly higher academic expectations, efficacy, self-empowerment, extrinsic motivation and perceptions of ability than the control group at post-test.

In another study, Cantwell (2005) studied the effectiveness of a strengths intervention in enhancing desired learning outcomes among students. While the control group engaged with their routine curriculum, the intervention group received course instruction from a distinct strengths-based perspective. Additionally, the latter received feedback from their Clifton Strengths Finder assessment. Findings suggested that intervention participants reported greater academic engagement and higher scores on relevant outcomes in comparison to the control group.

Another strengths-based programme directed towards flourishing classrooms and holistic school well-being is *Celebrating Strengths* (Fox Eades, 2008). This programme for primary school children in the UK merged the VIA strengths classification with school events and activities such as strengths identification in the class, recording student achievements and celebrating strengths. Findings based on programme evaluation have shown gains in participants' self-confidence, achievement motivation as well as emotional, cognitive and behavioural development (Govindji & Linley, 2007).

Seligman et al. (2009) evaluated the Strath Haven Positive Psychology Program wherein participants were randomly allocated to the intervention or control conditions. Pre-test, post-test and two year follow up data was collected from all students as well as their parents and teachers on all variables of interest. Pre-test to post-test comparisons revealed that intervention participants reported more enjoyment and engagement in school as compared to control group participants. Parents and teachers also reported enhancement in social skills of the intervention participants. However, no change in depression and anxiety scores was reported.

Madden, Green and Grant (2010) designed and evaluated a strengths-based programme in the Australian school setting. Based on the VIA character strengths framework, this 8-session curriculum helped participants identify their character strengths, set goals to use them in new ways and also write about their best future selves in the form of a 'letter from the future'. A within subject pre-test–post-test design was used. Results suggested that participants reported increased hope and engagement at post-test.

Proctor et al. (2011) studied the effectiveness of a character strengths curriculum called *Strengths Gym* (Proctor & Fox Eades, 2009) among school students in Great Britain. This programme was spread over 24 sessions (one session for each strength as per the VIA classification of strengths). Each session included the definition of the character strength in focus, two strengths builders exercises and a strengths challenge as a follow-up activity. The programme aimed to support identification of strengths (in self and others) and building of strengths among students. Age-appropriate strengths-based worksheets and exercises were used for students through Grades 7–9. Proctor et al. (2011) used a quasi-experimental pre-test–post-test design. Participants were assessed on measures of life satisfaction, positive and negative affect, and self-esteem. Results showed that the intervention group reported significantly higher life satisfaction, positive affect and self-esteem as compared to the control group.

Quinlan (2013) developed and delivered a classroom strengths programme called *Awesome Us* among grade 5–8 students in New Zealand. Programme resources included activities, video clips and hands-on work. Strategies such as strength spotting in self and others, linking them to VIA, setting valued goals and attaining them by using strengths were utilized. Preliminary results indicated improvement in participant scores on positive affect, engagement and relatedness. Qualitative feedback from students and teachers reflected that the programme facilitated focus on students' positive aspects and enabled corrective feedback and relatedness within the classroom setting (Quinlan, 2013; Quinlan, Swain, Cameron, & Vella-Brodrick, 2015).

Gratitude

Gratitude is a highly valued emotion that serves moral functions (McCullough, Kilpatrick, Emmons, & Larson, 2001) and is also understood to be linked to positive feelings and positive transformations of selfhood (Bono, Froh, & Emmons, 2012). A lot of evidence shows that gratitude has implications for the well-being of individuals as well as groups.

Recent research has shown that grateful youth exhibited higher tendency towards social integration (Froh, Bono, & Emmons, 2010), increased prosocial behaviour and reduced anti-social behaviour as compared to their counterparts who were low on gratitude (Bono, Froh, Emmons, & Card, 2013). All such findings and others indicate that gratitude fosters purposeful growth, life satisfaction, value for interpersonal relations—all of which are in sync with less materialism—a predominant social challenge (Chaplin & John, 2007).

The links between gratitude development and PYD (positive youth development) have also been suggested (Bono et al., 2013). In this context, it has been suggested that one of the first steps towards nurturing more grateful nations is assimilation of gratitude curricula in schools for children and adolescents (Lomas, Froh, Emmons, Mishra, & Bono, 2014). Besides being valuable for students, gratitude interventions have offered promising results with school teachers as well (e.g., Chan, 2010). Practicing gratitude can lead to flourishing schools and communities (Bono, Froh, & Forrett, 2014), which is in the truest sense aligned with the broader goals of PP.

However, research focused on gratitude and its applications for youth/in schools is still at an initial stage. There is a need for delving deeper into the experience and expression of gratitude across different cultures (Bono et al., 2014). The following section will concentrate on research and interventions dealing with gratitude in the school setting.

In a school-based study, Froh, Sefick and Emmons (2008) worked with 11–14-year-old students. Participants were assigned to one of the three conditions: listing gratitude, hassles or control. Listing blessings was found to lead to more optimism, satisfaction with life and less negative affect, as compared to listing hassles.

Shi and Zhu (2008) evaluated the effectiveness of a gratitude and well-being focused intervention among middle school students in China. Participants were distributed across three groups: 'counting blessings', 'counting blessings and group tutorship' and 'control group'. It was found that both intervention groups showed gains in gratitude, life satisfaction and positive affect as compared to the control group.

In a study involving 5–11-year-old school students in United States, Owens and Patterson (2013) compared the outcomes of a gratitude promotion and best possible selves intervention to a control condition. Participants engaged in weekly sessions where they were asked to draw a picture of something they were grateful for (gratitude condition), a future version of their own happiest selves (best possible self) or something they had done that day (control condition). Results showed no significance difference between the gratitude and control condition on outcome variables; however, best possible selves condition showed greater gains in self-esteem compared to both other conditions. The content of participants' drawings revealed their capability to express things for which they felt grateful and to picture their best future versions.

Froh et al. (2014) pioneered a programme named 'Nice Thinking! An Educational Intervention That Teaches Children to Think Gratefully'. An evolution of their previous work, this intervention was centred on the concepts of 'intention', 'cost' and 'benefit' in the context of thankfulness. These concepts were woven into a five-session curriculum for the intervention group while the control group participated in an attention neutral activity over the same duration. Elementary school classrooms were randomized across treatment or control conditions. It was found that the benefit–appraisal intervention was effective in altering appraisals of perceived intention, cost and value of interpersonal benefits. While participants in the benefit–appraisal condition showed growth over time in gratitude and positive affect, those in the attention control condition remained static. However, no effect on negative affect or satisfaction with life as a result of intervention participation was reported in this study. On the whole, this intervention was effective with from small to medium effect sizes.

It is undeniable that there is growing interest and corresponding research in the field of gratitude interventions for youth. However, greater clarity is required regarding the empirical significance of such work. Based on a meta-analysis of 20 original empirical journal articles focusing on gratitude in youth, Renshaw and Olinger Steeves (2016) found modest evidence for gratitude as an indicator of subjective well-being in youth. This study also raised concerns about the effectiveness of gratitude interventions (in schools and otherwise), necessitating the need for further intervention research, and a more robust and diverse evidence base in this area.

Hope

Hope is a human strength manifested in the ability to think of goals, pathways to attain them and be motivated to work towards such goals.

Among students, hope has been found to be strongly correlated with life satisfaction and mental health (Marques, Pais-Ribeiro, & Lopez, 2007; 2011) and negatively correlated with measures of internalizing and externalizing behaviour problems, psychological distress and school maladjustment (e.g., Gilman, Dooley, & Florell, 2006). Further, highly hopeful children (Merkas & Brajsa-Zganec, 2011) and adolescents (Gilman et al., 2006; Marques, Lopez, & Mitchell, 2013) have been found to report better mental health and life satisfaction as compared to less hopeful children.

An overarching case for the application of hope-based interventions in schools has been built by Snyder, Lopez, Shorey, Rand and Feldman (2003), who mentioned that 'hopeful thinking can empower and guide a lifetime of learning, and school psychologists can help to keep this lesson alive' (p. 134). Additionally, it has been found that hope, life satisfaction and self-worth have significant and meaningful relations with mental health and academic achievement—both of which are highly valued (Marques et al., 2011). All this research evidence prompts us to focus on some prominent hope-based interventions in the educational setting.

Green, Anthony and Rynsaardt (2007) conducted a hope-based intervention for female senior school students in Australia. Participants were randomly assigned to a coaching intervention (ten sessions with teacher coach) or a control group. It was reported that intervention group students showed increment in scores of hope and hardiness and decline in depression and anxiety. No such effects were seen in the control group. However, no significant differences in stress were observed.

Marques, Lopez, & Pais-Ribeiro (2009) carried out a programme 'Building Hope for the Future' targeting Grade 6 school students in Portugal. Parents and teachers of the intervention group students were also involved in the programme. The intervention spanned five weeks and was delivered through one-hour sessions each week, integrating solution-focused, narrative and cognitive-behavioural techniques. As a result of the intervention, participants showed change in hope, life satisfaction and self-worth but no change was found on academic achievement.

A meta-analysis of hope enhancement strategies in clinical and community settings was documented by Weis and Speridakos (2011). They evaluated whether these interventions were effective in increasing hope and life satisfaction and/or decreasing psychological distress among participants. Based on 27 studies that were shortlisted as per inclusion criteria, significant though small effect sizes for hope and life satisfaction were obtained. However, no significant relationship between hope interventions and psychological distress was reported. Meanwhile, Weis and Speridakos (2011) found that studies involving participants from educational and community settings showed marginally greater effect sizes as compared to those involving participants from clinical settings or with medical conditions.

Resilience

According to Fergus and Zimmerman (2005), resilience theory offers a conceptual model to understand how youth tackle adversity and use this information towards advancing strengths and positive aspects of youth and adolescence. The Penn Optimism Program (POP; Shatté, Gillham, & Reivich, 2000) is an extension of Seligman's work for teaching optimism to children. POP is a classroom-based group intervention spread over 12 weeks. It has a cognitive element (challenging irrational beliefs, solution focused thinking, etc.) and a skills training element (assertiveness, decision making, etc.). This was later renamed as the Penn Resilience Program (PRP; Gillham & Reivich, 2004).

An adaptation of PRP was implemented in the UK as UKPRP with the goal of promoting well-being and resilience among Grade 7 school students. This programme revolved around cognitive behavioural techniques that imparted assertiveness, relaxation and decision-making skills among a host of other skills aimed at boosting resilience. Challen, Noden, West and Machin (2011) evaluated this programme using both qualitative and quantitative assessment. Qualitative findings revealed positive feedback from both students and teachers involved with the programme. Further, significant enhancement was observed in scores of depression symptoms, school attendance and academic achievement in English and math scores. However, no gains were reported on behavioural and life satisfaction scores.

Seligman et al. (2009) reported the findings of PRP aimed at enhancing students' ability to deal with daily life stressors and common adolescent problems. A meta-analysis including PRP studies across diverse adolescent groups revealed that as compared to control groups, PRP reduces and prevents symptoms of depression, hopelessness, anxiety and may even reduce behavioural problems.

A classroom-based resilience and well-being intervention programme called *Bounce Back!* (McGrath & Noble, 2003) was originally developed in Australia. It has since been applied in many settings. The core areas included in this programme are prosocial values, coping skills, relationships skills, emotions and so forth. The programme comprises of activities and resources designed in accordance with developmental and age maturity. In the Scottish context, this programme has shown favourable impact in terms of well-being, connectedness and resilience among participating pupils. The programme was more effective in school settings with strong leadership, proactive staff teams and proper care towards programme implementation.

Peabody, Rhee and Leventhal (2010) have illustrated the findings of the Positive psychology, Emotional competence, Restorative practices and Communication for Youth (PERCY) school programme for middle school students. Also known as the CorStone Children's Resiliency Program, this was a mixed method intervention comprised of weekly sessions in small groups spread over 26 weeks. Participants were assessed at multiple times, and inputs were sought from teachers and facilitators about students' positive and negative behaviour as well as observed progress among participants. Results revealed an early and significant enhancement in level of optimism as well as decline in pessimism and external locus of control. While optimism and locus of control scores were sustained over time, improvement in pessimism scores began to dwindle later. Teachers and facilitators reported greater positive behaviour, coping skills and resilience among students. Students self-report revealed no change in physical fights with peers (Peabody et al., 2010).

A recent meta-analysis including 19 school-based interventions aimed at promoting resilience was carried out by Geesen (2014). The study focused on resilience, coping and self-esteem as outcome measures and considered two subgroups of primary and secondary school students. An overall small effect size of 0.24 on resilience was obtained, and no significant difference in effect sizes between the two subgroups was found. On the whole, Geesen (2014) reported small effects in school-based resilience interventions.

STRESS MANAGEMENT, RELAXATION AND MINDFULNESS

Diverse approaches are used to manage stress that include an array of relaxation techniques, meditation and so forth. For the purpose of this review, studies pertaining to stress management, relaxation and mindfulness training have been compiled in the same section. While each of these strategies have their own nuances, they do offer an overlapping area of research and practice and have therefore been considered as a whole.

Klein (2004) evaluated the impact of a randomized controlled trial of a classroom programme named Reaching New Heights. Participants recruited from three middle schools were allocated to immediate intervention and delayed intervention groups. They were assessed at pre-test, post-test and six-month follow up. The intervention comprised of 13 weekly sessions (each of 50 minutes duration) focused on enhancing students' stress—management and coping skills, and reducing anxiety as well as perfectionism. Participants showed improvement in problem solving skills and competency levels in school tasks. However, improved problem solving was not sustained at follow-up.

Keogh, Bond and Flaxman (2006) discussed a multi-method stress management intervention for school children. The intervention was delivered via 10 sessions in the form of a weekly hour-long workshop during school time. Results showed that the intervention group scored on an average 8 points higher than control group in exam performance, even when controlling for gender and intelligence. Keogh et al. (2006) also found that the increased motivation in intervention group was responsible for better exam performance.

Kraag et al. (2007) illustrated the process evaluation of Learn Young, Learn Fair—a stress management intervention for school students. This primary prevention programme aimed to enhance mental health in school by educating participants about coping skills and stress awareness. This programme comprised of eight weekly sessions, each session being of one-hour duration. Five booster sessions were given two months after the weekly session. Trained teachers delivered the programme by incorporating it in their curriculum. The intervention was positively evaluated by both students and teachers (Kraag et al., 2005) and found feasible for future implementation (Kraag et al., 2007).

Broderick and Metz (2009) evaluated a six-session mindfulness meditation programme delivered to American female school students. All participants were evaluated at pre-test and post-test. Findings showed that intervention group reported increment in feelings of self-acceptance, calmness and relaxation as well as reduction in negative affect as compared to the control group at post-test. At the end of the programme, improvement in emotion regulation and decline in somatic complaints was observed in the intervention participants.

Vierhaus, Maass, Fridrici and Lohaus (2010) studied a school-based stress prevention programme, spread over eight weekly sessions of 90 minutes each, involving adolescents in Germany. Participant group, in contrast to control group, showed a progression in regard to the phases of behavioural change after the first week but not after twelve weeks of the programme. This implies that the programme had effects which were not stable once the programme ended.

Huppert and Johnson (2010) described a classroom-based mindfulness training intervention delivered to adolescent English boys, delivered by a trained facilitator over four weekly sessions. A significant positive association was found between the amount of individual practice by participants, and improvement in well-being as well as mindfulness. No significant difference was seen in the results pertaining to the intervention group and the control group.

The effectiveness of a randomized-controlled trial of a mindfulness intervention spread over 12 weeks was reported by Mendelson et al. (2010). Urban school students from Grades 4 and 5 participated in yoga-based physical activity and supervised mindfulness practice to help with stress management. Findings revealed reduction in negative coping experiences such as rumination and emotional arousal among intervention participants.

Flook et al. (2010) evaluated a school-based intervention of mindful awareness practices for elementary school students. The eight-week-long programme was delivered in the form of biweekly sessions of 30 minutes each. Study results suggested that participants with relatively poor executive function score at baseline exhibited greater benefit from the intervention in terms of global executive control, behavioural control and metacognition. These findings were substantiated by both teacher and parent reports.

Liehr and Diaz (2010) conducted a randomized trial involving comparative analysis of a mindfulness-based intervention with a health education module. Participants (students from a disadvantaged background) were randomly allocated to either a mindfulness-based intervention or to a health education group. The former group received 10 sessions of 15 minutes each, spread over a period of two weeks, focused on mindful breathing and movement. Liehr and Diaz (2010) reported a significant decline in depression symptoms among participants of the mindfulness intervention while participants from both groups showed a reduction in anxiety at the time of immediate post-test assessment.

A quasi-experimental pre-test–post-test evaluation of a mindfulness-based education programme was reported by Schonert-Reichl and Lawlor (2010). The intervention emphasized the development of positive emotions and socio-emotional skills, facilitated by classroom teachers through daily lessons involving mindful attention training. Participants were pre-adolescents and early adolescents from schools in a Canadian district. They were rated by teachers on aspects of classroom-based socio-emotional competence. Study findings revealed that intervention group showed significant improvements in optimism, dimensions of teacher-rated social competence and self-concept as compared to control group.

In another US-based study, Nidich et al. (2011) evaluated the effect of the transcendental meditation programme on participants' well-being, social behaviour and academic performance. For three months, the experimental group students engaged in a 12-minute meditation session at the beginning and end of each school day. Meanwhile, the control group just participated in 12 minutes of quiet time each day. At the time of post-test, teachers reported that intervention group students were calmer, happier and more focused on school work than they were at pre-test. Participants in the meditation session also showed significant raises in their academic scores over the span of one year.

In a controlled trial in Hong Kong, Lau and Hue (2011) evaluated a school-based mindfulness intervention. Participants were secondary school-going adolescents with poor academic accomplishment. Preliminary outcomes revealed significant improvement in well-being as well as depressive symptoms among intervention participants as compared to those in the control group.

Foret et al. (2012) examined the feasibility and effectiveness of a relaxation response-based curriculum integrated into the school routine at a high school located in Massachusetts. This non-randomized cohort study included high school students assigned to control group and intervention group respectively. All participants were assessed on measures of perceived stress, locus of control, anxiety and self-esteem at pre-test and post-test. The intervention group engaged in eight sessions spread over four weeks during which they were exposed to a variety of relaxation response techniques such as yoga, meditation, breath focus, mindfulness among others. Aspects like informative sessions on stress awareness, PP activities like gratitude journaling and cognitive restructuring were also included. The classroom training was supplemented with instruction to practice the relaxation response at home using guided meditation audio tracks that were made accessible online. Results indicated significant betterment in perceived stress and anxiety in the intervention group as compared to the control group. Breathing and relaxation techniques were listed among the most preferred components of the programme.

Kuyken et al. (2013) evaluated the effectiveness of Mindfulness in Schools Program—a schools-based universal mindfulness intervention to enhance mental health and well-being. Participants in this nine-week-long study were assigned to the intervention group or continued with usual school routine. It was found that intervention group reported fewer depressive symptoms post-intervention. More well-being, lower stress and less depressive symptoms were reported in intervention group as compared to the control group at follow-up.

Frank, Bose and Schrobenhauser-Clonan (2014) assessed the effectiveness of a school-based yoga programme—Transformational Life Skills—aimed at enhancing socio-emotional wellness of high-risk adolescents in America. Sessions lasting approximately 30 minutes each were delivered in the classroom by trained yoga instructors. The programme dealt with issues of stress response, physical and emotional awareness, self-regulation and developing healthy interpersonal relations. Results indicated significant and meaningful decline in participant reports of anxiety, depression and global psychological distress. However, no significant differences were reported on scores of general positive or negative affect.

Edwards, Adams, Waldo, Hadfield and Biegel (2014) reported the outcomes of a pilot study to evaluate the impact of mindfulness groups on Latino adolescent school students. It was a structured eight session programme (50 minutes for each session) that used the mindfulness-based stress reduction (MBSR) for teens curriculum. Experiential mindful practices, group discussions and presentations were incorporated in the sessions, and participants were encouraged to practice mindfulness at home. Results revealed an enhancement in participants' level of mindfulness and self-compassion as well as a significant decline in their scores on depression and perceived stress.

Wendt et al. (2015) reported the impact of participation in a meditation-based programme called Quiet Time among high school students. The core idea of this programme was to provide participants a 15-minute time slot at the start and close of a school day, wherein they could practice transcendental meditation or any other quiet activity (e.g., reading silently). Results revealed that participants scored significantly lower on anxiety and higher on resilience at follow-up as compared to the control group. Participants who spent greater time meditating reported better resilience and academic outcomes and also perceived benefits in terms of their sleep, happiness and self-confidence.

Hashim and Zainol (2015) evaluated the effectiveness of a progressive muscle relaxation (PMR) based intervention among primary school children in Malaysia. The study compared the effects across three groups (6 sessions, 12 sessions and control group) on scores on emotional distress, short-term memory and attention. Results revealed no significant differences among the groups in anxiety, depression, stress and sustained attention. However, significant difference was seen in terms of short-term memory. Participants in the 12-session group exhibited more increase in memory as compared to the remaining two groups.

246 | Pulkit Khanna and Kamlesh Singh

In a meta-analysis of mindfulness-based interventions involving youth, Burke (2010) reviewed a total of 14 studies. All studies included some formal meditation and many included some form of psycho education as well. Review findings provided overall favourable evidence for mindfulness interventions. Positive intervention effects on social, academic, cognitive, physiological and behavioural functioning of participants were reported.

Findings of a meta-analytic study of mindfulness-based intervention in schools have been reported by Zenner, Herrnleben-Kurz and Walach (2014). A total of 24 studies (published and unpublished) from heterogeneous backgrounds were considered. Outcome variables were grouped into the categories of cognitive performance, emotional problems, resilience, stress, coping and third person ratings. Effect sizes derived in this analysis were comparable to the results of other meta-analyses of school-based prevention programmes. Studies involving home based practice were found to have greater impact. However, the sheer diversity of the studies included and the effects of the potential moderators constrain the generalizability of these findings to an extent.

MULTI-COMPONENT PROGRAMMES

This section includes studies that deal with more than one theme.

Martin (2008) evaluated a multi-dimensional intervention aimed at enhancing student motivation and engagement. The intervention was delivered to an all-male sample of Australian students. It was structured over 13 modules with a self-complete programme of activities. Each module was structured around the prepare–generate–reflect–closure procedure. Intervention group made positive motivation shifts in the areas of task management, anxiety and persistence.

McCabe-Fitch (2009) investigated the effectiveness of PP exercises in increasing self-reported happiness among school children aged 12–14 years. Participants were randomly allocated to the intervention or control condition. The intervention group completed the exercises pertaining to 'gratitude letter' (writing it and delivering it to the person they wanted to thank) and 'three good things in life'. While these exercises were done over a period of one week, the control group participants completed a task called 'life details' wherein they kept a note about three details of their day over one week. Results indicated that experimental group participants reported small increases in happiness at post-test but small to moderate effects at the time of follow up assessment. Importantly, the participating adolescents scored fairly high on happiness at the time of baseline assessment.

Suldo, Savage and Mercer (2013) worked on a PP-based group intervention for enhancing life satisfaction of middle school students. Participants were students who scored low on a screening measure of life satisfaction. A 10-week-long group wellness programme based on existing PP research was delivered. Results showed that participation in intervention was associated with students' enjoyment of the intervention as well as enhancement of global life satisfaction. No additional gains were reported on any dimension of mental health, psychopathology or subjective well-being.

Standage, Cumming and Gillison (2013) studied the effectiveness of the 'be the best you can be' (BtBYCB) programme to foster positive physical, psychological and social development among children. Using a cluster randomized controlled trial, 11–13-year-old participants from schools in England were randomly allocated to the intervention or control condition. Spread over 13 sessions, the programme included sessions on personal, social and health education, special talks and celebration events. Participants were assessed on outcome measures at three time points. A mixed-method approach was used to understand the different experiences of particular groupings within and across the intervention schools.

A promising culturally oriented PP initiative was proposed in China in the form of psychological suzhi—a native academic proposition of quality-based education (Wang & Zhang, 2012). The fundamental purpose of psychological suzhi is an application of PP traits that enable Chinese adolescents to deal positively with their school setting. Comprising of the key tenets of cognition quality, personality quality and adaptability, psychological suzhi is understood as the combination of implicit psychological characteristics and explicit adaptive behaviours (Wang & Zhang, 2012). Special strategies for training and imparting of psychological suzhi in the school setting have been developed. Initial findings showed positive outcomes like improvements in self-efficacy (Wang & Wang, 2008) and reduction in emotional regulation problems (Shao, Zhang, Wang, & Yi, 2010).

Proctor (2014) described a comprehensive PP-based well-being curriculum for years 1–13 that was developed and implemented at Haberdashers' Aske's Hatcham College in London. This programme included a gamut of individual evidence-based interventions. PPIs pertaining to happiness, flow, resilience, positive emotions and so forth were the core areas of focus for years 1–9. Later, positive education was the key focus area. With different focus areas, stages and evaluation outcomes for different levels, the programme involved weekly sessions through formal or informal channels. Based on preliminary findings, proctor (2014) reported that the programme was associated with enhancement in positive affect, life satisfaction, self-actualization and reduction in negative affect among intervention participants as compared to students from a comparison school.

Another prominent and promising well-being intervention from the recent times is the Positive Psychology Program (PPP; Gillham et al., 2013). The highlight of this programme was its underlying focus on assimilation within the school curriculum, and expanding its delivery not just through well-defined lesson plans but also through assignments and discussions that fit into routine academic lessons. Classrooms teachers act as the intervention facilitators. PPP includes 20–25 lessons imparted during the course of Grade 9. Areas of focus range from happiness, savouring, gratitude, optimism to character strengths, etc. Incorporation of these concepts and corresponding exercises is done in ways such that they may merge with routine class lessons. Preliminary findings have been favourable—indicating a boost in social skills, participant reports of school engagement as well as gains in academic achievement through Grade 11 (Gillham, Abenavoli, Brunwasser, Reivich, & Seligman 2013; Seligman et al., 2009).

Suldo et al. (2015) developed and evaluated a class wide PPI to boost subjective well-being among elementary school children. The programme spread over 11 sessions dealt with gratitude, kindness, character strengths and relationships within the classroom setting. Findings of a pilot study revealed gains in positive emotion, life satisfaction as well as contentment with self and social environment at post-test as well as follow-up. No benefits were reported in terms of negative affect.

In a study based in Netherlands, Elfrink, Goldberg, Schreurs, Bohlmeijer, & Clarke (2017) evaluated a pilot programme called 'Positive Education Program' to enhance student well-being and positive school climate. The programme involved workshops to promote values, life rules and engagement. Parent involvement was also incorporated through parent meetings. Initial evidence suggested gains for participants' self-reported well-being, problem behaviour, strengths and overall climate.

Roth, Suldo and Ferron (2017) studied the impact of a multicomponent programme involving middle school students and their parents. Students were assigned to intervention or waitlist control group. Findings revealed significant gains on life satisfaction, positive affect and negative affect as well as enduring gains on positive affect.

A meta-analysis by Waters (2011) reviewed 12 school-based PPIs designed to boost well-being and academic performance of students. These interventions primarily pertained to building positive emotions, character strengths and resilience. It was also noted that these interventions were implemented with students from diverse nations, ethnicities and across diverse school settings including co-educational as well as single gender schools. Findings indicated that PPIs were significantly linked with student well-being, academic outcomes as well as relationships.

In another meta-analysis, Bolier et al. (2013) evaluated 39 studies to understand effectiveness of PPIs for general public as well as those with some psychosocial problem. PPIs considered in this study were self-help interventions, individual training and group therapy. Results indicated that PPIs significantly enhanced well-being and reduced depressive symptoms. Small to moderate effect sizes were obtained. Small yet significant effect sizes for well-being were obtained even at 3–6 month follow up. Bolier et al. (2013) also mentioned the diversity in nature and quality of the studies as well as the presence of publication bias.

Dawood (2013) also reviewed the evidence base of school-based PP interventions. Studies pertaining to gratitude, hope, self-efficacy, life-satisfaction, etc., were reviewed. Findings indicated support for the efficacy of such interventions in promoting positive traits. However, lack of an adequately large evidence base as well as gaps in data were pointed out as impediments before beginning widespread implementation of PP in school settings.

SOCIAL AND EMOTIONAL LEARNING

SEL entails the development and application of skills essential to understand emotions, positive relationships, responsible decision-making, self-awareness and social-awareness (CASEL, 2008). SEL incorporates various strategies to promote mental health, and social and emotional skills, through curricula that form an important part of schooling (Zins, Bloodworth, Weissberg, & Walberg, 2004). While earlier literature maintained SEL as a distinct area, there is an emerging focus to integrate it with positive youth development towards consolidation of efforts to promote youth positive well-being. The following section focuses on interventions that have worked towards the advancement of SEL in the school setting.

Gordon (2001) examined the effectiveness of the 'roots of empathy' (ROE) programme among students from Grade 4 to Grade 7. Lessons relevant to empathy, sensitivity (corresponding with the SEL competencies of social awareness and relationship skills) were delivered. Programme participants exhibited greater prosocial behaviour (as per peer nominations) and lower aggressive behaviour (as per teacher rating) as compared to control group participants (Gordon, 2001). A subsequent evaluation of ROE (Schonert-Reichl, Smith, Zaidman-Zait, & Hertzman, 2012) reported enhanced prosocial behaviours and reduced aggression among participants.

Promoting alternative thinking strategies (PATHS; Greenberg, Kusche, Cook, & Quamma, 1995) was an SEL programme aimed at a school-wide implementation through regular classroom teachers. In an evaluation, Domitrovich, Cortes and Greenberg (2007) reported enhanced social competence and reduced social withdrawal among preschool participants.

Rimm-Kaufman, Fan, Chiu, & You (2007) examined the responsive classroom (RC) approach which focused on children's academic and social skills along with fostering a conducive environment for these skills. Participants reported a boost in positive feelings towards school, teachers, classmates and learning (Brock, Nishida, Chiong, Grimm, & Rimm-Kaufman, 2008). Further, programme participants showed better academic scores, prosocial behaviour, assertiveness and reduction in fear as compared to a control group (Rimm-Kaufman et al., 2007; Rimm-Kaufman & Chiu, 2007).

Jones, Brown and Lawrence Aber (2008) studied the 4Rs (reading, writing, respect and resolution) Programme dealing with conflict resolution, cultural difference and cooperation in the classroom. Brown, Jones, LaRusso and Lawrence Aber (2010) reported that after one year of implementation, 4Rs classrooms were rated higher by independent observers in quality of student–teacher interactions and teacher's sensitivity to student needs. Two years into the programme, participants were rated higher on social competence and attention as compared to counterparts in a control group (Jones, Brown, & Lawrence Aber, 2011).

Qualter, Whiteley, Hutchinson and Pope (2007) explored the effectiveness of an intervention to foster students' emotional intelligence (EI) competencies. Themes like bullying, relationships, self-esteem and emotions were addressed. Results suggested that students with high EI were able to cope better with transition than those with low EI. Further, the programme was more beneficial for those with low baseline EI scores.

In a study involving Norwegian school students, Holsen, Smith and Frey (2008) evaluated effectiveness of a universal social competence programme 'Second Step' on social competence, externalizing and internalizing problem. The programme focused on improving children's socio-emotional competence by helping develop skills in the area of empathy, problem solving, impulse control and anger management. Results showed generally positive outcomes but variation was reported across classrooms as well as gender of participants.

At the University of Oregon, United States of America, a prominent SEL programme called 'Strong Kids' was developed. This module encompassed curricula to nurture social and emotional skills, resilience, strengths and healthy coping skills among children and early adolescents. The programme catered to different age groups across school children through variants called 'Strong Start, Strong Kids and Strong Teens' further segregated to suit different grades. This programme has been widely researched. While some studies have reported significant decline in internalizing symptoms among programme participants (e.g., Caldarella, Christensen, Kramer, & Kronmiller, 2009; Faust, 2006; Isava, 2006, etc.), others have reported contrary findings (Gueldner & Merrell, 2011; Nakayama, 2008). Significant improvements in social and emotional learning among participants have been found (Castro-Olivio & Merrell, 2012; Gueldner & Merrell, 2011; Harlacher & Merrell, 2010). To sum up, there is abundant evidence in favour of 'Strong Kids' as an effective and socially valid SEL curriculum.

Social and Emotional Aspects of Learning (SEAL) was a government-funded programme in UK. It was offered as 'primary seal' and 'secondary seal' respectively, corresponding with the target students' age group. SEAL was characterized by a comprehensive approach and extensive research has been done to study the impact of SEAL programmes.

Humphrey, Kalambouka, Wigelsworth and Lendrum (2010) documented the effectiveness trial of a sub-aspect of the SEAL programme called 'Going for Goals'—a brief socio-emotional intervention for children. This eight-week-long study assessed intervention impact on socio-emotional skills, behaviour and well-being of the participants and checked if these impacts were sustained during a seven-week follow-up. Staff informant-report ratings of behavioural and emotional well-being showed that the intervention helped reduce overall difficulties. However, Humphrey et al. (2010) obtained null results from parental data.

Wigelsworth, Humphrey and Lendrum (2012) reported the findings of a SEAL study based upon a longitudinal quasi experimental pre-test–post-test control group design. Null results were obtained for this study as a whole wherein SEAL failed to significantly impact either the total sample or the at-risk sub-sample on the outcome variables.

Bidgood, Wilkie and Katchaluba (2010) evaluated the Supporting Tempers, Emotions, and Anger Management (STEAM) programme for elementary and adolescent children. Participants were teacher referred students from Grades 1 to Grade 8 from Canadian schools. Results revealed maximum significant change as a result of intervention in younger participants (Grades 1–3), and relatively little change in the other groups.

Hutchings et al. (2011) described a pilot study conducted to assess the benefits of the Incredible Years (IY) therapeutic programme for 5–9 year old 'at risk' participants. This study used the Therapeutic Dina (TD) programme—a component of IY that helps to mitigate conduct problems and enhances children's peer relationships and problem-solving skills (Webster-Stratton & Reid, 2003). Hutchings et al. (2011) reported no significant differences between intervention group and control group on outcome measures, but a sub-sample analysis of children classified as 'high risk' by school teachers exhibited significant benefits in problem-solving skill in case of the intervention group.

A socio-emotional resiliency skills programme called 'You Can Do It!' (YCDI) was evaluated by Bernard and Walton (2011) in Australia. YCDI included lessons in resilience, confidence, organization and persistence. Student assessment over one year showed that YCDI participants reported significant increments in various positive variables such as morale, connectedness with peers and school, and motivation. However, control group participants reported improvement only in student safety and classroom behaviour.

Di Fabio (2010) developed an emotional learning intervention rooted in the EI theory of Mayer and Salovey (1997) for high school students in Italy. The intervention was of 10 hours duration spread over four weeks. The sessions dealt with the themes of 'perceiving emotions', 'facilitating thought', 'understanding emotions' and 'managing emotions'. Results showed that the intervention was associated with improvement in EI and decline in indecision; these effects being sustained for a month after the intervention (Di Fabio & Kenny, 2011).

Another SEL intervention founded on the EI theory of Mayer and Salovey (1997) was the recognizing, understanding, labelling, expressing and regulating emotion (i.e., RULER) programme. This programme, focused on a feeling words curriculum, was used in schools in the United States. It observed the guiding principles laid down by CASEL in terms of involvement of school staff, and family, integration of programme with the standard lessons and assessment of programme outcomes. Findings suggested improvement in relationships, academic performance, interpersonal communication and reduction in behavioural issues among participants (Brackett, Rivers, Reyes, & Salovey, 2012).

In a meta-analysis of classroom-based social skills interventions, January, Casey and Paulson (2011) considered 23 articles published between 1981 and 2007. Only studies that involved the entire classroom (and not just students with difficulties) were considered. On the whole, interventions were found to have a small but positive effect on social behaviour. Moderate intervention outcomes were reported for several variables. Results indicated that classroom interventions targeting social skills were most effective among younger students. January et al. (2011) also found that effectiveness of such interventions rose around early adolescence—a phase of significant developmental shift.

Durlak, Weissber, Dymnicki, Taylor and Schellinger (2011) presented findings from a meta-analysis of school-based, universal SEL programmes. Most programmes were classroom-based—53 per cent were delivered by teachers and 21 per cent by non-school personnel. An 11 percentile gain in academic performance was reported. Contrary to their hypothesis and some existing literature (Catalano, Berglund, Ryan, Lonczak, & Hawkins, 2002), Durlak et al. (2011) did not find multicomponent programmes to be more beneficial than single-component programmes.

More recently, Taylor et al. (2017) reported meta-analytic findings based on 82 school-based SEL programmes spread across kindergarten to high school. Programme participants were found to fare significantly better than control group across indicators of well-being and social emotional skills. The most promising finding was that gains were consistent across diverse school locations, race and socio-economic backgrounds.

As demonstrated through this extensive review of school-based intervention work in various countries, it is clear that preventive and promotive wok in the field of mental health and well-being for students has been garnering attention. Having taken a look at the work happening globally, the next section will focus more specifically on the present scenario of such work in the Indian context.

PP AND STUDENT WELL-BEING IN INDIAN SCHOOLS: PRESENT SCENARIO

As mentioned earlier in this chapter, research in the area of PP in Indian schools is somewhat new and growing. Some work in the field appears to be happening on a purely experiential basis, without adequate scientific evidence base or rigorous documentation. Over the next few pages, we examine the present status of PP in Indian schools through the lens of documented research evidence. Given the availability of relatively limited research in this area, a few studies from higher education settings have also been included in this review.

We begin by describing our work with North Indian school-going adolescents that was taken up as part of the first author's doctoral research. Four independent intervention programmes (two of which have been included in the previous section) were delivered to a cross-section of school-going boys and girls aged 10–14 years.

In a study involving 11–14-year-old students from two schools, Khanna and Singh (2016) evaluated the effectiveness of Froh et al.'s (2014) 'Nice Thinking! An Educational Intervention That Teaches Children to Think Gratefully'. Froh et al. (2014) developed this classroom-based gratitude intervention revolving around social cognitions of intention, cost and benefit which are associated with the experience of gratitude. The five-week-long curriculum for both intervention and control groups was replicated in its entirety, with minor adaptations to better fit the Indian context. The first author delivered the sessions across all participating classrooms. Intervention participants scored better on self-reported measures of well-being, positive affect, life satisfaction and gratitude as compared to a control group, no relation between gratitude and negative affect; concurring with the findings of Froh and colleagues in their 2014 study. Findings also indicated mutual as well as cascading positive effect emanating from gratitude (Khanna & Singh, 2016).

In another study, Khanna (2016) evaluated the effectiveness of a stress management and gratitude journaling intervention originally conceptualized by Flinchbaugh, Moore, Chang, & May (2012). The original study by Flinchbaugh and colleagues (2012) was conducted over 12 weeks among management undergraduates using an online system. In the present study, participants were young adolescents aged 11–14 years recruited from two schools. They were allocated to four groups—stress management training, gratitude journaling, combination of both and control group—randomized by classrooms. The original curriculum put forth by Flinchbaugh et al. (2012) was replicated. However, the present study was conducted over eight weeks, using hard copy journals/booklets for students. These adaptations were made in view of the logistics and contextual setting. Participants were assessed on indicators of well-being, perceived stress, engagement, meaning and life satisfaction. Results revealed no significant intervention effects on self-reported measures of life satisfaction, perceived classroom engagement, stress and meaningfulness, although students found the intervention useful, interesting and relaxing. Specific stress management techniques, written components of programme and allocation of participants to different groups emerged as perceived criticisms of the programme. Overall findings indicated limited intervention effectiveness. The original study (Flinchbaugh et al., 2012) had shown relatively better outcomes. It has not been included in the present review as it was delivered to college students.

Using a well-researched intervention with Indian students, Khanna (2016) evaluated the effectiveness of 'Strengths Gym' (Proctor & Fox Eades, 2009) among 11–13-year olds from two schools. The 24-session curriculum was delivered to students over a 12-week period by classroom teachers. Before rolling out the curriculum in the classrooms, teachers were familiarized with the programme and handed over the curriculum material. Intervention fidelity was maintained through regular contact and exchange of feedback between the researchers and teachers. Aligned with the findings reported by Proctor et al. (2011), this study indicated that intervention participants scored significantly better than control group on self-reported measures of emotional well-being, happiness and affect. However, no significant intervention effect was reported on social and psychological well-being, life satisfaction and self-esteem. Overall findings broadly reinforced previous research which shows a positive association between character strengths, well-being and flourishing among youth (e.g., Brdar & Kashdan, 2010; Ruch et al., 2014).

A landmark study by Seligman, Steen, Park and Peterson (2005) delineated a web-based randomized controlled intervention using five happiness boosting exercises and one placebo control exercise. Five exercises—one on gratitude building (gratitude visit), two on raising awareness of one's own positive self and savouring (three good things in life, you at your best), and two exercises based on identification and use of character strengths (identifying signature strengths, using signature strengths in a new way) were used. Khanna & Singh (2019) evaluated the effectiveness of these exercises among Indian school-going adolescents aged 11–14 years. Participants were randomly allocated to any one of the five exercise groups or the placebo control group, and instructed to partake in their assigned activity over a one-week period. It is noteworthy that the participants in our study were randomly selected students unlike self-nominated adult volunteers in the original study by Seligman et al. (2005). Furthermore, they were provided individual booklets to keep a record of their week-long activity. The original study was web based. Results of the present study were promising yet quite modest in comparison with Seligman et al. (2005). In a nutshell, Khanna and Singh (2019) found that students who engaged in interactive activities such as the 'gratitude visit' and 'use of signature strengths in new ways' reported significant perceived gains on indicators of well-being, life satisfaction and happiness. Other exercises such as 'three good things in life' and 'you at your best', which had self-reflection and/or journaling at the heart of them did not show significant gains on well-being indicators. Contrary to Seligman et al. (2005), none of the participants showed any gains with respect to depressive symptoms.

The participants for each of the four interventions described above were mutually exclusive. For each study, participants' feedback for their respective programme was sought using a semi-structured interview schedule. Khanna and Singh (2014) reported that majority of the students enjoyed participation and perceived their respective programmes to be beneficial as an opportunity to learn more about themselves as also to express themselves. However, many students did not like the idea of attending such a programme at the cost of some other scheduled class/activity. They also expressed dislike for undertaking written work (assessments, journaling, etc.). The detailed findings have been published elsewhere.

Moving to other prominent work in India, an international organization, CorStone, has pioneered 'CorStone's Children's Resiliency Program for Girls'—a resilience curriculum to promote well-being among marginalized adolescent girls. Leventhal and Sachs (2011) reported the findings from a pilot project, wherein CorStone tested the programme content and delivery among 100 girls in a New Delhi slum school. The programme was delivered over six months, and participants were assessed both quantitatively and qualitatively. Statistically significant gains on various mental and emotional health indicators were reported (Leventhal & Sachs, 2011).

Further, CorStone evaluated CPRG among nearly 1,000 marginalized adolescent girls in Gujrat, India in 2011. Participants were equally distributed across intervention and control groups. Results revealed significant improvement on scores of mental health indicators, social skills and behavioural difficulties among programme participants as compared to controls (Leventhal & Sachs, 2011).

In a study situated in Bihar, India, Leventhal et al. (2015) evaluated the effectiveness of 'Girls First Resilience Curriculum'. This 5-month long school-based curriculum among rural adolescent girls was facilitated by local women. Participants completed self-report questionnaires at baseline and after programme completion. Leventhal et al. (2015) reported that participants gained on indicators of emotional resilience, self-efficacy, social-emotional assets, psychological well-being and social well-being as compared to controls. No significant impact was reported on depression. Findings from this study are particularly promising as they exemplify the potential gains from a brief school-based intervention delivered in a disadvantaged context. Programme facilitation by local women is also an excellent example of making such programmes accessible in a resource efficient manner as well empowering the local community in the process. These factors become exceedingly important in a developing and vast country like India.

In a subsequent study, Leventhal et al. (2016) examined the effects of 'Girls First', a curriculum involving psychosocial as well as physical health components. The programme with a focus on resilience spanned 23 weekly sessions and was delivered to adolescent girls in rural middle schools. Sessions were facilitated by school-based peer groups as well as local women trained for this purpose. A significant aspect of this study was that it evaluated the combined effect of psychosocial and physical heath curricula, indicating greater benefits from the combination as compared to either curriculum alone. Further, study findings help build a strong case for school-based interventions to boost psychosocial well-being with a view to their additional positive impact on physical health outcomes. Leventhal et al. (2016) regarded their resilience curriculum as a vital element to foster adolescent physical health.

Bharath and Kishore (2010) pioneered a school mental health programme called the NIMHANS (National Institute of Mental Health & Neurosciences) model of LSE. Study participants were 14–16-year-old students from two schools. Teachers previously trained for this programme served as programme facilitators. This promotional LSE curriculum relied on interactive techniques like role-play, games and group discussions, steering clear of didactic methodology. An intervention group—control group design—was used and all participants were assessed on measures of self-esteem, adjustment, self-efficacy among other classroom indicators. Students who engaged in the programme reported better coping skills and school adjustment as compared to the control group. Teachers also reported positive change in classroom behaviour among programme participants.

In another initiative catering to the needs of children and adolescents at school, NIMHANS put forth a comprehensive model for promotion of their mental health and well-being. Following an extensive needs analysis, 15 key areas were identified. A series of interactive and experiential activities addressing diverse themes like life skills, sexuality, gender issues, peer pressure, suicide prevention and academic stress were designed. This universal mental health promotion programme was created envisioning teachers as facilitators. This resource efficient module aimed to foster resilience and psychosocial skills and has been field tested in multiple schools in South India (Vranda, 2015).

With a view to alleviate stress and well-being, Anand and Sharma (2011) studied the impact of an MBSR programme among adolescents. The intervention was delivered over eight weekly sessions of 40 minutes each during school hours. The programme was based on existing programmes like the MBSR programme by Kabat-Zinn (1990) and the stress reduction workbook for teens by Biegel, Brown, Shapiro and Schubert

(2009). Anand and Sharma (2011) reported significant reductions in stress levels, difficulties with peers and emotional symptoms besides improvement in academic self-concept and well-being of the participants.

Nair and Meera (2014) studied the impact of in-class PMR on academic stress among secondary school students from South India. Participants undertook the PMR exercise over a six-week period, 30 minutes daily for five days a week. Results suggest that the exercise was effective in reducing academic stress among all participants post-intervention, as compared to their baseline scores.

In a pilot study examining the effectiveness of the PRP among urban Indian adolescents, Sankaranarayanan and Cycil (2014) studied the attribution style of participants, and whether PRP could change students' explanatory styles. Participants were divided into intervention and control conditions. Results revealed that the programme was effective in increasing optimistic orientation and reducing pessimistic explanatory style among intervention group as compared to controls.

Working with Indian undergraduate students, Singh and Choubisa (2009) evaluated the effectiveness of a self-focused intervention programme for enhancing well-being. The programme entailed 12-weekly sessions (including pre and post assessment) conducted during tutorial classes for students enrolled in a PP course. Sessions revolved around the themes of self-management strategies (such as introspection, writing about best possible selves, relaxation techniques, etc.) as well as interpersonal relations (effects of altruism, gratitude). Towards the end, participants were asked to recall and provide feedback about the sessions. Significant improvement in students' scores on a few subscales of self-management and resilience was reported. However, no significant results were found on dimensions of mindfulness, happiness, meaning in life and life satisfaction (Singh & Choubisa, 2009).

Another programme created and evaluated among Indian college students was a mental health promotion programme called Feeling Good and Doing Well (Mehrotra, Elias, Chowdhury, & Gupta, 2013). It has eight sessions spanning a total of 20 hours, spread over one and a half months. This module is centred on the themes of discovery and application of strengths, pursuing goals, emotion regulation and motivation.

Mehrotra (2013) studied the effectiveness of this programme among South Indian college students by employing a pre-post-follow up control group design. Significant increase in psychological well-being, positive affect and improvement in efficacy in managing sadness, anxiety and anger was reported among intervention group when compared with control group. Overall results suggested significant differences between the intervention and waitlist control group on life satisfaction and positive affect even after controlling for baseline variables. On the whole, findings indicate the potential of this programme.

This review of PP-based work with Indian youth is clearly indicative of the growing eminence of this field in India. It must also be acknowledged that there is other ongoing work within the broader realm of promoting student well-being (e.g., workshops, after school activities, life skills sessions, etc.) that may well be beneficial but often not scientific or evidence based in approach. The next section examines some such prominent initiatives.

OTHER INITIATIVES TO PROMOTE MENTAL HEALTH AND WELL-BEING AMONG INDIAN YOUTH: GOVERNMENT, NGO AND PRIVATE CONTRIBUTION

Programmes of this nature are being driven by government as well as non-government organizations (NGOs) and private parties. While the former (relatively few in number) usually garner wide publicity and attention, information on the latter is often limited to their own webpages and media handles. This section begins by discussing some government backed programmes and then moves on to those run by other agencies.

Keeping in mind the challenges associated with multidimensional changes experienced during adolescence, the NCERT conceptualized the Adolescence Education Program in 2005 guided by the National Curriculum Framework. This programme is coordinated by the NCERT in collaboration with the Ministry for Human Resource Development (MHRD) and the United Nations Population Fund (UNPF), and targets students in the age group of 13–18 years (NCERT, n.d.). The programme works through assimilation of relevant information within learning materials of National Institute of Open Schooling (NIOS) as well as a stratified training approach wherein master trainers guide nodal teachers who in turn facilitate the school level programme delivery. Training materials addressing myriad themes like gender, sexuality, relationships and substance abuse are used as part of this programme (NCERT, n.d.).

The Central Board of Secondary Education (CBSE)—a prominent board of school education under the Government of India—introduced CBSE Life Skills training as an integral part of the curriculum for Grades 6–10. To offer standardization and programme fidelity, life skills manuals for Grades 6–8 have been published. These manuals offer guidelines and age appropriate activities to foster each of the 10 core life skills that have been listed by the WHO (CBSE, 2013). While this is a large-scale programme covering many schools across the country, to the best of our knowledge there isn't any publicly available research data to assess the effectiveness of this initiative.

A new and promising endeavour that generated much enthusiasm has been the 'Happiness Curriculum' launched in Delhi government schools in July 2018. This curriculum has been designed in accordance with the guidelines of the National Curriculum Framework (NCERT, 2005) and encompasses various interventions such as mindfulness, storytelling, group discussions among others, delivered in the form of 45-minute-long daily sessions for students through Grades 1–8. The frequency of sessions is twice per week for younger students. As part of the programme, teachers will periodically gauge students' progress using a 'Happiness Index' (Katyal, 2018; Kundu, 2018). Due to the recency of this initiative, empirical evidence for it remains to be seen. Nevertheless, it comes as a very welcome step given the highly competitive and stressful milieu in which these students exist.

As part of a state-level government initiative, the Madhya Pradesh government has launched Anand Mantralaya (Ministry of Happiness). This initiative encompasses programmes for different segments of the population, including a flagship programme called Anand Sabha, which is offered to school students. Anand Sabha aims to promote life skills and positive constructs such as forgiveness, gratitude and others through special modules and experiential sessions led by teachers in the school setting. The core idea is to supplement the usual school curriculum with these activities and sessions with a view to enhance positive development of youth.[1]

In response to the growing stress levels among students, the District Administration of Gurugram (situated in the state of Haryana) has launched an initiative called 'Project Zindagi' (Project Life) across 15 government schools with 45 teachers trained as counsellors and programme facilitators. The programme aims to help students express their feelings, nurture positive peer relations and deal effectively with anger and stress. Regular yoga sessions as well as a telephonic helpline which would facilitate students' access to psychological help are planned as part of this programme.

While government-led initiatives are gradually picking pace, many NGOs are also working in the sector of mental health promotion and remedial work in Indian education sector. The MINDS Foundation, Manas Foundation, Counseling India, New Horizon's Child Development Center, and the De Sousa Foundation are some of the leading organizations working in this sector. Although extensive work is being carried out, much of it remains undocumented or isn't backed by empirical evidence. Nevertheless, a lot seems headed in the right direction.

Sangath, a Goa-based NGO working towards holistic health services in the community, has spearheaded various programmes and interventions to promote adolescent and youth mental health. Unlike most contemporaries in the field, Sangath rigorously field tests their programmes and backs them with robust scientific documentation and investigation. Some of their key research projects in this area include Pride (psychosocial interventions for school-going adolescents with mental health concerns), Atman (development of intervention to mitigate self-harm in young people), SEHER (Strengthening the Evidence base on effective scHool-based intErventions for pRomoting adolescent health programme), POWERTXT (programme for effective health interventions in under-resourced settings for adolescents), and Young Lives Matter (a study to examine risk and protective factors for suicide among young people in India). Most of these are ongoing funded research projects being handled

---

[1] https://www.anandsansthanmp.in/en/index

by Sangath.[2] Such steps clearly help meet the crying need for adapting child and adolescent mental health interventions to cater to resource deficient settings like Indian schools and community spaces (e.g., Divan, 2017).

At this point, it merits attention that Indian schools too acknowledge the idea of promoting happiness and well-being among their students. There is an emerging (albeit gradual) shift in the focus of schools from mere academic achievement towards more well-rounded development. This is visible in the form of schools following the philosophy of alternative education, integrated education as well as a return to indigenous ways of teaching and learning with a view to promote student happiness. Some prominent examples of private educational institutions include the 'Mirambika' school in New Delhi that is part of the Mirambika Research Centre for Integral Education and Human Values. This is a free progress school that espouses the philosophy of Sri Aurobindo and The Mother. Another school rooted in the philosophy of Sri Aurobindo and The Mother, with a view to nurture holistic development of students, is 'MatriKiran' based in Gurugram in NCR. Other examples include the 'Global Indian International School' in NCR which emphasizes happiness among students and has devised a 'Happiness Index' comprising some relevant parameters to monitor the effectiveness of its initiatives. In Tamil Nadu, the 'Isha Home School' (led by Sadhguru of Isha Foundation) follows an unconventional pedagogical approach to facilitate holistic development of students in an unrestricted space. An extensive educational initiative that is still in the pipeline is the Riverbend School slated to open in Chennai (Tamil Nadu) with a cardinal mission to promote student happiness, which can in turn enable students to deal with life positively. A quick online search reveals the existence of some 'Gurukul' schools across the country which root themselves in spiritual values and rich indigenous culture, often as an antidote to the stresses and problems faced by youth in contemporary times. In case of many of these schools, their philosophy is reflected in not just their curriculum but also their architecture. We'd like to reiterate that this is not meant to be a comprehensive review of schools that claim to nurture student well-being. These are just some

---

[2] http://www.sangath.in

prominent examples of schools working in this area. However, empirical evidence to support most of these practices or their impact on student-related outcomes are conspicuous by their absence.

These are all steps in the positive direction and deserve encouragement and appreciation in that regard. One cannot ignore the enormity of challenges such as resource deficiency, large numbers and inadequate infrastructure that come in the way of such initiatives. Nevertheless, attention to aspects such as intervention fidelity, randomization of sample, use of intervention and control groups, and assessment of outcome variables would tremendously enhance the scientific acceptance and validity of many aforementioned initiatives. Having looked at an overview of both evidence-based and purely experiential initiatives towards student well-being and application of PP in Indian schools, the concluding segment of this chapter discusses the way forward towards a more scientific and comprehensive application of PP in India.

THE WAY FORWARD

This chapter bears testimony to the widespread work happening in the domain of positive youth development and well-being programmes for students. However, it is noteworthy that majority of the empirical work in this area has taken place in the West, with relatively limited contribution from other parts of the world, particularly developing nations which are home to substantially large youth populations. Thus, there is a definite imbalance in terms of where most of this research is happening and where the need exists. There exists a dearth of literature pertaining to PP initiatives for Indian youth. In addition to the broader insufficiency of intervention-based research focused on this demographic group, the majority of Indian research in this area deals with problem rectification or targeting those identified as being at risk.

Consequently, it merits emphasis that investment in the holistic health and mental well-being children will have a strong bearing on the future of the nation. Clearly, with growing awareness, the application of PP in Indian schools is evolving. The last section of this chapter offers some recommendations for the way ahead, towards a more inclusive and comprehensive application of PP in Indian schools.

1. *Promoting cross-cultural research and validation*: The true success of PP-based (and other) programmes lies in their development beyond pilot studies, engaging with large and diverse samples (Waters, 2011). Gilman, Huebner and Furlong (2014) have discussed the paucity of research addressing the needs of youth populations outside of United States. It is the need of the hour to build upon and expand existing scholarly knowledge by adopting global best practices and tested interventions, and studying their applicability in different contexts (e.g., Khanna & Singh, 2016). Such cross-cultural and validation research can pave the way for meeting indigenous requirements through customized initiatives.

2. *Tailor made programmes for diverse populations*: A 'one size fits all' approach is not likely to be beneficial in meeting the mental health and well-being goals of diverse populations. It has already been stated that majority of scientific work pertaining to PP in schools comes from American and European settings. Given this scenario, the importance of an etic approach of using this rich knowledge base for cross-cultural research and the larger good of students is undeniable (see previous point). At the same time, taking an emic approach to customize and create tailor made programmes to address local needs of diverse populations is also essential. This is in sync with the core nature of TR that deals with the reciprocal influence of global and local knowledge while focusing on evidence-based practices (Palinkas & Soydan, 2012). This approach is important to identify specific needs and offer contextually relevant interventions for the Indian setting.

3. *Utilizing existing indigenous and sociocultural best practices*: In addition to adopting globally successful and deliberate interventions, it is equally important to recognize and foster existing sociocultural practices that may be associated with positive mental health and well-being. For example, yoga programmes in schools offer an excellent means to boost student health and wellness. Given the sensory overload and multitude of distractions available to students in contemporary times, Hagen and Nayar (2014) emphasize the value of yoga as a tool to foster physical and mental well-being among students. They highlight how integrating yoga in the school routine can go a long way in enhancing emotional regulation, resilience and stress management. Further, there is preliminary evidence for the benefits of yoga interventions

among Indian college students' general and subjective well-being (e.g., Bansal, Gupta, Agarwal, & Sharma, 2013; Jadhav & Havalappanavar, 2009). A recent systematic review of documented research for yoga interventions in schools (Khalsa & Butzer, 2016) suggests the emerging focus on this area as one that merits ongoing research. Existing studies in this field have many limitations such as weak research designs, inadequate information about optimal dose, intervention fidelity and sustainability (Greenberg & Harris, 2012; Khalsa & Butzer, 2016). Similarly, other rich indigenous practices like the Gurukul culture—a traditional schooling approach focused on value education—and other such practices that may already be a part of the Indian milieu should be identified and strengthened.

In this regard, Ramakrishnan Baccari, Ramachandran, Ahmed, & Koenig (2018) studied Indian teachers' and parents' perspectives on introducing religious–spiritual education in school as a means of health promotion. They examined participants' views about merits and challenges of integrating such education within the school curriculum and found that an empirically backed and clinically validated curriculum would be acceptable to both stakeholders. They further held the view that religious–spiritual education had the potential to enhance students' social and emotional health.

4. *Resource efficient and collaborative approach*: Among challenges like geographic and cultural diversity, India as a developing nation also deals with a resource crunch, especially in terms of trained personnel for imparting mental health services. Additionally, schools in particular are characterized by packed schedules and busy staff members. Consequently, for any intervention to be sustainable in this context, these challenges must be duly considered.

A resourceful solution lies in a collaboration between education and research institutions as well as community members towards the shared goal of cultivating emotional hygiene and interventions for youth well-being. In case of Indian schools, prospective initiatives may look to joining hands with community representatives like parent associations (urban areas) and *anganwadi* workers (rural areas). Kranzler et al. (2014) have elaborated on the constructive role of lay persons and paraprofessionals in intervention delivery in the domain of youth resilience and well-being. Such a process is aligned with the

TR approach to foster communication between academia and communities (Wethington, 2015). This is essential to nurture sustainable practices instead of 'flash in the pan' programmes which may not be beneficial in the long run.

5. *Involvement of key stakeholders from children's social environment*: Majority of Indian studies included in this review involve students alone and rely heavily on their self-report data. Besides, school-based programmes are often limited to the school (with no participation from parents, etc.). A more holistic and lasting impact may be achieved by including other stakeholders like family and peers within the purview of future interventions. Moreover, these stakeholders have an indispensable role to play in maintaining children's well-being.

6. *Robust documentation*: In addition to innovative and customized programmes, it is important to acknowledge various ongoing localized initiatives to boost student well-being (e.g., thematic assemblies, workshops, counselling programmes, etc.) in schools and the larger community, some of which may be truly effective. However, intervention fidelity as well as the scope for generalization seems dodgy in the absence of any proper documentation. Robust documentation and scientific research practices will not only help provide a more objective approach but also help gather empirical evidence going forward.

In conclusion, youth mental health and well-being has tremendous social and economic implications for India owing to its particularly large youth population. As if in acknowledgement of this fact, there exist widely known government schemes such as the Mid-Day Meal Scheme and Sarva Shiksha Abhiyan (Education for All Movement) to promote child nutrition and literacy. In the same vein, a holistic approach to mental health requires policy level strategic initiatives to promote well-being in addition to remedial work to tackle mental illness. The previous section draws attention to some steps (e.g., AEP, Delhi Government's Happiness Curriculum, etc.) that have already been taken in this direction. However, there is a long way to go in order to adequately address the needs of young people in India and bridge the gap between theory and practice, to truly translate the potential of PP into benefits at the grassroots level. Much can be learnt from the inspirational example of Bhutan, a young South Asian democracy in India's neighbourhood. Aligned with Bhutan's now acclaimed overarching goal of Gross National Happiness, the nation works towards Educating for Gross National Happiness (EGNH). EGNH highlights the significance of simultaneously nurturing contemporary knowledge and skills as well as the legacy of national culture and values (Dema, 2018). This is a perfect example of using indigenous knowledge to promote youth well-being.

Aligned with Lemon et al.'s (2013) mapping of phases of TR, testing of interventions, evaluating intervention effectiveness and guiding policy constitute integral phases. This chapter reviews school-based PPIs through the same lens. To give momentum to the emerging field of PP in Indian schools, there is a need for policy makers, government and non-governmental agencies as well as researchers and the community at large to come together and contribute meaningfully.

REFERENCES

Abraham, M., & Neogi, S. (1997). The tension is killing. *The Week, 15*(7), 16–20.

Anand, U., & Sharma, M. P. (2011). Impact of a mindfulness-based stress reduction program on stress and well-being in adolescents: A study at a school setting. *Journal of Indian Association of Child & Adolescent Mental Health, 7*(3), 73–97.

Austin, D. (2005). *The effects of a strengths development intervention program upon the self-perception of students' academic abilities* (Doctoral dissertation). *Dissertation Abstracts International, 66,* 1631A.

Bansal, R., Gupta, M., Agarwal, B., & Sharma, S. (2013). Impact of short-term yoga intervention on mental well being of medical students posted in community medicine: A pilot study. *Indian Journal of Community Medicine, 38*(2), 105–108

Benninga, J. S., Berkowitz, M. W., Kuehn, P., & Smith, K. (2006). Character and academics: What good schools do. *Phi Delta Kappan, 87*(6), 448–452.

Bernard, M., & Walton, K. (2011). The effect of You Can Do It! education in six schools on student perceptions of wellbeing, teaching, learning and relationships. *Journal of Student Wellbeing, 5*(1), 22–37.

Bharath, S., & Kishore, K. K. V. (2010). Empowering adolescents with life skills education in schools—School mental health program: Does it work? *Indian Journal of Psychiatry, 52*(4), 344–349.

Bidgood, B. A., Wilkie, H., & Katchaluba, A. (2010). Releasing the steam: An evaluation of the supporting tempers, emotions, and anger management (STEAM) program for elementary and adolescent-age children. *Social Work with Groups, 33*(2–3), 160–174.

Biegel, G. M., Brown, K. W., Shapiro, S. L., & Schubert, C. (2009). Mindfulness-based stress reduction for the treatment of adolescent psychiatric outpatients: A randomized clinical trial. *Journal of Clinical & Consulting Psychology, 7*(5), 855–866.

Bolier, L., Haverman, M., Westerhof, G. J., Riper, H., Smit, F., & Bohlmeijer, E. (2013). Positive psychology interventions: a meta-analysis of randomized controlled studies. *BMC Public Health, 13,* 119. doi:10.1186/1471-2458-13-119

Bono, G., Froh, J. J., & Emmons, R. A. (2012). Searching for the developmental role of gratitude: A 4-year longitudinal analysis. In J. Froh (Chair), *Helping youth thrive: Making the case that gratitude matters.* Symposium conducted at the meeting of the American Psychological Association, Orlando, FL.

Bono, G., Froh, J. J., Emmons, R. A., & Card, N. (2013, April). The benefits of gratitude to adolescent development: Longitudinal models of gratitude, well-being and prosocial behaviour. In G. Bono (Chair), *Promoting gratitude as a skill for building positive connections between adolescents and society.* Symposium conducted at the Society for Research on Child Development, Seattle, WA.

Bono, G., Froh, J. J., & Forrett, R. (2014). Gratitude in school: Benefits to students and schools. In M. Furlong, R. Gilman, & E. S. Huebner (Eds.), *Handbook of positive psychology in schools* (2nd ed., pp. 67–81). New York, NY: Routledge.

Brackett, M. A., Rivers, S. E., Reyes, M. R., & Salovey, P. (2012). Enhancing academic performance and social and emotional competence with the RULER feeling words curriculum. *Learning and Individual Differences, 22*(2), 218–224.

Brdar, I., & Kashdan, T. B. (2010). Character strengths and well-being in Croatia: An empirical investigation of structure and correlates. *Journal of Research in Personality, 44*(1), 151–154.

Brock, L. L., Nishida, T. K., Chiong, C., Grimm, K. J., & Rimm-Kaufman, S. E. (2008). Children's perceptions of the classroom environment and social and academic performance: A longitudinal analysis of the contribution of the Responsive Classroom approach. *Journal of School Psychology, 46*(2), 129–149.

Broderick, P., & Metz, S. (2009). Learning to BREATHE: A pilot trial of a mindfulness curriculum for adolescents. *Advances in School Mental Health Promotion, 2*(1), 35–46.

Brown, J. L., Jones, S. M., LaRusso, M. D., & Lawrence Aber, J. (2010). Improving classroom quality: Teacher influences and experimental impacts of the 4Rs program. *Journal of Educational Psychology, 102*(1), 153–167.

Burke, C. (2010). Mindfulness-based approaches with children and adolescents: A preliminary review of current research in an emergent field. *Journal of Child and Family Studies, 19*(2), 133–144.

Caldarella, P., Christensen, L., Kramer, T. J., & Kronmiller, K. (2009). The effects of Strong Start on second grades students' emotional and social competence. *Early Childhood Education Journal, 37*(1), 51–56.

Cantwell, L. (2005). A comparative analysis of strengths-based versus traditional teaching methods in a freshman public speaking course: Impacts on student learning and engagement. *Dissertation Abstracts International, 67*(02A), 478–700.

Castro-Olivo, S., & Merrell, K. W. (2012). Validating cultural adaptations of a school-based social emotional learning program for use with Latino immigrant adolescents. *Advances in School Mental Health Promotion, 5*(2), 78–92.

Catalano, R. F., Berglund, M. L., Ryan, J. A. M., Lonczak, H. S., & Hawkins, J. D. (2002). Positive youth development in the United States: Research findings on evaluations of positive youth development programs. *Prevention & Treatment, 5*(1).

Center on the Developing Child. (2010). *The foundations of lifelong health are built in early childhood.* Retrieved from www.developingchild.harvard.edu

Central Board of Secondary Education. (2013). Teacher's Manual–Life Skills for Class-VIII. Retrieved from http://cbseacademic.nic.in/web_material/doc/2014/9_Life%20Skills_Class_VIII.pdf

Challen, A., Noden, P., West, A., & Machin, S. (2011). *UK resilience programme evaluation: Final report* (Research reports, DFE-RR097). London, UK: Department for Education.

Chan, D. (2010). Gratitude, gratitude intervention and subjective wellbeing among Chinese school teachers in Hong Kong. *Educational Psychology, 30*, 139–153. doi:10.1080/01443410903493934

Chaplin, L. N., & John, D. R. (2007). Growing up in a material world: Age differences in materialism in children and adolescents. *Journal of Consumer Research, 34*(4), 480–493.

Collaborative for Academic Social and Emotional Learning. (2008). *Connecting social and emotional learning with mental health.* Retrieved from http://casel.org/wp-content/uploads/2011/04/SELandMH.pdf

Dawood, R. (2013). Positive psychology in school-based psychological intervention: A study of the evidence-base. *The European Journal of Social & Behavioural Sciences, 5*(2), 954–968.

Deb, S., Strodl, E., & Sun, J. (2015). Academic stress, parental pressure, anxiety and mental health among Indian high school students. *International Journal of Psychology and Behavioral Sciences, 5*(1), 26–34.

Dema, S. (2018). *Educating for Gross National Happiness* (Masters dissertation). Retrieved from http://dspace.library.uvic.ca/bitstream/handle/1828/9913/Dema_Sonam_MEd_2018.pdf?sequence=1&isAllowed=y

Di Fabio, A. (2010). *Enhancing emotional intelligence at school: Guidelines for training.* Florence: Giunti O.S.

Di Fabio, A., & Kenny, M. E. (2011). Promoting emotional intelligence and career decision making among Italian high school students. *Journal of Career Assessment, 19*(1), 21–34.

Divan, G. (2017). Editorial perspective: 'From there to here': Adapting child and adolescent mental health interventions for low-resource settings. *Journal of Child Psychology and Psychiatry, 58*(3), 325–327

Domitrovich, C. E., Cortes, R. C., & Greenberg, M. T. (2007). Improving young children's social and emotional competence: A randomized trial of the preschool 'PATHS' curriculum. *Journal of Primary Prevention, 28*(2), 67–91.

Durlak, J. A., Weissberg, R. P., Dymnicki, A. B., Taylor, R. D., & Schellinger, K. B. (2011). The impact of enhancing students' social and emotional learning: A meta-analysis of school-based universal interventions. *Child Development, 82*(1), 405–432.

Edwards, M., Adams, E. M., Waldo, M., Hadfield, O. D., & Biegel, G. M. (2014). Effects of a mindfulness group on Latino adolescent students: Examining levels of perceived stress, mindfulness, self-compassion, and psychological symptoms. *The Journal for Specialists in Group Work, 39*(2), 145–163.

Elfrink, T. R., Goldberg, J. M., Schreurs, K. M. G, Bohlmeijer, E. T., & Clarke, A. M. (2017). Positive educative programme: A whole school approach to supporting children's well-being and creating a positive school climate: A pilot study. *Health Education, 117*(2), 215–230. doi:10.1108/HE-09-2016-0039

Epstein, M. H. (2004). *Behavioral and emotional rating scale: A strength-based approach to assessment, examiner's manual* (2nd ed). Austin, TX: PRO-ED.

Fatusi, A. O., & Hindin, M. J. (2010). Adolescents and youth in developing countries: Health and development issues in context. *Journal of Adolescence, 33*(4), 499–508.

Faust, J. J. (2006). *Preventing depression and anxiety: An evaluation of a social-emotional curriculum.* Unpublished education specialist project, University of Wisconsin, Whitewater.

Fergus, S., & Zimmerman, M. A. (2005). Adolescent resilience: A framework for understanding healthy development in the face of risk. *Annual Review of Public Health, 26*, 399–419.

Flinchbaugh, C. L., Moore, E. W., Chang, Y. K., & May, D. R. (2012). Student well-being interventions: The effects of stress management techniques and gratitude journaling in the management education classroom. *Journal of Management Education, 36*(2), 191–219.

Flook, L., Smalley, S. L., Kitil, M. J., Galla, B. M., Kaiser-Greenland, S., Locke, J., … Kasari, C. (2010). Effects of mindful awareness practices on executive functions in elementary school children. *Journal of Applied School Psychology, 26*(1), 70–95.

Foret, M. M., Scult, M., Wilcher, M., Chudnofsky, R., Malloy, L., Hasheminejad, N., … Park, E. R. (2012). Integrating a relaxation response-based curriculum into a public high school in Massachusetts. *Journal of Adolescence, 35*(2), 325–332.

Forster, J. (1991). Facilitating positive changes in self-constructions. *Journal of Constructivist Psychology, 4*(3), 281–292.

Fox Eades, J. M. (2008). *Celebrating strengths: Building strengths-based schools.* Coventry: CAPP Press.

Frank, J. L., Bose, B., & Schrobenhauser-Clonan, A. (2014). Effectiveness of a school-based yoga program on adolescent mental health, stress coping strategies, and attitudes toward violence: Findings from a high-risk sample. *Journal of Applied School Psychology, 30*(1), 29–49.

Fredrickson, B. L. (2001). The role of positive emotions in positive psychology: The broaden-and-build theory of positive emotions. *American Psychologist, 56*(3), 218–226.

Froh, J. J., Bono, G., & Emmons, R. A. (2010). Being grateful is beyond good manners: Gratitude and motivation to contribute to society among early adolescents. *Motivation & Emotion, 34*(2), 144–157.

Froh, J. J., Bono, G., Fan, J., Emmons, R. A., Henderson, K., Harris, C., ... Wood, A. (2014). Nice thinking! An educational intervention that teaches children how to think gratefully. *School Psychology Review, 43*(2), 132–153.

Froh, J. J., Sefick, W. J., & Emmons, R. A. (2008). Counting blessings in early adolescents: An experimental study of gratitude and subjective well-being. *Journal of School Psychology, 46*(2), 213–233.

Garcia, J., & Cohen, G. L. (2012). A social-psychological approach to educational intervention. In E. Shafir (Ed.), *Behavioral foundations of policy* (pp. 329–350). Princeton, NJ: Princeton University Press.

Geesen, F. (2014). *Resilience in the educational system: A meta-analysis of school-based interventions aimed at promoting resilience* (Unpublished manuscript). Retrieved from http://essay.utwente.nl/65710/1/Geesen,%20F.J.%20%20s1097334%20 (verslag).pdf

Gillham, J. E., Abenavoli, R. M., Brunwasser, S. M., Linkins, M., Reivich, K. J., & Seligman, M. E. P. (2013). Resilience education. In S. David, I. Boniwell, & A. C. Ayers (Eds.), *Oxford handbook of happiness* (pp. 609–630). Oxford: Oxford University Press.

Gillham, J., Adams-Deutsch, Z., Werner, J., Reivich, K., Coulter-Heindl, V., Linkins, M. ... Seligman, M. E. P. (2011). Character strengths predict subjective well-being during adolescence. *Journal of Positive Psychology, 6*(1), 31–44.

Gillham, J. E., & Reivich, K. J. (2004). Cultivating optimism in childhood and adolescence. *Annals of Political and Social Science, 591*(1), 146–163.

Gillum, W. M. (2005). *The effects of strengths instruction on under-performing high school students in mathematics* (Doctoral dissertation). *Dissertation Abstracts International, 66*(01A), 86–248.

Gilman, R., Dooley, J., & Florell, D. (2006). Relative levels of hope and their relationship with academic and psychological indicators among adolescents. *Journal of Social and Clinical Psychology, 25*(2), 166–178.

Gilman, R., Huebner, E. S., & Furlong, M. J. (2014). Towards a science and practice of positive psychology in schools: A conceptual framework. In M. J. Furlong, R. Gilman, & E. S. Huebner (Eds.), *Handbook of positive psychology in schools* (2nd ed., pp. 3–11). New York, NY: Routledge.

Gordon, M., (2001). *Roots of empathy training manual.* Ontario: Early Years.

Govindji, R., & Linley, P. A. (2007). Strengths use, self-concordance and well-being: Implications for strengths coaching and coaching psychologists. *International Coaching Psychology Review, 2*(2), 143–153.

Green, S. (2014). Positive education: An Australian perspective. In M. Furlong, R. Gilman, & E. S. Huebner (Eds.), *Handbook of positive psychology in schools* (2nd ed., pp. 401–415). New York, NY: Routledge.

Green, S., Anthony, T., & Rynsaardt, J. (2007). Evidence-based life coaching for senior high school students: Building hardiness and hope. *International Coaching Psychology Review, 2*(1), 24–32.

Greenberg, M. T. (2010). School-based prevention: Current status and future challenges. *Effective Education, 2*(1), 27–52.

Greenberg, M. T., & Harris, A. R. (2012). Nurturing mindfulness in children and youth: Current state of research. *Child Development Perspectives, 6*(2), 161–166.

Greenberg, M. T., Kusche, C. A., Cook, E. T., & Quamma, J. P. (1995). Promoting emotional competence in school-aged children: The effects of the PATH curriculum. *Development and Psychopathology, 7*(1), 117–136.

Gueldner, B. A., & Merrell, K. W. (2011). The effectiveness of a social and emotional learning program with middle school students in the general education setting and the effect of consultation on student outcomes. *Journal of Educational and Psychological Consultation, 21*, 1–27.

Hagen, I., & Nayar, U. S. (2014). Yoga for children and young people's mental health and well-being: Research review and reflections on the mental health potentials of yoga. *Frontiers in Psychiatry, 5*, 35. doi:10.3389/fpsyt.2014.00035

Harlacher, J. E., & Merrell, K. W. (2010). Social and emotional learning as a universal level of student support: Evaluating the follow-up effect of strong kids on social and emotional outcomes. *Journal of Applied School Psychology, 26*(3), 212–229.

Hashim, H. A., & Zainol, N. A. (2015). Changes in emotional distress, short term memory, and sustained attention following 6 and 12 sessions of progressive muscle relaxation training in 10–11 years old primary school children. *Psychology, Health & Medicine, 20*, 623–628. doi:10.1080/13548506.2014.1002851

Holsen, I., Smith, B. H., & Frey, K. S. (2008). Outcomes of the social competence program Second Step in Norwegian elementary schools. *School Psychology International, 29*(1), 71–88.

Hosie, P. J., & Sevastos, P. P. (2010). A framework for conceiving of job-related affective wellbeing. *Management Revue: The International Review of Management Studies, 21*(4), 406–436.

Huebner, E. S., Gilman, R., Reschly, A. L., & Hall, R. (2009). Positive schools. In S. J. Lopez & C. R. Synder (Eds.), *The Oxford handbook of positive psychology* (2nd ed., pp. 561–568). New York, NY: Oxford.

Huebner, E. S., Hills, K. J., Siddall, J., & Gilman, R. (2014). Life satisfaction and schooling. In M. J. Furlong, R. Gilman, & E. S. Huebner (Eds.), *Handbook of positive psychology in schools* (2nd ed, pp. 192–207). New York, NY: Routledge.

Humphrey, N., Kalambouka, A., Wigelsworth, M., & Lendrum, A. (2010). Going for goals: An evaluation of a short, social–emotional intervention for primary school children. *School Psychology International, 31*(3), 250–270.

Huppert, F. A., & Johnson, D. M. (2010). A controlled trial of mindfulness training in schools: The importance of practice for an impact on well-being. *The Journal of Positive Psychology, 5*(4), 264–274.

Hutchings, J., Bywater, T., Gridley, N., Whitaker, C. J., Forbes, P. M., & Gruffydd, S. (2011). The incredible years therapeutic social and emotional skills programme: A pilot study. *School Psychology International, 33*(3), 285–293.

Isava, D. M. (2006). *An investigation of the impact of a social-emotional learning curriculum on problem symptoms and knowledge gains among adolescents in a residential treatment center* (Unpublished doctoral dissertation). Eugene: University of Oregon.

Jadhav, S. G., & Havalappanavar, N. B. (2009). Effect of yoga intervention on anxiety and subjective well-being. *Journal of the Indian Academy of Applied Psychology, 35*(1), 27–31.

Jain, M. (1996, April). The adult child. *India Today, 21*, 92–97.

January, A. M., Casey, R. J., & Paulson, D. (2011). A meta-analysis of classroom-wide interventions to build social skills: Do they work? *School Psychology Review, 40*(2), 242–256.

Jones, S. M., Brown, J. L., & Lawrence Aber, J. (2008). Classroom settings as targets of intervention and research. In M. Shinn & H. Yoshikawa (Eds.), *Toward positive youth development: Transforming schools and community programs* (pp. 58–77). New York, NY: Oxford University Press.

———. (2011). Two-year impacts of a universal school-based social, emotional and literacy intervention: An experiment in translational developmental research. *Child Development, 82*(2), 533–554.

Kabat-Zinn, J. (1990). *Full catastrophe living: Using the wisdom of your body and mind to face stress, pain and illness.* New York, NY: Dell Publishing.

Kasprzak, C., Jones, E., & Marshall, J. (2011). *National Early Childhood Technical Assistance Center (NECTAC) annual evaluation performance report.* Unpublished manuscript. Retrieved from https://fpg.unc.edu/node/9005

Katyal, R. (2018). Need to inculcate happiness curriculum in India schools. *Hindustan Times,* 28 February. Retrieved from https://www.hindustantimes.com/education/need-to-inculcate-happiness-curriculum-in-india-schools/story-eupLPGOlVRjENE8n4M4BSN.html

Keogh, E., Bond, F. W., & Flaxman, P. E. (2006). Improving academic performance and mental health through a stress management intervention: Outcomes and mediators of change. *Behaviour Research and Therapy, 44*(3), 339–357.

Keyes, C. L. M., & Cartwright, K. (2013). Well-being in the West: Hygieia before and after the demographic transition. In A. Morandi & A. N. Narayanan Nambi (Eds.), *An integrated view of health and well-being: Bridging Indian and western knowledge* (pp. 3–23). Dordrecht: Springer.

Keyes, C. L. M., & Westerhof, G. J. (2012). Chronological and subjective age differences in flourishing mental health and major depressive episode. *Aging & Mental Health, 16*(1), 67–74.

Khalsa, S. B. S., & Butzer, B. (2016). Yoga in school settings: A research review. *Annals of the New York Academy of Sciences, 1373*(1), 45–55.

Khanna, P. (2016). *Validation of positive psychological interventions for Indian school students* (Unpublished doctoral dissertation). New Delhi: Indian Institute of Technology Delhi.

Khanna, P., & Singh, K. (2014). Perceived effectiveness of positive psychology intervention programs among North Indian school students. *International Research Journal of Human Resources and Social Sciences, 1*(7), 1–18.

———. (2016). Effect of gratitude educational intervention on well-being indicators among North Indian adolescents. *Contemporary School Psychology, 20*(4), 305–314.

———— (2019). Do All positive psychology exercises work for everyone? Replication of Seligman et al.'s (2005) Interventions among adolescents. *Psychological Studies, 64*(1), 1–10.

Kieling, C., Baker-Henningham, H., Belfer, M., Conti, G., Ertem, I., Omigbodun, O., … Rahman, A. (2011). Child and adolescent mental health worldwide: Evidence for action. *The Lancet, 378*(9801), 1515–1525.

Klein, S. M. (2004). *Reaching new heights: A primary prevention program for gifted middle school students* (Unpublished dissertation). Bowling Green, OH: Department of Psychology, Graduate College of Bowling Green State University.

Kraag, G., Breukelen, G. V., Lamberts, P., Vugts, O., Kok, G., Fekkes, M., … Huijer Abu-Saad, H. (2007). Process evaluation of 'Learn Young, Learn Fair': A stress management programme for 5th and 6th Graders. *School Psychology International, 28*(2), 206–219.

Kraag, G., Kok, G., Huijer Abu-Saad, H., Lamberts, P., & Fekkes, M. (2005) Development of a stress management programme—Learn Young, Learn Fair—for 5th and 6th formers in the Netherlands using intervention mapping. *International Journal of Mental Health Promotion, 7*(3), 37–44.

Kranzler, A., Hoffman, L. J., Parks, A. C., & Gillham, J. E. (2014). Innovative models of dissemination for school-based interventions that promote youth resilience and well-being. In R. Gilman, E. S. Huebner, & M. J. Furlong (Eds.), *The handbook of positive psychology in schools* (2nd ed, pp. 381–398). London: Routledge.

Kumar, A., & Reshmi, R. S. (2014). Adolescent health in India & development implications. *International Journal of Development Research, 4*(10), 2078–2083.

Kundu, P. (2018). 'Happiness Curriculum' introduced in Delhi govt schools: In world obsessed with marks, studies can still be source of joy. *Firstpost.* Retrieved from https://www.firstpost.com/india/happiness-curriculum-introduced-in-delhi-govt-schools-in-a-world-obsessed-with-marks-studies-can-still-be-a-source-of-joy-4755651.html

Kuyken, W., Weare, K., Ukoumunne, O. C., Vicary, R., Motton, N., Burnett, R., & … Huppert, F. (2013). Effectiveness of the mindfulness in schools:

Non-randomised controlled feasibility study. *The British Journal of Psychiatry, 203*, 126–131. doi:10.1192/bjp.bp.113.126649

Lau, N., & Hue, M. (2011). Preliminary outcomes of a mindfulness-based programme for Hong Kong adolescents in schools: Well-being, stress and depressive symptoms. *International Journal of Children's Spirituality, 16*(4), 315–330.

Lemon, S. C., Bowen, D., Rosal, M. C., Pagoto, S. L., Schneider, K., Pbert, L., … Ockene, J. K. (2013). Translational research phases in the behavioral and social sciences: Adaptations from the biomedical sciences. In K. A. Riekert, J. K. Ockene, & L. Pbert (Eds.), *The handbook of health behavior change* (pp. 483–497). New York, NY: Springer.

Leventhal, K. S., DeMaria, L. M., Gillham, J. E., Andrews, G., Peabody, J., & Leventhal, S. M. (2016). A psychosocial resilience curriculum provides the 'missing piece' to boost adolescent physical health: A randomized controlled trial of Girls First in India. *Social Science & Medicine, 161*, 37–46.

Leventhal. K. S., Gillham, J., DeMaria, L., Andrew, G., Peabody, J., & Leventhal, S. (2015). Building psychosocial assets and wellbeing among adolescent girls: A randomized controlled trial. *Journal of Adolescence, 45*, 284–295.

Leventhal, K. S., & Sachs, K. (2011). *CorStone Children's Resiliency Program for Girls in India (CRPG): Summary of research findings.* Retrieved from https://20f33m3zkof52bpkx344t8kf-wpengine.netdna-ssl.com/wp-content/uploads/2015/05/CorStone-2011-CRPG-India_Summary-of-Research-Findings_Oct-2011.pdf

Liehr, P., & Diaz, N. (2010). A pilot study examining the effect of mindfulness on depression and anxiety for minority children. *Archives of Psychiatric Nursing, 24*, 69–71.

Linley, P. A., Joseph, S., Maltby, J., Harrington, S., & Wood, A. M. (2009). Positive psychology applications. In S. J. Lopez (Ed.), *Handbook of positive psychology* (2nd ed., pp. 35–48). Oxford: Oxford University Press.

Lomas, T., Froh, J. J., Emmons, R. A., Mishra, A., & Bono, G. (2014). Gratitude interventions: A review and future agenda. In. A. Parks & S. Schueller (Eds.), *Handbook of positive psychological interventions* (pp. 3–19). Maiden, MA: Wiley-Blackwell.

Lopez, S. J., Magyar-Moe, J. L., Peterson, S. E., Ryder, J. A., Krieshok, T. S., O'Byrne, K. K., … Fry, N. A. (2006). Counselling psychology's focus on positive aspects of human functioning. *The Counselling Psychologist, 34*(2), 205–227.

Lovat, T., Toomey, R., & Clement, N. (Eds.), (2010). *International research handbook on values education and student wellbeing.* Dordrecht: Springer.

Lyubomirsky, S., Sheldon, K. M., & Schkade, D. (2005). Pursuing happiness: The architecture of sustainable change. *Review of General Psychology, 9*, 111–131. doi:10.1037/1089-2680.9.2.111

Madden, W., Green, S., & Grant, T. (2010). A pilot study evaluating strengths-based coaching for primary school students: Enhancing engagement and hope. *International Coaching Psychology Review, 6*(1), 71–83.

Marques, S. C., Lopez, S. J., & Mitchell, J. (2013). The role of hope, spirituality and religious practice in adolescents' life satisfaction: Longitudinal findings. *Journal of Happiness Studies, 14*(1), 251–261.

Marques, S. C., Lopez, S. J., & Pais-Ribeiro, J. L. (2009). 'Building hope for the future': A program to foster strengths in middle-school students. *Journal of Happiness Studies, 12*, 139–152.

Marques, S. C., Pais-Ribeiro, J. L., & Lopez, S. J. (2007). Validation of a Portuguese version of the Students' Life Satisfaction Scale. *Applied Research in Quality of Life, 2*(2), 83–94.

Marques, S. C., Pais-Ribeiro, J. L., & Lopez, S. J. (2011). The role of positive psychology constructs in predicting mental health and academic achievement in children and adolescents: A two-year longitudinal study. *Journal of Happiness Studies, 12*(6), 1049–1062.

Martin, A. J. (2008). Enhancing student motivation and engagement: The effects of a multidimensional intervention. *Contemporary Educational Psychology, 33*(2), 239–269.

Mayer, J. D., & Salovey, P. (1997). What is emotional intelligence? In P. Salovey & D. Sluyter (Eds.), *Emotional development and emotional intelligence: Implications for educators* (pp. 3–31). New York, NY: Basic Books.

McCabe-Fitch, K. A. (2009). *Examination of the impact of an intervention in positive-psychology on the happiness and life satisfaction of children* (Doctoral dissertation). Storrs, CT: University of Connecticut. Retrieved from https://opencommons. uconn.edu/dissertations/AAI3361015/

McCullough, M. E., Kilpatrick, S. D., Emmons, R. A., & Larson, D. B. (2001). Is gratitude a moral affect? *Psychological Bulletin, 127*(2), 249–266.

McGrath, H., & Noble, T. (2003). *Bounce Back! A classroom resiliency program. Teacher's handbook. Teacher's resource books, Level 1: K–2; Level 2: Yrs 3–4; Level 3: Yrs 5–8.* Sydney: Pearson Education.

Mehrotra, S. (2013). Feeling good and doing well? Testing efficacy of a mental health promotive intervention program for Indian youth. *International Journal of Psychological Studies, 5*(3), 28–42.

Mehrotra, S., Elias, J. K, Chowdhury, D., & Gupta, A. (2013). Feeling good and doing well: Development of a mental health promotion program for youth. *Psychological Studies, 58*(1), 54–57.

Mendelson, T., Greenberg, M. T., Dariotis, J. K., Gould, L. F., Rhoades, B. L., & Leaf, P. J. (2010). Feasibility and preliminary outcomes of a school-based mindfulness intervention for urban youth. *Journal of Abnormal Child Psychology, 38*(7), 985–994.

Merkas, M., & Brajsa-Zganec, A. (2011). Children with different levels of hope: Are there differences in their self-esteem, life satisfaction, social support, and family cohesion? *Journal of Child Indicators Research, 4*(3), 499–514.

Millar, G. M., Lean, D., Sweet, S. D., Moraes, S. C., & Nelson, V. (2013). The psychology school mental health initiative: An innovative approach to the delivery of school-based intervention services. *Canadian Journal of School Psychology, 28*(1), 103–118.

Ministry of Statistics and Programme Implementation. (2012). *Children in India 2012: A Statistical Appraisal.* New Delhi: Central Statistics Office, Government of India.

————. (2017). *Youth in India.* New Delhi: Central Statistics Office, Government of India.

Mohanraj, R., Subbhiah, K., & Watson, B. (2010). Risk and protective factors to depressive symptoms in school-going adolescents. *Journal of Indian Association of Child and Adolescent Mental Health, 6*(4), 101–119.

Moreira, P. A. S., Cloninger, C. R., Dinis, L., Sá, L., Oliveira, J. T., Dias, A. ... Oliveira, J. (2015). Personality and well-being in adolescents. *Frontiers in Psychology, 5*, 1494. doi:10.3389/fpsyg.2014.01494

Mukherjee, A. (2011). Student suicides soar 26% in 5 years, education system blamed. *The Times of India.* Retrieved from http://articles.timesofindia.indiatimes.com/2011-11-02/india/30349474_1_student-suicides-education-system-higher-education

Myers, D. G. (2000). The funds, friends, and faith of happy people. *American Psychologist, 55*(1), 56–67.

Nair, P. P., & Meera, K. P. (2014). Effectiveness of progressive muscle relaxation in reducing academic stress of secondary schools students of Kerala. *IOSR Journal of Humanities and Social Science, 19*(8), 29–32.

Nakayama, N. J. (2008). *An investigation of the impact of the Strong Kids curriculum on social-emotional knowledge and symptoms of elementary aged students in a self-contained special education setting* (Unpublished doctoral dissertation). Eugene: University of Oregon.

National Council of Educational Research and Training (NCERT). (n.d.) *Adolescence education programme.* Retrieved from http://www.aeparc.org/

Nidich, S., Mjasiri, S., Nidich, R., Rainforth, M., Grant, J., Valosek, L., ... Zigler, R. (2011). Academic achievement and transcendental meditation: A study with at-risk urban middle school students. *Education, 131*(3), 556–564.

Noggle, J. J., Steiner, N. J., Minami, T., & Khalsa, S. B. (2012). Benefits of yoga for psychosocial well-being in a US high school curriculum: A preliminary randomized controlled trial. *Journal of Developmental and Behavioral Pediatrics, 33*(3), 193–201. doi:10.1097/DBP.0b013e31824afdc4.

Owens, R. L, & Patterson, M. M. (2013). Positive psychological interventions for children: A comparison of gratitude and best possible approaches. *The Journal of Genetic Psychology: Research and Theory on Human Development, 174*(4), 403–428.

Palinkas, L. A., & Soydan, H. (2012). New horizons of translational research and research translation in social work. *Research on Social Work Practice, 22*(1), 85–92.

Park, N., & Peterson, C. (2006). Moral competence and character strengths among adolescents: The development and validation of the values in action inventory of strengths for youth. *Journal of Adolescence, 29*(6), 891–905.

Peabody, J., Rhee, E., & Leventhal, S. (2010). *Promoting emotional resilience in middle school students: Evaluation of the PERCY school program.* Retrieved from http://www.corstone.org/html/downloads/Promoting%20Emotional%20 Resilience%20in%20Middle%20School%2 0Students_%20Evaluation%20 of%20the%20PERCY%20School%20Program.pdf

Peterson, C., & Seligman, M. E. P. (2004). Character strengths and virtues: A handbook and classification. New York, NY: Oxford University Press and Washington, DC: American Psychological Association.

Popov, L. K. (2000). *The virtues project: Simple ways to create a culture of character: Educator's guide.* Los Angeles, CA: Jalmar Press.

Proctor, C. (2014). Enhancing well-being in youth: Positive psychology interventions for education in Britain. In M. J. Furlong, R. Gilman, & E. S. Huebner (Eds.), *Handbook of positive psychology in schools* (2nd ed, pp. 416–432). New York, NY: Routledge.

Proctor, C., & Fox Eades, J. (2009). *Strengths gym: Year 8.* St. Peter Port: Positive Psychology Research Centre.

Proctor, C., Tsukayama, E., Wood, A. M., Maltby, J., Eades, J. F., & Linley, P. A. (2011). Strengths gym: The impact of a character strengths-based intervention on the life satisfaction and well-being of adolescents. *The Journal of Positive Psychology, 6*(5), 377–388.

Proyer, R. T., Gander, F., Wellenzohn, S., & Ruch, W. (2015). Strengths-based positive psychology interventions: A randomized placebo-controlled online trial on long-term effects for a signature strengths vs. a lesser strengths-intervention. *Frontiers in Psychology, 6,* 456.

Pushkarna, M., & Veeraraghavan, V. (2014). Adolescent's well-being and role of school. *Indian Journal of Youth and Adolescent Health, 1*(3–4), 2–6.

Qualter, P., Whiteley, H. E., Hutchinson, J. M., & Pope, D. J. (2007). Supporting the development of emotional intelligence competencies to ease the transition from primary to high school. *Educational Psychology in Practice: Theory, Research and Practice in Educational Psychology, 23*(1), 79–95.

Quinlan, D. M. (2013). *Awesome us: The individual, group and contextual effects of a strengths intervention in the classroom* (Doctoral dissertation). University of Otago. Retrieved from http://hdl.handle.net/10523/4114

Quinlan, D. M., Swain, N., Cameron, C., & Vella-Brodrick, D. A. (2015). How 'other people matter' in a classroom-based strengths intervention: Exploring interpersonal strategies and classroom outcomes. *Journal of Positive Psychology, 10,* 77–89. doi:10.1080/17439760.2014.920407

Ramakrishnan, P., Baccari, A., Ramachandran, U., Ahmed, S. F., & Koenig, H. G. (2018). Teachers' and parents' perspectives on a curricular subject of 'religion and spirituality' for Indian schools: A pilot study toward school mental health program. *Journal of Religion and Health*, 57(4), 1330–1349. https://doi.org/10.1007/s10943-017-0474-1

Rath, T. (2007). *StrengthsFinder 2.0*. New York, NY: Gallup Press.

Renshaw, T. L., & Olinger Steeves, R. M. (2016). What good is gratitude in youth and schools? A systematic review and meta-analysis of correlates and intervention outcomes. *Psychology in the Schools, 53*, 286–305. doi:10.1002/pits.21903

Rimm-Kaufman, S. E., & Chiu, Y. I. (2007). Promoting social and academic competence in the classroom: An intervention study examining the contribution of the responsive classroom approach. *Psychology in the Schools, 44*(4), 397–413.

Rimm-Kaufman, S. E., Fan, X., Chiu, Y. J., & You, W. (2007). The contribution of the responsive classroom approach on children's academic achievement: Results from a three-year longitudinal study. *Journal of School Psychology, 45*(4), 401–421.

Roth, R. A., Suldo, S. M., & Ferron, J. M. (2017). Improving middle school students' subjective well-being: Efficacy of a multicomponent positive psychology intervention targeting small groups of youth. *School Psychology Review, 46*(1), 21–41.

Ruch, W., Weber, M., Park, N., & Peterson, C. (2014). Character strengths in children and adolescents: Reliability and initial validity of the German Values in Action Inventory of Strengths for Youth (German VIA-Youth). *European Journal of Psychological Assessment, 30*, 57–64.

Sankaranarayanan, A., & Cycil, C. (2014). Resiliency training in Indian children: A pilot investigation of the PENN resiliency program. *International Journal of Environmental Research and Public Health, 11*, 4125–4139. doi:10.3390/ijerph110404125.

Schonert-Reichl, K. A., & Lawlor, M. S. (2010). The effects of a mindfulness-based education program on pre- and early adolescents' well-being and social and emotional competence. *Mindfulness, 1*(3), 137–151.

Schonert-Reichl, K. A., Smith, V., Zaidman-Zait, A., & Hertzman, C. (2012). Promoting children's prosocial behaviors in school: Impact of the 'Roots of Empathy' program on the social and emotional competence of school-aged children. *School Mental Health, 4*(1), 1–21.

Seligman, M. E. P., Ernst, R. M., Gillham, J., Reivich, K., & Linkins, M. (2009). Positive education: Positive psychology and classroom interventions. *Oxford Review of Education, 35*(3), 293–311.

Seligman, M. E. P., Steen, T. A., Park, N., & Peterson, C. (2005). Positive psychology progress: Empirical validation of interventions. *American Psychologist, 60*(5), 410–421.

Shao, J., Zhang, D., Wang, J., & Yi, Q. (2010). An experimental study on enhancing pupils' difficulties in emotion regulation in Chinese teaching. *Psychological Development and Education, 26*, 390–394.

Shastri, P. C. (2009). Promotion and prevention in child mental health. *Indian Journal of Psychiatry, 51*(2), 88–95.

Shatté, A. J., Gillham, J. E., & Reivich, K. J. (2000). Promoting hope in children and adolescents. In J. E. Gillham (Ed.), *The science of optimism and hope: Research essays in honor of Martin E. P. Seligman* (pp. 215–234). Philadelphia, PA: Templeton Foundation Press.

Sheldon, K. M., Fredrickson, B. L., Rathunde, K., Csikszentmihalyi, M., & Haidt, J. (2000). *Positive psychology manifesto* (electronic version). Retrieved from www.positivepsychology.org/akumalmani festo.html

Sheldon, K. M., & Lyubomirsky, S. (2006). How to increase and sustain positive emotion: The effects of expressing gratitude and visualizing best possible selves. *The Journal of Positive Psychology, 1*(2), 73–82.

Shi, G., & Zhu, W. (2008). The intervention of gratitude and subjective well-being for junior middle school students. *Psychological Exploration, 28*(3), 63–66.

Singh, K., Bassi, M., Junnarkar, M., & Negri, L. (2015). Mental health and psychosocial functioning in adolescence: An investigation among Indian students from Delhi. *Journal of Adolescence, 39*, 59–69.

Singh, K., & Choubisa, R. (2009). Effectiveness of self-focused intervention for enhancing students' well-being. *Journal of the Indian Academy of Applied Psychology, 35* (Special issue), 23–32.

Singh, K., Junnarkar, M., & Jain, A. (2015). Factors affecting mental health of north Indian adolescents. *Psychological Studies, 62*(2), 168–177.

Snyder, C. R., Lopez, S. J., Shorey, H. S., Rand, K. L., & Feldman, D. B. (2003). Hope theory, measurements, and applications to school psychology. *School Psychology Quarterly, 18*(2), 122–139.

Standage, M., Cumming, S. P., & Gillison, F. B. (2013). A cluster randomized controlled trial of the 'be the best you can be' intervention: Effects on the psychological and physical well-being of school children. *BMC Public Health, 13*(1), 666.

Suldo, S. M., Hearon, B. V., Bander, B., McCullough, M., Garofano, J., Roth, R. A., … Tan, S. Y. (2015). Increasing elementary school students' subjective well-being through a classwide positive psychology intervention: Results of a pilot study. *Contemporary School Psychology, 19*, 300–311. doi:10.1007/s40688-015-0061-y

Suldo, S. M., Savage, J. A., & Mercer, S. (2013). Increasing middle school students' life satisfaction: Efficacy of a positive psychology group intervention. *Journal of Happiness Studies, 15*, 19–42. doi:10.1007/s10902-013-9414-2

Taylor R. D., Oberle, E., Durlak, J. A., & Weissberg, R. P. (2017). Promoting positive youth development through school-based social and emotional learning interventions: A meta-analysis of follow-up effects. *Child Development, 88*(4), 1156–1171.

Tran, O. K., Gueldner, B. A., & Smith, D. (2014). Building resilience in schools through social and emotional learning. In M. Furlong, R. Gilman, & E.

S. Huebner (Eds.), *Handbook of positive psychology in schools* (2nd ed., pp. 298–312). New York, NY: Routledge.

Turner, J. L. (2004). *Strengths quest counseling applied to high school freshmen.* Los Angeles, CA: CASP Scientist-Practitioner Grant.

United Nations. (2013). *World youth report.* New York, NY: United Nations.

Van Eeden, C., Wissing, M. P., Dreyer, J., Park, N., & Peterson, C. (2008). Validation of the Values in Action Inventory of Strengths for Youth (VIA-Youth) among South African learners. *Journal of Psychology in Africa, 18*(1), 145–156.

Vierhaus, M., Maass, A., Fridrici, M., & Lohaus, A. (2010). Effects of a school-based stress prevention program on adolescents in different phases of behavioural change. *Educational Psychology: An International Journal of Experimental Educational Psychology, 30*(4), 465–480.

Vranda, M. N. (2015). Promotion of mental health and well-being of adolescents in schools: A NIMHANS Model. *Journal of Psychiatry, 18*(5), 303.

Wagner, L., & Ruch, W. (2015). Good character at school: Positive classroom behavior mediates the link between character strengths and school achievement. *Frontiers in Psychology, 6*, 610. doi:10.3389/fpsyg.2015.00610

Wang, X. Q., & Zhang, D. J. (2012). The criticism and amendment for the dual-factor model of mental health: From Chinese psychological suzhi research perspectives. *International Journal of Clinical medicine, 1*, 7–13.

Wang, Y., & Wang, Y. (2008). A review of intervention studies on increasing subjective well-being. *Psychological Science, 31*(6), 1441–1442.

Warner, C. M., & Fox, J. K. (2012). Advances and challenges in school-based intervention for anxious and depressed youth: Identifying and addressing issues of sustainability. *School Mental Health, 1*, 4. doi:10.1007/s12310-012-9087-8

Waters, L. (2011). A review of school-based positive psychology interventions. *The Australian Educational and Developmental Psychologist, 28*(2), 75–90.

Webster-Stratton, C., & Reid, M. J. (2003). Treating conduct problems and strengthening social and emotional competence in young children (ages 4–8): The DINA dinosaur treatment program. *Journal of Emotional and Behavioural Disorders, 11*(3), 130–143.

Weis, R., & Speridakos, E. C. (2011). A meta-analysis of hope enhancement strategies in clinical and community settings. *Psychology of Well-Being, 1*(1), 5.

Wendt, S., Hipps, J., Abrams, A., Grant, J., Valosek, L., & Nidich, S. (2015). Practicing transcendental meditation in high schools: Relationship to well-being and academic achievement among students. *Contemporary School Psychology, 19*, 12–319. doi:10.1007/s40688-015-0066-6

Wethington, E. (2015). Translational sociology. In R. A. Scott & S. Kosslyn (Eds.), *Emerging trends in the social and behavioral sciences: An interdisciplinary, searchable, and linkable resource* (pp. 1–8). New York, NY: J. Wiley & Sons.

Wigelsworth, M., Humphrey, N., & Lendrum, A. (2012). Evaluation of a school-wide preventive intervention for adolescents: The secondary social and emotional aspects of learning (SEAL) program. *School Mental Health, 5*(2), 96–109.

Yeager, D. S., Walton, G., & Cohen, G. L. (2013). Addressing achievement gaps with psychological interventions. *Kappan, 94*(5), 62–65.

Zenner, C., Herrnleben-Kurz, S., & Walach, H. (2014). Mindfulness based interventions in schools- a systematic review and meta-analysis. *Frontiers in Psychology, 5,* 1–20.

Zins, J. E., Bloodworth, M. R., Weissberg, R. P., & Walberg, H. J. (2004). The scientific base linking social and emotional learning to school success. In J. Zins, R. Weissberg, M. Wang, & H. J. Walberg (Eds.), *Building academic success on social and emotional learning: What does the research say?* (pp. 3–22). New York, NY: Teachers Press, Columbia University.

Chapter 7

Web-based Interventions to Improve Quality of Life

Shilpa Bandyopadhyay and Kamlesh Singh

In contemporary times, as more individuals seek help online, web-based psychotherapeutic interventions have been emerging and changing the traditional view of psychotherapy. They serve as an example of the application of translational research in the field of behavioural sciences. Currently, with the ongoing effort to digitalize India, the Ministry of Health and Family Planning, Government of India, has come up with a large number of web and mobile-based health care services for public use. However, the field of mental health care itself has not received its due attention, which makes it difficult to accept the usefulness of these web-based programmes at face value. This chapter reviews the literature on documented psychotherapeutic and other well-being enhancing programmes both in India and in the West. Furthermore, it provides recommendations for future research in this field. It attempts to emphasize the significance of web-based interventions in improving the quality of life (QoL) and psychological well-being while highlighting some of the challenges encountered by online practitioners. Several legal, ethical and professional issues arise in the delivery of online mental health services. This chapter highlights these issues and provides recommendations and suggestions for better service delivery with special reference to the Indian context.

Translational research in the medical sciences focuses on the discovery of medicines, health care devices and better treatment approaches. Similarly, translational research in psychology needs to emphasize designing interventions, which aim at improving mental well-being. Web-based interventions that could enhance the overall QoL can be considered as an example of the application of translational research in psychology.

This chapter brings to light some of the existing web-based interventions both in India and globally. It also reviews the appearance of Internet use in mental health service delivery; the features of web-based psychotherapeutic interventions; status of research on such interventions both globally and in India; the current position of web-technology in India; legal, ethical and professional issues in online mental health service delivery; and recommendations for better practice and future research in this field, with special emphasis on the Indian context.

THE EMERGENCE OF INTERNET USE IN COUNSELING AND PSYCHOTHERAPY

The delivery of mental health services was never solely dependent upon face-to-face communication. At some point or the other, some if not all, mental health professionals have used letters and phone calls to communicate with their client (Perle, Langsam, & Nierenberg, 2011). Over time, the Internet has become the preferred mode of distance communication technology. The notion of Internet use in the delivery of mental health services emerged in the 1990's (Binik, Cantor, Ochs, & Meana, 1997; Colón, 1996; Huang & Alessi, 1996; Murphy & Mitchell, 1998; Sampson, Kolodinsky, & Greeno, 1997; Shapiro & Schulman, 1996). Online counselling also appeared during this time (Anthony, Jung, Rosenauer, Nagel, & Goss, 2010), thus representing one of the first outcomes of this emerging idea.

Web-based psychotherapy has been changing the traditional conceptualization of psychotherapy as a face-to-face therapeutic encounter between a client and a skilled therapist. The contemporary conceptualization of psychotherapy in cyberspace involves either a two-way synchronous (e.g., instant messages) or asynchronous (e.g., email) communication between a client and a therapist (Fenichel et al., 2002). It has the potential to serve as an independent form of therapeutic intervention that can also supplement traditional face-to-face therapy (Li, Lau, Jaladin, & Abdullah, 2013). It is referred to as computerized therapy, computer-mediated therapy, e-therapy, Internet-based psychotherapeutic interventions, cyber therapy (Chester & Glass, 2006) or designated as 'Telehealth' (Jerome et al., 2000; Liss, Glueckauf, & Ecklund-Johnson, 2002; Nickelson, 1998; Tsan & Day, 2007).

WEB-BASED PSYCHOTHERAPEUTIC INTERVENTIONS: DEFINITION AND FEATURES

According to Barak, Klein and Proudfoot (2009, p. 5–12) the diverse range of mental health services being delivered online may be categorized into four groups:

- *Online counselling and therapy*: 'A mental health intervention between a patient (or a group of patients) and a therapist, using technology as the modality of communication' (Barak & Grohol, 2011, p. 157).
- *Web-based interventions*: 'A primarily self-guided intervention programme that is executed by means of a prescriptive online programme operated through a website and used by consumers seeking health- and mental-health related assistance. The intervention programme itself attempts to create positive change and or improve/enhance knowledge, awareness, and understanding via the provision of sound health-related material and use of interactive web-based components' (Barak et al., 2009, p. 5).
- *Internet operated therapeutic software*: Barak et al. (2009) differentiate between web-based interventions and Internet operated therapeutic software. The latter make use of highly advanced computer programming, including artificial intelligence and language recognition software.
- *Personal publications, online support groups, and online assessments*: Web-based psycho-educational resources, self-help therapies, therapist-guided treatment interventions, and online support groups.

Online practitioners have various options at their disposal for service dissemination including the email, instant messaging, chat, video sessions and a combination of these along with face-to-face sessions (Cipolletta & Mocellin, 2016). However, people tend to express themselves differently through auditory, visual and text media. Hence, prior to deciding the mode of communication, psychologists need to be aware of the ethical and pragmatic challenges associated with each mode (Childress, 2000). Among the different modes, email has been found to be the most commonly used (Chester & Glass, 2006; Heinlen, Welfel, Richmond, & Rak, 2003). Being asynchronous in nature, it allows both parties to communicate at their own convenience and enables the client to vent his emotions while the trigger is still present. Text-based communication also provides them the advantage of editing their text and choosing their words carefully unlike in face-to-face conversations.

It has been found that members of the lesbian, gay, bisexual, transgender and queer community, survivors of sexual abuse, celebrities, the hearing-disabled, business travellers, individuals with issues related to sex (Barak & Fisher, 2001), the chronically ill (Shaw & Shaw, 2006), those with social anxiety and agoraphobia (Allenman, 2002; Li et al., 2013), demanding work schedule (Peterson & Beck, 2003) or family commitments (Maples & Han, 2008) may find it more convenient to avail of web-based mental health services in the comfort of their home or office (Fenichel et al., 2002; Manhal-Baugus, 2001). Research findings indicate that among the primary factors motivating clients to seek online services are privacy and anonymity, autonomy and a sense of control, greater accessibility and experiencing a sense of personal and real connection to the therapist, which is relatively more comfortable for the younger generation to establish via texting (Gibson & Cartwright, 2014; Gatti, Brivio, & Calciano, 2016).

WEB-BASED INTERVENTIONS: A FORM OF TRANSLATIONAL RESEARCH FOR ENHANCING QOL

Well-being research encompasses the examination, investigation and exploration of a large number of psychological constructs, which gained momentum after the birth of positive psychology. Resilience, hardiness, hope, optimism, happiness, gratitude and QoL are among a few of those variables. Out of the vast array of well-being related variables, the present chapter focuses on QOL, which is defined as 'the satisfaction of an individuals's values, goals and needs through the actualization of their abilities or lifestyle' (Emerson, 1985, p. 282; in Felce & Perry, 1995, p. 58). Hence, QoL encompasses an indiviual's assessment of 'the "goodness" of multiple aspects of their life', including 'one's emotional reactions to life occurences, disposition, sense of fulfillment and satisfaction, and satisfaction with work and personal relationships' (Theofilou, 2013, p. 151).

There are several psychometrically sound instruments to measure one's QoL, some of which are used to measure the QoL of the general population, such as the World Health Organization Quality of Life–Brief (Skevington, Lotfy, & O'Connell, 2004) and the European Quality of Life (EuroQol group, 1990). Others are disease-specific measures, including the Kidney Disease Quality of Life (Hays, Kallich, Mapes, Coons, & Carter, 1994), the Minnesota Living with Heart Failure Questionnaire (Rector & Cohn, 1992), and the Arthritis Impact Measurement Scales (Meenan, Gertman, & Mason, 1980).

One's QoL is influenced by a large number of psychosocial factors, some of which may not be amenable to immediate change. For example, it is only recently, in 2018, that the Supreme Court of India decriminalized homosexuality. It took years of struggle for the members of the LGBTQ community in India to see such a positive change. Social, political and legal factors have major impact on one's QoL. However, they take years to resolve. Similarly, one may have to spend her entire life in abject poverty. Although such issues cannot be eradicated by psychologists alone, yet psychologists can play a major role in uplifiting the QoL of society at large. This they can do by addressing those factors which are under an individual's control, because QoL is determined by a multitude of personal resources too along with the social ones. These include self-efficacy, self-esteem, hardiness, emotional intelligence, personal meaning and others which can be enhanced through evidence-based psychological interventions developed for each of these constructs. In fact, incorporation of these constructs into relevant policies can help in enhancing the QoL of different segments of Indian society in a relatively cost-effective manner. For a country like India which is struggling with its developmental priorities, translational research outcomes from psychologists can go a long way in helping it to improve its Human Development Index.

The increase in human longevity has raised major concerns about 'adding life to the years' (Havighurst, 1961, p. 8) and not just 'years to life'. This increasing concern with the QoL makes it essential to investigate its antecedent conditions. There is a large-scale consensus about the role of lifestyle factors that has resulted in the development of a broad range of lifestyle applications on meditation (Headspace, Omvana, Meditation in Hindi), sleep (Relax and Sleep Well, Runtastic Sleep Better), happiness (Happy Habits: Choose Happiness, Smile – Motivation and Happiness, Happiness Journal), productivity apps (Productivity Challenge Timer, Smarter Time, Forest: Stay focused), and so on, easily found on the Google Play Store. However, in the absence of empirical testing it is inconclusive if they are indeed effective, although it does make one reflect on how cost-effective and convenient it would be to address QoL if these apps are indeed found to be efficacious in serving their intended purpose.

There are two ways of going about this: one approach would be to develop and test mobile and web-based interventions, and, if found to be effective, make them available online. The other approach would be to conduct a thorough survey of the various lifestyle-based applications currently available online, make a list of some of those apps which seem to have a good face value (for example, good review from users, highest number of downloads), and after obtaining due permission, conduct an intervention study using those apps. Implementation of the second approach would be actually faster. However, in following either of these two approaches in India, researchers need to bear in mind the importance of the language being used. Since 41.03 per cent of the Indian population speaks and understands Hindi (Census of India, 2011), it makes perfect sense for Hindi to be the preferred language of these apps. That said, it needs to be borne in mind, if the translational research is to have an impact in a pluralistic country like ours, translating the content to other regional languages becomes crucial.

Apart from the android and iPhone-based apps, another form of web-based technology that impacts our day to day lives is social media. From a translational research point of view, social media is a rich source of big data and helps in formulating predictive algorithms. In the course of posting their opinions, images, 'liking' the comments on their posts, and of posts shared by others, and through sharing other content on their social media profiles, users leave behind their digital footprints. Their recent digital footprints coupled with their previous behavioral residues feed predictive algorithms. These manifest in the form of recommendations to join Facebook groups which align with their interests, or ads curated explicitly for the specific users.

Psychology researchers have also been using big data and predictive algorithms in well-being research. For example, Guntuku, Yaden, Kern, Ungar and Eichstaedt (2017) made significant deductions regarding the ability of social media profiles in helping detect the users' mental state. Apart from these, one of the most extensive studies on psychological well-being, using big data and algorithms, was conducted by researchers at the University of Pennsylvania in 2013. Their World Well-being Project created a country level well-being map of all the US countries, using big data analysis of geographically located 'tweets' of the US residents (Schwartz et al., 2013).

Virtual and augmented reality is another technology which has made its way to the well-being research. While virtual reality (VR) immerses the users in an artificial digital environment, augmented or mixed reality (AR) superimposes virtual objects in the real-world environment. They broadly fall under the category of immersive interactive technologies. Their value in well-being research lies in their ability to elicit positive emotional states and experiences in the user by creating a powerful illusion of the reality. The immersion in the experience is so intense that the user's body and mind are hoodwinked into behaving and responding to the VR as though it is the real environment.

Virtual and augmented or mixed reality headsets, which are cost-effective can be incorporated into the traditional psycho-social activities of positive interventions. For example, they can be integrated into the interventions for terminally ill children or adults, and those with loco-motor disabilities, to help them encounter positive experiences, such as that of walking and exploring the streets of Paris or climbing the Everest.

Recupero, Tribertu, Modesti and Talamo (2018) recommend the use of mixed reality resources in helping immigrants deal with their home-sickness and in bringing ease in the process of their cultural integration into the host country. Digital memories and digital storytelling help in combating loneliness and in smoother cultural integration, respectively. Besides, AR provides the digital medium to enable exchanges between people from different cultural, social and economic backgrounds. Not only does it make AR a potential tool for addressing prejudices but also makes it a viable medium for enriching cross-cultural research.

The immersive interactive technologies may incorporate some of the following features into their design so as to be more efficacious in well-being research (Kitson, Prpa, & Riecke, 2018):

- Targeting specific sensory changes which have been scientifically proved to support relaxation, contentment and harmony or peace of mind
- Bringing changes to the virtual environment using biofeedback
- Incorporating natural elements, minimalism, and playful elements into their design

Each of the technologies described above is broadly categorized under 'positive technology', for their utility in inducing positive experience and positive change. 'Positive technology' comprises of those technologies which either contribute to the measurement of well-being or have value as an intervention. Among these technologies, AR is also being used successfully as a form of educational technology.

Turan, Meral and Sahin (2018) tested the effectiveness of AR technology in mobile platforms on students' achievement levels and the cognitive load exerted on them. The academic subject chosen for this intervention study was geomorphology, which falls under the subject of geography. The results of one way MANOVA showed that there was a significant difference in the achievement scores as well as cognitive load levels of the experimental and control group. Further, the results of their qualitative interviews revealed the positive attitude of the students towards this technology. They reported higher level of interest, motivation and attention as a result of AR technology use. Another key feature of this intervention is its cost-effectiveness; in fact, it was prepared using a free sotware called Aurasma which can be used on both iPhones and Android phones.

The effectiveness of AR technology in improving learning outcomes lies in its ability to combine elements from the real and virtual world/

environment. This helps in transforming complex abstract concepts into concrete ones, and it provides a learning environment for the students which resembles the real world. This in turn makes it easier for them to grasp the concepts, puts a lesser degree of cognitive load on them, improves their learning outcomes and makes the learning process interesting for them (Cai, Wang, & Chiang, 2014; Turan, Meral, & Sahin, 2018). These have implications for the QoL of the students as wide consensus exists on the role of academic performance on students' QoL (DeBerard, Glen & Julka, 2004; Henning et al., 2013; Shareef et al., 2015).

Besides, AR, VR technology has also been found to be effective as a tool for training. Sorathia, Sharma, Bhowmick and Kamidi (2017) used VR technology to design a mobile phone enabled Head Mounted Virtual Reality (HMVR) platform called Pragati. Further, they compared the effectiveness of Pragati with traditional mobile phone based 2D videos and 360-degree videos. The primary difference between Pragati and the 2D and 360-degree videos was that only Pragati allowed users to move inside the virtual environment. Pragati was developed as a learning and simulated training tool for Accredited Social Health Activists (ASHA's) of Assam (India). They serve as health promoters in rural India. However, ASHAs often do not receive sufficient training or receive training through the traditional classroom mode where they do not receive any hands-on training.

The researchers had initially conducted focus group discussions (FGDs) with ASHAs and ASHA trainers to gain a nuanced understanding of the challenges involved in their teaching, training and learning process. A unique challenge identified through the FGDs was the complexity in envisioning difficult health care concepts such as the position of the baby inside the womb and also the discrepancy between the field reality and the classroom teaching which drastically lowered their confidence. To address these limitations of traditional teaching and training, Bhowmick, Darbar and Sorathia (2018) designed Pragati. The teaching modules were based on maternal and child health care as per the recommendation of the National Health Mission for the state of Assam. This is in line with the state agenda of reducing the maternal and infant mortality rate.

Since their focal area was Assam, they created a virtual simulation of the traditional Assamese rural environment. They even designed two characters—ASHA *baidew* (sister) and Meera, a young pregnant woman—who were modelled around Assamese women. The ASHA *baidew* was the mentor for the learners and spoke in the local Assamese language.

The training modules involved interactive questions and hands-on tasks. In one such task, the learners had to clean a new-born infant. For this, the learner had to walk toward the infant using a joystick. Once she was near the infant, her hands were automatically prompted to clean the baby. The entire process happens in such a way that the user feels as if she herself is cleaning the baby—such is the enigma of VR technology.

The positive learning outcomes of using Pragati for the ASHA workers included increase in their self-efficacy, higher level of engagement and presence in the learning process as compared to learning via 2D and 360-degree videos. Among these variables, self-efficacy has a strong positive correlation with QoL as found in a number of studies (Cramm, Strating, Roebroeck, & Nieboer, 2013; Kostka & Jachimowicz, 2010; Prati, Pietrantoni, & Cicognani, 2010; Rodney, Royse, Benitez, & Pekmezi, 2014). Thus, Pragati has implications for improving the QoL of ASHA workers through its indirect effect on self-efficacy and increased confidence of the workers regarding their work. Apart from this, it is a VR intervention which serves as a cost-effective form of translational research. Without delving deep into the technicalities of the technology used, we would mention a few points which highlight the cost effectiveness of Pragati:

- The virtual rural Assamese environment and the two Assamese characters were created using free 3D computer animation software called Maya.
- Google cardboard which is not only economical but also adaptable to most smartphones was used as the HMD viewer.
- For the user to navigate inside the virtual environment, a joystick was used (joysticks are available for as low as ₹240 online).
- The 2D and 360-degree video group watched the modules on a Google LG Nexus 5.
- Users of Pragati used Google cardboard viewer using the same mobile phone.
- All the participants listened to the audio through Sony earphones (which are also available at a relatively lower cost now).

With the current decline in the price of HDM, using VR to investigate the role of immersive interactive technologies (via mobile or web-based platforms) in enhancing our QoL has great potential as a form of translational research.

However, researchers using these technologies must not lose sight of the ethical concerns, some of which include the following:

• The digital divide both within the developing world and between the developing and developed world raises the issue of inequitable distribution of technology.
• The modification of mental states using technologies such as VR or AR raises the question of controlling human experiences and therefore threatening their autonomy.
• The issue of safety regarding the use of VR or AR devices
• If such experiences are made easily accessible, they may cease to have a positive effect. Since our mental states will become amenable to manipulation through the use of emerging technologies, it is imperative to have ethical guidelines about their usage.

In contemporary times, not only have psychologists moved away from the use of paper-and-pencil tests to digital surveys but also ventured into the world of web-based interventions. Similarly, counselling in cyberspace represents another critical unification of psychology with technology. However, psychologists are comparatively less aware of the potential uses of the latest technologies in well-being research. Perhaps, it is time for us to revisit the interdisciplinary orientation of psychology, and collaborate with information technology experts for learning more about the various emergent technologies which can add value to well-being research.

We will now examine a few potential web-based platforms whose effectivness if evaluated can serve as promising examples of translational research. These include the YouTube channles of the Indian religious/spiritual (R/S) leaders and organizations who have been very active lately. Channles of Sadhguru, Isha Foundation, Gaur Gopal Das, Gurudev Sri Sri Ravi Shankar, The Art of Living have a large number of subscribers.

Many of their videos are widely shared by subscribers on social media platforms too.

Currently, there is a worldwide research focus on R/S activities and their impact on QoL (e.g., Baker, 2003; Idler, McLaughlin, & Kasl, 2009; Young, 2012). In this context, Indian researchers could perhaps explore whether at all the youtube videos of these R/S leaders have a significant impact on well-being indicators of the subscribers.

Similarly, there are several national and international motivational speakers and social media influencers who also have a large number of followers. Their short duration but highly engaging videos receive thousands of views within minutes of being uploaded. This is also accompanied by highly positive comments by the viewers. Although no research evidence exists of their effectiveness in increasing well-being, at the surface level (from the large number of views, positive comments and large number of shares), however, it seems to have at least a momentary impact. Since they only require one to have a smartphone and an Internet connection and are highly cost-effective and can reach a huge audience at the same time, their potential for enhancing QoL can be examined.

The primary aim of this section was to highlight the potential of web-based platforms and technologies in enhancing QoL and to show how effective intervention studies using such technologies can serve as forms of translational research. In the next section there will be a shift in perspective from 'potential' and promising forms of web-based interventions to 'actual' studies on web-based interventions, both globally and nationally.

SOME OF THE CURRENTLY AVAILABLE WEB-BASED PSYCHOTHERAPEUTIC INTERVENTIONS GLOBALLY

In this section, we consider some of the evidence-based psychotherapeutic interventions which are based on web technology. A few other interventions have also been reported which although not evidence-based, are in widespread use (see Tables 7.1–7.5).

Table 7.1 *Web-based Clinical Interventions*

Intervention	Key Features	Research
The Panic Center (http://sg.paniccenter.net/support/)	• A web-based CBT intervention for anxiety and panic disorders. • One can post questions anonymously and get a response from an expert. • Provision of group support. • Psycho-educational resources on panic and anxiety disorders.	–
MoodGYM (https://www.moodgym.com.au/)	• A self-help CBT programme for depression and anxiety. • Available in German and English.	Twomey and O'Reilly (2016), Farrer, Christensen, Griffiths and Mackinnon (2012), Powell et al. (2013) and Twomey et al. (2014)
Beating the Blues (http://www.beatingtheblues.co.uk/)	• A brief 8 session web-based CBT intervention for individuals with mild to moderate levels of anxiety and depression. • Users receive e-mail reminders if they have not logged in for a while.	Proudfoot et al. (2003)
The DEAL Project (DEpression-ALcohol) (https://dealproject.org.au/)	• A four-module web-based intervention for those within 18–25 years with co-occurring depression and alcohol use problems. • Use of CBT techniques and principles of motivation enhancement. • Based on certain modifications of the SHADE (Self Help for Alcohol/other drug use and Depression) programme, with the aim to make it more youth-centric. • Includes case studies on experiences of youths with comorbid depression and anxiety issues.	Deady, Kay-Lambkin, Teesson and Mills (2014)

(Continued)

Table 7.1 (*Continued*)

Intervention	Key Features	Research

ES[S]PRIT
Developed by Bauer, Moessner, Wolf, Haug and Kordy (2009)
	• A web-based programme for the prevention and intervention of eating disorder among college students.
	• Preliminary screening of each user is done based on an online assessment.
	• An individualized strategy is adopted for each student depending upon their needs.
	• A stepped care approach with the following elements:
	  ○ Psycho-educational resources on eating disorders.
	  ○ Weekly monitoring of the symptoms along with feedback.
	  ○ Provision of peer-support through online forums
	  ○ One-to-one counselling session with experts
	  ○ Referral to university student counselling center in case of severe deterioration.
		Lindenberg, Moessner, Harney, McLaughlin and Bauer (2011)

I-Sleep (for use with breast cancer patients) Developed by Dozeman, Verdonck-de Leeuw, Savard and van Straten (2017)	• I-Sleep is a Dutch-based CBT intervention for insomnia. • I-Sleep is a 6-session CBT programme tailored to suit the needs of breast cancer patients. • It involves maintenance of a daily sleep diary, case presentations of other breast cancer patients with insomnia, information about sleep hygiene, relaxation techniques and dysfunctional thoughts about sleep.	van Straten & Cuijpers (2009), JernelÖv et al. (2012), Zachariae, Lyby, Ritterband and O'Toole (2015), Seyffert, Lagisetty, Landgraf, Chopra and Pfeiffer (2016)

Source: Authors.

Table 7.2 *Web-based Positive Psychology Interventions*

Interventions	Key Features	Research

In-Joy Developed by Redzic et al. (2014)	• An Internet-based positive psychology programme which is psycho-educational in nature.
	• Based on the principles of CBT and positive psychology.
	• Aims at the prevention of depression among school children.
	• Addresses four risk factors—cognitive factors, stress, poor interpersonal relationships and subsyndromal depression.
	• Has a provision of group support.
	• As part of the programme participants are taught about:
	  ○ The concepts of happiness, pleasure, and meaning in life.
	  ○ The skills to manage and regulate their emotions, to challenge their irrational thoughts and habits, to set short and long-term goals.
	  ○ Mindfulness training, relaxation exercises and identification of signature strengths. The final session is designated as 'My Roadmap', where the participants are given a record of their achievements as part of the programme.
		–

An early intervention to promote well-being and flourishing and reduce anxiety and depression Developed by Schotanus-Dijkstra et al. (2017)	• Based on the use of a positive self-help book, *This is Your Life* (Bohlmeijer & Hulsbergen, 2013) which is designed for the non-clinical population with low to moderate levels of well-being, along with the use of e-mail support. • The study was a randomized control trial which lasted for nine weeks. • Participants had low or moderate levels of well-being, either assigned to the experimental group or to the wait-list control group. • The self-help book which was used as part of this programme utilizes the principles of positive psychology in improving well-being. • Participants received a weekly personal e-mail from a counsellor who provided positive reinforcement, feedback, support, helped to promote their self-efficacy and clarified any doubts related to the exercises which were part of the book.	–

(Continued)

Table 7.2 (*Continued*)

Interventions	Key Features	Research
Web-based training intervention to develop positive psychological capital Developed by Luthans, Avey and Patera (2008)	• A brief two-hour web-based training intervention which aims at fostering the development of psychological capital among employees. • Based on the use of a multimedia approach and personalization. • It was conducted in two sessions of 45 minutes each. • The first session addressed the development and nurturing of resilience and efficacy. There were exercises which required them to list down and work out solutions for challenging situations they have encountered, or anticipate encountering in the future in their workplace. • Development of hope and optimism was the core focus of the second session. The exercises of this session encouraged the participants to transfer the learning acquired during the programme to situational problems and challenges in their workplace settings.	—

Source: Authors.

Table 7.3 *Web-based Organizational Psychology Intervention*

Intervention	Key Features	Research
ENAI Solutions: Employee Needs Assessment Inventory (https://www.enaisolutions.com/)	• An online counselling management system developed for Malaysian private and public sector employees. • ENAI counselling approach involves web-based assessment and data analysis. • Employees first take an online psychological assessment and indicate their critical personal and work-related problems. • The employee decision as to whether he or she wants to seek therapy is also indicated. • The intervention approach of ENAI is labelled as an 'Ecological Approach Intervention' which covers, individual/group counselling, workshops, awareness programmes and transforming company policy. • The unique feature of ENAI is the inclusion of the employees, the counsellor as well the employer as part of the counselling management process. • Being aware of the significant workplace-related issues of the employees will help the management modify its work-related policies accordingly.	Hashim, Othman, Madian and Syafiq (2013)

Source: Authors.

Table 7.4 *Web-based Crisis Intervention*

Intervention	Key Features	Research
SAHAR (http://www.sahar.org.il/?categoryId=91345)	<ul><li>A free-online counselling service in Israel providing psychological first-aid to victims of trauma, abuse and those with suicidal ideation</li><li>Use of the regional language, Hebrew. This makes it more comfortable and easier for the Israeli and other Hebrew speaking population to express and communicate their thoughts and feelings.</li><li>Although it is an emergency or crisis based intervention for suicidal clients, it serves other functions:<ul><li>One-to-one synchronous and asynchronous counselling in non-crisis situations</li><li>Provision for group support</li><li>Psycho-educational resources</li></ul></li></ul>	Barak (2007)

Source: Authors.

Table 7.5 *Web-based Interventions for Non-clinical and Sub-clinical Population*

Intervention	Key Features	Research
7 Cups of Tea (https://www.7cups.com/)	• Synchronous and asynchronous messaging options with professionals as well as trained active listeners. • Paid online sessions with trained professionals and free sessions with interns or trained listeners. • It has a web portal as well as a mobile application. • Numerous self-help resources and guides. • Support groups for addiction, anxiety, bipolar disorder, depression, eating disorder, borderline personality disorder and disability support among many others. • Discussion forums and the feed which acts as a form of social connectivity among members and listeners. • Mindfulness exercises and personalized growth paths which all members can access for free.	Baumel (2015), Baumel and M Schueller (2016), Baumel, Correll and Birnbaum (2016)
Lantern (https://golantern.com/)	• A computerized cognitive behavioural therapy along with asynchronous support from an assigned coach. • Online psychological assessment of the user to help determine the pace of the programme best suited for him. • The user is asked to select any three areas of his life where he wants improvement. • Individualized programme for each user. • The user is provided with information about the credentials and qualifications of the personal coach.	–

(Continued)

Table 7.5 (Continued)

Intervention	Key Features	Research
ELIZA (http://www.masswerk.at/elizabot/) Developed by Weizenbaum (1966)	• A Chabot which emulates a Rogerian therapist. • It is the first well-documented example of a computer programme used for therapeutic purposes.	Mallen, Vogel, Rochlen and Day (2005)
Manage Your Life Online (MYLO) (manageyour-lifeonline.org/mylo-web)	• An automated self-help programme based upon the Method of Levels (MoL) Therapy which was developed by Carey (2006). • The three guiding principles of MoL are control, conflict and reorganization. • MYLO helps clients become more aware of their conflicts and aims to create a higher level of awareness about one's problems. • It works by evaluating the key terms and themes of the content typed by the user. It then asks questions based on those terms and themes. • Thus, by engaging an individual in problem-solving and greater clarity regarding his conflict, MYLO helps to reduce psychological distress.	Gaffney, Mansell, Edwards and Wright (2014)

Online Pestkoppenstoppen (Stop Bullies Online/Stop Online Bullies) Developed by Foody, Samara and Carlbring (2015)	• A web-based intervention designed for victims of cyber-bullying. • Based on the principles of Rational Emotive Therapy. • It teaches them effective strategies to deal with the depression, anxiety, psychological distress and social withdrawal which occur on account of cyber-bullying.

Get Real Developed by Stafford, Hides and Kavanagh (2015)	• A free web-based programme for young people who have had Psychotic-like Experiences (PLEs).
	• 'Psychotic-like experiences (PLEs) are subclinical delusional ideas and perceptual disturbances that lie on a phenotypic continuum with psychotic symptoms and disorders' (Stafford et al., 2015, p. 266).
	• The objectives of Get Real include:
	  ○ Helping users identify and understand PLEs,
	  ○ Lessen the distress experienced by them on account of PLEs by imparting specific cognitive-behavioural coping skills such as mindfulness, problem-solving, cognitive restructuring and behavioural activation.
	• It attempts to normalize PLEs by providing information about the frequency of their occurrence in the general population.

Source: Authors.

RESEARCH FINDINGS ON WEB-BASED PSYCHOTHERAPEUTIC INTERVENTIONS: GLOBAL SCENARIO

Although web-based mental health services have become increasingly popular, certain legal, ethical, professional and pragmatic issues related to providing such services necessitate research-based evidence to warrant it's further expansion and continuation (Dowling & Rickwood, 2013).

Chester & Glass (2006, p. 146) classified research on online mental health services into the following two categories:

- Research focusing on website analyses.
- Research focusing on the direct survey of online practitioners. In this second category, we may also include online clients.

Website analyses involve the screening and evaluation of the webpage of mental health professionals or professional organizations rendering web-based psychotherapeutic services. For example, Heinlen et al. (2003) conducted a survey of 136 websites delivering online mental health services through synchronous or asynchronous mode. They analysed the websites on the basis of the professional credentials of the service providers, the fees being charged for the service and compliance with the ethical guidelines of the National Board for Certified Counselors (NBCC) for web counselling. First, their analysis revealed that 64 per cent of the professionals delivering online mental health services had a license or a certified degree in the field of mental health. Second, e-mail was the most commonly used medium for communication between the client and the counsellor. Third, some of the service providers did not charge any fee, while others charged a fee ranging between 20$ to 25$ per e-mail. Finally, while certified professionals had 50 per cent compliance with the NBCC norms, the uncertified professionals had even lower or no compliance at all. Moreover, the measures taken to ensure the privacy of the communication were meager, including the absence of encryption technology in the majority of the websites. The only privacy measure taken was in the fee payment segment. Eight months after their data collection, they found that more than a third of the websites they had analysed ceased to exist.

An example of the second category of research is that conducted by Cipolletta and Mocellin (2016). Their research on 289 licensed Italian psychologists revealed that only 18.3 per cent of them had prior experience with online counselling and 62.6 per cent of them had a positive attitude towards the use of online modality for delivering mental health interventions. However, there was an absence of clarity regarding the ethical and legal issues involved in online counselling. Such lack of clarity was perhaps responsible for the creation of certain degree of scepticism in the Italian practitioners regarding the efficacy of web-based services.

The willingness of mental health professionals to deliver mental health services through the use of web-based technology partly depends upon their attitude towards it (Lazuras & Dokou, 2016; Simms, Gibson, & O'Donnell, 2011). Prior knowledge has also been found to be a significant determinant of one's attitude toward such services (Centore & Milacci, 2008; Perle et al., 2013; Rochlen, Beretvas, & Zack, 2004).

An interesting research finding related to online clients is that of their low hope, high levels of psychological distress and life dissatisfaction and high levels expectations from the outcome of the treatment (Dowling & Rickwood, 2016).

There are various other categories of research which have been conducted on web-based psychotherapeutic services so far. They include research on the effectiveness of online sessions as compared to in-person sessions and pharmacological treatments, predictors of the willingness to use web-based psychotherapeutic services, including gender and personality variables. These and various other researches on web-based interventions will be explored in the following paragraphs.

Research on the demographic characteristics of online clients has shown that, females and individuals belonging to the middle to higher socio-economic status are more likely to seek online therapy (Chester & Glass, 2006; Cook & Doyle, 2002; Liebert & Archer, 2006; Swan & Tyssen, 2009; Whitlock, Powers, & Eckenrode, 2006). Tsan & Day (2007) found that women were more probable than men to seek help both online and through face-to-face sessions. Previous research by Sharma and Aradhana (2000) also found that there is a greater possibility of women seeking psychological aid than men, and they also hold a more favourable attitude towards the different modes of counselling. They also investigated personality variables as predictors of online counselling. Contrary to previous research findings of Amichai-Hamburger, Wainapel and Fox (2002), Tuten and Bosnjak (2001), Hamburger and Ben-Artizi (2000) and Swickert, Rosentreter, Hittner and Mushrush (2002), neuroticism did not turn out to be a significant predictor in case of their research findings. According to their research extraverts hold a more favourable attitude toward online counselling.

We shall now consider some of the research findings which provide evidence for the effectiveness of the various web-based psychotherapeutic interventions.

Cohen and Kerr (1998) compared the effectiveness of online counselling in relation to in-person therapy in a group of American adolescents seeking help for anxiety. Their study found no significant differences between the two modes of counselling. Similarly, Fukkink and Hermanns (2009) compared online and telephone counselling. Their investigation revealed, for both online and telephone counselling, an immediate positive impact on the client well-being, although the effect size was smaller for telephone counselling. Both groups of clients also felt more emotionally relieved after their counselling session. A one-month follow-up study showed that the level of well-being and relief was stable for both groups. Another comparative study between online and telephone counselling, however, revealed different results. The study of King et al. (2006) which compared the differences between online and telephone counselling at Kids Helpline Australia found telephone counselling to be more effective than online sessions.

Short Messaging Service (SMS) or text-messaging has been found to be useful as a mode of therapeutic treatment in the reduction of aggressive behaviour among adolescents with excessive aggressive behaviour. Rajabi, Ghasemzadeh, Ashrafpouri and Saadat (2012) subjected such adolescents to SMS based therapy for two months wherein they received two messages per day. Their behavioural change was compared to that of the control group, and the outcome was found to be statistically significant. The nature of the messages was such that they helped increase self-awareness and self-control. SMS based therapy has also been found to be effective in helping clients with issues of overeating (Joo & Kin, 2007). As a form of therapeutic medium, text messaging works by promoting self-regulatory behaviour and through the provision of individualized feedback to the clients regarding their behaviour. The former aspect of text messaging helps increase the client's feelings of self-efficacy (Wing, Epstein, Nowalk, & Lamparski, 1986).

Christensen et al. (2014) investigated the effectiveness of an online intervention for generalized anxiety disorder as compared to pharmacological treatment using selective serotonin reuptake inhibitor (SSRI). Their results revealed both forms of treatment to be equally effective in helping to reduce the symptoms of generalized anxiety disorder.

In fact, web-based sessions have been found to be effective for clients who have depression, anxiety or those who are in some form acute distress (Barak, 2007; Barak, Hen, Boneil-Nissim, & Shapira, 2008; Reger & Gahm, 2009).

The chat-based counselling sessions are perceived by clients to be most helpful under two circumstances: first, when they are efficacious in revealing significant and relevant information from the client, which are related to the 'real' issue for which he opted for counselling; second, when they are free from miscommunication and misunderstanding (Stommel, 2016).

Single-session counselling is another interesting phenomenon which has emerged from a review of research on online counselling services. Rodda, Lubman, Cheetham, Dowling and Jackson (2015) conducted a qualitative study (using thematic analysis) on the primary problems and the content of single session web-based communication of 85 clients with gambling-related problem. Their analysis revealed that the problems of clients seeking single session therapy were of an immediate nature. Some sought help for a crisis situation, while others required help in managing a relatively non-urgent problem. There was a general trend among the clients to emphasize more on story-telling than discussing their mental readiness to change, feelings of self-efficacy related to the 'problem gambling' situation or the different plans of action that could be adopted for resolving their issues. This study highlights the significance of 'story-telling' in single session therapy. Richards and Vigano (2013) proposed that the element of story-telling itself is therapeutic in nature, similar to the act of writing which is another unique characteristic of online counselling.

Similar to the findings of Rodda et al. (2015), Chardon, Bagraith and King (2011) also found that in single session counselling, the clients are more focused on telling their stories and less on discussing potential solutions.

Another interesting research was that of Danaher et al. (2015) in which they conducted a randomized controlled trial to evaluate the efficacy of using Nicotine lozenges in addition to an Internet-based tobacco cessation programme called MyLastDip. Participants who were assigned to the experimental group (being given nicotine lozenges in addition to being enrolled in MyLastDip) were found to show higher levels of engagement in the programme. Moreover, their adherence to non-smoking behaviour was also higher in the long run (as evidenced in a three and six-month follow-up programme).

Research by Ho et al. (2016) revealed that there is a significant correlation between peer support (in the form of comments, likes and posts) and the long-term use of a web-based intervention. Their Project TECH (teens engaged in collaborative health), based on the techniques of cognitive behavioural therapy (CBT) and peer connectivity, investigated the impact of peer-support on treatment adherence to a web-based intervention for depression among the adolescents.

This section highlighted only a few of the researches which have been conducted so far on web-based psychological interventions. We briefly looked at the demographic characteristics of clients seeking online therapy and practitioners delivering online therapy; we also considered a few specific interventions and their effectiveness and explored single session counselling. A few researches evaluating the central issues of online clients have also been reported. The effectiveness of web-based therapy, as opposed to in-person or telephone sessions, has also been considered. However, the list is not exhaustive; it only provides a brief overview of some of the significant milestones which have been reached so far in research on web-based interventions.

THE INDIAN CONTEXT: WEB TECHNOLOGY AND CYBER THERAPY

The Economic Times (2017) provides the latest reports of the Internet and Mobile Association of India, according to which the number of Internet users in India was approximately 450–465 million in June 2017. However, there is still scope of greater penetration of Internet services in rural India. As per the 2011 Census reports, only 163 million of the 906 million rural Indians use the Internet, whereas, out of the 444 million living in urban India, 269 million use Internet. This highlights the existence of the Digital Divide in India between the rural and urban population (Economic Times, 2017). Higher penetration of Internet in rural India could help the proliferation of web-based mental health interventions among rural Indians.

Currently, with the ongoing effort to digitalize India, the Ministry of Health and Family Planning, Government of India, has come up with a large number of web- and mobile-based health care services.

Another recent progress in the field of mental health care in India has been in the form of the Mental Health Care Act, 2017. It is 'an Act to provide for mental health care and services for persons with mental illness and to protect, promote and fulfill the rights of such persons during delivery of mental health care and services and for matters connected therewith or incidental thereto' (The Mental Health Care Act, 2017, p. 1).

Although it has its own limitations and has been subject to criticisms from psychologists throughout India, the inclusion of two statements in the Mental Health Act relating to e-therapy improves the possibility of advocating web-based interventions for the Indian population. These statements have been quoted below:

A person with mental illness admitted in a mental health establishment may send and receive mail through electronic mode including through e-mail. (Mental Health Care Act, 2017, p. 14)

Where a person with mental illness informs the medical officer or mental health professional in charge of the mental health establishment that he does not want to receive mail or email from any named person in the community, the medical officer or mental health professional in charge may restrict such communication by the named person with the person with mental illness" (Mental Health Care Act, 2017, p. 14)

However, for mental health services to be delivered efficiently to the entire Indian population, through web-based services, it is necessary that the Internet services reach the rural population. Moreover, the field of mental health care itself must receive due attention. Ethics for online counselling, web-based psychological interventions backed by research evidence, an association of online practitioners in India, courses on cyber-counselling are areas which remain to be explored if cyber therapy is to be made successful in India. Perhaps the immediate need is for a revision of the Code of Conduct (1995) of the Indian Association of Clinical Psychologists (IACP). The recognition of web-based counselling services, and the ethical and legal issues therein need to be incorporated and addressed as part of the revised Code of Conduct of the IACP.

EXISTING WEB-BASED INTERVENTIONS IN INDIA

Government Initiatives

mCessation Programme: Quit Tobacco for Life[1]: This is a text-based messaging programme for curbing tobacco use among Indians. It was developed by the Ministry of Health and Family Welfare, Government of India, in collaboration with the World Health Organization and the International Telecommunications Union. The Centre for Addiction Medicine of National Institute of Mental Health & Neurosciences (NIMHANS) located in Bengaluru, India developed the content of the web-based messaging system. Individuals who seek to quit tobacco need to register online or simply give a missed call on a number mentioned on the web page. Thereafter, they start receiving motivational messages on a daily basis that act as a reminder of their initiative to quit tobacco.

No More Tension[2]: A stress-reliever mobile-based application, it is another initiative of the Government of India, Ministry of Health and Family Welfare. It has a stress-meter which enables the user to evaluate his current level of stress by answering certain questions; it also acts as a medium to enlighten users about stress, its indicators, causes and measures to be adopted to relieve stress. However, the most interesting aspect of this self-help application is perhaps the 'music section', which has instrumental music for five mood states: angry, calm, happy, rebellious and sad. Although primarily psycho-educational, the music which is available for

---

[1] https://www.nhp.gov.in/quit-tobacco-about-programme_mtl
[2] https://www.nhp.gov.in/mobile-no-more-tension

free on the application does have a soothing effect and if the desired one may use it for their meditation or yoga sessions.

Private Sector Initiatives

Your DOST[3]: It offers one-to-one chat-based sessions with experts and also provides the option of video or voice call sessions. It has online discussion forums, blogs, self-tests and offers personalized development programmes. The personalized programmes offered by Your DOST includes programmes on strengthening marital relationships, overcoming pre-marital jitters or anxiety, bereavement and coping, becoming more self-confident, making better career choices and the likes. The website mentions that these programmes are supported by research findings. Besides these, the website has a wide variety of psycho-educational resources.

Family Counselling: Your Online Psychologist[4]: It is an India-based counselling website run by a mental health professional who delivers online as well as telephone-based counselling services. According to the information mentioned in the website, she offers Individual counselling and life coaching, counselling for children and on parenting, counselling for reducing stress and anxiety, and relationship and marriage counselling. The website has several self-help articles; it mentions the advantages of online counselling; confidentiality and privacy being offered to the clients are also clarified, including SSL certificate which ensures that a client's navigation on the website and his payment transactions are not compromised.

Inner Space Counseling and Assessment[5]: It is a counselling center located in Mumbai (India) which offers both in-person and paid online consultations. The online counselling services offered to clients cover pre-marital and marital counselling therapy for children, adolescents and children and sex counselling. The website has a host of resources (articles, blogs) which are psycho-educational in nature. Inner Space also conducts psychometric assessment, corporate wellness programmes and workshops.

---

[3] https://yourdost.com/!
[4] https://familycounselling.co.in/
[5] http://innerspacetherapy.in/

It encourages the visitors of the website to leave an e-mail or make a call to inquire about its online mental health services.

Counseling India[6]: This is another cyber therapy service provider based in India. It offers face-to-face as well as telephonic counselling sessions. It renders counselling services related to family issues and parenting, marital discord, relationship issues and offers counselling services for children, adolescents and adults.

YUVA: It is a yet to be launched web-based service in India. It is an e-health intervention for helping adolescents deal with psychological distress. The researchers working on YUVA (Srivastava, Pant, & Nagar, 2017) have reported their proposed plan and the aim of the intervention-besides promoting mental well-being of adolescents, it also aims to address their health and education-related issues. The various initiatives adopted by the Government of India for the youth are also proposed to be a part of the website. The primary focus of this initiative is the adolescent population in India, a significant portion of the nation's current population. In fact, according to the Population Census report of 2011, every fifth person in India is an adolescent. Self-assessment, health-based information, including phone numbers of pharmacies in one's vicinity and the opportunity to connect with counsellors, dieticians and sports instructors are all proposed to be incorporated in this web as well as mobile based service.

Banjara Academy[7]: It is an online platform for the delivery of free online counselling service (free online counselling by e-mail) for those in need of emotional support. It offers support through e-mails. The Banjara Academy is a member of the World Federation for Mental Health, an international multi-disciplinary organization which is an advocate of mental health. The Banjara Academy also offers free in-person therapy sessions at its office in Bengaluru, India. The introduction of counselling through e-mails was mainly a way of reaching out to the larger community, those residing outside Bengaluru. There are numerous downloadable audio and video clips on mental health issues, which have been shared on the website. Apart from rendering online mental health service, the Banjara Academy also organizes training sessions for counsellors and

---

[6] http://counselingindia.com/
[7] http://www.banjaraacademy.org/

offers career counselling services. The primary aim of the academy is the improvement of the QoL.

RESEARCH FINDINGS ON WEB-BASED PSYCHOTHERAPEUTIC INTERVENTIONS: INDIAN SCENARIO

Indian studies on well-being interventions have primarily been delivered through the offline mode, either in group or classroom settings (Choubsia, 2011). This relative lack of emphasis on web-based interventions could be attributed to a number of factors. The relative absence of sound technical knowledge regarding information and communication technology among psychology researchers perhaps has deterred them from venturing into online delivery of well-being interventions. The majority of the interventions designed by Indian researchers deal with the effectiveness of yoga, meditation and a variety of other psycho-spiritual interventions which are not readily amenable to the online or web-based mode (Choubsia, 2011; Mehrotra & Tripathi, 2011). Moreover, offline interventions are easier to administer to the rural population who are at a greater need of well-being interventions; the poor Internet connectivity or lack of it in most rural areas coupled with their computer illiteracy makes it beneficial to design offline interventions which can be used by both the rural and urban Indians.

In this section, we report the few web-based interventions in India, all research-based. The Student Well-being Enhancement Program designed by Choubsia (2011) is a web-based well-being intervention for college students. It comprises of four sessions: time, stress and self-management, and emotional intelligence. This research study was based on a randomized control trial, and each of its sessions was found to be efficacious in well-being enhancement of the participants. The simplicity of the web interface coupled with engaging online skill-based tasks and exercises are two of the chief characteristics of this well-being intervention explicitly designed for Indian college students.

Among the web-based programmes developed for use with clinical patients is the Internet-based application designed by Malhotra et al. (2015). It has been developed with the aim to diagnose and manage common mental health disorders. The results of their research revealed that the patients using the service and their caregivers are satisfied with the application.

An interesting intervention has been suggested for preventing farmer suicides in India (Lorne, Rosalin, Kurundvade, & Ratra, 2017). However, it is yet to be implemented. It is essentially a social experiment which intends to garner the support of the non-governmental organizations in providing mental health consultation through wireless technology and telemedicine, for farmers contemplating suicide. Being an emergency or crisis intervention it may be efficacious in reducing the suicide rate among farmers in India. However, in the absence of its implementation and any research-based evidence, such outcomes are only probabilistic.

Research-based evidence on the feasibility of web-based interventions in India is limited as well as scattered. One such study relates to the feasibility of asynchronous 'telepsychiatry' in the Indian state of Maharashtra (Balasinorwala, Shah, Chatterjee, Kale, & Matcheswalla, 2014). Its results show that mental health service delivery through the asynchronous mode is efficacious in bridging the gap between service demand and supply.

The lack of sufficient research in India on web-based interventions or their feasibility highlights the immediate need for research. It is essential to test the efficacy of the already existing interventions which have been developed by private stakeholders or which are the outcomes of various government initiatives. Although web-based counselling services being offered by Your Dost, Banjara Academy and Inner Space are being used by the Indian population, there is an absence of research-based evidence. In the absence of such evidence, it is difficult to claim that they are scientifically robust and have a positive outcome for the users. There is also a dearth of research on the perception of in-person therapists and the general population towards web-based counselling and interventions.

Although the offline interventions have been significant in number, there is a need to shift base to the online mode of delivering interventions in order to reach a larger population in order to overcome the insufficiency of mental health practitioners in India. Moreover, the stigma attached with visiting a mental health professional may act as a mental block for many and prevent them from seeking help. In the presence of an online intervention, where one remains anonymous, and which can be used in the comfort of one's home, the fear of being stigmatized is greatly curtailed. This may indeed help in creating awareness and addressing the mental health needs of Indians, provided research is conducted and the interventions so designed are implemented for use with the general population.

Ethical, Legal and Professional Issues in the Delivery of Web-based Mental Health Services

The application of psychotherapy in cyberspace raises novel ethical, pragmatic, professional and legal concerns not encountered in traditional therapeutic sessions (Childress, 2000; Fenichel et al., 2002; Suler, 2002). A few of these issues have been discussed below.

There is a greater possibility of breach of confidentiality in the delivery of web-based mental health services (Childress, 1999). Online practitioners should inform the general public about their professional qualification, and the risks and benefits associated with online psychotherapy. They should also take measures to secure information, including secure chat rooms, digital signatures, encryption technology and the use of secret passwords to restrict access to their computers (Kanz, 2001). Time also acquires a different meaning in online therapy. The therapist should avoid making quick un-empathetic responses which may hurt the client. Working online requires one to choose and use words with skill and caution because they are the only therapeutic tools at his disposal. For online practitioners, geographical distance is another issue because, in most instances, they are not legally authorized to engage in clinical practice outside the boundaries of the state in which they hold the legal license (Seeman, 1999). Cultural and social boundaries and time and language barriers are other issues relevant to geographical distance. Another concern for practitioners who do not deal with minors is not being able to verify the age of the online client and thereby treating minors without parental consent (Childress, 2000; Callahan & Inckle, 2012). Practitioners also need to be cautious while dealing with suicidal clients, those encountering physical and sexual abuse or threatening to harm others.

Despite these challenges, psychologists have a professional responsibility to provide e-therapy if consumers raise such demands (Childress, 2000). Lack of response on their part will lead consumers to seek e-therapy from untrained and unlicensed practitioners (Childress, 1992; Colón, 1996), and although in its infancy, computer-mediated psychotherapy has been in demand from the general public (Grover, Wu, Blanford, Holcomb, & Tidler, 2002).

The American Psychological Association (APA) has constructed Guidelines for the Practice of Telepsychology. The guidelines suggest that online practitioners should take the required steps to ensure the confidentiality of the client and impart information about the issues related to web-based psychotherapy to the clients in the informed consent form. They should strive to enhance their level of competence before venturing to provide online mental health services and acquaint themselves with the legal provisions relating to mental health practice of their country and that of their client before the onset of the therapeutic relationship (Force & Guidelines, 2013).

NBCC, the International Society for Mental Health Online (ISHMO), the American Counseling Association (ACA), the British Association for Counselling and Psychotherapy (BACP) and the like have also developed their own guidelines for the practice of web-based psychotherapy.

Suggestions for Better Practice

There is a gap between the demand for mental health services and the supply of it in India. This is mainly on account of the insufficient numbers of mental health professionals. In fact, according to the report of the Minister of Health and Family Welfare, Government of India, the number of registered clinical psychologists in India was 898 as of December 2015 (Ministry of Health and Family Welfare, 2015). This highlights the existing shortage of in-person clinical psychologists in our country. Under such circumstances, web-based interventions may help reduce this existing gap by making mental health service available to greater number of Indians. In this section, we shall consider a few ways in which we can make web-based interventions more client-centric, and thereby accessible to the general public, with a special focus on India.

There has been a trend of many web-based services emerging and soon becoming dysfunctional. These are often entrepreneurial ventures which have failed to sustain. Any new organization aiming to set up such a service should carefully analyse the factors which may have contributed to the failure of other such service providers. They should remember that this service relates to a crucial aspect of human life, mental well-being. The sudden shutdown of their service may be detrimental to the psychological well-being of those few clients availing of their service.

Therefore, one should not venture into establishing an online mental health service without a proper market survey. It is also essential to involve psychologists from the preliminary stages of project development itself. Organizations should refrain from moving ahead with their business model or modify it if preliminary research reveals the likelihood of future loss and shutdown. However, once they start their service, it should essentially be client-centric.

Universities and colleges have a crucial role to play in promoting mental health, and its related services. In North America, for example, most of the universities have counselling centres (Vonk, Markward, & Arnold, 2000). In the context of Indian society, the government should make it mandatory for all institutes of higher learning to have a student counselling center run by trained professional counsellors and clinical psychologists.

The number of college and university student suicides in India is alarming: According to the National Crime Records Bureau, around 40,000 students committed suicide between 2011 and 2015; in 2015 alone, 8,934 cases were reported (*Hindustan Times*, 2017). Hence, educational institutions should also initiate web-based counselling services for the students in addition to the traditional counselling centres. Implementing such a service free of cost may help address issues such as academic stress and coping, ragging and sexual assault encountered by the students can help in bringing down the rate of student suicides and aid in the early detection and treatment of depression, schizophrenia and other mental health issues among the students. Moreover, college and university life is a phase of transition (Dyson & Renk, 2006; Rosenthal & Schreiner, 2000) for adolescents, many of whom move to towns and cities for the purpose of education, leaving behind their rural or semi-rural background and family. This relocation necessitates a certain degree of adjustment and emotional, social and informational support from counsellors within the anonymous world of cyberspace may help ease this transition.

However, such counsellors should be well-equipped to address the needs of the client within the domain of cyberspace. Therapeutic alliance is perhaps more challenging to establish online, in the absence of visual, auditory and behavioural cues. Training modules need to be developed for such therapists along with internship opportunities prior to exposure in the real online counselling set-up. Simulations and roleplay in an online environment may be incorporated as part of their training and internship. Moreover, the psychology departments of the educational institutions across India could consider initiating courses on online therapy at the undergraduate and postgraduate level.

As for the online counsellors, before venturing into online practice, they need to honestly evaluate their competence in delivering an online clinical service (Lehman & Berg, 2007). They should receive training in Internet and computer technology, theory, applications and ethics of online psychotherapy, and should have a clear understanding of the demands of online clinical work (Kanz, 2001). Goss (2010) emphasizes the need for psychotherapists to be aware of and competent in social networking, maintenance of therapeutic boundaries, VR, computerized CBT, blogs, blended media, psychological profiling of online clients and web2.0 among many others. During the initial days of their web-based practice, supervised sessions by an experienced professional is recommended for online practitioners. Oravec (2000) points out the significance of informing the client about the same: its necessity and the implications it holds for him or her. Only after taking the informed consent of the client regarding the accessibility of the records of the counselling session should the counsellor commence the therapeutic relationship.

Murphy and Mitchell (1998) recommend that online practitioners should incorporate presence, pacing and spacing techniques as part of their online practice. Presence techniques aim to provide the client with a 'therapeutic space', that is, an emotionally secure and empathic relationship with the therapist wherein he can analyse his feelings, problems and search various alternative solutions to his issues (Corcoran, 1981). Murphy and Mitchell (1998) devised two such presence techniques: emotional bracketing and descriptive immediacy. In emotional bracketing, the therapist expresses the non-verbal elements within brackets along with his written message. In descriptive immediacy, the therapist describes the immediate physical setting around him/her in order to give the client a more realistic experience of the therapy session in the virtual world of cyberspace. It helps to intensify the bond between the counsellor and the client. Both of these techniques can be used to accentuate the therapeutic experience of the client.

Ragusea and VandeCreek (2003) recommend that counsellors request their clients to be present in their own private space during the therapy session as a precautionary measure. This will prevent them from being intruded upon during a video session as well as arrest the possibility of another person (family member or co-worker) reading their e-mail or message exchanges with the therapist.

As for the legal issues relating to web-based mental health services, Zack (2008) suggests that counsellors should thoroughly familiarize themselves with the existing laws of their respective country about the same. Besides, if they have a client who lives outside the jurisdiction of their own country, they should acquaint themselves with the laws of the client's jurisdiction.

Counselling in cyberspace is not free from the possibility of transference, counter transference and excessive dependence of the client on the counsellor. Therefore, it is imperative for the therapist to discuss the issue of therapeutic boundaries with the online client before initiating the first session (Li et al., 2013).

According to Kanani and Regehr (2003), counsellors should refrain from sending immediate responses to the client. Instead, they should set up a time frame for responding and inform the client about the same. This may act as a form of boundary setting between the two parties.

Li et al. (2013) indicate the importance of developing sensitivity to other cultures because web-based services often transcend inter-state and inter-country boundaries.

With regards to language use in online therapy Fenichel et al. (2002) recommend that counsellors keep themselves updated with the language used in the Internet and social media in current times, especially by adolescents. It has developed its own unique features including abbreviations such as LOL (laugh out loud), TTYL (talk to you later), ASAP (as soon as possible) and the absence of some grammatical rules such as 'whatcha doing' 'gotta go', or not using appropriate punctuations. These may make it difficult for a therapist to comprehend the thoughts being conveyed unless he is aware of language usage in texting and in the cyber-community.

Manhal-Baugus (2001) suggest that the websites rendering mental health services should include information about suicide helplines and hotlines, and provide the emergency contact details of the hospitals present in the state or country in which the website is based.

Moreover, service providers should ensure that even if no professional is available to respond to client requests immediately, the feature of text messaging or email should be such that it enables clients to know whether their message was delivered and read. This provides them the assurance that it will be read, and they will eventually be contacted. Besides, some individuals may choose to write a message when the practitioner is offline as it gives them a greater sense of anonymity and may facilitate self-disclosure. Thus, 'limited accessibility' to online services may be proactive for specific clients, giving them a greater sense of control (Gatti et al., 2016, p. 33).

It is necessary for organizations rendering web-based interventions to develop their own code of ethics based on the ethical guidelines of the APA, BACP and NBCC, and other professional organizations (Hunt, 2002). This is particularly essential for such organizations in India due to the lack of ethical guidelines for web-based counselling at present. Some of the professionals enrolled as 'experts' in these private online counselling organizations in India have provided their professional credentials in their profile while many haven't; even among those who have, it has been observed that they only have a postgraduate degree in psychology or applied psychology. In India, one cannot practice or designate oneself as a clinical psychologist or a counselling psychologist unless he or she has an MPhil degree or a certificate/diploma degree in clinical psychology and counselling, respectively. Lack of awareness of these issues is perhaps responsible for enrolment of uncertified and unqualified individuals as 'experts'. The organizations delivering mental health services in India should adhere to guidelines and standards of the Rehabilitation Council of India (RCI) while enrolling clinical psychologists, rehabilitation psychologists, and special educators as part of their workforce.

All such organizations must make arrangements for training of recruits who do not have prior exposure to or training on cyber counselling. They should ideally recruit well-trained and well-experienced online counsellors as part of their training department. While recruiting trainers, they should ensure that they have received training from an institute which is recognized by the BACP, APA or NBCC. Although it involves large-scale investment, in the long run, it will lead to a higher profit for the organization.

The organizations should also introduce stress management programmes for their counsellors and psychologists. Mental health professionals are as susceptible to illness and burnout as other professionals. Moreover, there should be arrangements for therapy sessions for all the mental health practitioners of the organization to vent after a problematic or triggering chat session with a client.

Mental health professionals delivering computer-mediated programmes for health promotion and/or disease prevention need to ensure that such services are both effective and engaging for universal (clients without any form of psychopathology) as well as targeted populations (e.g., individuals with social anxiety disorder or anorexia nervosa).

Moreover, the service providers of web-based psychological interventions need to evaluate the treatment outcome of their clients periodically. If their service is not leading to client recovery, improvement and satisfaction, then it is perhaps time for them to modify their delivery model and system after a thorough analysis of the shortcomings in their service.

Service providers could also design their websites in such a manner that it is amenable to translation in the major regional languages of the state within whose jurisdiction it operates or if it runs on a global level, then the most commonly used international languages should be available. However, this also requires psychologists or counsellors who have a working knowledge of that language. SAHAR, for example, is an Israel-based website which is operational only in Hebrew language, and it has achieved great success in reducing suicide among the Israeli population. Similarly, for those who intend to start such in a venture in India, need to consider the possibility of not being able to fit the needs of the rural population if the application or website only runs in English. If the aim is to reach out to 'Indians', then certain local languages need to be taken in consideration, and if not all, at least the major languages of all the states need to be taken into consideration. Language is thus one issue which should be considered during website or application planning and designing.

Although computer-mediated psychotherapeutic interventions hold great potential, they require both parties to be aware of the risks involved and their personal responsibilities. Practitioners should carefully consider the benefits and shortcomings of online counselling before venturing into the field (Centore & Milacci, 2008). The academic and professional organizations have an essential role to play in this regard. Training sessions, seminars, workshops, courses need to be organized in order for practitioners to be aware of their professional responsibilities, legal and ethical issues, guidelines to deal with the same, and the possible constraints and benefits of delivering mental health services online (Perle & Nierenberg, 2013; Simms et al., 2011).

It is necessary for clients to be more cautious consumers who are aware of their own rights. They should verify the identity and the qualifications of the therapist before enrolling for therapy. Moreover, they must read the informed consent and terms and conditions form carefully before signing up for it. This will make them aware of their legal liabilities and personal responsibilities as a consumer of online mental health services (Cipolletta & Mocellin, 2016).

There is also a need for International collaboration and cooperation between mental health professionals, researchers and academicians (Finn & Barak, 2010). An example of one such currently existing professional organization is ISMHO. However, it is rather unfortunate that there are only three Indian mental health professionals who are currently members of the ISMHO. One reason could be a lack of awareness of the existence of such an association. This highlights the significance of promotional activities. Existing members of different countries could play a role in promoting the cause of the ISMHO by sharing the information on their LinkedIn and Research Gate profile or their own personal website or even on social media.

At present all countries do not have laws or ethical guidelines or standards on web-based psychotherapeutic interventions. This raises an immediate need to draft guidelines specific to online clinical practice. Therefore, in the interest of consumers, 'practicing psychologists must cobble together an understanding about relevant laws regarding informed consent, patient confidentiality, privacy and security' (Baker & Bufka, 2011, p. 410).

DIRECTIONS FOR FUTURE RESEARCH

It is necessary to explore and assess the ongoing changes in computer-mediated therapy periodically. This will make practitioners aware of the ways in which these extant technological trends might impact the future development of psychological services delivered through cyberspace.

Research is the only significant pathway for observing and evaluating such changes. Future research is needed to establish and substantiate the efficiency of the various web-based clinical services and interventions which are currently being used, including synchronous and asynchronous chat, audio and video communication, online forums, group support and web-based psychotherapeutic applications such as structured CBT, dialectical behavioural therapy programmes or m-health applications (Dowling & Rickwood, 2016). Perhaps, the most effective way to investigate the long-term impact of such interventions is through longitudinal studies (Menon & Rubin, 2011; Perle & Nierenberg, 2013), and to date there is a dearth of such studies.

A critical question is whether the learning from an online therapeutic session transforms into positive behavioural changes in real-world settings. For example, for a socially phobic person receiving therapeutic interventions online, it is essential that this online learning have an impact on his/her social behaviour in real-world settings.

Research investigating whether there are any significant differences in the outcome of online treatment of clients with different categories of mental health issues such as mood disorder, anxiety disorder and stress disorder is equally significant (Dowling & Rickwood, 2016).

There is also a need to examine if gender, age, theoretical orientation, previous knowledge and experience play a role in determining the attitude of practitioners towards web-based mental health services (Cipolletta & Mocellin, 2016).

So far, among the different web-based interventions, various studies have established the efficacy of online counselling. However, the presence of a large number of communication options (such as video-conferencing, e-mails, instant messaging), make it necessary to investigate which individuals are more inclined to seek help through which medium (Mallen, Vogel, & Rochlen, 2005). In web-based counselling, single-session counselling is a relatively unexplored area (Rodda et al., 2015) as compared to multi-session therapy (Richards & Vigano, 2013). The research questions that might help better understand this phenomenon in online counselling are as follows:

- What are the chief characteristics of clients who opt for single session counselling?
- What are their pre-dominant problems?
- Are they generally satisfied with the single counselling session?
- Do they seek help from multiple sources (several single sessions from different online practitioners)?
- Do they have a higher level of self-efficacy as compared to clients who opt for multi-session therapy?

There is an immediate need for researchers to work in collaboration with online practitioners, to derive a theoretical and practical module to determine ways to use cyber therapy with clients having severe forms of psychopathology. Currently, most practitioners refrain from dealing with such clients through the online medium (Callahan & Inckle, 2012; Childress, 2000; Haberstroh, Parr, Bradley, Morgan-Fleming, & Gee, 2008; Lovejoy, Demireva, Grayson, & McNamara, 2009). Their cause of concern is indeed valid because it is difficult to address the needs of the client with manic-depressive psychosis, borderline personality disorder, schizophrenia or other such disorders solely through the online medium. Rather, web-based services can act as additional sources of support for them. In the meanwhile, organizations and professionals rendering online services may consider providing informational and emotional support services to the caregivers of such clients.

The literature on help-seeking behaviour seems to indicate that men, introverts and those individuals with high levels of neuroticism have an unfavourable attitude towards seeking help for personally relevant problems (Addis & Mahalik, 2003; Fischer & Farina, 1995; Fischer & Turner, 1970). Thus, if they do enter into therapy, they are more likely to discontinue (Cohen & Kerr, 1998; MacNair & Corazzini, 1994; Nocita & Stiles, 1986). This makes it necessary to investigate if web-based interventions can be tailored to their needs, and whether they may develop a more favourable attitude towards such help.

In their review on the determinants which facilitate the involvement of users in web-based interventions, Schubart, Stuckey, Ganeshamoorty and Sciamannan (2011) highlighted the significance of individualized programmes for clients. This may help increase adherence to the programme and prevent early dropout rates of clients. Their review brings to light the need for research to determine whether individualized programmes are more effective than programmes tailored for specific target populations (Dozeman et al., 2017).

There is also a lack of psychometrically sound instruments to evaluate the perception or attitude of practitioners or current or prospective clients towards web-based interventions. Other vital constructs include the perception of communication satisfaction with the online counsellor and the satisfaction with the overall service. This highlights the need to develop reliable and valid psychometric instruments assessing these constructs to further research on these aspects of web-based psychotherapeutic interventions.

According to the report of the 'Health Information Technology and Mental Health: the Way Forward', a technical expert panel set up by the Agency for Healthcare Research and Quality and the National Institute of Mental Health, future research on behavioural intervention technologies including web-based interventions should emphasize upon adherence, barriers, cost and the reach of these diverse technologies in the field of mental health. It also calls for improvements in the evaluation strategies and highlights the need for theoretical models to guide researchers working on behavioural intervention technologies in mental health.

Apart from applied research, basic research is also equally important. For example, there is a need for development and refinement of theoretical models of psychotherapy in cyberspace. Today, the Internet is a living space in itself, and analogous to role theory which posits that one needs to efficiently manage all his roles in order to achieve a healthy balance in life, 'cyberspace living is … another manifestation of this shifting, juggling maneuver' (Suler, 2002, p. 456). Hence, a comprehensive theoretical model of web-based or computer-mediated psychotherapeutic interventions should also help explain human behaviour in cyberspace.

Researchers reporting randomized controlled trials (RCTs) of web-based mental health interventions should refer to the CONSORT E-HEALTH (Consolidated Standards of Reporting Trials of Electronic and Mobile Health Applications and Online Telehealth) guidelines. It acts as a checklist for researchers reporting randomized controlled trials of eHealth and mHealth interventions. The first Journal to adopt the CONSORT E-HEALTH guidelines was the *Journal of Medical Internet Research* (Eysenbach & CONSORT-EHEALTH Group, 2011). It is hoped that other Journals will also follow suit keeping in view the importance of the CONSORT E-HEALTH statements in improving the quality of web-based psychotherapeutic research using RCTs.

In order to better understand the current trend in research on web-based interventions in various countries, collaboration among researchers is equally significant. They could also have their own association or professional organization. Academic discussions, presentation of research findings on web-based mental health services, brainstorming sessions could be made part of their online or face-to-face annual or biannual meetings (Cipolletta & Mocellin, 2016).

CONCLUSION

The spirit of the times has a consequential role in the acceptance or rejection of a particular idea or innovation by the scientific as well as non-academic community. The current 'zeitgeist' seems conducive to the acceptance and further development, refinement and enhancement of web-based mental health interventions. The entire community of mental health practitioners, researchers and academicians possess the responsibility of utilizing this favourable environment, for efficiently aligning psychological interventions with technology. In the course of doing so, the help of law and policymakers and information and communication technology specialists is indispensable. However, in this journey of promoting web-based psychological services, it is important to remember that 'online therapy will never be for every client or every practitioner' (Anthony et al., 2010, p. 484). There is always a possibility of disapproval from a section of consumers and practitioners who believe there can never be any substitute for in-person clinical services. Such scepticism has always been characteristic of any field trying to incorporate novel scientific ideas even though they are supported by research based-evidence.

It is hoped that law and policymakers will show a positive attitude towards web-based interventions and shall help clarify the legal issues pertaining to the delivery of mental health services online, besides framing laws related to the same if deemed necessary. However, it will definitely take time before ethical, legal and professional guidelines for web-based psychotherapeutic interventions are framed in India. Until then, perhaps, we will continue to see the trend of rapid upsurge and consequent downfall of a large number of online counselling websites, influenced in part by the 'start-up culture' currently prevalent in India.

REFERENCES

Addis, M. E., & Mahalik, J. R. (2003). Men, masculinity, and the contexts of help seeking. *American Psychologist, 58*(5), 5–17.

Allenman, J. (2002). Online counselling: The internet and mental health treatment. *Psychotherapy, 39*(2), 199–209.

Amichai-Hamburger, Y., Wainapel, G., & Fox, S. (2002). On the internet no one knows I'm an introvert: Extraversion, neuroticism, and internet interaction. *Cyberpsychology & Behavior, 5*(2), 125–128.

Anthony, K., Jung, A., Rosenauer, D., Nagel, D. M., & Goss, S. (2010). Interview with Audrey Jung, President of the International Society for Mental Health Online (ISMHO), presented at the Online Counseling and Therapy in Action conference, 25 April 2009. *British Journal of Guidance and Counselling, 38*(4), 483–494.

Baker, D. C. (2003). Studies of the inner life: The impact of spirituality on quality of life. *Quality of Life Research, 12*(1), 51–57.

Baker, D., & Bufka, L. (2011). Preparing for the telehealth world: Navigating legal, regulatory, reimbursement, and ethical issues in an electronic age. *Professional Psychology: Research and Practice, 42*(6), 405–411.

Balasinorwala, V., Shah, N., Chatterjee, S., Kale, V., & Matcheswalla, Y. (2014). Asynchronous telepsychiatry in Maharashtra, India: Study of feasibility and referral pattern. *Indian Journal of Psychological Medicine, 36*(3), 299–301.

Barak, A. (2007). Emotional support and suicide prevention through the Internet: A field project report. *Computers in Human Behavior, 23*(2), 971–984.

Barak, A., & Fisher, W. A. (2001). Toward an internet driven, theoretically based innovative approach to sex education. *Journal of Sex Research, 38*(4), 324–332.

Barak, A., & Grohol, J. M. (2011). Current and future trends in internet-supported mental health interventions. *Journal of Technology in Human Services, 29*(3), 155–196.

Barak, A., Hen, L., Boneil-Nissim, M., & Shapira, N. (2008). A comprehensive review and meta-analysis of the effectiveness of Internet-based psychotherapeutic interventions. *Journal of Technology in Human Services, 26*(2–4), 109–160.

Barak, A., Klein, B., & Proudfoot, J. (2009). Defining Internet-supported therapeutic interventions. *Annals of Behavioral Medicine, 38*(1), 4–17.

Bauer, S., Moessner, M., Wolf, M., Haug, S., & Kordy, H. (2009). ES[S]PRIT: An internet-based programme for the prevention and early intervention of eating disorders in college students. *British Journal of Guidance and Counselling, 37*(3), 327–336.

Baumel, A. (2015). Online emotional support delivered by trained volunteers: Users' satisfaction and their perception of the service compared to psychotherapy. *Journal of Mental Health, 24*(5), 313–320.

Baumel, A., Correll, C., & Birnbaum, M. (2016). Adaptation of a peer-based online emotional support program as an adjunct to treatment for people with schizophrenia-spectrum disorders. *Internet Interventions, 4*(1), 35–42.

Baumel, A., & Schueller, S. M. (2016). Adjusting an available online peer support platform in a program to supplement the treatment of perinatal depression and anxiety. *Journal of Medical Internet Research* (JMIR) *Mental Health, 3*(1), e:11. doi:10.2196/mental.5335

Binik, Y. M., Cantor, J., Ochs, E., & Meana, M. (1997). From the couch to the keyboard: Psychotherapy in cyberspace. In S. Kiesler (Ed.), *Culture of the internet* (pp. 71–100). Mahwah, NJ: Erlbaum.

Bohlmeijer, E., & Hulsbergen, M. (2013). *This is your life. Experience the effects of positive psychology.* Amsterdam: Uitgeverij Boom.

Cai, S., Wang, X., & Chiang, F. K. (2014). A case study of augmented reality simulation system application in a chemistry course. *Computers in Human Behavior, 37*(8), 31–40.

Callahan, A., & Inckle, K. (2012). Cybertherapy or psychobabble? A mixed methods study of online emotional support. *British Journal of Guidance and Counselling, 40*(3), 261–278.

Carey, T. (2006). *The method of levels: How to do psychotherapy without getting in the way.* Hayward: Living Control Systems Publishing.

Census of India. (2011). Retrieved from http://censusindia.gov.in/2011-prov-results/paper2/data_ files/india/ Rural_Urban_2011.pdf

Centore, A. J., & Milacci, F. (2008). A study of mental health counselors' use of and perspectives on distance counseling. *Journal of Mental Health Counseling, 30*(3), 267–282.

Chardon, L., Bagraith, K. S., & King, R. (2011). Counseling activity in single-session online counseling with adolescents: An adherence study. *Psychotherapy Research, 21*(5), 583–592.

Chester, A., & Glass, C. A. (2006). Online counseling: A descriptive analysis of therapy services on the Internet. *British Journal of Guidance and Counselling, 34*(2), 145–160.

Childress, C. A. (1992). Interactive email journaling: A model for providing psychotherapeutic interventions using the internet. *Cyberpsychology & Behavior, 2*(3), 213–221.

———— (1999). Parenting skills research: Limitations and issues in e-mail consultation. Retrieved from http://www.geocities.com/Heartland/Oaks/3068/limitations.html

———— (2000). Ethical issues in providing online psychotherapeutic interventions. *Journal of Medical Internet Research, 2*(1), e:5. doi: 10.2196/jmir.2.1.e5

Choubsia, R. (2011). *Enhancing college students well-being through a web-based intervention module: An empirical investigation* (Unpublished doctoral thesis). Retrieved from http://eprint.iitd.ac.in/bitstream/2074/5827/1/TH-4124.pdf

Christensen, H., Mackinnon, A. J., Batterham, P. J., O'Dea, B., Guastella, A. J., Griffiths, K. M., ... Hickie, I. (2014). The effectiveness of an online e-health application compared to attention placebo or Sertraline in the treatment of Generalised Anxiety Disorder. *Internet Interventions, 1*(4), 169–174.

Cipolletta, S., & Mocellin, D. (2016). Online counseling: An exploratory survey of Italian psychologists attitudes towards new ways of interaction. *Psychotherapy Research, 28*(6), 1–16.

Cohen, G. E., & Kerr, B. A. (1998). Computer-mediated counseling: An empirical study of a new mental health treatment. *Computers in Human Services, 15*(4), 13–26.

Colón, Y. (1996). Chattering through the fingertips: Doing group therapy online. *Women & Performance: A Journal of Feminist Theory, 9*(1), 205–215.

Cook, J., & Doyle, C. (2002). Working alliance in online therapy as compared to face-to-face therapy: Preliminary results. *Cyberpsychology & Behavior, 5*(2), 95–105.

Corcoran, K. J. (1981). Experiential empathy: A theory of a felt-level experience. *Journal of Humanistic Psychology, 21*(1), 29–38.

Cramm, J. M., Strating, M. H., Roebroeck, M. E., & Nieboer, A. P. (2013). The importance of general self-efficacy for the quality of life of adolescents with chronic conditions. *Social Indicators Research, 113*(1), 551–561.

Danaher, B. G., Severson, H. H., Crowley, R., Meter, N. V., Tyler, M. S., Widdop, C., … Ebbert, J. O. (2015). Randomized controlled trial examining the adjunctive use of nicotine lozenges with MyLastDip: An e-health smokeless tobacco cessation intervention. *Internet Interventions, 2*(1), 69–76.

Deady, M., Kay-Lambkin, F., Teesson, M., & Mills, K. (2014). Developing an integrated, internet-based self-help programme for young people with depression and alcohol use problems. *Internet Interventions, 1*(3), 118–131.

DeBerard, M. S., Glen, I. S., & Jhulka, C. D. (2004). Predictors of academic achievement and retention among college freshman: A longitudinal study. *College Student Journal, 38*(1), 66–80.

Dowling, M., & Rickwood, D. (2013). Online counseling and therapy for mental health problems: A systematic review of individual synchronous interventions using chat. *Journal of Technology in Human Services, 31*(1), 1–21.

——— (2016). Exploring hope and expectations in the youth mental health online counselling environment. *Computers in Human Behavior, 55*, 62–68.

Dozeman, E., Verdonck-de Leeuw, I. M., Savard, J., & van Straten, A. (2017). Guided web-based intervention for insomnia targeting breast cancer patients: Feasibility and effect. *Internet Interventions, 9*, 1–6.

Dyson, R., & Renk, K. (2006). Depressive symptoms, stress, and coping. *Journal of Clinical Psychology, 62*(10), 1231–1244.

Economic Times. (2017, 1 March). *Economic Times Telecom.* Retrieved from https://telecom.economictimes.indiatimes.com/news/indias-internet-user-base-to-reach-450-465-million-by-june-2017-iamai-imrb-report/57410229

Emerson, E. B. (1985). Evaluating the impact of deinstitutionalization on the lives of mentally retarded people. *American Journal of Mental Deficiency, 90*(3), 277–288.

Eysenbach, G., & CONSORT-EHEALTH Group. (2011). CONSORT_EHEALTH: Improving and standardizing evaluation reports of web-based and mobile health interventions. *Journal of Medical Internet Research, 13*(4), e:126. doi: 10.2196/jmir.1923

Farrer, L., Christensen, H., Griffiths, K., & Mackinnon, A. (2012). Web-based cognitive behavior therapy for depression with and without telephone tracking in a national helpline: Secondary outcomes from a randomized controlled trial. *Journal of Medical Internet Research, 14*(3), e:68. doi: 10.2196/jmir.1859

Felce, D., & Perry, J. (1995). Quality of life: Its definition and measurement. *Research in Developmental Disabilities, 16*(1), 51–74.

Fenichel, M., Suler, J., Barak, A., Zelvin, E., Jones, G., Munro, K., … Walker-Schmucker, W. (2002). Myths and realities of online clinical work. *Cyberpsychology & Behavior, 5*(5), 481–497.

Finn, J., & Barak, A. (2010). A descriptive study of e-counsellor attitudes, ethics, and practice. *Counselling and Psychotherapy Research, 10*(4), 268–277.

Fischer, E. H., & Farina, A. (1995). Attitudes toward seeking professional psychological help: A shortened form and considerations for research. *Journal of College Student Development, 36*(4), 368–373.

Fischer, E. H., & Turner, J. J. (1970). Orientations to seeking professional help: Development and research utility of an attitude scale. *Journal of Consulting and Clinical Psychology, 35*(1), 79–90.

Foody, M., Samara, M., & Carlbring, P. (2015). A review of cyberbullying and suggestions for online psychological therapy. *Internet Interventions, 2*(3), 235–242.

Force, J. T., & Guidelines, T. (2013). Guidelines for the practice of telepsychology. *American Psychologist, 68*(9), 791–800.

Fukkink, R., & Hermanns, J. (2009). Counseling children at a helpline: Chatting or calling? *Journal of Community Psychology, 37*(8), 939–948.

Gaffney, H., Mansell, W., Edwards, R., & Wright, J. (2014). Manage Your Life Online (MYLO): A pilot trial of a conversational computer-based intervention for problem-solving in a student sample. *Behavioral and Cognitive Psychotherapy, 42*(6), 731–746.

Gatti, F. M., Brivio, E., & Calciano, S. (2016). 'Hello! I know you help people here, right?' A qualitative studyof young people's acted motivations in text-based counseling. *Children and Youth Services Review, 71*, 27–35.

Gibson, K., & Cartwright, C. (2014). Young people's experiences of mobile phone text counselling: Balancing connection and control. *Children and Youth Services Review, 43*, 96–104.

Goss, S. (2010). Online counselling: A handbook for practitioners (book review). *British Journal of Guidance and Counselling, 38*(3), 364–367.

Grover, F. J., Wu, H. D., Blanford, C., Holcomb, S., & Tidler, D. (2002). Computer-using patients want Internet services from family physicians. *Journal of Family Practice, 51*(6), 570–572.

Guntuku, S. C., Yaden, D. B., Kern, M. L., Ungar, L. H., & Eichstaedt, J. C. (2017). Detecting depression and mental illness on social media: An integrative review. *Current Opinion in Behavioral Sciences, 18*, 43–49.

Haberstroh, S., Parr, G., Bradley, L., Morgan-Fleming, B., & Gee, R. (2008). Facilitating online counseling: Perspectives from counselors in training. *Journal of Counseling & Development, 86*(4), 460–470.

Hamburger, Y. A., & Ben-Artizi, E. (2000). The relationship between extraversion and neuroticism and the different uses of the internet. *Computers in Human Behavior, 16*(4), 441–449.

Hashim, W. N., Othman, M. R., Mardian, S., & Syafiq, M. I. (2013). Development of a usable online counseling management system. *Procedia – Social and Behavioral Sciences, 97*, 761–765.

Havighurst, R. J. (1961). Successful aging. *The Gerontologist, 1*(1), 8–13.

Hays, R. D., Kallich, J. D., Mapes, D. L., Coons, S. J., & Carter, W. B. (1994). Development of the Kidney Disease Quality of Life (KDQOL) instrument. *Quality of Life Research, 3*(5), 329–338.

Heinlen, K. T., Welfel, E. R., Richmond, E. N., & Rak, C. F. (2003). The scope of webcounseling: A survey of services and compliance with NBCC standards for the ethical practice of webcounseling. *Journal of Counseling & Development, 81*(1), 61–69.

Henning, M. A., Krägeloh, C., Thompson, A., Sisley, R., Doherty, I., & Hawken, S. J. (2015). Religious affiliation, quality of life and academic performance: New Zealand medical students. *Journal of Religion & Health, 54*(1), 3–19.

Hindustan Times. (2017). Red alert—Rising cases of student suicides sound alarm bells across India. *Hindustan Times,* 5 May. Retrieved from http://www.hindustantimes.com/brandstories/tatateajaagore/rising-cases-of-student-suicides-sound-alarm-bells-across-India.html

Ho, J., Corden, M. E., Caccamo, L., Tomasino, K. N., Duffecy, J., Begale, M., ... Mohr, D. C. (2016). Design and evaluation of a peer network to support adherence to a web-based intervention for adolescents. *Internet Interventions, 6,* 50–56.

Huang, M. P., & Alessi, N. E. (1996). The internet and the future of psychiatry. *The American Journal of Psychiatry, 153*(7), 861–869.

Hunt, S. (2002). In favour of onlinecounselling? *Australian Social Work, 55*(4), 260–267.

Idler, E. L., McLaughlin, J., & Kasl, S. (2009). Religion and the quality of life in the last year of life. *The Journal of Gerontology: Social Science, 64*(4), 528–537.

JernelÖv, S., Lekander, M., Blom, K., Rydh, S., Ljotsson, B., Axelsson, J., ... Kaldo, V. (2012). Efficacy of a behavioral self-help treatment with or without therapist guidance for comorbid and primary insomnia: A randomized controlled trial. *BMC Psychiatry, 12*(1), 5.

Jerome, L. W., DeLeon, P. H., James, L. C., Folen, R., Earles, J., & Gedney, J. J. (2000). The coming age of telecommunications in psychological research and practice. *American Psychologist, 55*(4), 407–421.

Joo, N. S., & Kin, B. T. (2007). Mobile phone short message service messaging for behavior modification in a community-based weight control programme in Korea. *Journal of Telemedicine and Telecare, 13*(8), 416–420.

Kanani, K., & Regehr, C. (2003). Clinical, ethical, and legal issues in e-therapy. *Families in Society, 84*(2), 155–162.

Kanz, J. (2001). Clinical supervision.com: Issues in the provision of online supervision. *Professional Psychology: Research and Practice, 32*(4), 415–420.

Kitson, A., Prpa, M., & Riecke, B. E. (2018). Immersive interactive technologies for positive change: A scoping review and design consideration. *Frontiers in Psychology, 9,* 1–19.

Kostka, T., & Jachimowicz, V. (2010). Relationship of quality of life to dispositional optimism, health locus of control and self-efficacy in older subjects living in different environments. *Quality of Life Research, 19*(3), 351–361.

Lazarus, L., & Dokou, A. (2016). Mental health professionals' acceptance of online counseling. *Technology in Society, 44*, 10–14.

Lehman, R. M., & Berg, R. A. (2007). *147 tips for synchronous and blended technology teaching and learning.* Madison, WI: Atwood Publishing.

Li, L. P., Jaladin, A. M., & Abdullah, S. H. (2013). Understanding the two sides of online counseling and their ethical and legal ramifications. *Procedia—Social and Behavioral Sciences, 103*, 1243–1251.

Liebert, T., & Archer, J. (2006). An exploratory study of client perceptions of Internet counselling and the therapeutic alliance. *Journal of Mental Health Counselling, 28*(1), 69–84.

Lindenberg, K., Moessner, M., Harney, J., McLaughlin, O., & Bauer, S. (2011). E-health for individualized prevention of eating disorders. *Clinical Practice & Epidemiology in Mental Health, 7*, 74–83.

Liss, H. J., Glueckauf, R. L., & Ecklund-Johnson, E. P. (2002). Research on telehealth and chronic medical conditions: Critical review, key issues, and future directions. *Rehabilitation Psychology, 47*(1), 8–30.

Lorne, F., Rosalin, R., Kurundvade, N., & Ratra, H. (2017). Social experiment for rural India: Addressing Indian farmers suicide problems via wireless technology. *Frontiers in Management Research, 1*(4), 126–140.

Lovejoy, T., Demireva, P., Grayson, J., & McNamara, J. (2009). Advancing the practice of online psychotherapy: An application of Rogers' diffusion of innovations theory. *Psychotherapy: Theory, Research, Practice, Training, 46*(1), 112–124.

Luthans, F., Avey, J. B., & Patera, J. L. (2008). Experimental analysis of a web-based training intervention to develop positive psychological capital. *Academy of Management Learning & Education, 7*(2), 209–221.

MacNair, R. R., & Corazzini, J. G. (1994). Client factors influencing group therapy dropout. *Psychotherapy: Theory, Research, Practice, Training, 31*(2), 352–362.

Malhotra, S., Chakrabarti, S., Shah, R., Sharma, M., Sharma, K., & Singh, H. (2015). Diagnostic accuracy and feasibility of a net-based application for diagnosing common psychiatric disorders. *Psychiatry Research, 230*(2), 369–376.

Mallen, M. J., Vogel, D. L., & Rochlen, A. B. (2005). The practical aspects of online counseling: Ethics, training, technology, and competency. *The Counseling Psychologist, 33*(6), 776–818.

Mallen, M. J., Vogel, D. L., Rochlen, A. B., & Day, S. X. (2005). Online counseling: Reviewing the literature from a counseling psychology framework. *The Counseling Psychologist, 33*(6), 819–871.

Manhal-Baugus. (2001). E-therapy: Practical, ethical, and legal issues. *Cyberpsychology & Behavior, 4*(5), 551–563.

Maples, M. F., & Han, S. (2008). Cybercounseling in the United States and South Korea: Implications for counseling college students of the millennial generation and the networked generation. *Journal of Counseling 7 Development, 86*(2), 178–183.

Meenan, R. F., Gertman, P. M., & Mason, J. H. (1980). Measuring health status in arthritis: The arthritis impact measurement scales. *Arthritis & Rheumatism, 23*(2), 146–152.

Mehrotra, S., & Tripathi, R. (2011). Positive psychology research in India: A review and critique. *Journal of the Indian Academy of Applied Psychology, 37*(1), 9–26.

Menon, G. M., & Rubin, M. (2011). A survey of online practitioners: Implications for education and practice. *Journal of Technology in Human Services, 29*(2), 133–141.

Ministry of Health and Family Welfare. (2015). *Answer of the Minister of Health and Family Welfare, Government of India, to starred question number 253 to the Rajya Sabha.* New Delhi: Author.

Murphy, L. J., & Mitchell, D. L. (1998). When writing helps to heal: E-mail as therapy. *British Journal of Guidance and Counselling, 26*(1), 21–32.

Nickelson, D. W. (1998). Telehealth and the evolving health care system: Strategic opportunities for professional psychology. *Professional Psychology: Research and Practice, 29*(6), 537–535.

Nocita, A., & Stiles, W. B. (1986). Client introversion and counseling session impact. *Journal of Counseling Psychology, 33*(3), 235–241.

Oravec, J. A. (2000). Online counseling and the internet: Perspectives for mental health care supervision and education. *Journal of Mental Health, 9*(2), 121–135.

Perle, J. G., Langsam, L. C., & Nierenberg, B. (2011). Controversy clarified: An updated review of clinical psychology and telehealth. *Clinical Psychology Review, 31*(8), 1247–1258.

Perle, J. G., Langsam, L. C., Randel, A., Lutchman, S., Levine, A. B., Odland, A. P., … & Marker, C. D. (2013). Attitudes toward psychological telehealth: Current and future clinical psychologists' opinions of Internet-based interventions. *Journal of Clinical Psychology, 69*(1), 100–113.

Perle, J. G., & Nierenberg, B. (2013). How psychological telehealth can alleviate society's mental health burden: A literature review. *Journal of Technology in Human Services, 31*(1), 22–41.

Peterson, M. R., & Beck, R. L. (2003). E-mail as an adjunctive tool in psychotherapy: Response and responsibility. *American Journal of Psychotherapy, 57*(2), 167–181.

Powell, J., Hamborg, T., Stallard, N., Burls, A., McSorley, J., Bennett, K., … Christensen, H. (2013). Effectiveness of a web-based cognitive-behavioral tool to improve mental well-being in the general population: Randomized controlled trial. *Journal of Medical Internet Research, 15*(1), e:68. doi: 10.2196/jmir.1859

Prati, G., Pietrantoni, L., & Cicognani, E. (2010). Self-efficacy moderates the relationship between stress appraisal and quality of life among rescue workers. *Anxiety, Stress & Coping: An International Journal, 23*(4), 463–470.

Proudfoot, J., Swain, S., Widmer, S., Watkins, E., Goldberg, D., Marks, I., ... Gray, J. A. (2003). The development and beta-test of a computer-therapy program for anxiety and depression: Hurdles and preliminary outcomes. *Computers in Human Behavior, 19*(3), 277–289.

Ragusea, A. S., & VandeCreek, L. (2003). Suggestions for the ethical practice of online psychotherapy. *Psychotherapy: Theory, Research, Practice, Training, 40*(1–2), 94–102.

Rajabi, A., Ghasemzadeh, A., Ashrafpouri, Z., & Saadat, M. (2012). Effects of counseling by mobile phone short message service (SMS) on reducing aggressive behavior in adolescence. *Procedia—Social and Behavioral Sciences, 46*, 1138–1142.

Rector, T. S., & Cohn, J. N. (1992). Assessment of patient outcome with the Minnesota Living with Heart Failure Questionnaire: Reliability and validity during a randomized, double-blind, placebo-controlled trial of pimobendan. *American Heart Journal, 124*(4), 1017–1025.

Recupero, A., Triberti, S., Modesti, C., & Talamo, A. (2018, July). Mixed reality for cross-cultural integration: Using positive technology to share experiences and promote communication. *Frontiers in Psychology, 9*, 1–5.

Redzic, N. M., Taylor, K., Chang, V., Trockle, M., Shorter, A., & Taylor, C. B. (2014). An internet-based positive psychology program: Strategies to improve effectiveness and engagement. *The Journal of Positive Psychology, 9*(6), 494–501.

Reger, M., & Gahm, G. (2009). A meta-analysis of the effects of internet and computer-based cognitive-behavioral treatments for anxiety. *Journal of Clinical Psychology, 65*(1), 53–75.

Richards, D., & Vigano, N. (2013). Online counseling: A narrative and critical review of the literature. *Journal of Clinical Psychology, 69*(9), 994–1011.

Rochlen, A. R., Berevtas, S. N., & Zack, J. S. (2004). The online and face-to-face counseling attitudes scales: A validation study. *Measurement and Evaluation in Counseling and Development, 37*(2), 95–111.

Rodda, S. N., Lubman, D. I., Cheetham, A., Dowling, N. A., & Jackson, A. C. (2015). Single session web-based counselling: A thematic analysis of content from the perspective of the client. *British Journal of Guidance and Counselling, 43*(1), 117–130.

Rodney, J. P., Royse, K. E., Benitez, T. J., & Pekmezi, D. W. (2014). Physical activity and quality of life among university students: Exploring self-efficacy, self-esteem, and affect as potential mediators. *Quality of Life Research, 23*(2), 659–667.

Rosenthal, B. S., & Schreiner, A. C. (2000). Prevalence of psychological symptoms among undergraduate students in an ethnically diverse urban public college. *Journal of American College Health, 49*(1), 12–18.

Sampson, J. P., Kolodinsky, R. W., & Greeno, B. P. (1997). Counseling on the information highway: Future possibilities and potential problems. *Journal of Counseling & Development, 75*(3), 203–212.

Schotanus-Dijkstra, M., Drossaert, C. H., Pieterse, M. E., Boon, B., Walburg, J. A., & Bohlmeijer, E. T. (2017). An early intervention to promote well-being and flourishing and reduce anxiety and depression: A randomized controlled trial. *Internet Interventions, 9*, 15–24.

Schubart, J. R., Stuckey, L., Ganeshamoorty, A. B., & Sciamannan. (2011). Chronic health conditions and internet behavioral interventions: a review of factors to enhance user engagement. *CIN: Computers, Informatics, Nursing, 29*(2), 81–92.

Schwartz, H. A., Eichstaedt, J. C., Kern, M. L., Dziurzynski, L., Ramones, S. M., Agrawal, M., … Ungar, L. H. (2013). Personality, gender, and age in the language of social media: The open-vocabulary approach. *PLoS One, 8*(9), e73791.

Seeman, M. V. (1999). E-psychiatry: The patient-psychiatrist relationship in the electronic age. *Canadian Medical Association Journal, 161*(9), 1147–1149.

Seyffert, M., Lagisetty, P., Landgraf, J., Chopra, V., & Pfeiffer, P. N. (2016). Internet-delivered cognitive behavioral therapy to treat insomnia: A systematic review and meta-analysis. *PLoS One, 11*(2), e0149139.

Shapiro, D. E., & Schulman, C. E. (1996). Ethical and legal issues in e-mail therapy. *Ethics and Behavior, 6*(2), 107–124.

Shareef, M., Abdullhadi, A. A., Abdulrahman, A. A.-K., Zainab, A., Mohammed, A. A., Sanderlla, I. Z., … Mariam, J. T. (2015). The interplay between academic performance and quality of life among preclinical students. *BMC Medical Education, 15*(1), 193.

Sharma, V., & Aradhana. (2000). Is seeking help a threat to self-worth? *Psychological Studies, 45*(1–2), 65–68.

Shaw, H. E., & Shaw, S. F. (2006). Critical ethical issues in online counseling: Assessing current practices with an ethical intent checklist. *Journal of Counseling & Development, 84*(1), 41–53.

Simms, D. C., Gibson, K., & O'Donnell, S. (2011). To use or not to use: Clinician's perceptions of telemental health. *Canadian Psychology, 52*(1), 41–51.

Skevington, S. M., Lotfy, M., & O'Connell, K. A. (2004). The World Health Organization's WHOQOL-BREF quality of life assessment: Psychometric properties and results of the international field report: A report from the WHOQOL Group. *Quality of Life Research, 13*(2), 299–310.

Sorathia, K., Sharma, K., Bhowmick, S., & Kamidi, P. (2017). Pragati: A mobile-based virtual reality (VR) platform to train and educate community health workers. In R. Bernhaupt, G. Dalvi, A. Joshi, D. Balkrishan, J. O'Neill, & M. Winckler (Eds.), *Human-Computer Interaction-INTERACT 2017* (pp. 459–463). Cham: Springer.

Srivastava, S., Pant, M., & Nagar, A. (2017). YUVA: An e-health model for dealing with psychological issues of adolescents. *Journal of Computational Science, 21,* 150–163.

Stafford, E., Hides, L., & Kavanagh, D. J. (2015). The acceptability, usability and short-term outcomes of Get Real: A web-based program for psychotic-like experiences (PLEs). *Internet Interventions, 2*(3), 266–271.

Stommel, W. (2016). Information giving or problem discussion? Formulations in the initial phase of web-based chat counseling sessions. *Journal of Pragmatics, 105,* 87–100.

Suler, J. R. (2002, October). Identity management in cyberspace. *Journal of Applied Psychoanalytic Studies, 4*(4), 455–459.

Swan, A., & Tyssen, E. (2009). Enhancing treatment access: Evaluation of an Australian web-based alcohol and drug counselling initiative. *Drug and Alcohol Review, 28*(1), 48–53.

Swickert, R. J., Rosentreter, C. J., Hittner, J. B., & Mushrush, J. E. (2002). Extraversion, social support processes, and stress. *Personality and Individual Differences, 32*(5), 877–879.

The Mental Health Care Act. (2017). *The Gazett of India.* New Delhi: Ministry of Law and Justice. Retrieved from http://www.prsindia.org/uploads/media/Mental%20Health/Mental%20Healthcare%20Act,%202017.pdf

Theofilou, P. (2013). Quality of life: Definition and measurement. *Europe's Journal of Psychology, 9*(1), 150–162.

Tsan, J. Y., & Day, S. X. (2007). Personality and genderas predictors of online counseling use. *Journal of Technology in Human Services, 25*(3), 39–55.

Turan, Z., Meral, E., & Sahin, I. F. (2018). The impact of mobile augmented reality in geography education: Achievements, cognitive loads and views of university students. *Journal of Geography in Higher Education, 42*(3), 1–15.

Tuten, T. L., & Bosnjak, M. (2001). Understanding differences in web usage: The role of need for cognition and the five-factor model of personality. *Social Behavior and Personality, 29*(4), 391–398.

Twomey, C., & O'Reilly, G. (2016). Effectiveness of a freely available computerised cognitive behavioural therapy programme (MoodGYM) for depression: Meta-analysis. *Australian and New Zealand Journal of Psychiatry, 51*(3), 260–269.

Twomey, C., O'Reilly, G., Byrne, M., Bury, M., White, A., Kissane, S., … Clancy, N. (2014). A randomized controlled trial of the computerized CBT programme, MoodGYM, for public mental health service users waiting for interventions. *British Journal of Clinical Psychology, 53*(4), 433–450.

van Straten, A., & Cuijpers, P. (2009). Self-help therapy for insomnia: A meta-analysis. *Sleep Medicine Reviews, 13*(1), 61–71.

Vonk, M. E., Markward, M. M., & Arnold, E. (2000). Social work practice in higher education: Two case studies. *Journal of Social Work Education, 36*(2), 359–371.

Weizenbaum, J. (1996). ELIZA: A computer program for the study of natural language communication between man and machine. *Communications of the Acm, 9*(1), 36–45.

Whitlock, J., Powers, J., & Eckenrode, J. (2006). The virtual cutting edge: The internet and adolescent self-injury. *Developmental Psychology, 42*(3), 407–417.

Wing, R. R., Epstein, L. H., Nowalk, M. P., & Lamparski, D. M. (1986). Behavioral self-regulation in the treatment of patients with diabetes mellitus. *Psychological Bulletin, 99*(1), 78–89.

Young, K. W. (2012). Positive effects of spirituality on quality of life for people with severe mental illness. *International Journal of Psychosocial Rehabilitation, 16*(2), 62–77.

Zachariae, R., Lyby, M. S., Ritterband, L. M., & O'Toole, M. S. (2016). Efficacy of internet-delivered cognitive-behavioral therapy for insomnia: A systematic review and meta-analysis of randomized controlled trials. *Sleep Medicine Reviews, 30*, 1–10.

Zack, J. S. (2008). How sturdy is that digital couch? Legal considerations for mental health professionals who deliver clinical services via the internet. *Journal of Technology in Human Services, 26*(2–4), 333–359.

Chapter 8

Employee Well-Being in Organizations

Mahima Raina and Kamlesh Singh

Translational research or the emphasis on converting basic science research into implementable interventions is gaining ground in the area of psychology. Despite its promise, translation research is still rare owing in part to the lack of familiarity with translational methods on part of the psychologists. In the corporate sector, employee well-being and efforts to increase the same are being increasingly focussed upon. Less focus on employee health and well-being can have compelling implications for organizations. This chapter discusses these implications at the outset, followed by how health and well-being initiatives impact physical and mental health of employees. The chapter ends with some recommendations for future initiatives that would be useful for both organizational and research purposes.

EMPLOYEE WELL-BEING IN ORGANIZATIONS

Across the globe, importance of well-being at work is being underscored, given which avid research has ensued to improve quality of work experiences. According to Manpower Group Survey (2005), Indians put in the highest number of hours at work compared to peers across the globe.

This ultramarathon of clocking away longest work hours across the world has put India at the lower end in terms of quality of life. Unprecedented competition, jet-set life, increased spatial segregation from support sources compromises not only personal well-being of the workforce but also impacts company's productivity and profitability as they lose talent in the absence of a work family-friendly environment. Recent surveys indicate that the ambit of well-being at work is increasing for Indians, who are seeking more quality experiences at work that contribute to a meaningful life. For instance, a whopping 87 per cent of people expressed in the Outlook Business Survey (2010) the need for work–life balance, with a pervasive and persistent message: 'Give us ME time, or else…'. The Michael Page India (2017) survey notes that skill enhancement and work–life balance are currently the most sought-after job aspects for Indian millennials. Another study conducted by the Tata Institute of Social Sciences and Key-Consumer Diagnostics (2013) studied millennials' attitudes towards work. The study claims that the younger generation is seeking 'life–work' balance and not 'work–life' balance, indicating the new generation worker's search for meaningful experiences at work that lead to a productive, balanced and quality life.

The mentioned work issues are compounded due to the advent of globalization. The early 1990s ushered in an era of economic reforms with the introduction of New Economic Policy (NEP) in 1991. The two major facets of the policy were globalization and privatization. This caused an upsurge of foreign trade investment, spurt in corporate activities and West-based companies setting up businesses in India (Gopinath, 1998). A transition was also experienced in demographics in the workplaces with more women joining the workforce, and also a rise in the number of dual earning couples was registered (Kalliath, Kalliath, & Singh, 2011). While the avenues for employment have increased after the implementation of NEP, globalization has caused major shifts in the way employees conduct and manage their work. At the outset, globalization has caused migration of people to bigger cities for employment, which has led to a spatial disconnect from the families. This has resulted in a marked reduction in the support available to the millennials. While the entrepreneurial spirit of India was seeing an upsurge like the ancient times (Kumar & Sethi, 2005), increasing affluence had its effect on the fabric of the Indian society.

Although the collectivistic orientation is largely intact, these changes have stimulated individualism (Sinha, 2014). Mishra (1994) reported that urbanized and more educated youngsters were more individualistic compared to the older generation.

Thus, to conclude, Indian mindset is essentially adapting and accommodating new ideas and experiences into its folds while having a firm foundation in its old traditions, thoughts and patterns. This foundation drives and influences how we work as well. Despite the ways work culture is evolving with technological advances, shifts in workplace demographics and organizational cultures promoting work-centric attitudes by implicitly forcing longer work hours; the dynamics are rooted in traditional shared values and patterns.

While understanding and facilitating well-being at work is a universal concern, it should step up as top priority for Indian organizations and policymakers given the revelations from recent surveys. As employees spend extended hours at work in India, the relevance of well-being at work gets more pronounced. Workplace is an important location for successful prevention strategies as employers can contribute meaningfully to employee well-being by fostering a supportive environment and offering well-being interventions, which in turn would increase their profitability and productivity. The scoping literature review identifies the effects of workplace health and well-being programmes on employees as well as employers.

WELL-BEING INTERVENTIONS AT WORK

The top reason for employers seeking well-being interventions for their employees is to improve quality of life, facilitate work engagement and enhance the productivity of the employees, thus cutting economic losses due to sickness, absenteeism and employee turnover. However, well-being interventions serve other purposes as well, like decreasing vulnerability to mental and physical illnesses as a result of available support, reducing spillover on co-workers, families and supervisors, reducing insurance and health-related costs to employers, and developing a positive corporate image due to increased employee morale and job satisfaction.

Shain and Kramer (2004) show that health as we experience it is a combination of individual and psychosocial elements. Individual elements can include personal resources, health beliefs, attitudes, values and hereditary factors. The psychosocial elements, on the other hand, include the physical environment of the workplace (impacts occupational safety), and the workplace psychosocial environment, or the way the management expects and influences employees' decisions to organize their work. For instance, an organization having a work–family friendly culture would be more flexible to employees organizing their work according to their needs (Kossek & Lautsch, 2012; Thompson, Beauvais, & Lyness, 1999). The physical and psychosocial components of the workplace interact to have a cumulative effect on the health of an employee (Polanyi et al., 2000). In fact, these physical and psychosocial components of the workplace also influence an employee's abilities to utilize and maintain their own personal resources. Thus, interventions having a multi-pronged approach (i.e., including both physical and psychosocial elements of work) offer the best results in terms of improving employee health (Hymel et al., 2011).

The World Health Organization (WHO) has proposed three main categories of health interventions, primary health care, disease prevention and health promotion. Health interventions at workplace can be organized on three levels (Goetzel & Ozminkowski, 2006, p. 304): primary, secondary and tertiary. Primary interventions are targeted at the healthy employed population, for example, developing programmes that focus on encouraging fitness, exercise, healthy eating, nutrition, stress management, use of safety belts in cars, moderate alcohol consumption, etc. Secondary interventions target working individuals who are at high risk of acquiring a lifestyle disease, for instance, substance abuse, poor nutrition, high stress and so on. Interventions are introduced at the workplace to provide support to such employees and include access to a counsellor/psychologist, smoking cessation programmes, stress and weight management programmes. Tertiary interventions are targeted at people who are living with physical or lifestyle diseases such as diabetes, hypertension, musculoskeletal diseases, etc. However, in the organizational context, primary and secondary interventions are more common, and more effective in reducing the negative impact of diseases, as well as return-to-work time (Proper & van Mechelen, 2008). Plethora of workplace well-being interventions such as access to a gym, smoking cessation programmes, stress and substance abuse management have been known to be very effective.

The literature review in the chapter covers three major target areas of well-being interventions: physical health in the workplace, health promotion at work and mental health/work-related stress at work. This section is followed by the current state of well-being interventions in India, and the chapter concludes with future recommendations.

PHYSICAL HEALTH IN THE WORKPLACE

The WHO and the World Economic Forum consider the workplace as an important setting for health promotion and prevention of non-communicable diseases like obesity. To that end, many interventions that tackle the issue of physical health at work have surfaced with encouraging results. The desirable changes affected through these interventions include increased physical activity resulting in decreased body fat percentage, improved cardiovascular fitness and building healthy eating habits. The overarching aim of these interventions is to propel employees towards a more productive lifestyle, decrease the risk of non-communicable diseases and facilitate organizational changes like decreased absenteeism.

A systematic review involving 47 studies found strong evidence that workplace health promotion programmes aimed at improving nutrition or physical activity or both are effective in reducing body weight and BMI (Anderson et al., 2009). Conn, Hafdahl, Cooper, Brown, & Lusk (2009) carried out a meta-analysis of the health and physical activity outcomes of workplace health promotion programmes. They synthesized standardized mean difference effect size data from approximately 38,231 subjects and found significant positive effects for a range of health outcomes, including physical activity behaviour, fitness, lipids, anthropometric measures, work attendance and job stress. Katz et al. (2005) conducted a systematic review of studies aimed at prevention and control of obesity at workplace. It was concluded that multi-component interventions including nutrition and physical activity focused interventions were effective in affecting changes related to lifestyles of employees. The interventions included strategies such as nutrition education, dietary prescription, physical activity prescriptions, group activities and behavioural skills training. Kahn et al. (2002) also stressed the individually tailored behavioural skills training. The review pointed to the relevance of strategies like encouraging the use of stairs to increase physical activity was likely to be effective across wide range of working population. Further, creating spaces to encourage physical activity was likely to promote physical health at work. Engbers, van Poppel, Paw, & van Mechelen (2005) also reported similar findings in their review. Strong evidence from multi-centre trails indicated that environmental modifications had positive impact on dietary intake. Such modifications included food labelling, provision for healthy eating options in the canteen and vending machines at work. Matson-Koffman, Brownstein, Neiner, & Greaney (2005) reviewed experimental and quasi-experimental studies aimed at policy or environmental interventions to promote physical activity and good nutrition at work. The studies included impact of using prompts to encourage staircase use, creating places and opportunities to engage in physical activity, using worksite approaches like education, employee and peer group support, providing access to exercise facilities, availability of nutritious food and access to counselling on diet, training and health care issues and so on. Strong evidence was reported for affecting change via such policy and environmental modifications. A systematic review by Bellew (2008), Dugdill, Brettle, Hulme, McCluskey and Long (2008), and Robroek, Van Lenthe, Van Empelen and Burdorf (2009) reported similar findings as well.

MENTAL HEALTH IN THE WORKPLACE

According to the *Mental Health at Work Report 2017*, about 60 per cent of employees have experienced mental health issues due to work-related problems at some point of their career. About 31 per cent of this population was clinically diagnosed with a mental health issue. The figures are striking, and point to the fact that workplaces form a versatile site for mental health interventions as well as call for employers and employees to come together to resolve mental health issues. While corporations have long been involved in providing monetary resources (e.g., insurance programmes; Conrad, 1988), other occupational health and safety interventions like ergonomic workplaces (Larson, 1998), and improved ventilation at workplaces (Frazer, 1998), workplace interventions targeting mental health have evolved slowly.

The mental health interventions work on primary, secondary and tertiary levels. The primary interventions aim at prevention of mental health issues by reducing work-related risk factors. The secondary interventions promote mental health by accentuating positive aspects of work as well as the employee. The tertiary interventions address the existing mental health issues of employees regardless of their origin. The primary level interventions may include HR policies, training programmes, corporate social responsibility initiatives in addition to health promotion at work (Singh & Junnarkar, 2017; Vijaimadhavan & Raju, 2013). *HR policies* target employee well-being by introducing health, safety, talent and career management initiatives at work. This can include career breaks, flexible working hours/days, childcare leave, and such work–life balance initiatives. They may also include initiatives for career and talent progression of an employee and providing aid in coaching, mentoring, time management, conflict management and conducting trainings to enhance employees' skill sets (Vijaimadhavan & Raju, 2013). *Corporate social responsibility* initiatives include community outreach programmes that have the dual aim of having employees engage in social welfare, such as blood donation, charitable fundraising and reducing stress of employees, thereby increasing employees' productivity. The productivity of employees is also dependent on their psychosocial environment; hence, many primary interventions target at modifying the same. Mattila, Elo, Kuosma and Kylä-Setälä (2006) investigated the impact of participative work conference[1] on psychosocial work environment which included aspects such as job control, work climate, supervisory support, role clarity and information flow. About 525 participants working in a large municipal organization participated in this intervention that lasted two days and included a follow up six months post intervention. The work climate levels remained stable in intervention group and deteriorated in the control group, indicating significant improvement in intervention group. Pryce, Albertsen and Nielsen (2006) assessed the impact of open rota system on health, job satisfaction and work–life balance of 177 psychiatric nurses in a 20-month-long

---

[1] Work conference method is an intensive participation method aimed at involving employees in organizational planning and decision-making.

intervention programme. The experimental groups were made to attend a one-day workshop where case studies related to work scheduling were presented. The groups were then asked to develop an intervention that suited them the best. The groups followed the chosen work schedule intervention for 20 months, post which a follow up was conducted to gauge the efficacy of the intervention. Significant changes were noted in key areas such as work–life balance, social support, job satisfaction and sense of community. The autonomy to take decisions about their daily work helped the employees maintain high levels of energy and satisfaction at work. Primary interventions that aim at modifying psychosocial environment are also being used to reduce absenteeism at work. Nielsen, Kristensen and Smith-Hansen (2002) conducted a large intervention study at 52 worksites involving 2,068 employees in Denmark. The study showed that five basic work stressors—psychological demands, control, meaning of work, predictability and social support—had positive impact on reducing absenteeism. Lavoie-Tremblay et al. (2005) also showed how psychosocial work environment—commitment from organization, work constraints and autonomy to make decisions about work constraints and the ways to solve them—reduced absenteeism.

Many studies evaluating the efficacy of secondary interventions show promising results as well. For instance, Te Brake, Gorter, Hoogstraten and Eijkman (2001) evaluated if a counselling programme reduced demotivation and reduced burnout in dentists. Over six months, the results revealed significant positive impact on sense of personal accomplishment as well as emotional health. Another 12-week-long study conducted by Eriksen et al. (2002) reported participants describing positive subjective effects of the intervention on their health, physical fitness, muscle pain and ability to deal with stress. This study evaluated the effect of a stress management programme on 860 employees in Norway which aimed at improving coping abilities of employees using a cognitive behavioural–approach. Horan (2002) tested effectiveness of a workplace stress intervention called Chicken Soup for the Soul™ in employee groups. This involved reading inspirational workplace stories once a week for a period of 11 weeks. Results indicated that the experimental group improved in terms of using their cognitive skills in dealing with stressful work situations. The group also reportedly improved their mental well-being and confidence. Other studies have also reported efficacy of educational programmes and wellness seminars in reducing work-related stress (e.g. Bolt, Hare, Vitale, & Newman, 2004; Featherstone, James, Powell, Milne, & Maddison, 2004; Judkins, Reid, & Furlow, 2006; Rahe et al., 2002; SiddeGowda, 2004; Van Dierendonck, Garssen, & Visser, 2005; Yung, Fung, Chan, & Lau, 2004; Żołnierczyk-Zreda, 2002). Recently, web-based well-being interventions are being conducted; for example, Kawakami, Kobayashi, Takao and Tsutsumi (2005) conducted a web-based intervention study to improve supervisory support and psychological well-being to subordinate workers. The three-week intervention involved circulation of material via web that focused on knowledge about and attitude to mental health at work, role of supervisors in mental health of employees and overall improvement of work environment to reduce stress. The study reported significant shift in supervisors' ability to listen to and deal with subordinates facing mental health issues post this web-based training. Subordinates' rating of their supervisors in terms of their willingness to listen to their issues and perceived support also improved significantly post this intervention.

POSITIVE PSYCHOLOGY MOVEMENT IN ORGANIZATIONS

Acknowledging Seligman and Pawelski's (2003) assertion that psychology as a field over-emphasized on 'fixing' mental illness rather than focusing on positive aspects, Positive Organizational Behaviour (POB; Luthans & Youssef, 2007) came into existence. POB is the 'study and application of positively oriented human resources strengths and psychological capacities that can be measured, developed and effectively managed for performance improvement in today's workplace' (Luthans, 2002, p. 59). Grounded in positive psychology, many interventions exist to foster health and well-being of employees (e.g., Ouweneel, Le Blanc, & Schaufeli, 2013; Page & Vella-Brodrick, 2013). These usually consist of short writing exercises, for example, *best possible selves* intervention (King, 2001), which requires participants to think of their best version either in a past or a future situation (also, Sheldon & Lyubomirsky, 2006). There are *gratitude* interventions like *three good things* requires participants to journal three good events of a day and their reasons for the same. Other examples of positive psychology-based interventions are *kindness* interventions (perform or record acts of kindness towards others; Otake, Shimai,

Tanaka-Matsumi, Otsui, & Fredrickson, 2006), and *signature strengths* interventions (Park, Peterson, & Seligman, 2004). It has been reported that these interventions immediately boost positive resources within, promote effective self-regulation (King, 2001), strengthen relationships, help the participants notice positive aspects of the environment (Watkins, Uhder, & Pichinevskiy, 2015), and help them identify opportunities in the future to build positive resources (Wood, Froh, & Geraghty, 2010). The impact of these interventions have also been claimed on the overall happiness experienced (Mongrain & Anselmo-Matthews, 2012), life satisfaction (Manthey, Vehreschild, & Renner, 2016; Rust, Diessner, & Reade, 2009) and well-being (Bolier et al., 2013; Sin & Lyubomirsky, 2009). Apart from this, positive resource-building interventions are picking pace in the recent times. Resources are anything that help people build or achieve desired outcomes (Halbesleben, Neveu, Paustian-Underdahl, & Westman, 2014; Hobfoll, 2001). Job demands–resource (JD-R) model defines resources as constructs that '(a) are functional in achieving goals, (b) protect from threats and the associated physical and psychological costs, and (c) stimulate personal growth and development' (Xanthopoulou, Bakker, Demerouti, & Schaufeli, 2009, p. 236). Resource-building interventions help build a resilient and psychologically fit workplace, as also foster well-being by developing resources to cope with adversities (Reivich, Seligman, & McBride, 2011). The targeted components of work within these interventions encompass supervisory coaching and feedback (Xanthopoulou et al., 2009), conscientiousness and resilience (Halbesleben et al., 2014), optimism and power (Ten Brummelhuis & Bakker, 2012), health, home, stamina, food, money and home appliances (Hobfoll, 2011). Resources can be psychological, cognitive or physiological in nature (Rich, Lepine, & Crawford, 2010). Under the psychological resources, constructs such as positive mood states (Gable, Reis, Impett, & Asher, 2004; Sheldon & Lyubomirsky, 2006), happiness (Lambert et al., 2013; Seligman, Steen, Park, & Peterson, 2005), subjective well-being (King, 2001), vitality (Ryan et al., 2010) and vigour (Sonnentag & Natter, 2004) have been studied avidly. Resource-building interventions are also targeted at replenishing resources (sometimes also referred to as momentary personal resources [Trougakos & Hideg, 2009]) that get depleted daily due to negative work environments (Ten Brummelhuis & Bakker, 2012). Such resources are considered volatile and malleable in nature, which means they are easily depleted but at the same time can be influenced by interventions. These resources are not just restricted to work environments and, hence, can be beneficial both on and off work. Moreover, the effect of such resources can easily spill over to others around, like co-workers and family (Bono & Ilies, 2006). Personal resources can benefit in successful work performance in multiple ways, for example, they can affect team processes such as decision-making (Håkonsson et al., 2016), team cohesion (Dovidio, Gaertner, Isen, & Lowrance, 1995). Finally, these resources not only reduce stress but also create a reserve of resources leading to eustress or well-being (Hobfoll, 1989).

Gilbert, Foulk and Bono (2018) have evaluated the efficacy of five resource-building interventions/techniques that are used primarily in clinical settings but can be beneficial in organizational settings as well. Following five interventions are widely practiced and have shown promising positive effects (Gilbert et al., 2018).

Expressive writing: Pioneered by Pennebaker and Francis (1996), expressive writing involves having participants engage in multiple brief writing sessions across some days explaining their thoughts and emotional reactions around a particular traumatic event. There are several theoretical explanations to why this intervention helps develop positive psychological resources (Smyth & Pennebaker, 2008). For instance, expressive writing could be akin to catharsis, the benefits are manifested when the participant is able to 'release' the hurt feelings through expression (Frattaroli, 2006). The assertion is also supported by cognitive processing theory (Klein & Boals, 2001). It helps others make sense of the negative event since writing gives an opportunity to engage with the event actively. The comprehension drawn from this active engagement frees up the cognitive resource capacity by reducing avoidant or intrusive thoughts (Sloan, Marx, & Epstein, 2005). Further, as posited by exposure theory, facing negative thoughts and events actively can produce desensitization, similar to phobia treatments. Actively working through the traumatic event could increase participant's self-efficacy in dealing with traumatic events in the future (Greenberg, Stone, & Wortman, 1996). Overall, the cumulative arguments help us conclude that expressive writing leads to positive resource generation and resource gains because active engagement with a negative event makes the participant less and less obsessed with negative thoughts and feelings (Gilbert et al., 2018). The intervention has shown a range of positive impacts which include-physiological benefits—improved immunity (Pennebaker, Kiecolt-Glaser, & Glaser, 1988), improved lung functioning (Smyth, Stone, Hurewitz, & Kaell, 1999), lowered medical visits and blood pressure (Pennebaker & Beall, 1986), fewer physical health symptoms (Poon & Danoff-Burg, 2011), improved physical health (Ashley, O'Connor, & Jones, 2013); cognitive and psychological benefits—increased working memory (Klein & Boals, 2001), positive affect (Burton & King, 2004), self-esteem (O'connor et al., 2011), psychological health (Yang, Tang, Duan, & Zhang, 2015), increased emotional intelligence, and reduced workplace incivility (Kirk, Schutte, & Hine, 2011).

Social sharing or capitalization: Langston (1994) coined the word 'capitalization' to understand how sharing positive events with others helps an individual. Recently, many experimental studies (Ilies, Keeney, & Scott, 2011) delineate the impact of positive self-disclosure using diary studies and experience sampling methodology. Some theorists believe that capitalization leads to amplification of positive effects of a positive event. As one shares a positive event with others, it prolongs the experience of the event. This active and prolonged engagement with the positive incident increases positive construal of the event thereby generating positive self-evaluations (Gable et al., 2004). Other theorists (Ilies et al., 2011) believe that sharing a positive event with others makes it more real. Continual sharing eventually leads to enhanced self-evaluations and social relationships. Positive self-disclosure leads to enhanced positive affect (Gable et al., 2004; Lambert et al., 2013), happiness (Demir, Dougan, & Procsal, 2013), life satisfaction (Gable et al., 2004) and vitality (Lambert et al., 2013). Ilies et al. (2011) identified benefits of sharing positive work events with the spouse. Extending this positive self-disclosure to co-workers has also been known to be an effective agency to build volatile positive resources (Gilbert et al., 2018).

Work breaks: Work breaks are time off or leisurely breaks during the working hours that can help employees develop personal resources. They are based on the premise that they help an employee replenish depleted resources by providing an opportunity to halt the work demands (Westman, Hobfoll, Chen, Davidson, & Laski, 2004) to replace work activities with alternate activities that might help rebuild depleted resources. Sonnentag and Fritz (2007) explain that when people can choose how they spend their breaks, it can lead to mental detachment from work demands, which in turn, can induce build-up of positive resources within (Trougakos & Hideg, 2009). Presumably, due to the same reason, engaging in low-demand activities or leisurely activities during the work breaks induce positive affect or feeling of relaxation by causing a temporary disconnection from work demands. It has been proved that interventions focusing on helping people learn how to best utilize their break time have shown promising results (Hahn, Binnewies, Sonnentag, & Mojza, 2011). Work breaks have been classified according to their length. Any length of work break (microbreaks, lunch breaks, evening, weekend or vacations breaks) has been shown to result in building of positive volatile personal resources. These have been found to enhance vitality (Zacher, Brailsford, & Parker, 2014), positive affect (Sonnentag & Bayer, 2005), well-being (Fritz & Sonnentag, 2005), cognitive liveliness and flexibility (De Bloom, Ritter, Kühnel, Reinders, & Geurts, 2014), positive emotions (Bakker, Demerouti, Oerlemans, & Sonnentag, 2013; Sonnentag, Binnewies, & Mojza, 2008), improved health indicators (Westman, Etzion, & Danon, 2001), reduced injury and strain (Taylor, 2005), cortisol levels (Engelmann et al., 2011) and discomfort (Barredo & Mahon, 2007).

Mindfulness: Mindfulness is defined as attention to and awareness of the present moment (Brown & Ryan, 2003) and generally involve *focused attention* (a deliberate attempt to maintain focus on an object or breathing) and *open monitoring* (the awareness of being in the present moment without external point of focus or judgement). Recently, mindfulness-based interventions, meditation techniques, are being avidly used in organizational settings (Good et al., 2016; Wolever et al., 2012). Research points to the evidence that neurobiological changes are observed during meditation (Cahn & Polich, 2006) that result in physical health benefits (Bonadonna, 2003; Brown & Ryan, 2003) and psychological quality (Ryback, 2006). Meditation or mindfulness-based interventions foster ability to listen to one's inner voice (Miller, 2000) and contemplation (Bodhi, 2011). They also improve psychological health as they can reduce maniac symptoms (Yorston, 2001), depression (Collip et al., 2013;

Williams et al., 2014), anxiety (Miller, Fletcher, & Kabat-Zinn, 1995; Treven, 2010; Waelde et al., 2008) and post-traumatic stress (Kalill, Treanor, & Roemer, 2014). The mindfulness-based stress reduction (Kabat-Zinn, 2003) is one of the most popular interventions and research on the same has been avidly documented (Long & Christian, 2015). It is understood that mindfulness induces a cascading effect on all three types of resources. It stimulates cognitive resources by improving working memory and executive functioning (Mrazek, Franklin, Phillips, Baird, & Schooler, 2013; Zeidan, Johnson, Diamond, David, & Goolkasian, 2010), and visual-spatial processing (e.g., see Zeidan et al., 2010). It also prompts neutral appraisals and curtails negative affectivity causing well-being (Keng, Smoski, & Robins, 2011), life satisfaction (Mackenzie, Poulin, & Seidman-Carlson, 2006) and resiliency (Aikens et al., 2014), thereby stimulating psychological resources. Moreover, mindfulness generates the positive impact on physiological resources by reducing stress reactions and pain tolerance (Liu, Wang, Chang, Chen, & Si, 2013), and improves immune functioning (Davidson et al., 2003). In the organizational settings, mindfulness improves workforce performance (Marques & Dhiman, 2009) and contributes to mindful negotiation (Freshman, Hayes, & Feldman, 2002)

Nature exposure: This intervention involves exposure to natural environment, which may include viewing nature (e.g., viewing pictures of nature or seeing a view from a window), being in nature (e.g., among trees, driving through a scenic place) and being actively involved with nature (e.g., playing outdoor games, hiking). Psycho evolutionary theory (Ulrich et al., 1991) explains that humans have a tendency to feel positive emotional response in unthreatening natural surroundings. Attention restoration theorists (Hartig, Mitchell, De Vries, & Frumkin, 2014; Kaplan & Kaplan, 1989) explain that mechanized, built environments and the tasks that we do repeatedly and routinely require sustained and focused attention to be completed. In the process, these activities deplete us of the resources, causing stress and strain. Nature provides the opportunity to remove ourselves from demanding environments, provides aesthetic stimuli that replace the depleted resources and gives us an opportunity to engage in reflection (Kaplan & Kaplan, 1989), helping rebuild cognitive (Hartig et al., 2014) and psychological (Johnsen, 2011) resources. Thus, we can say natural settings offer something unique that induces a positive reaction which promotes resource gains. Indeed, nature exposure has been documented to impact vitality (Ryan et al., 2010), happiness (MacKerron & Mourato, 2013), health and recovery (Moore, 1981; Ulrich, 1984), better stress tolerance (Ulrich et al., 1991) and working memory (Berman, Jonides, & Kaplan, 2008). Barton and Pretty (2010) reported positive effects of outdoor exercise on self-esteem and mood, and McMahan and Estes (2015) reported its positive impact on affect.

SPIRITUALITY IN ORGANIZATIONS

Within the folds of positive psychology, some recent advances have been made to understand the role of spirituality in workplaces (Pawar, 2008; 2009). Organizations are shifting from an economic focus to a caring and nurturing one (Capra, 1993), as there has been a call for inclusive growth and ethical business. Moreover, spirituality is known to accentuate employees' morale and improve productivity of an organization (Pradhan, Jena, & Soto, 2017). Komala and Ganesh (2007) found positive association between spirituality at work and job satisfaction, and a negative association with burnout.

The scholars have defined spirituality at workplace in multiple ways over the years. For instance, it has been defined in terms of oneness of life and perception of reality (Neck & Milliman, 1994); meaningful work and sense of community (Mirvis, 1997); interconnectedness (Mitroff & Denton, 1999); transcendence through work process and sense of community (Giacalone & Jurkiewicz, 2003); spiritual connection, meaning and purpose of work and mystical experience (Kinjerski & Skrypnek, 2006).

As Indian culture especially embodies spiritual values, some conceptualizations based on Indian spiritual thought have also been put forth (Krishnan, 2007; Pardasani, Sharma, & Bindlish, 2014; Sharma, 2007). These primarily consist of the essential components of concepts such as meaningful work, interconnectedness, transcendence of self at an individual level as well as organizational values and holistic growth and development on an organizational level.

Meaningful work in the Indian worldview is understood in terms of the spiritual principle of karma yoga. The karma theory explains that 'all actions that are done have the power to ordain for their doers joy or sorrow in future, depending upon the action whether it is good or bad' (Mulla & Krishnan, 2009, p. 26). It comprises working in a righteous manner with utmost devotion and fortitude. The person should maintain an equanimity of emotions in the wake of failure and success, and continue to work without expectation of rewards, also described as nishkama karma in the Bhagavad Gita (Chakraborty & Chakraborty, 2006; Singh & Raina, 2015).

Interconnectedness has been explained in terms of *Loksangraha* (Radhakrishnan, 1970), which stands for unity and interconnectedness of all living beings. In terms of business organizations, this implies that employees as well as the organization on the whole should act in a way that is for the greater good; shift from being obsessively focused on economic gains and perform responsible and ethical business.

Transcendence of self implies a connection to something greater than the self (McCormick, 1994). This connection entails transcending beyond the *tri-gunas*, which are the three basic attributes of personality according to the Indian spiritual through. The *sattvik* personality is characterized by attributes such as cleanliness, truthfulness, discipline, mental equilibrium, contentment, sense control, determination, etc.; the *rajasik/rajasic* personality by a desire for sense gratification, little interest in spiritual elevation, dissatisfaction with one's position, envy, etc.; and *tamasik* personality by mental imbalance, anger, ignorance, arrogance, depression, etc. As a person transcends these three unique attributes of personality, s/he reaches a complete state of *Sat-Chit-Ananda* or highest level of well-being and happiness that is not affected by external life circumstances (Singh, Khari, Amonkar, Arya, & Kumar, 2013).

As organizational values define the work culture to a large extent, it is imperative for the organizations to espouse spiritual values and thus promote a work culture that encourages ethical business transactions and integrity. It should take cognizance of the fact that their actions must lead to welfare of employees, customers, stakeholders and overall society. When this is practiced, an alignment with organizational values is achieved. Indian scholars have suggested that such work culture is promoted as we work on ourselves to acquire *daivi sampat* (characteristics of Gods), characterized by sacrifice, self-control, purity, calmness and curb *asuri sampat* (characteristics of demons) characterized by delusions, egoism, desires (Desai, 2009).

While these conceptualizations have been tested to some extent and have showed promising positive impact on productivity and performance of employees (Rego & Cunha, 2008; Petchsawanga & Duchon, 2009), the need for designing and implementing interventions based on these conceptualizations is underscored (Pardasani et al., 2014).

WORKPLACE INTERVENTIONS IN INDIA

According to India's National Sample Survey data, about 40 per cent of the population is employed and only 10 per cent of the population comes under insurance cover (Babu, Madan, Veluswamy, Mehra, & Maiya, 2014). Another survey by Indian Council of Medical Research found high prevalence of risk factors associated with cardiovascular diseases. Lifestyle diseases accounted for 27 per cent of illnesses among working people in India, and organizations lose approximately 14 per cent of their annual working days due to sickness (Chadha, Mehdi, & Malik, 2007). Many developed countries have benefitted by inclusion of workplace health and wellness programmes; however, implementation of such programmes for employee health in India is still at a very nascent stage (Carnethon et al., 2009; Couch et al., 2013). However, the need for introduction of such wellness programmes in India has been underscored given the fact that deaths by non-communicable diseases are expected to rise from 40 per cent in 1990 to a whopping 75 per cent by 2030 (Patel et al., 2011). It has been estimated that cardiovascular diseases and cancer push 10 per cent and 25 per cent of families in India towards poverty, respectively. Some studies have focused on effectiveness of workplace interventions on health in India. For instance, Prabhakaran et al. (2005) reported effectiveness of a multicomponent educational programme on cardiovascular health. Pimple et al. (2012) reported that an integrated intervention approach using psycho-education, screening and behavioural therapy was effective in tobacco cessation in factory workers. The WHO India has started an Initiative for

Cardiovascular Health Research in Developing Countries in collaboration with All India Institute of Medical Sciences. Under this research initiative, workplace-based health education intervention model has been developed that utilizes multi-pronged approach to tackle issue of non-communicable diseases. The model utilizes mass awareness to addressing issues such as lack of physical activity, unhealthy diets and tobacco use. Around 11 per cent of Indian population is suffering from common mental disorders such as depression, bipolar disorder, etc. (NIMHANS, 2016). This roughly translates to about 150 million Indians who are in need of active interventions and support. The awareness about mental health is far less compared to occupational health and safety. However, big enterprise stress on workplace health and wellness intervention which is reflected in Right Management Survey. The survey reported that 63 per cent of Indians felt that their companies invested adequately in health and wellness initiatives. Indeed, the wellness initiatives of Wipro, Accenture and Larsen & Toubro are some of the best initiatives known in the country. Many India-based fitness apps like HealthifyMe, GetActive, Orobind and ReTiSense are also picking pace, especially among urban Indian population. The apps help keep a track of diet, daily calories expenditure, exercise and gives access to online fitness trainers and nutritionists.

FUTURE RECOMMENDATIONS

Globalization has brought about rapid changes in urban India, which constitutes a small fraction of working population in India, yet these workplaces are spearheading the change to included workplace health and wellness programmes. Yet, Indian workplaces lag far behind in terms of physical and mental health promotion. The foremost reason for this is the lack of legislation for the unorganized sector which constitutes larger proportion of workforce in India (Sakthivel & Joddar, 2006). About 52 per cent of workforce is self-employed, while another 18 per cent are engaged in casual labour. Mostly, workers are engaged in small or medium enterprises which lack organizational structure, and are typically not covered under health insurance programmes, thus excluded from workplace health and well-being programmes as well (Elis, Alam, & Gupta, 2000). This is a serious concern further amplified because of the shortage of occupational health and safety research as well as practitioners in India. For successful health promotion and to address safety and mental health concerns of the Indian workforce, wellness initiatives need to be implemented in unorganized sector through innovative and cost-effective means.

As leaders shape and institutionalize a culture in the organization, leaders must spearhead these wellness programmes and might prove to be a sophisticated way to engage employees in such initiatives. It must be ensured that the health progress is assessed and monitored on regular basis to keep these initiatives productive and on track. Active collaboration with public–private stakeholders is necessary to create impact and affect meaningful change. Employees can also be offered incentives to encourage participation since in the longer run, it will help organizations stay more productive and healthy.

CONCLUSIONS

The chapter reviewed the impact of varied well-being initiatives/wellness programmes in organizations. It further highlighted the status and challenges in implementing well-being programmes in India. With the commitment of leadership, public–private collaboration, we can ensure health and well-being of our workforce. In doing so, employers will benefit greatly as this will enhance employees' productivity and reduce health-care cost.

REFERENCES

Aikens, K. A., Astin, J., Pelletier, K. R., Levanovich, K., Baase, C. M., Park, Y. Y., ... Bodnar, C. M. (2014). Mindfulness goes to work: Impact of an online workplace intervention. *Journal of Occupational and Environmental Medicine*, 56(7), 721–731.

Anderson, L. M., Quinn, T. A., Glanz, K., Ramirez, G., Kahwati, L. C., Johnson, D. B., ... Katz, D. L. (2009). The effectiveness of worksite nutrition and physical activity interventions for controlling employee overweight and obesity: A systematic review. *American Journal of Preventive Medicine*, 37(4), 340–357.

Ashley, L., O'Connor, D. B., & Jones, F. (2013). A randomized trial of written emotional disclosure interventions in school teachers: Controlling for positive expectancies and effects on health and job satisfaction. *Psychology, Health & Medicine*, 18(5), 588–600.

Babu, A. S., Madan, K., Veluswamy, S. K., Mehra, R., & Maiya, A. G. (2014). Worksite health and wellness programs in India. *Progress in Cardiovascular Diseases*, 56(5), 501–507.

Bakker, A. B., Demerouti, E., Oerlemans, W., & Sonnentag, S. (2013). Workaholism and daily recovery: A day reconstruction study of leisure activities. *Journal of Organizational Behavior, 34*(1), 87–107.

Barredo, R. D. V., & Mahon, K. (2007). The effects of exercise and rest breaks on musculoskeletal discomfort during computer tasks: An evidence-based perspective. *Journal of Physical Therapy Science, 19*(2), 151–163.

Barton, J., & Pretty, J. (2010). What is the best dose of nature and green exercise for improving mental health? A multi-study analysis. *Environmental Science & Technology, 44*(10), 3947–3955.

Bellew, B. (2008). Primary prevention of chronic disease in Australia through interventions in the workplace setting: A rapid review. *Sax Institute for the Chronic Disease Prevention Unit, Victorian Government Department of Human Services.*

Berman, M. G., Jonides, J., & Kaplan, S. (2008). The cognitive benefits of interacting with nature. *Psychological Science, 19*(12), 1207–1212.

Bodhi, B. (2011). What does mindfulness really mean? A canonical perspective. *Contemporary Buddhism, 12*(1), 19–39.

Bolier, L., Haverman, M., Westerhof, G. J., Riper, H., Smit, F., & Bohlmeijer, E. (2013). Positive psychology interventions: A meta-analysis of randomized controlled studies. *BMC Public Health, 13*(1), 119.

Bolt, D. M., Hare, R. D., Vitale, J. E., & Newman, J. P. (2004). A multigroup item response theory analysis of the psychopathy checklist-revised. *Psychological Assessment, 16*, 155–168. doi:10.1037/1040-3590.16.2.155

Bonadonna, R. (2003). Meditation's impact on chronic illness. *Holistic Nursing Practice, 17*(6), 309–319.

Bono, J. E., & Ilies, R. (2006). Charisma, positive emotions and mood contagion. *The Leadership Quarterly, 17*(4), 317–334.

Brown, K. W., & Ryan, R. M. (2003). The benefits of being present: mindfulness and its role in psychological well-being. *Journal of Personality and Social Psychology, 84*(4), 822.

Burton, C. M., & King, L. A. (2004). The health benefits of writing about intensely positive experiences. *Journal of Research in Personality, 38*(2), 150–163.

Cahn, B. R., & Polich, J. (2013). Meditation states and traits: EEG, ERP, and neuroimaging studies. *Psychological bulletin, 132*(2), 180.

Capra, F. (1993). A systems approach to the emerging paradigm. In M. Ray and C. A. Rinzler (Eds.), *The new paradigm in business: Emerging strategies for leadership and organizational change* (pp. 230–237). New York, NY: Tarcher Books.

Carnethon, M., Whitsel, L. P., Franklin, B. A., Kris-Etherton, P., Milani, R., Pratt, C. A., … Wagner, G. R. (2009). Worksite wellness programs for cardiovascular disease prevention: a policy statement from the American Heart Association. *Circulation, 120*(17), 1725–1741.

Chadha, A., Mehdi, A., & Malik, G. (2007). *Impact of preventive health care on Indian industry and economy.* New Delhi: Indian Council for Research on International Economic Relations.

Chakraborty, D., & Chakraborty, S. K. (2006). The 'Nishkam Karma' principle: Its relevance to effectiveness and ethics. *IIMB Management Review, 18*(2), 115–125.

Collip, D., Geschwind, N., Peeters, F., Myin-Germeys, I., van Os, J., & Wichers, M. (2013). Putting a hold on the downward spiral of paranoia in the social world: A randomized controlled trial of mindfulness-based cognitive therapy in individuals with a history of depression. *PloS One, 8*(6), e66747.

Conn, V. S., Hafdahl, A. R., Cooper, P. S., Brown, L. M., & Lusk, S. L. (2009). Meta-analysis of workplace physical activity interventions. *American Journal of Preventive Medicine, 37*(4), 330–339.

Conrad, P. (1988). Health and fitness at work: A participants' perspective. *Social Science & Medicine, 26*(5), 545–550.

Couch, P., O'Flaherty, M., Sperrin, M., Green, B., Balatsoukas, P., Lloyd, S., ... Buchan, I. (2013). e-Labs and the stock of health method for simulating health policies. *Studies in Health Technology and Informatics, 192*, 288–292.

Davidson, R. J., Kabat-Zinn, J., Schumacher, J., Rosenkranz, M., Muller, D., Santorelli, S. F., ... Sheridan, J. F. (2003). Alterations in brain and immune function produced by mindfulness meditation. *Psychosomatic Medicine, 65*(4), 564–570.

De Bloom, J., Ritter, S., Kühnel, J., Reinders, J., & Geurts, S. (2014). Vacation from work: A 'ticket to creativity'? The effects of recreational travel on cognitive flexibility and originality. *Tourism Management, 44*, 164–171.

Demir, M., Dougan, A., & Procsal, A. D. (2013). I am so happy 'cause my friend is happy for me: Capitalization, friendship, and happiness among US and Turkish college students. *The Journal of Social Psychology, 153*(2), 250–255.

Desai, M. P. (2009). Spiritual psychology: A way to effective management. *African Journal of Marketing Management, 1*(7), 165–171.

Døjbak Håkonsson, D., Eskildsen, J. K., Argote, L., Mønster, D., Burton, R. M., & Obel, B. (2016). Exploration versus exploitation: Emotions and performance as antecedents and consequences of team decisions. *Strategic Management Journal, 37*(6), 985–1001.

Dovidio, J. F., Gaertner, S. L., Isen, A. M., & Lowrance, R. (1995). Group representations and intergroup bias: Positive affect, similarity, and group size. *Personality and Social Psychology Bulletin, 21*(8), 856–865.

Dugdill, L., Brettle, A., Hulme, C., McCluskey, S., & Long, A. F. (2008). Workplace physical activity interventions: A systematic review. *International Journal of Workplace Health Management, 1*(1), 20–40.

Ellis, R. P., Alam, M., & Gupta, I. (2000). Health insurance in India: Prognosis and prospectus. *Economic and Political Weekly*, 207–217.

Engbers, L. H., van Poppel, M. N. M., Paw, M. J. M. C. A., & van Mechelen, W. (2005). Worksite health promotion programs with environmental changes: A systematic review. *American Journal of Preventive Medicine, 29*(1), 61–70.

Engelmann, C., Schneider, M., Kirschbaum, C., Grote, G., Dingemann, J., Schoof, S., ... Ure, B. M. (2011). Effects of intraoperative breaks on mental and somatic operator fatigue: A randomized clinical trial. *Surgical Endoscopy*, 25(4), 1245–1250.

Eriksen, H. R., Ihlebaek, C., Mikkelsen, A., Grønningsæter, H., Sandal, G. M., & Ursin, H. (2002). Improving subjective health at the worksite: A randomized controlled trial of stress management training, physical exercise and an integrated health programme. *Occupational Medicine, 52*(7), 383–391.

Featherstone, K., James, I. A., Powell, I., Milne, D., & Maddison, C. (2004). A controlled evaluation of a training course for staff who work with people with dementia. *Dementia, 3*(2), 181–194.

Frattaroli, J. (2006). Experimental disclosure and its moderators: A meta-analysis. *Psychological Bulletin, 132*(6), 823.

Frazer, H. T. (1998). RMs can curb indoor-air problems. *National Underwriter Property & Casualty-Risk Benefits Management, 102*, 23–78.

Freshman, C., Hayes, A. M., & Feldman, G. C. (2002). Adapting meditation to promote negotiation success: A guide to varieties and scientific support. *The Harvard Negotiation Law Review, 7*, 67.

Fritz, C., & Sonnentag, S. (2005). Recovery, health, and job performance: Effects of weekend experiences. *Journal of Occupational Health Psychology, 10*(3), 187.

Gable, S. L., Reis, H. T., Impett, E. A., & Asher, E. R. (2004). What do you do when things go right? The intrapersonal and interpersonal benefits of sharing positive events. *Journal of Personality and Social Psychology, 87*(2), 228.

Giacalone, R. A., & Jurkiewicz, C. L. (2003). Right from wrong: The influence of spirituality on perceptions of unethical business activities. *Journal of business Ethics, 46*(1), 85–97.

Gilbert, E., Foulk, T., & Bono, J. (2018). Building personal resources through interventions: An integrative review. *Journal of Organizational Behavior, 39*(2), 214–228.

Goetzel, R. Z., & Ozminkowski, R. J. (2006). What's holding you back: why should (or shouldn't) employers invest in health promotion. *Surgery and Science Combine to Unlock the Secrets of Diabetes, 67*(6), 428.

Good, D. J., Lyddy, C. J., Glomb, T. M., Bono, J. E., Brown, K. W., Duffy, M. K., … Lazar, S. W. (2016). Contemplating mindfulness at work: An integrative review. *Journal of Management, 42*(1), 114–142.

Gopinath, C. (1998). Alternative approaches to indigenous management in India. *MIR: Management International Review*, 257–275.

Greenberg, M. A., Stone, A. A., & Wortman, C. B. (1996). Health and psychological effects of emotional disclosure: A test of the inhibition-confrontation approach. *Journal of Personality and Social Psychology, 71*(3), 588–602.

Hahn, V. C., Binnewies, C., Sonnentag, S., & Mojza, E. J. (2011). Learning how to recover from job stress: Effects of a recovery training program on recovery, recovery-related self-efficacy, and well-being. *Journal of Occupational Health Psychology, 16*(2), 202.

Halbesleben, J. R. B., Neveu, J.-P., Paustian-Underdahl, S. C., & Westman, M. (2014). Getting to the 'COR' understanding the role of resources in conservation of resources theory. *Journal of Management, 40*(5), 1334–1364.

Hartig, T., Mitchell, R., De Vries, S., & Frumkin, H. (2014). Nature and health. *Annual Review of Public Health*, *35*, 207–228.

Hobfoll, S. E. (1989). Conservation of resources: A new attempt at conceptualizing stress. *American Psychologist*, *44*(3), 513.

———. (2001). The influence of culture, community, and the nested-self in the stress process: Advancing conservation of resources theory. *Applied Psychology*, *50*(3), 337–421.

———. (2011). Conservation of resource caravans and engaged settings. *Journal of occupational and organizational psychology*, *84*(1), 116–122.

Horan, A. P. (2002). An effective workplace stress management intervention: Chicken soup for the soul at work™ employee groups. *Work*, *18*(1), 3–13.

Hymel, P. A., Loeppke, R. R., Baase, C. M., Burton, W. N., Hartenbaum, N. P., Hudson, T. W., ... Konicki, D. L. (2011). Workplace health protection and promotion: A new pathway for a healthier—and safer—workforce. *Journal of Occupational and Environmental Medicine*, *53*(6), 695–702.

Ilies, R., Keeney, J., & Scott, B. A. (2011). Work–family interpersonal capitalization: Sharing positive work events at home. *Organizational Behavior and Human Decision Processes*, *114*(2), 115–126.

Johnsen, S. Å. K. (2011). The use of nature for emotion regulation: Toward a conceptual framework. *Ecopsychology*, *3*(3), 175–185.

Judkins, S., Reid, B., & Furlow, L. (2006). Hardiness training among nurse managers: Building a healthy workplace. *The Journal of Continuing Education in Nursing*, *37*(5), 202–207.

Kabat-Zinn, J. (2003). Mindfulness-based interventions in context: Past, present, and future. *Clinical Psychology: Science and Practice*, *10*(2), 144–156.

Kahn, E. B., Ramsey, L. T., Brownson, R. C., Heath, G. W., Howze, E. H., Powell, K. E., ... Corso, P. (2002). The effectiveness of interventions to increase physical activity: A systematic review. *American Journal of Preventive Medicine*, *22*(4), 73–107.

Kalill, K. S., Treanor, M., & Roemer, L. (2014). The importance of non-reactivity to posttraumatic stress symptoms: A case for mindfulness. *Mindfulness*, *5*(3), 314–321.

Kalliath, P., Kalliath, T., & Singh, V. (2011). When work intersects family: A qualitative exploration of the experiences of dual earner couples in India. *South Asian Journal of Management*, *18*(1), 37.

Kaplan, R., & Kaplan, S. (1989). *The experience of nature: A psychological perspective*. CUP Archive.

Katz, D. L., O'Connell, M., Yeh, M.-C., Nawaz, H., Njike, V., Anderson, L. M., ... Dietz, W. (2005). Public health strategies for preventing and controlling overweight and obesity in school and worksite settings: A report on recommendations of the Task Force on Community Preventive Services. *Morbidity and Mortality Weekly Report: Recommendations and Reports*, *54*(10), 1–12.

Kawakami, N., Kobayashi, Y., Takao, S., & Tsutsumi, A. (2005). Effects of web-based supervisor training on supervisor support and psychological distress among workers: A randomized controlled trial. *Preventive Medicine*, *41*(2), 471–478.

Keng, S.-L., Smoski, M. J., & Robins, C. J. (2011). Effects of mindfulness on psychological health: A review of empirical studies. *Clinical Psychology Review*, *31*(6), 1041–1056.

King, L. A. (2001). The health benefits of writing about life goals. *Personality and Social Psychology Bulletin*, *27*(7), 798–807.

Kinjerski, V., & Skrypnek, B. J. (2006, August). Measuring the intangible: Development of the spirit at work scale. In *Academy of management proceedings* (Vol. 2006, No. 1, pp. A1–A6). Briarcliff Manor, NY: Academy of Management.

Kirk, B. A., Schutte, N. S., & Hine, D. W. (2011). The effect of an expressive-writing intervention for employees on emotional self-efficacy, emotional intelligence, affect, and workplace incivility. *Journal of Applied Social Psychology*, *41*(1), 179–195.

Klein, K., & Boals, A. (2001). Expressive writing can increase working memory capacity. *Journal of Experimental Psychology: General*, *130*(3), 520.

Komala, K., & Ganesh, L. S. (2007). Individual spirituality at work and its relationship with job satisfaction and burnout: An exploratory study among healthcare professionals. *The Business Review*, *7*(1), 124–129.

Kossek, E. E., & Lautsch, B. A. (2012). Work–family boundary management styles in organizations: A cross-level model. *Organizational Psychology Review*, *2*(2), 152–171.

Krishnan, V. R. (2007). Effect of transformational leadership and leader's power on follower's duty-orientation and spirituality. *Great Lakes Herald*, *1*(2), 48–70.

Kumar, R., & Sethi, A. K. (2005). The Rise of India: India and the West—Institutional Contrasts. In *Doing Business in India* (pp. 27–42). New York, NY: Palgrave McMillan.

Lambert, N. M., Gwinn, A. M., Baumeister, R. F., Strachman, A., Washburn, I. J., Gable, S. L., ... Fincham, F. D. (2013). A boost of positive affect: The perks of sharing positive experiences. *Journal of Social and Personal Relationships*, *30*(1), 24–43.

Langston, C. A. (1994). Capitalizing on and coping with daily-life events: Expressive responses to positive events. *Journal of Personality and Social Psychology*, *67*(6), 1112.

Larson, M. (1998). Worklife quality: Ergonomic workstations boost productivity. *Quality*, *37*(3), 44.

Lavoie-Tremblay, M., Bourbonnais, R., Viens, C., Vézina, M., Durand, P. J., & Rochette, L. (2005). Improving the psychosocial work environment. *Journal of Advanced Nursing*, *49*(6), 655–664.

Liu, X., Wang, S., Chang, S., Chen, W., & Si, M. (2013). Effect of brief mindfulness intervention on tolerance and distress of pain induced by cold-pressor task. *Stress and Health*, *29*(3), 199–204.

Long, E. C., & Christian, M. S. (2015). Mindfulness buffers retaliatory responses to injustice: A regulatory approach. *Journal of Applied Psychology*, *100*(5), 1409.

Luthans, F. (2002). The need for and meaning of positive organizational behavior. *Journal of Organizational Behavior*, *23*(6), 695–706.

Luthans, F., & Youssef, C. M. (2007). Emerging positive organizational behavior. *Journal of Management, 33*(3), 321–349.

Mackenzie, C. S., Poulin, P. A., & Seidman-Carlson, R. (2006). A brief mindfulness-based stress reduction intervention for nurses and nurse aides. *Applied Nursing Research, 19*(2), 105–109.

MacKerron, G., & Mourato, S. (2013). Happiness is greater in natural environments. *Global Environmental Change, 23*(5), 992–1000.

Manthey, L., Vehreschild, V., & Renner, K.-H. (2016). Effectiveness of two cognitive interventions promoting happiness with video-based online instructions. *Journal of Happiness Studies, 17*(1), 319–339.

Marques, J. F., & Dhiman, S. K. (2011). *Buddhist psychology in the workplace: A relational perspective*. Unpublished PhD thesis. Tilburg University, The Netherlands.

Matson-Koffman, D. M., Brownstein, J. N., Neiner, J. A., & Greaney, M. L. (2005). A site-specific literature review of policy and environmental interventions that promote physical activity and nutrition for cardiovascular health: What works? *American Journal of Health Promotion, 19*(3), 167–193.

Mattila, P., Elo, A.-L., Kuosma, E., & Kylä-Setälä, E. (2006). Effect of a participative work conference on psychosocial work environment and well-being. *European Journal of Work and Organizational Psychology, 15*(4), 459–476.

McCormick, D. W. (1994). Spirituality and management. *Journal of managerial psychology, 9*(6), 5–8.

McMahan, E. A., & Estes, D. (2015). The effect of contact with natural environments on positive and negative affect: A meta-analysis. *The Journal of Positive Psychology, 10*(6), 507–519.

Miller, B. (2000). Spirituality for business leadership. *Journal of Management Inquiry, 9*(2), 132–133.

Miller, J. J., Fletcher, K., & Kabat-Zinn, J. (1995). Three-year follow-up and clinical implications of a mindfulness meditation-based stress reduction intervention in the treatment of anxiety disorders. *General Hospital Psychiatry, 17*(3), 192–200.

Mirvis, P. H. (1997). Crossroads—'soul work' in organizations. *Organization Science, 8*(2), 192–206.

Mishra, R. C. (1994). *Individualist and collectivist orientations across generations*. San Francisco, CA: Jossey-Bass Publishers.

Mitroff, I. I., & Denton, E. A. (1999). *A spiritual audit of corporate America: A hard look at spirituality, religion, and values in the workplace* (Vol. 140, pp. 257–263). San Francisco, CA: Jossey-Bass Publishers.

Mongrain, M., & Anselmo-Matthews, T. (2012). Do positive psychology exercises work? A replication of Seligman et al. (2005). *Journal of Clinical Psychology, 68*(4).

Moore, E. O. (1981). A prison environment's effect on health care service demands. *Journal of Environmental Systems, 11*(1), 17–34.

Mrazek, M. D., Franklin, M. S., Phillips, D. T., Baird, B., & Schooler, J. W. (2013). Mindfulness training improves working memory capacity and GRE performance while reducing mind wandering. *Psychological Science*, 24(5), 776–781.

Mulla, Z. R., & Krishnan, V. R. (2009). Do Karma-Yogis make better leaders? Exploring the relationship between the leader's Karma-Yoga and transformational leadership. *Journal of Human Values*, 15(2), 167–183.

Neck, C. P., & Milliman, J. F. (1994). Thought self-leadership: Finding spiritual fulfilment in organizational life. *Journal of Managerial Psychology*, 9(6), 9–16.

Nielsen, M. L., Kristensen, T. S., & Smith-Hansen, L. (2002). The Intervention Project on Absence and Well-being (IPAW): Design and results from the baseline of a 5-year study. *Work & Stress*, 16(3), 191–206.

O'connor, D. B., Hurling, R., Hendrickx, H., Osborne, G., Hall, J., Walklet, E., ... Wood, H. (2011). Effects of written emotional disclosure on implicit self-esteem and body image. *British Journal of Health Psychology*, 16(3), 488–501.

Otake, K., Shimai, S., Tanaka-Matsumi, J., Otsui, K., & Fredrickson, B. L. (2006). Happy people become happier through kindness: A counting kindnesses intervention. *Journal of Happiness Studies*, 7(3), 361–375.

Ouweneel, E., Le Blanc, P. M., & Schaufeli, W. B. (2013). Do-it-yourself: An online positive psychology intervention to promote positive emotions, self-efficacy, and engagement at work. *Career Development International*, 18(2), 173–195.

Page, K. M., & Vella-Brodrick, D. A. (2013). The working for wellness program: RCT of an employee well-being intervention. *Journal of Happiness Studies*, 14(3), 1007–1031.

Pardasani, R. R., Sharma, R., & Bindlish, P. (2014). Facilitating workplace spirituality: Lessons from Indian spiritual traditions. *Journal of Management Development*, 33(8–9), 847–859.

Park, N., Peterson, C., & Seligman, M. E. P. (2004). Strengths of character and well-being. *Journal of Social and Clinical Psychology*, 23(5), 603.

Patel, V., Chatterji, S., Chisholm, D., Ebrahim, S., Gopalakrishna, G., Mathers, C., ... Reddy, K. S. (2011). Chronic diseases and injuries in India. *The Lancet*, 377(9763), 413–428.

Pawar, B. S. (2008). Two approaches to workplace spirituality facilitation: A comparison and implications. *Leadership & Organization Development Journal*, 29(6), 544–567.

———. (2009). Workplace spirituality facilitation: A comprehensive model. *Journal of Business Ethics*, 90(3), 375.

Pennebaker, J. W., & Beall, S. K. (1986). Confronting a traumatic event: Toward an understanding of inhibition and disease. *Journal of Abnormal Psychology*, 95(3), 274.

Pennebaker, J. W., & Francis, M. E. (1996). Cognitive, emotional, and language processes in disclosure. *Cognition & Emotion*, 10(6), 601–626.

Pennebaker, J. W., Kiecolt-Glaser, J. K., & Glaser, R. (1988). Disclosure of traumas and immune function: Health implications for psychotherapy. *Journal of Consulting and Clinical Psychology*, 56(2), 239.

Petchsawang, P., & Duchon, D. (2012). Workplace spirituality, meditation, and work performance. *Journal of Management, Spirituality & Religion*, 9(2), 189–208.

Pimple, S., Pednekar, M., Majmudar, P., Ingole, N., Goswami, S., & Shastri, S. (2012). An integrated approach to worksite tobacco use prevention and oral cancer screening among factory workers in Mumbai, India. *Asian Pacific Journal of Cancer Prevention*, 13(2), 527–532.

Polanyi, M. F. D., Frank, J. W., Shannon, H. S., Sullivan, T. J., Lavis, J. N., & Bertera, R. L. (2000). Promoting the determinants of good health in the workplace. In B. D. Poland, L. W. Green, & I. Rootman (Eds.), *Settings for health promotion: Linking theory and practice* (pp. 138–160). Thousand Oaks, CA: SAGE Publications.

Poon, A., & Danoff-Burg, S. (2011). Mindfulness as a moderator in expressive writing. *Journal of Clinical Psychology*, 67(9), 881–895.

Prabhakaran, D., Shah, P., Chaturvedi, V., Ramakrishnan, L., Manhapra, A., & Reddy, K. S. (2005). Cardiovascular risk factor prevalence among men in a large industry of northern India. *National Medical Journal of India*, 18(2), 59.

Pradhan, R. K., Jena, L. K., & Soto, C. M. (2017). Workplace spirituality in Indian organisations: Construction of reliable and valid measurement scale. *Business: Theory and Practice*, 18, 43.

Proper, K., & van Mechelen, W. (2008). *Effectiveness and economic impact of worksite interventions to promote physical activity and healthy diet*. Geneva: World Health Organization.

Pryce, J., Albertsen, K., & Nielsen, K. (2006). Evaluation of an open-rota system in a Danish psychiatric hospital: A mechanism for improving job satisfaction and work–life balance. *Journal of Nursing Management*, 14(4), 282–288.

Radhakrishnan, S. (1970). *The Bhagavad Gita*. London: George Allen and Unwin.

Rahe, R. H., Taylor, C. B., Tolles, R. L., Newhall, L. M., Veach, T. L., & Bryson, S. (2002). A novel stress and coping workplace program reduces illness and healthcare utilization. *Psychosomatic Medicine*, 64(2), 278–286.

Rego, A., & Cunha, M.P. (2008). Workplace spirituality and organizational commitment: An empirical study. *Journal of Organizational Change Management*, 21(1), 53–75.

Reivich, K. J., Seligman, M. E. P., & McBride, S. (2011). Master resilience training in the US Army. *American Psychologist*, 66(1), 25.

Rich, B. L., Lepine, J. A., & Crawford, E. R. (2010). Job engagement: Antecedents and effects on job performance. *Academy of Management Journal*, 53(3), 617–635.

Robroek, S. J. W., Van Lenthe, F. J., Van Empelen, P., & Burdorf, A. (2009). Determinants of participation in worksite health promotion programmes: A systematic review. *International Journal of Behavioral Nutrition and Physical Activity*, 6(1), 26.

Rust, T., Diessner, R., & Reade, L. (2009). Strengths only or strengths and relative weaknesses? A preliminary study. *The Journal of Psychology*, 143(5), 465–476.

Ryan, R. M., Weinstein, N., Bernstein, J., Brown, K. W., Mistretta, L., & Gagne, M. (2010). Vitalizing effects of being outdoors and in nature. *Journal of Environmental Psychology*, *30*(2), 159–168.

Ryback, D. (2006). Self-determination and the neurology of mindfulness. *Journal of Humanistic Psychology*, *46*(4), 474–493.

Sakthivel, S., & Joddar, P. (2006). Unorganised sector workforce in India: Trends, patterns and social security coverage. *Economic & Political Weekly*, *41*(21), 2107–2114.

Seligman, M. E. P., & Pawelski, J. O. (2003). Positive psychology: FAQS. *Psychological Inquiry*, *14*(2), 159–163.

Seligman, M. E. P., Steen, T. A., Park, N., & Peterson, C. (2005). Positive psychology progress: Empirical validation of interventions. *American Psychologist*, *60*(5), 410.

Shain, M., & Kramer, D. M. (2004). Health promotion in the workplace: Framing the concept; reviewing the evidence. *Occupational and Environmental Medicine*, *61*(7), 643–648.

Sharma, S. (2007). *New mantras in corporate corridors: From ancient roots to global routes*. New Delhi: New Age International (P) Limited.

Sheldon, K. M., & Lyubomirsky, S. (2006). How to increase and sustain positive emotion: The effects of expressing gratitude and visualizing best possible selves. *The Journal of Positive Psychology*, *1*(2), 73–82.

SiddeGowda, Y. S. (2004). Social work intervention with white collared employees and their families. *International Journal for the Advancement of Counselling*, *26*(4), 421–432.

Sin, N. L., & Lyubomirsky, S. (2009). Enhancing well-being and alleviating depressive symptoms with positive psychology interventions: A practice-friendly meta-analysis. *Journal of Clinical Psychology*, *65*(5), 467–487.

Singh, K., & Junnarkar, M. (2017). The well-being of information technology professionals. In L. G. Oades, M. Steger, A. D. Fave, & J. Passmore (Eds.), *The Wiley Blackwell handbook of the psychology of positivity and strengths-based approaches at work* (pp. 491–507). Chicago, IL: John Wiley & Sons.

Singh, K., Khari, C., Amonkar, R. S., Arya, N. K., & Kumar, S. K. (2013). Development and validation of a new scale: Sat-Chit-Ananda Scale. *International Journal on Vedic Foundations of Management*, *1*(2), 102–122.

Singh, K., & Raina, M. (2015). Development and validation of a test on Anasakti (non-attachment): An Indian model of well-being. *Mental Health, Religion & Culture*, *18*(9), 715–725.

Sinha, J. B. P. (2014). *Psycho-social analysis of the Indian mindset*. New Delhi: Springer.

Sloan, D. M., Marx, B. P., & Epstein, E. M. (2005). Further examination of the exposure model underlying the efficacy of written emotional disclosure. *Journal of Consulting and Clinical Psychology*, *73*(3), 549.

Smyth, J. M., & Pennebaker, J. W. (2008). Exploring the boundary conditions of expressive writing: In search of the right recipe. *British Journal of Health Psychology*, *13*(1), 1–7.

Smyth, J. M., Stone, A. A., Hurewitz, A., & Kaell, A. (1999). Effects of writing about stressful experiences on symptom reduction in patients with asthma or rheumatoid arthritis: A randomized trial. *Journal of the American Medical Association, 281*(14), 1304–1309.

Sonnentag, S., & Bayer, U.-V. (2005). Switching off mentally: Predictors and consequences of psychological detachment from work during off-job time. *Journal of Occupational Health Psychology, 10*(4), 393.

Sonnentag, S., Binnewies, C., & Mojza, E. J. (2008). 'Did you have a nice evening?' A day-level study on recovery experiences, sleep, and affect. *Journal of Applied Psychology, 93*(3), 674.

Sonnentag, S., & Fritz, C. (2007). The recovery experience questionnaire: Development and validation of a measure for assessing recuperation and unwinding from work. *Journal of Occupational Health Psychology, 12*(3), 204.

Sonnentag, S., & Natter, E. (2004). Flight attendants' daily recovery from work: Is there no place like home? *International Journal of Stress Management, 11*(4), 366.

Taylor, W. C. (2005). Transforming work breaks to promote health. *American Journal of Preventive Medicine, 29*(5), 461–465.

Te Brake, H., Gorter, R., Hoogstraten, J., & Eijkman, M. (2001). Burnout intervention among Dutch dentists: Long-term effects. *European Journal of Oral Sciences, 109*(6), 380–387.

Ten Brummelhuis, L. L., & Bakker, A. B. (2012). A resource perspective on the work–home interface: The work–home resources model. *American Psychologist, 67*(7), 545.

Thompson, C. A., Beauvais, L. L., & Lyness, K. S. (1999). When work–family benefits are not enough: The influence of work–family culture on benefit utilization, organizational attachment, and work–family conflict. *Journal of Vocational Behavior, 54*(3), 392–415.

Treven, S. (2010). Individual methods for reducing stress in work settings. *Interbeing, 4*(2), 1.

Trougakos, J. P., & Hideg, I. (2009). Momentary work recovery: The role of within-day work breaks. In S. Sonnentag, P. L. Perrewe, & D. C. Ganster (Eds.), *Current perspectives on job-stress recovery* (pp. 37–84). Bingley: Emerald Group Publishing.

Ulrich, R. S. (1984). View through a window may influence recovery from surgery. *Science, 224*(4647), 420–421.

Ulrich, R. S., Simons, R. F., Losito, B. D., Fiorito, E., Miles, M. A., & Zelson, M. (1991). Stress recovery during exposure to natural and urban environments. *Journal of Environmental Psychology, 11*(3), 201–230.

Van Dierendonck, D., Garssen, B., & Visser, A. (2005). Burnout prevention through personal growth. *International Journal of Stress Management, 12*(1), 62.

Vijaimadhavan, P., & Venkatarama Raju, D. (2013). An empirical study on relationship among quality of work life and its factors. *Journal of Business and Management, 12*(3) 20–28.

Waelde, L. C., Uddo, M., Marquett, R., Ropelato, M., Freightman, S., Pardo, A., ... Salazar, J. (2008). A pilot study of meditation for mental health workers following Hurricane Katrina. *Journal of Traumatic Stress, 21*(5), 497–500.

Watkins, P. C., Uhder, J., & Pichinevskiy, S. (2015). Grateful recounting enhances subjective well-being: The importance of grateful processing. *The Journal of Positive Psychology, 10*(2), 91–98.

Westman, M., Etzion, D., & Danon, E. (2001). Job insecurity and crossover of burnout in married couples. *Journal of Organizational Behavior, 22*(5), 467–481.

Westman, M., Hobfoll, S. E., Chen, S., Davidson, O. B., & Laski, S. (2004). Organizational stress through the lens of conservation of resources (COR) theory. In P. Perrewé, J. Halbesleben, & C. Rosen (Eds.), *Exploring interpersonal dynamics* (pp. 167–220). Bingley: Emerald Group Publishing.

Williams, J. M. G., Crane, C., Barnhofer, T., Brennan, K., Duggan, D. S., Fennell, M. J. V, ... Shah, D. (2014). Mindfulness-based cognitive therapy for preventing relapse in recurrent depression: A randomized dismantling trial. *Journal of Consulting and Clinical Psychology, 82*(2), 275.

Wolever, R. Q., Bobinet, K. J., McCabe, K., Mackenzie, E. R., Fekete, E., Kusnick, C. A., ... Baime, M. (2012). Effective and viable mind-body stress reduction in the workplace: A randomized controlled trial. *Journal of Occupational Health Psychology, 17*(2), 246.

Wood, A. M., Froh, J. J., & Geraghty, A. W. A. (2010). Gratitude and well-being: A review and theoretical integration. *Clinical Psychology Review, 30*(7), 890–905.

Xanthopoulou, D., Bakker, A. B., Demerouti, E., & Schaufeli, W. B. (2009). Work engagement and financial returns: A diary study on the role of job and personal resources. *Journal of Occupational and Organizational Psychology, 82*(1), 183–200.

Yang, Z., Tang, X., Duan, W., & Zhang, Y. (2015). Expressive writing promotes self-reported physical, social and psychological health among Chinese undergraduates. *International Journal of Psychology, 50*(2), 128–134.

Yorston, G. A. (2001). Mania precipitated by meditation: A case report and literature review. *Mental Health Religion & Culture, 4*(2), 209–213.

Yung, P., Fung, M. Y., Chan, T. M. F., & Lau, B. W. K. (2004). Relaxation training methods for nurse managers in Hong Kong: A controlled study. *International Journal of Mental Health Nursing, 13*(4), 255–261.

Zacher, H., Brailsford, H. A., & Parker, S. L. (2014). Micro-breaks matter: A diary study on the effects of energy management strategies on occupational well-being. *Journal of Vocational Behavior, 85*(3), 287–297.

Zeidan, F., Johnson, S. K., Diamond, B. J., David, Z., & Goolkasian, P. (2010). Mindfulness meditation improves cognition: Evidence of brief mental training. *Consciousness and Cognition, 19*(2), 597–605.

Żołnierczyk-Zreda, D. (2002). The effects of worksite stress management intervention on changes in coping styles. *International Journal of Occupational Safety and Ergonomics, 8*(4), 465–482.

Conclusion
Psychology and Translational Research—
The Way Ahead

Suman Sighora and Kamlesh Singh

This chapter will focus on the retrospect and prospects of translational research in applied psychology in India. After giving an overall critical review of the field, beginning with happiness, it will summarise the current status of TR in various sectors in Indian settings—rural areas, education sector (especially schools), corporate sector, before moving on to web-based interventions besides the personal religious and spiritual (R/S) practices. Given the kind of research presented and reviewed in earlier chapters and as a result of those researches and translational work being already done, the focus of this chapter would be on how TR could grow in various directions, how psychological findings may be utilized in better ways to improve the overall quality of life (QoL) and how the psychologists should explore the existing sociocultural practices that may help in maintaining and increasing well-being, mental health and QoL. The chapter will end by recommending future directions for the field.

As we mention in the 'Introduction', TR has become a priority the world over. However, India needs to catch up to the rest of the world in this race to bring scientific discoveries to the people. Although, the government has already initiated the process in biomedical sciences, a stronger thrust is required not only by the government but also by other stakeholders, especially in the field of applied psychology, where focused TR is still rare.

This book has been an endeavour to review the progress that has been made so far by means of TR in applied psychology. We began by reviewing the status of TR the world over in various fields with a special focus on psychology and identified the potential to develop and implement effective interventions across varied communities as well as address the differences and reduce the gaps. The first chapter reviewed the status of translation research in general, from its definitions to the still perplexing nature and processes or phases that mark TR. The chapter next considered its relevance in social and behavioural sciences, with a special focus on applied psychology. In addition, we regarded the importance entailed to TR by different regions and countries, as reflected through policy emphasis and setting up of various agencies. Finally, we presented its significance within the Indian context, in applied psychology, and we highlight that TR can contribute significantly because of its panoptic vision to engage directly with the stakeholders, researchers, academicians and the people alike. Besides, it can provide a holistic understanding of basic sociocultural and behavioural processes that affect mental health and lead to better QoL.

Community participation is the salient feature of both TR and applied psychology. This is made amply clear by Shokeen and Singh in 'Knowledge Translation and Translational Research'. Given the staggering amount of knowledge produced worldwide, it should ideally be helping people everywhere, however, reality is much different from this ideal. Hardly any of this knowledge is translated into effective programmes to help people deal with their numerous challenges. This chapter examines various gaps or 'death valleys' in knowledge translation (KT) and their impact on health care service delivery in both developed and developing countries. It also studies the ways being used to try to address and bridge these valleys by means of different KT strategies. Among other barriers, language and communication has emerged as a major issue in India because psychological research is primarily disseminated in English. Since about 70 per cent of Indian population is rural, and is conversant with Hindi and/or other vernacular languages, effective communication and interaction strategies are needed to translate the knowledge, emphasized no less in the KT literature worldwide. Hence, language plays a vital role in dissemination of social science research/literature. Shokeen and Singh discuss the role of translation in TR and highlight how translation can result in many language challenges and needed revisions to achieve 'equivalence' such that the items remain consistent, valid and meaningful in the new languages for use in different cultures. More importantly, they challenge the common assumption that data translation is a merely technical task where the translator could 'objectively and faithfully' transfer meaning of research data from source language to target language. They suggest that applied research in Indian setting should travel on all levels from research to translational research–knowledge translation (TR-KT) for benefits to the laymen so as to have flourishing communities and societies. Better documentation is as important an aspect of this. There is also a need felt for the lab to reach the field rather than the other way round so that the students who are supposed to work in applied fields gain first hand exposure and practical knowledge. Platforms to translate such research in different Indian languages and dialects and to train researchers/translators to facilitate KT journey are also required. They also lament that psychological science is often neither communicated by psychologists with diverse backgrounds nor in a manner that takes the audience's cultural diversity into account. They call for a systematic culture change within psychology if it is to address these limitations. They assert the need to realize that translational efforts need to be constant and integral component of psychology's social contract with society.

A distinct element of any research, applied psychology more so, given its practical utility in providing solution to real-world issues, is the research method used for knowledge production. Research methods need to be effective, consider the human element involved and to have policy-relevant outcomes for TR and KT. Analogous to the advancements in applied psychology, equivalent advancement has been achieved in the research methods used. Since the choice of the research method not only depends upon the research question but also upon the core constructs of the subfield, this chapter's focus is timely and necessary while discussing TR in applied psychology. The different methods discussed highlight the progression of not only the field via its methods but also the focus that is continuously shifting towards application or, in other words, the translation of research into practice. Singh and Bandyopadhyay review the various methods that researchers use in their chapter 'Research Methods in Applied Psychology: An Evaluation'. They conclude that no one approach offers a holistic picture of the complexity of human nature and experience and suggest an eclectic approach or pluralistic methodology to overcome this limitation. The choice of method/s should be based upon the research question; practical considerations of time, availability of participants, finances, etc.; and the individual skill in the method/s used. They assert that any study must include the participation of the targeted community members and a mixed research methodology, including qualitative and quantitative, if it is to yield significant positive outcomes. Their recommendations include the need for proficiency in both usage of software and knowledge of statistics in order to interpret the results. They recommend that theorists and researchers collaborate in order to achieve better results in the field. Similarly, there is a need for active discourse and collaboration between psychologists and other social science researchers such as economists, sociologists and linguists. Techniques and insights from one discipline would add to the techniques and insights from the other, and would thus address the issues at hand from multiple perspectives as is required given the complexity of the individual and the society.

In 'Applications of Psychology in Rural India', Kaur and Singh shift the focus of the book to the most important yet neglected part of India, the rural India. In this chapter, they present a holistic picture of all mental health development measures and initiatives undertaken by the government of India, local bodies, NGOs, private sector organizations, etc., to help the people lead more fulfilling lives. They offer a consolidated review of psychology-based translational researches/programmes undertaken across rural India as well as different mediums used for the same. The chapter documents research and intervention programmes aimed at improving well-being of people living in rural areas. While the Government of India maintains its overall focus on the development of the rural Indian society, Kaur and Singh show that these efforts have failed to motivate rural communities to mobilize local resources for their developmental activities. People do not get involved even in the development plans that intimately affect their lives. Community participation has failed to materialize despite planning and preparations, all a result of their apathy and alienation. It is time that psychology researches and findings are implemented in community to empower and enable rural people to deal with the fast-changing environment. While efforts by various sections of people are underway to provide psychological interventions in rural areas, this chapter, apart from the review of the interventions, provides suggestions, which actively involve the role of applied psychologists. Applied psychologists, with their ability to translate psychological research into tools and interventions will contribute greatly in improving the well-being and QoL of rural people. They suggest effective use of technology, training people, using TED talks, launching mental health programmes for different sectors in rural areas, propose translation of measures in local languages, using community-based participatory research (CBPR), better understanding of local conditions and utilizing the strengths of Indian rural communities to promote well-being. Integrating community with intervention programmes may boost the desired outcomes and therefore recommend that translational professionals/researchers working in rural communities to plan intervention programmes keeping in mind not just the individual but his/her family/core group and the community members to ensure success. Such successfully planned and implemented interventions will go a long way in improving the QoL. This would not only benefit the individuals but also communities at large and make them thrive. Like Shokeen and Singh, Kaur and Singh also posit that translational psychologists and researchers need to begin by assessing rural communities on various psychological and sociocultural parameters by looking closely at the factors responsible for enhancing the QoL in rural areas as well as factors responsible for its deterioration. Also, the diversity in India needs to be kept in mind, which may render psychological parameters of one region uniquely different from others. And like Shokeen and Singh, they also clarify the important role being played by NGOs in translation of research and its implementation in real-life settings.

Happiness appears to be one of the basic indicators of mental health and QoL, which is why Singh, Takahashi and Kaur in Chapter 4, titled 'Perceived Happiness and Its Determinants', engage with happiness. They explain the differing Western and Eastern conceptions of this intriguing topic by describing the former's focus on subjective well-being, psychological well-being, social well-being, and so on, and the latter's focus on the inner self—inner harmony, peace of mind, *Sat-Chit-Anand* (inner source of happiness), etc. An empirical study on happiness from the Indian state of Haryana, on more than a hundred participants that collected data via face-to-face interviews and responses on data collection booklet, it focuses on a layperson's perception of happiness and life satisfaction with reference to past, present and future. Divided into four sections, the study explores the participants' living and housing conditions and their perception of their standard of living, their perception of happiness from various angles, differences between happiness and satisfaction (if any), and the correlation among different measures used in the study. The results are encouraging indeed. They found that more than half (56.5%) of the participants perceived their standard of living as average and nearly 26 per cent perceived it to be reasonably or very comfortable. More than half of the participants were seen to be thriving with averages in all domains (happiness, ideal happiness, future happiness and life satisfaction) above 7. Family, work, financial security, health (of self and family) and positive interpersonal relationships emerged as the factors that support happiness and satisfaction. Personal freedom and spirituality were also cited as reasons for being happy. From among those who believed that happiness and satisfaction differed, it emerged that happiness was considered as external and short lived while satisfaction was thought to be internal and long lived. Dissatisfaction also revolved around family, work, health and interpersonal relationships. Interestingly, participants strongly believe that policies of the government strongly influence happiness in their day-to-day lives and that of community as a whole, and government intervention can lead to increased happiness by eradicating unemployment, providing people with basic amenities, controlling cost inflation, poverty, working towards women empowerment, decreasing corruption, addressing social issues and casteism. The study also found significant positive correlation between the measures of happiness and satisfaction used in the study.

The strength of their study lies in their implementation, mixed methodology approach and reporting. However, a limitation of the study is that it reports results as a whole and not in the light of the socio-demographic variables, it will not be surprising if notions of happiness also differ from one Indian state to another due to not only the cultural diversity of India but also its vast urban–rural divide. Replicating this study within or outside India would yield interesting results besides encouraging TR. One of the most interesting outcomes of the chapter is the people's perception of the role of the government in affecting happiness of its people. Taking it as a signal, further research and planning may be carried out in this direction since prior knowledge about what makes its citizens happy would be helpful to governments and policymakers.

Moving on to Chapter 5, 'Role of Religious and Spiritual Practices in Mental Health', Sharma and Singh address various ways in which religion and spirituality contribute to the promotion of overall well-being. The chapter documents different spiritual practices, religious rituals and interventions promoting mental health in the Indian setting. It is a significant contribution to TR in applied psychology as it offers a sampling of different scientific researches and indigenous practices that can be applied to communities to improve health and QoL. They find that the participants perceive prosocial behaviour, gratitude and forgiveness, among other virtues, as the most significant ones different religions promote. These three, along with spirituality, are considered as the major contributors to positive mental health. Indian culture celebrates different socially embedded religious traditions that promote positive virtues like prosocial behaviour, altruism, forgiveness and oneness, which further strengthen the relationship between religion and positive mental health. The ability to find answers through religion acts as an important support to an individual's well-being and happiness, and spirituality induced by different religious rituals and practices plays a central role in further promoting positive virtues in individuals. Also, there is relatively little understanding and inclusion of these practices in the scientific and clinical work.

Their research is thus useful in integrating common practices promoting mental health with mainstream research, and there is ample scope for more work in this area. The recent religion-accommodative cognitive therapy would benefit if it includes Eastern perspectives. They suggest accommodating religion and spirituality in clinical practice and assert that addressing a client's R/S beliefs and providing services accordingly may be an important step, since religion and spirituality may be an underlying dimension of certain problems and may play a role in transformation of patients who are explicitly religious. According to them, 'R/S cannot be considered as separate constructs, especially in the Indian setting. Rather, spirituality is one of the outcomes of religion; and although it can exist outside the domains of religion, it nevertheless forms a significant part of religion and religious practices'. Sharma and Singh also suggest more rigour in TR in R/S studies, where the focus should be on empirical evaluation of the question whether incorporation of R/S in existing psychotherapy for R/S clients improves efficacy or not, and an assessment of R/S is important for it to be integrated in clinical practice. Although various measures of Indian R/S constructs have been constructed and validated, a series of researches should be promoted to confirm and revalidate them in order to establish them in mainstream psychology. A greater specialization with respect to measurement of R/S and R/S practices might lead to a greater understanding of how their individual components might influence mental health status of the client. There is also a need to decipher knowledge available as alternative health care systems in combating physical and mental illness. Examining its import to enhance therapeutic services can contribute a lot, which can be achieved by developing methodologies and mindsets to learn from this rich heritage. They contend that road to optimizing mental health care cannot be paved by a single discipline, hence, it is vital for sociologists, economists, policy researchers, social workers and psychologists to make concerted efforts to bridge the gap between science and practice in mental health care, especially in India.

The next chapter, 'Applications of Positive Psychology in Indian School Setting', focuses on another important segment of the population in India, the children in schools. Positive psychological interventions fulfil the main objective of positive psychology (PP), that is, to contribute to the flourishing or optimal functioning of people, groups and institutions. Khanna and Singh review the current status of mental health and overall well-being in schools, before moving on to a comprehensive review of intervention programmes in the school setting. As in the case of the corporate sector, globally there has been an increasing focus on the assimilation of PP within the school milieu, however, a lot remains to be done in the Indian school system still marked by neglect and a deficit-focused approach towards mental health. Indian children and youth's mental health has not received sufficient attention due to preoccupation with physical health concerns. More so because children are usually presumed to be physically healthy, and hence, their mental health issues receive lower priority. Khanna and Singh say that the situation is compounded due to children growing up in misery that poverty, disease, illiteracy and crime proffer. Increasing population and the expanse of India do not foster an environment conducive to the delivery of government as well as voluntary programmes. Increasing incidence of school going children and adolescents experiencing social, emotional and behavioural difficulties have marked the past few decades. It hampers normal growth and functioning. Schools emerge as a very relevant backdrop to develop, nurture and reinforce psychological assets and strengths of the young.

The chapter shows assimilating evidence-based interventions into the school setting can prove very beneficial while addressing the larger public health goal of bridging the gap between those who need intervention and the availability of actual services. It then seems only logical to work in schools to provide interventions in order to promote well-being. The review clearly shows that there is some ongoing work within the broader realm of promoting student well-being (e.g., workshops, after school activities and life skills sessions) that may be beneficial to the students but is often not scientific or evidence based in approach. It is noteworthy that majority of the empirical work in this area has taken place in the Western nations, with relatively limited contribution from other parts of the world, particularly developing nations which are home to substantially large youth populations. There exists a dearth of literature pertaining to PPIs for Indian youth. In addition to the broader insufficiency of intervention-based research focused on this demographic group, the majority of Indian research in this area deals with problem rectification or targeting those identified as being at risk. Like elsewhere, the chapter brings to light the important role played by the NGOs in this realm. However, the efforts need to be coordinated, streamlined and consolidated if desired results in terms of health outcomes for the youth are to be achieved.

The chapter reiterates that investment in holistic health and mental well-being of children will have a strong bearing on the future of the nation. For a more inclusive and comprehensive application of PP in Indian schools, it recommends promoting cross-cultural research and validation, tailor made programmes for diverse populations that utilise existing indigenous and sociocultural best practices, a resource efficient and collaborative approach and involvement of key stakeholders from children's social environment besides robust documentation since youth mental health and well-being has tremendous social and economic implications for India.

Contemporary times, marked by rapid development and spread of Internet, social media and other technologies, have also led to more individuals seeking help online. Bandyopadhyay and Singh in 'Web-based Interventions to Improve Quality of Life', discuss web-based psychotherapeutic interventions that have been emerging and changing the traditional view of psychotherapy, examples of the application of TR in the field of behavioural sciences. The authors reveal that the Government of India with its ongoing effort to digitalize India has come up with a large number of web- and mobile-based health care services for the people; however, the field of mental health care itself has not received much attention, which makes it very difficult to accept the usefulness of these web-based programmes merely at face value.

This chapter begins with a review of literature on documented psychotherapeutic and other well-being enhancing programmes. It has attempted to emphasize the significance of web-based interventions in improving the QoL and psychological well-being while at the same time highlighting some of the challenges encountered by online practitioners. It discusses various legal, ethical and professional issues that arise in the delivery of online mental health services. This chapter ends with recommendations and suggestions for better service delivery with special reference to the Indian context.

Moving from cyberspace to the corporate sector, Raina and Singh emphasize the need of well-being in the fast paced and high stress corporate world in 'Employee Well-Being in Organizations'. According to them, given the high stress levels seen in the increasingly privatized and globalized workplaces, the corporate sector is increasingly focusing on employee well-being because employee health and well-being can have compelling implications for the organizations. The chapter discusses these implications before moving on to various health and well-being initiatives and their impact on physical and mental health of employees. Raina and Singh aver that the Indian mindset is continually adapts and accommodates new ideas and experiences into its folds while at the same time maintains a firm foundation in its traditions, which in turn drives and influences the way people work, among other things. Despite an evolving work culture in sync with the technological advances, workplace demographic shifts and work-centric organizational culture forcing longer work hours; the dynamics are rooted in traditional shared values and patterns. Given this scenario, they discuss some recent advances in PP in order to understand the role of spirituality in workplaces because spirituality is known to accentuate employees' morale. The economic focus is seen giving way to a caring and nurturing one, besides there has been a call for inclusive growth and ethical business.

Given the lack of insurance cover for the population and high prevalence of risk factors associated with cardiovascular diseases and lifestyle diseases in India, they posit that since many developed countries have benefited by inclusion of workplace health and wellness programmes, India would also do so. India is still at a nascent stage when it comes to implementation of such programmes for employee health. However, while wellness initiatives of Wipro, Accenture and Larsen & Toubro are some of the best industry initiatives known in the country, and many India-based fitness apps such as HealthifyMe, GetActive, Orobind and ReTiSense are also increasingly becoming popular in the urban Indian population, they recommend that for successful health promotion and for addressing safety and mental health concerns of Indian workforce, wellness initiatives need to be implemented in the unorganized sector through innovative and cost-effective means and should be incentivised to encourage participation. These wellness programmes must get the attention of the leaders for better implementation as well as be assessed and monitored on regular basis to keep these initiatives productive and on track. They advocate active collaboration between public–private stakeholders to create impact and affect meaningful change, which will benefit the employers besides enhancing employees' productivity and reducing health care costs.

Having surveyed and critically analysed the prevalent practices and issues as well as the role of various practitioners and agencies, regarding TR and its applications in applied psychology, we now summarize its current status, especially in India. We also enunciate future directions that the field may take in order to achieve the desired results in mental health.

PRESENT STATUS AND FUTURE DIRECTIONS

This section provides our recommendations for future TR in applied psychology as well as for the policymakers. To begin with, it is important to have more clarity on the definitions and a better understanding of discipline-wise adaptation of TR. TR in applied psychology needs to be framed better in order to be understood more. The reviews and studies reveal the array of research available wherein most of the current frameworks of interventions are focused on the immediacy of needs, which leave certain sections such as women, older adults or children unattended, more so in rural areas. There is a need to prioritize the health of these sections of population. New interventions should consider their individualized and systemic needs and should pursue more highly integrated health care frameworks encompassing individual's needs, familial problems and systemic social issues. These interventions should be designed to help them understand the importance of personal health and should have ease of accessibility for successful implementation. Health care organizations or community health centres should have adequately trained staff along with sufficient resources to manage care. Since resources might pose a problem, at least for staffing, instead of opting for new appointments, local mental health centres can partner community health centres. NGOs would also form an important link in this delivery chain. A rethink on the tools used for intervention can also help, mobile and telehealth interventions (Kuhn et al. [2014] also point towards this) or media like television or video (Humphreys, Tsoh, Kohn, & Gerbert, 2011) could be effective in reaching out to the population living in rural or remote areas. There should be an openness to add or adapt more relevant methods if the current ones are not helping. For example, in the domain of psychological testing, scholars are using various tests to collect both quantitative and qualitative data and an effort is being made to overcome their respective limitations by using a combination of the two.

Further, rural settings require both top-to-bottom and bottom-to-top approaches. Psychological interventions are an excellent example of top-to-bottom approach, while identification and promotion of sociocultural factors that facilitate their QoL would constitute the bottom-to-top approach. The latter would also be suitable to identify the factors hampering their well-being and QoL, and interventions could be devised in order to reduce their impact.

TR to KT can happen via several frameworks of KT that may be adopted in bridging the know–do gap. They include Promoting Action on Research Implementation in Health Services framework, Ottawa Model of Research Use framework, The Knowledge to Action framework, Framework for Research Dissemination and Utilization, Consolidated Framework for Implementation Research, Research and Policy in Development model, Assessing country level efforts linking research to action (Linking RTA), Canadian Health Services Research Foundation Self-Assessment tool, Supporting Policy relevant Reviews and Trials tools, etc. (Sudsawad, 2007). Pronovost, Berenholtz and Needham (2008) have proposed a model of KT that shows five phases through which KT should go through to be effective. These are specifying a summary of the interventions expected to generate positive outcomes based on research evidence, identifying local barriers to their implementation, measuring the outcome variables against the baseline and making sure of the 4Es of engagement, education, execution and evaluation.

In organizational setups, promotion of QoL and well-being can happen with an increased focus on different activities such as yoga, meditation and other incentivized well-being promoting activities linked to employee performance. The example of the Gujarat diamond merchant gifting cars, flats, jewellery, etc., to his employees based on their performance and loyalty is one example of this incentive-driven performance approach. Another out of the box incentive given to his employees was a 10-day family trip to Uttarakhand, a state known for its religious and spiritual significance and home to various holy sites. What was of immense significance was his accompanying them on this yatra. The company became a family rather than just a place of work.

In India, such spiritual and religious activities, travel to holy places, go through hardships in order to cleanse one of one's sins and attain salvation, double up as activities that promote well-being and QoL, or the classic examples of *dawa aur dua*, invocation that becomes medicine. Another good example would be the Indian television serial *Satyamev Jayate*, which focuses on various social issues such as female foeticide, sexual abuse, dowry system, honour killings, casteism, water crisis, medical malpractices, etc. It is significant because it talks about the issues that plague the society by focusing on the common people, and the star power of the famous actor host is no less an attraction for the masses to watch the show and in the process understand some aspects of those problems. Acknowledgement is one step towards solution.

Educational institutions, that is, schools and colleges, are ideal places to promote values, character strengths and QoL. It would lead to not only a strengthening of an individual's personality but also contribute to his/her overall development. There is a need to introduce, improve and foster value education in schools, colleges and even in services. Unlike other subjects of study, value education needs to learn by practice in the field, with the people and by example. There is a need to formulate new ways of promoting this value education.

Known for its diversity of spoken dialects, India presents a unique challenge in its need to do and promote TR in local languages so that it reaches the masses and has maximum impact. Tied with this diversity of languages is the presence of multitudinous local communities, which need to be understood in order to be helped. Given the paucity of manpower and limitations of staffing, the challenge of understanding that appears mind boggling and insurmountable initially can be met to a certain extent with the help of NGOs, which are working in the field. All that is required is better documentation, as mentioned earlier. Another requirement is the reinforcement of the extension work in research, like that happening in agricultural universities across India. Applied psychologists can look to them for data collection as well implementation, since all of them work with the common men, in the rural settings, and for those who require interventions most and yet have the least access to it or least resources to access it.

CONCLUSION

Since TR is still in its infancy in India, more so in applied psychology and its interventions, there is a need to recognize the importance of work being done, we have tried to do so as a first step in this direction as well as caution in moving ahead. New components should be added after keeping the successful elements of already implemented interventions intact and keeping in mind the uniqueness of individual and community experiences. This will help foster self-efficacy and well-being, and lessen the stigma attached (if any).

Based on our interventions, we find that in order to address the long-term comprehensive goals of public health care, mental well-being and QoL, there is a need to root the future interventions in psychological theories of change as they contribute towards an understanding of required outcomes. A focus on these will help identify processes that bring a change and thus explain why certain interventions work while others do not. Theoretical frameworks, such as cognitive behavioural framework, empowerment theory, resilience theory among others, have already been used successfully to alleviate depression, post-traumatic stress, increase positivity and resilience (Graham-Bermann & Miller, 2013; Iverson et al., 2011; Kubany et al., 2004; Masten 2001; Miller, Howell, & Graham-Bermann, 2014; Ungar, 2012). They can help in measuring the mechanisms of change that may affect elements like self-efficacy or social support, which make interventions fail or succeed. This can in turn help increase the effectiveness of interventions.

Governmental initiative and support are one thing that is pointed out every time by different stakeholders. Although, it is taking some steps in this direction, like insurance for all (Pradhan Mantri Jeevan Jyoti Bima Yojna), and psychologists have been dealing with poverty, malnutrition, health, etc., a much more focused approach is required by both the government and the researchers. We see that behavioural scientists are more or less missing, in policy initiatives or their implementation. There is an urgency to include them in various think tanks, steering committees and policy decision-making bodies since they would not only bring an understanding of the people but also help in including indigenous healing practices in interventions. What is required is a holistic understanding of problems, and a push towards TR in applied psychology is sure to not only increase theoretical understanding but also lead to solutions of different real local social problems and issues. And they would benefit from harnessing the potential of the technological know how that India has.

REFERENCES

Graham-Bermann, S. A., & Miller, L. E. (2013). Intervention to reduce traumatic stress following intimate partner violence: An efficacy trial of the Moms' Empowerment Program (MEP). *Psychodynamic Psychiatry, 41*(2), 329–349.

Humphreys, J., Tsoh, J. Y., Kohn, M. A., & Gerbert, B. (2011). Increasing discussions of intimate partner violence in prenatal care using video doctor plus provider cueing: A randomized, controlled trial. *Women's Health Issues, 21*(2), 136–144.

Iverson, K. M., Gradus, J. L., Resick, P. A., Suvak, M. K., Smith, K. F., & Monson, C. M. (2011). Cognitive–behavioral therapy for PTSD and depression symptoms reduces risk for future intimate partner violence among interpersonal trauma survivors. *Journal of Consulting and Clinical Psychology, 79*(2), 193–202.

Kubany, E. S., Hill, E. E., Owens, J. A., Iannce-Spencer, C., McCaig, M. A., Tremayne, K. J., ... Williams, P. L. (2004). Cognitive trauma therapy for battered women with PTSD (CTT-BW). *Journal of Consulting and Clinical Psychology, 72*(1), 3.

Kuhn, E., Greene, C., Hoffman, J., Nguyen, T., Wald, L., Schmidt, J., ... Ruzek, J. (2014). Preliminary evaluation of PTSD coach, a smartphone app for post-traumatic stress symptoms. *Military Medicine, 179*(1), 12–18.

Masten, A. S. (2001). Ordinary magic: Resilience processes in development. *American Psychologist, 56*(3), 227.

Miller, L. E., Howell, K. H., & Graham-Bermann, S. A. (2014). The effect of an evidence-based intervention on women's exposure to intimate partner violence. *American Journal of Orthopsychiatry, 84*(4), 321–328.

Pronovost, P. J., Berenholtz, S. M., & Needham, D. M. (2008). Translating evidence into practice: A model for large scale knowledge translation. *British Medical Journal, 337*, a1714.

Sudsawad, P. (2007). *Knowledge translation: Introduction to models, strategies, and measures.* Austin, TX: Southwest Educational Development Laboratory, National Center for the Dissemination of Disability Research.

Ungar, M. (Ed.). (2012). *The social ecology of resilience: A handbook of theory and practice.* New York, NY: Springer.

About the Editors and Contributors

EDITORS

Kamlesh Singh, PhD (Psychology), is an Associate Professor of Psychology at Indian Institute of Technology (IIT) Delhi. She has teaching and research experience of about 22 years. The main areas of her interest are applied positive psychology, psychometrics, community psychology, and rural women and adolescents. Kamlesh Singh has to her credit 85 published papers in peer-reviewed national and international journals and 14 book chapters. She has co-authored the book *Measures of Positive Psychology*, published in 2016. With her ongoing teaching and various research projects in positive psychology, Kamlesh Singh is a member of the advisory committee of the International Positive Psychology Association (IPPA). She has also initiated an Indian association named National Positive Psychology Association (NPPA; http://nppassociation. org/) with several positive psychology specialists. Detailed information on her publications and other academic activities can be found at http:// web.iitd.ac.in/~singhk/

Suman Sigroha, PhD, is a researcher and teacher at IIT Mandi, Himachal Pradesh. With her training in the field of literary studies and in psychology, she engages with texts through psycho-social concepts such as stereotyping, implicit bias, memory and representation. She deals with intersections of art, history and fiction, besides myths and oral history. Her recent research focuses on contemporary literature from troubled regions of India, rich with unsettling questions about nationalism, belonging, identity and ideals of love amid terrorism and militarization. She has published in various national and international journals.

CONTRIBUTORS

Shilpa Bandyopadhyay is currently pursuing her PhD in Psychology from IIT Delhi. She is a Junior Research Fellow (JRF) under the UGC (University Grants Commission) scheme. Her research broadly explores the aging experience of older North Indians. The areas of her research interest include online counselling, aging and web-based well-being interventions.

Jasleen Kaur, a doctorate in Psychology, is currently serving as a visiting psychologist in the Indian Air Force. Her areas of interest include developmental psychology, positive psychology, and child and adolescent mental health. She has recently co-authored the book *Measures of Positive Psychology*.

Pulkit Khanna completed her PhD in Psychology from IIT Delhi in 2016. She is certified in the field of positive psychology (research, education and application in community health) from NIMHANS, Bangalore. Her research interests include well-being, interventions for students and positive youth development. She has presented as well as published her research at various national and international platforms, including the International Positive Psychology Association, over the past few years. Besides working in the academic domain, she also garnered exposure to the corporate setting during her stint as a human resources professional.

Mahima Raina recently received her doctorate in psychology from IIT Delhi. Her thesis focussed on work–life boundary management in Indian context. Mahima has Master's in Organizational/Industrial Psychology from University of Jammu. She has been engaged in a cross-cultural research on work–family conflict with Humboldt University of Berlin before joining IIT Delhi. She has published research in Indian psychology with the core focus on psychometrics, developing tests on various indigenous psychological constructs. Mahima has also been the recipient of the prestigious FONDS scholarship for visiting researchers at UQAM, Canada, during her doctoral work.

Swati Sharma is a PhD candidate in psychology at IIT Delhi. She holds a Senior Research Fellowship (SRF) from UGC, India. Before joining IIT Delhi, she worked as an Assistant Professor at Indraprastha College for Women, University of Delhi. Her key research and teaching areas are positive psychology, psychometrics and organizational behaviour. She has published five research papers in national and international peer-reviewed journals, three articles in top national dailies in India and overseas and has presented her research work in over five international conferences including International Congress of Psychology and European Congress of Psychology. She is currently a member of research staff at Mercer Mettl, India.

Bharti Shokeen is a Research Scholar at Jawaharlal Nehru University, New Delhi. She is presently working as an Assistant Professor of English in an engineering college affiliated to Guru Gobind Singh Indraprastha University, New Delhi. She has also worked as an English Language Instructor at IIT Delhi. Besides teaching, she is also associated with Indian Institute of Dalit Studies, New Delhi, as an editor. Her teaching and research areas include ELT, communication skills and computer-aided language learning (CALL).

Yoshiaki Takahashi joined Nakasone Peace Institute as a Senior Research Fellow in 2016. He was Associate Professor at the University of Tsukuba. His main research topics are cultural differences and measurement issues of happiness. He introduced happiness studies into government work in Japan. He wrote the White Paper on the National Lifestyle in 2008 when he was the Director of Research, Department of Quality of Life, Cabinet Office. From 2009 to 2011, he was the Head of Happiness Studies Unit in the Cabinet Office and contributed to development of Japan's National Well-being Indicators. To date, his research team has conducted qualitative and quantitative surveys in Bhutan, India, the Philippines, Thailand, Costa Rica, the Netherlands and Japan. He was also an advisory member when the Organisation for Economic Co-operation and Development developed the guidelines for measuring subjective well-being (2011–2013) and the head of Japanese advisory team for the GNH2015 survey conducted by the Centre for Bhutan Studies and GNH

Research (2014–2017). He is currently the head of advisory board for opinion surveys for suicide prevention in Nippon Foundation (2016–present) and Principle Investigator for JSPS Bilateral Open Partnership Research Project with EHERO, the Netherlands (2017–present). He holds MSc degrees from University of London and University of Southampton in the United Kingdom and PhD in International Studies from Waseda University, Japan.

Index